Managing Change Successfully

Using Theory and Experience to Implement Change

Managing Change Successfully

Using Theory and Experience to Implement Change

Allan P. O. Williams, Sally Woodward
and Paul Dobson

THOMSON

Australia • Canada • Mexico • Singapore • Spain • United Kingdom • United States

THOMSON

Managing Change Successfully

Copyright © Allan P. O. Williams, Sally Woodward and Paul Dobson 2002

The Thomson logo is a registered trademark used herein under licence.

For more information, contact Thomson, High Holborn House, 50–51 Bedford Row, London, WC1R 4LR or visit us on the World Wide Web at: http://www.thomsonlearning.co.uk

British Library Cataloguing-in-Publication Data
A catalogue record for this book is available from the British Library

ISBN 1-86152-981-3

Typeset by Ian Kingston Editorial Services, Nottingham

Printed in Great Britain by TJ International, Padstow, Cornwall

Contents

List of tables and figures

Preface

In a constantly changing business climate, all managers must be able to manage change in their organization. Managers recognize that the most difficult aspect of this process is implementing change rather than formulating strategy. Only top managers are involved in the latter, whereas all are involved in the former. Moreover, implementing change has a direct and immediate impact on employees' jobs, working relationships, rewards and working conditions. No one will deny that managers need to enhance their leadership skills in this very practical and topical area. Many books have attempted to do this. In the main their approach has been to summarize available knowledge in the area, and to promote a preferred approach. *Managing Change Successfully* is different, and the differential cue lies in the sub-title 'Using theory and experience to implement change'.

Managing Change Successfully advocates an active approach to learning that builds on our knowledge of how adults learn. The objective is to increase the understanding of managers or potential managers so that they are better equipped to take a leading role in implementing change. Central to the learning process is the development of visual representations of the mental models influencing their thinking, thereby bringing the assumptions they have acquired, through experience, to the educational setting. These models are reviewed and modified in the light of the interactions taking place with fellow learners and the practical knowledge derived from influential theories.

This is not a comprehensive textbook summarizing available knowledge, nor is it a book to be used as a prescriptive guide. The theories that are discussed have been selected as examples of how theories can provide practical guidelines to practitioners. These theories are helpful through the insights that they give in gaining the cooperation of others in implementing change and in helping others cope with the stress of change. The focus on these two topics was identified from the findings of 15 case histories collected specially for the book.

The book is divided into three parts:

- Part 1 is an introduction to the learning approach and tools.
- Part 2 contains 15 case histories recounted by managers involved in implementing change in diverse settings.
- Part 3 covers learning to use the experiences embedded in the cases, theories in the literature, and one's own beliefs about change to develop effective leadership skills in implementing change.

While the book has a preferred learning sequence, it caters for the tutor and manager who prefer to impose their own structure on the learning process. The preface for each case history chapter will enable you to select those case histories that you identify as most suitable for your audience or yourself, given your learning objectives. The abstract to each chapter is also intended to be helpful where a tailor-made learning programme is being devised.

The book will be found most valuable on those programmes where learning outcomes include improving an individual's ability to implement change successfully. Natural readers will therefore be those running or attending executive development, MBA and other post-graduate programmes incorporating change management.

While *Managing Change Successfully* may appear to be the result of a trio of authors, there are many others who have made valuable contributions. First and foremost are those managers who were prepared to share their experiences with us and others. In order to preserve their anonymity, and that of their organisations, we have applied appropriate camouflage to the names, places and some of the dates in the case histories. Second, the City Corporation (through the City Educational Trust) provided the financial support that enabled the case histories to be researched. Third, we are very grateful for the wise inputs made by Professor Sylvia Downs in the numerous discussions she attended during the developmental stages of the book, and to Dr Rosalie Silverstone for her assistance in collecting some of the data. Finally, we acknowledge with gratitude the help and encouragement we received in preparing the manuscript, including publishers and colleagues.

■ PART ONE ■

Introduction

CHAPTER ONE

Introduction: orientation

This chapter aims to set the scene by: (1) reminding you that although you are continually learning to adapt to change your learning can be enhanced; (2) making you aware of the leadership responsibility that you have for your own learning and for helping others to learn; (3) posing typical dilemmas faced when implementing change; and (4) proposing an approach to learning which builds on our understanding of how people learn. The overall aim of the book is to familiarize you with this approach as you increase your understanding of the process of implementing change. Increased understanding of both the learning approach and the implementation of the change process will be reflected in your beliefs – some prior beliefs will be reinforced but others will be changed.

We all recognize that the only constant thing around us is change. This means that we have to learn to cope with change if we are to achieve our career ambitions, that we have to help our subordinates cope with change if they are going to continue to work for us, and that we have to play our part in enabling our organization to change if it is to grow and survive. All of us have had experiences of change, but how many of us can successfully generalize from these to the new situations that we encounter? Most of us have read or heard about various theories relating to change, but how many of us can apply these to situations we find ourselves managing?

A job for life is no longer a realistic expectation. Individuals now have to think in terms of continuing education in order to maintain their employability. Large organizations with a great deal of fat may be competitive when they are in a privileged position to dominate the market, but when a fundamental market shift takes place such companies are often too slow to change. IBM is a classic case, but so are most of the other organizations put on a pedestal in 1982 as exemplars of excellently managed companies (Peters and Waterman, 1982).

Members of the management team have an important part to play in enabling the process of adaptation to occur in their organization. In this book we are focusing on one part of the cycle of change – implementation. Several authors have pointed out that this is often where a change programme fails. In some ways this is surprising, because most managers will have had plenty of experience of change, and the management and behavioural science literatures are not short of guidelines and theories. While part of the explanation must be put down to the inherent difficulties of managing the dynamics of change within a social system, much of it can also be explained by our own learning inadequacies. Two factors contribute to this. First, when our experiences are based on a narrow front (e.g. only based on a food retailing company) it becomes more difficult for us to generalize and apply this learning to very different situations (e.g. the British Army). How one goes about implementing change in unionized and non-unionized organizations, such as in the Institute of Bankers and in Abbey National, or in Sony in Japan and in Phillips in the UK, may well require different approaches for success to be achieved. Second, knowledge derived from the experiences of others or from scientific research is often difficult to digest for the purpose of application when delivered through the passive channels of one-way communication. Learning in order to pass an invigilated examination and learning in order to apply the concepts and experience of managing others in change require different levels of understanding. These situational differences are not always recognized in the learning methods used on management training programmes.

Observations such as these suggest that managers or potential managers should not depend upon superiors, trainers or lecturers to provide them with the range of experiences that they should have, or to create the conditions for understanding the dynamics of implementing change. In the highly competitive and political world we live in, individuals need to be prepared to take responsibility for managing their own careers and for managing their own learning. Those who can show that they have the knowledge and skill to manage change successfully will enhance their employability and hence their employment opportunities. In order to gain the loyalty and commitment of our subordinates, we should do what we can to encourage them to manage their careers and their own learning.

This book is intended to help those managers and potential managers (and those supporting them) who are keen to increase their understanding and skill in the processes of implementing change, and in creating learning conditions to enable others to do the same.

Table 1.1 illustrates a selection of questions that managers ask themselves when implementing change. Which questions weigh most

TABLE 1.1: Practical questions relating to the implementation of change

- Should a change programme be led and coordinated by a team or an individual?
- Should the changes be introduced gradually or in one fell swoop?
- If several things have to be changed, what should determine the sequence?
- Do we need external consultants for the implementation process?
- How do we reassure stayers when others are made redundant?
- How do we motivate people to implement change when they have nothing to gain from it?
- To what extent do we need to take historical factors or culture into account when introducing change?
- What kinds of leadership are best when implementing change?
- How can we help staff cope with the stress of change?
- How do we get individuals to adopt 'mental sets' compatible with the changes being introduced?

on your mind? How confident are you in answering these questions? What basic beliefs are influencing your responses? Do you for instance believe in allowing your subordinates maximum influence over how change is to be implemented, or do you believe that you should only consult subordinates after you have determined the broad approach to be adopted? If this book achieves its intended aims you should (in interacting with other learners/facilitators) achieve the following: the questions in Table 1.1 should hold a lot more meaning for you than they do now; you will be disposed to question some of your long-held beliefs about implementing change; and the way you think about successful change, or the mental models you use to interpret change events, will change. The aim is not to provide prescriptive solutions for you to adopt, but to help you understand more clearly the beliefs that you and others hold about implementation, so that you can appraise their validity in the light of any new understanding you develop. Acting on the ideas and approaches contained in this book is one way in which you can take on greater responsibility for your own learning, learning which is likely to be generalizable beyond the current work context in which you find yourself.

Reading on your own is a convenient way of becoming familiar with the beliefs of others, and to compare and contrast these with your own beliefs. But it can be expensive to apply these at work without first testing them out in 'simulated situations' with colleagues. Most of us will normally do this, although we may call it 'consulting' rather than 'testing'. Consulting serves three main purposes: briefing others; allowing others influence in problem solving; and giving us an opportunity to test out our ideas, or what we plan to do, in order to eliminate pitfalls or to identify better solutions that we may not have considered. It is this 'testing out' aspect of consulting which plays an important role in our learning. Purposeful reading is consulting the ideas of others, but when done in isolation there is no way of checking out that we have understood their ideas because of the lack of feedback. Nor is there the opportunity to check out the validity of these ideas except in the context of our own limited experience. Face-to-face interactions, either with the originator of these ideas or with others who are also trying to understand the same ideas, can generate the feedback and range of experiences required for effective learning to take place. This is the function of group exercises and discussions.

Successful change

The main title of this book is *Managing Change Successfully*. The implicit message conveyed by 'successfully' needs to be elaborated. Anyone can implement change so long as the consequences of change are unimportant or undefined. Those who aspire to leadership in the process of implementing change need to develop mental models with clear criteria of success and valid pathways to achieving these criteria. Individuals who attach little importance to the human consequences of change are likely to have different mental models from those who hold opposing beliefs. The former may only be interested in accruing enough power to force through particular changes; the latter will seek to enhance their understanding of the functioning of people and organizations. The dominant culture in today's democratic countries requires leaders with mental models closer to the latter than the former – hence the potential value of the learning experiences embedded in this book.

Principles of learning

Before outlining the approach to learning underlying this book it is worth reminding ourselves of some basic principles which apply to adult learning. These have been succinctly summarized by Sylvia Downs (1995) and are reproduced in Table 1.2.

TABLE 1.2: Ten principles for adult learning (Downs, 1995)

1 Learners need to know where they are going and have a sense of progress towards their objectives.

2 The learning environment has to be one of trust, respect, openness and acceptance of differences.

3 Being aware of and owning the responsibility for learning lies with the learner. Others can only give information and support and provide feedback.

4 Learners need to participate actively in the learning process.

5 Learning should be related to and use the learner's experience and knowledge.

6 Learning is not only a basic capability but also a group of skills which can be developed/learned.

7 Facts, concepts and skills are learned in different ways.

8 Getting ideas wrong can be a valuable aid to developing understanding.

9 For learning to be processed and assimilated, time must be allowed for reflection.

10 Effective learning depends on realistic, objective and constructive feedback.

- **Learners need to know where they are going and have a sense of progress towards their objectives.** The aim of this book is to provide learning material, and appropriate guidelines, that will enable potential and experienced managers to review and improve their skills in the implementation of change. Progress in this context will be felt by the learner in terms of the insights gained and the confirming and disconfirming generalizations arrived at. The intention is that these subjective experiences of progress will eventually translate themselves into effective performance. You may of course have your own additional learning objectives when studying parts of this book, and progress will be determined according to whether your expectations are met. Theories supporting this learning principle are extensive, and we shall return to them in Chapter 2.

- **The learning environment has to be one of trust, respect, openness and acceptance of differences.** One of the reasons why management training courses are often held in a residential centre, away from the work environment, is to reduce the influence of the formal authority structure. In most hierarchical organizations, formal relationships suppress creativity and are intolerant of individual differences. For our stated learning objective to be achieved, individuals must feel safe in revealing their beliefs on issues discussed, so that they can test out their ideas against others and give and receive honest feed-back. 'Ice-breaking' sessions at the start of a course attempt to speed up this process of facilitating open communication.

- **Being aware of and owning the responsibility for learning lies with the learner. Others can only give information and support and provide feedback.** We are often encouraged to be passive learners, with the responsibility for determining what and how learning takes place resting with a lecturer or trainer. This is unfortunate, since learning is not an easy process, and giving someone encouragement and responsibility for their own learning will release the necessary motivation. Everyone has the capacity to learn. Where help is appro-priate is in selecting methods of learning according to the material to be learned, and in arranging for honest feedback to be available.

- **Learners need to participate actively in the learning process.** Much of management training involves changing those beliefs and mental models that determine how managers interpret the information and activities they encounter (Weick, 1995). Many authors have shown the value of active learning experiences in bringing about new insights (Revans, 1983; Kolb, 1984). The role of a trainer or colleague in active learning is that of a facilitator of the learning process – by asking questions, encouraging reflection, and providing support in terms of resources, including feedback.

- **Learning should be related to and use the learner's experience and knowledge.** To speed up understanding and to facilitate remem-bering it is important to build on what the learner already knows. Group methods of learning encourage this approach; also, experi-enced members can aid the learning of the less experienced.

- **Learning is not only a basic capability but also a group of skills which can be developed/learned.** Much is made in the management literature of learning how to learn, but relatively few guidelines are provided. Applying some of the principles already discussed (e.g. active learning, taking on responsibility for one's own learning) will be facilitated if learners are made aware of the need to acquire certain basic learning skills, such as memorizing, questioning, problem solving or reflecting on a learning experience.

- **Facts, concepts and skills are learned in different ways.** To acquire a physical skill one needs to practise it; to learn facts one needs to memorize them; and to learn to use concepts one needs to under-stand them. Each of these requires different methods of learning. In developing understanding of concepts managers need to relate them to experience, comparing and contrasting things, looking at things from different points of view and so on. Memorizing a definition of a concept (e.g. organizational culture) for the purposes of passing an examination is not helpful when it comes to dealing with a situation where an understanding of that concept is needed.

- **Getting ideas wrong can be a valuable aid to developing understanding.** Correcting errors of fact is straightforward – it is either right or wrong. Correcting misunderstandings of ideas and concepts is quite another thing. Advances in the understanding of concepts come when we are forced to reassess them in the light of new experiences, or when we test them out on others. In order for the latter to occur it is obviously important to have a learning environment of trust and openness, as already mentioned.

- **For learning to be processed and assimilated, time must be allowed for reflection.** In the learning of new information and concepts it is important for periods to be inserted during which the learner can integrate new knowledge with old knowledge. This process can be aided by encouraging group methods of learning, i.e. the sharing and discussion of ideas. The role of reflection will be returned to in the next chapter within the context of Experiential Learning Theory (Kolb, 1984).

- **Effective learning depends on realistic, objective and constructive feedback.** Realistic feedback means that it should, whenever possible, refer to concrete and observable things. Objective feedback is that which is not biased by personal feelings. Constructive means that feedback includes comments about things which were well done and should be repeated, as well as suggestions as to how to improve those things which were not so well done.

REFLECTION

Consider the 10 learning principles in Table 1.2. In the light of your own learning agenda, which of these would you see as being easy to apply, and which would prove more difficult?

Management development and organization development

A further clarification of the aims and limitations of this book is necessary. It is aimed at contributing toward the process whereby individual managers acquire the knowledge and understanding that will lead to effective behaviours in implementing change. As such, it is concerned with management development. If, on the other hand, the primary aim of the book was to show organizations what they had to do in order to bring about change, the approach would have been different. This is the province of organizational development (OD), whereby one is trying to facilitate organizational learning. To achieve its purpose this would involve learning interventions encompassing a range of social units within the organization, and resulting in changes expected to enhance organizational learning or adaptation. These changes would be likely to encompass strategic, structural and cultural changes (French and Bell, 1995).

These two approaches are complementary, and should reinforce one another. There is an argument for saying that the management development approach should precede the OD approach, particularly if it was targeted at those managers with the power to make things happen within their organization. A good example of where this sequence is followed is in the design of the Managerial Grid (Blake and Mouton, 1964), where phase 1 aims at giving individual managers an understanding of the relevant concepts and methods; phase 2 is aimed at using the learning of the first phase to improve intragroup team-work; phase 3 aims at improving intergroup teamwork; and phases 4 to 6 focus on long-range planning, implementation of planned changes, review and stabilization. Blake and Mouton saw phases 1 and 2 as falling in the MD category, and phases 3 to 6 as falling in the OD category. *The approach adopted in this book is designed to encourage individuals to examine the assumptions they are making when implementing change, to compare and contrast these with the assumptions being made by others operating in similar and different situations, and with relevant theories, and to assimilate any insights gained.*

The main criticism levelled at the Managerial Grid was that it tried to impose an ideal culture and managerial style on all users, regardless of their history and the environment in which they operated. It encouraged uniformity in its main assumptions. In this book we are leaning in the direction of nurturing diversity, recognizing the learning benefits to be gained in trying out new ideas; that is, new to individual learners, not necessarily to everyone. The case for valuing diversity as a source of creativity within an organization has been well made by Herriot and Pemberton (1994).

REFLECTION

Given your understanding of learning and the problems of implementing change, what are the advantages and disadvantages of initially adopting a management development approach as opposed to an OD approach?

Applying the principles of learning

The first aim of this book is to help you, the learner, to become more effective in implementing change by increasing your understanding of the processes involved. The second aim is to achieve this by adopting an approach to learning which attempts to incorporate the 10 principles of learning outlined above. By experiencing the application of these principles at first hand you will be more likely to 'learn how to learn' and 'help others to learn' – skills which will prove invaluable in coping, and mentoring others to cope, with the turbulent and uncertain world we live in.

How then have we gone about the task that we have set ourselves? This first chapter is designed to help you to orientate yourself in relation to the learning experiences embodied in the book. It is part of the process of ensuring that you have realistic objectives and expectations, and that the learning experiences you will encounter have practical application now and in the future. This should motivate you to continue to explore the offerings before you! In the next chapter we examine in more depth our knowledge relating to learning – a critical area, since learning and change can be said to be two sides of the same coin. Goal-oriented change is preceded by learning (i.e. we learn that if we do things in a certain way we are more likely to achieve our goals), and in turn feedback relating to change results in modifying or reinforcing our learning. Discussion of learning leads us to two vehicles for gaining insight, and developing understanding, into the complexity of organizational change – case studies and visual models. The part on case studies will prepare you for studying the real-life cases collected for this volume. The one on visual models will familiarize you with the basic tools for externalizing and communicating your beliefs (particularly cause–effect relationships) about the important variables and processes involved in implementing change. The exercise at the end of Chapter 2 is designed for you to review your beliefs in this area before and after reading how others have gone about implementing change, and before and after exchanging views with other participating learners.

Part 2 (Chapters 3–9) is given to the 15 original cases. A wide range of different change situations are represented, as indicated by the chapter headings: fundamental organizational change; developing a marketing orientation; downsizing and outsourcing; reorganizing support services; merging organizations; integrating IT into the business; and unplanned change in a market research agency. The main characteristics of each case are given at the start of the chapters so that you can decide which ones are most likely to meet your learning needs. We recognize that few people will have the time to study all 15 cases, and that you are more likely to be motivated to study those which appear to have immediate relevance to situations you are in or you may be entering in the foreseeable future.

Part 3 is concerned with conceptualizing the relevant experiences of yourself and others, and refining those conceptualizations by drawing upon useful theories (i.e. conceptualizations based on academic research and scholarship). Chapter 10 presents the results of one of our attempts at carrying out the exercise that you were asked to do after studying a selection of the cases. It is recommended that this chapter is read after you have carried out the exercise. It is included not as 'the right answer' (we shall all come to this exercise with differing knowledge and experiences), but so that individuals or groups of learners can have a 'model' against which to compare and contrast their own model. The process of testing our model against others (identifying similarities and differences and explaining them) will result in the confirmation and disconfirmation of particular beliefs. This learning experience will affect the generalizations we feel are important, and carry sufficient validity, to influence our behaviour when implementing change.

This iterative process of confirming and disconfirming beliefs regarding the implementation of change is taken further in the remainder of the volume. In Chapter 11 you are encouraged to list those competencies or qualities that you hypothesize are particularly relevant for managers to acquire if they are to be effective in implementing change in a variety of situations. Your list will naturally be influenced by the model you have adopted to convey the generalizations you previously arrived at. The rest of the chapter will present a list based on an examination of the relevant knowledge, and summarize a preliminary test of this list that was carried out during the course of collecting data for the case studies. You will be encouraged to review your original list in the light of the additional information provided in this chapter. Using your revised list you will then be encouraged to identify those competencies where you feel a need for further training.

Chapters 12, 13 and 14 demonstrate the value of the theoretical literature to those who aspire to be effective leaders in the implementation of change. Relevant theories will enrich our mental models and enhance their validity. Chapter 12 focuses on some generic models for thinking about change. Chapter 13 samples the theories that help us to understand why individuals cooperate or not in times of change, and draws attention to useful theories that provide guidelines as to how to bring about cooperative behaviour. Chapter 14 focuses in some depth on the topic of stress – the *bête noire* of implementing change. All these topics have an extensive literature. The intention in Part 3 is to demonstrate the value of using available knowledge when building one's own model of implementing change, and not to write a comprehensive summary of the relevant knowledge in this area.

Finally, in the concluding comments you are encouraged to further review your model, and your list of competencies, in the light of the theories and models that you and your 'learning colleagues' have encountered and discussed.

REFLECTION

In the light of the contents of this chapter, to what extent does the learning approach adopted in this book apply the 10 principles of learning? Within the framework of your personal agenda, how can you ensure that effective learning takes place?

■ CHAPTER TWO ■

Learning, mental models and case histories

This chapter spells out in more depth our beliefs about the nature of learning; drawing mainly upon the literature on experiential learning, action learning and action research. We then explore the role of mental models in learning. The purpose and process of eliciting mental models are discussed, and the essentials of four alternative diagrammatic frameworks for presenting these are outlined. Finally, the use of case histories for learning about the implementation of change is proposed. We outline the methods we employed in gathering data on 15 cases, and describe the structure we have adopted in their presentation. Guidelines are provided for their use in achieving learning objectives.

Introduction

We are writing this book with the overall aim of helping learners become better managers of change. We believe that understanding the learning process is a key to achieving this aim. While there are a variety of theories in this area, we shall focus on those theories that are particularly relevant to the approach we are adopting.

We start by explaining some of our beliefs about the nature of learning, and discuss how, in the design of structured learning situations, and materials like this book, we need to acknowledge that different participants come with different goals and needs. We then present an influential model, from educational theory, of how adults learn – the 'experiential learning cycle' (Kolb, 1984). We follow this with details of an approach that applies this theory to help people increase the effectiveness of their actions. It does this through designing a learning environment that is structured in two key ways. First, a 'set' is established for a group of learners to make time to reflect on action and experience; second, learning is enabled through the practice of Socratic dialogue. Not surprisingly, this is termed 'action learning' (Revans, 1983). We then make a slight digression to look at the nature of knowledge before a discussion of the theory of 'action research' (Argyris and Schon, 1978). This approach seeks to link the practice and theory dimensions, not at the level of the individual, but at the level of the organization and the social sciences. It aims to enable learning and change to occur in organizations through structured enquiry. We conclude this first section by giving our views on the value of these theories for people who are interested in managing change.

The second section introduces the concept of mental models and their impact on our perceptions. Our mental models can only be elicited with difficulty. One method is to identify the beliefs or assumptions that appear to influence our behaviour. Four alternative diagrammatic frameworks are presented as ways of communicating to others the key beliefs that we hold about a given subject. In the final section of the chapter we turn to the use of case histories as part of the process of learning to implement change. We outline the methods we employed in gathering data on 15 cases, and describe the structure we have adopted in their presentation. We provide guidelines for using the cases to achieve learning objectives.

The nature of learning

Four aspects of learning are worth highlighting here.

1. Learning is an active process

We hope, and intend, that after reading this book you will take certain learning outcomes away with you. Some of our agenda for this is detailed in the text, such as spelling out our values and assumptions, and reasons for choosing to promote certain theories and frameworks. Some of the agenda is hidden and consists of messages that we may not communicate directly, but which can be inferred, such as our belief of the need for cooperative partnerships in learning.

But, as well as taking away some of our intended outcomes, each reader will actively reflect, in the light of their unique histories and experiences, and may reject and modify some of what is being said, and may use the material of the book in new ways. Through this process unintended learning outcomes will arise. Some will be negative, such as misunderstandings because we have not expressed what we mean in terms the reader understood; some positive, such as when the reader has taken our meaning and it has produced further insight in their understanding.

Our task in writing this book, and in promoting its use in structured situations, is therefore to promote 'thought' rather than merely to transmit 'knowledge'.

REFLECTION

At what points in your reading so far has your attention been engaged by what has been said? Why?

---

2. Learning is a social activity

This means that we all learn as individuals, but there are structures within which learning occurs, e.g. home, school, work or clubs. Each structure provides us with different learning experiences, different sorts of knowledge, and different roles and role expectations. Throughout history these structures assumed differing importance. For primitive people, key learning took place within the structures of family and tribe, and this learning was transmitted by word of mouth. When learning was recorded, first by hand and then by mechanical means, access to others' recorded learning depended on reading and writing skills. Schools and universities arose to teach these skills and to transmit bodies of knowledge.

One form of 'learning', which we have all experienced, is that gained by attending an educational institution. This formal learning mechanism was traditionally developed from Greek times to enable the transmission of knowledge through the generations. In the first half of the last century, learning at school was followed, in many cases, by movement into a work organization. There, people progressed steadily up the hierarchical career ladder, for forty years or more, to retirement. Additional learning took place 'on the job'.

Recently, as a consequence of a number of changes encompassed by the term 'the information age' (including globalization of information and financial flows, increased business competition, knowledge increasing exponentially, automation of routine work) it has been proposed that many people in today's society will need to participate in 'lifelong learning'. This means a willingness and capacity of individuals to learn new skills and knowledge over their lifetime, as new jobs emerge and old ones fade.

The traditional demarcation lines between education (knowledge and skills gained for 'life'), training (knowledge and skills relating to a specific job or task) and development (knowledge and skills to release potential for future jobs/positions) are breaking down. This also means that the divide between theoretical knowledge and practical knowledge is being removed. Hence there is an increase in alliances and joint ventures between educational institutions (traditionally holding the 'theoretical' bodies of knowledge), professional bodies (guarding areas of expertise and developing new knowledge), and work organizations (an ageing workforce means that people already employed will need re-skilling and/or continuous updating).

Similarly, learning will need to take place, not only at the individual level but in the structures themselves; hence the increased interest in the concept of organizational learning.

REFLECTION

In what ways are changes impinging on your life? What learning implications do they hold?

---

3. Theory and practice are intimately related

A body of knowledge relating to a particular area such as management is not static but is constantly changing and growing. Berger and Luckmann (1966, p. 95) state:

> We can assume that, because of the division of labour, role-specific knowledge will grow at a faster rate than generally relevant and accessible knowledge. The multiplication of specific tasks brought about by the division of labour requires standardized solutions that can be readily learned and transmitted. These in turn require specialised knowledge of certain situations, and the means/end relationships in terms of which situations are socially defined.

With increasing specialization there has been a growth in the professions, that is, the institutions who are 'guardians' of particular bodies of knowledge. Their practitioners address selected problem areas, establish the validity and legitimacy of knowledge in these areas and lay claim to their ownership and practice. For example, a problematic situation at work can be diagnosed in terms of human relations problems by a personnel professional; in terms of cash flow or liability problems by a finance professional; or in terms of distribution outlets and advertising strategy problems by marketing professionals. As further division of labour takes place, new knowledge arises and people form networks to exchange experience of practice. As this becomes codified and refined formal knowledge systems become established, and education, training and qualifications develop.

REFLECTION

To what extent is management a profession? If it is, can it lay claim to the area of knowledge identified with managing organizational change?

---

4. Incidental learning and structured events

Much of our learning happens incidentally, but, where learning events are designed, consideration of certain factors will enable learning to occur more effectively. Kolb and colleagues (Kolb *et al.*, 1995), for example, have identified five characteristics they consider important in the creation of effective learning environments for adults:

(a) *The psychological contract of reciprocity*
    Rather than the traditional model of the teacher as 'giver' and the pupil as the passive 'target', an adult learning environment enables all involved to learn cooperatively from each other's experiences. Participants both suggest new ideas and perspectives and appreciate and integrate others' ideas and perspectives.

(b) *Experience and problem-based learning*
    Motivation for learning comes from the participant's need to learn for a purpose. Generally, adults attend a learning event or read a book voluntarily. Motivation from external factors, such as grades or a teacher's comments, is not as important as intrinsic satisfaction gained from seeing the solution to a problem or increasing insight into an area.

(c) *Personal application*
    Because the need for learning arises from people's experience and problem solving considerations, an important goal is to be able to apply the learning to these areas; theory and the interaction of application through practice are key. Finding out what works and what does not creates 'why' knowledge, i.e. propositions and hypotheses for testing and so on, around the learning cycle.

(d) *Learning is individual and self-directed*
    Not only is every person's experience different, but so too are their learning goals and learning preferences. Some people like to

interact with theoretical ideas; some are more comfortable with experiential exercises. Others are good at reflecting, while, in contrast, some never seem to learn from their experiences. Those responsible for constructing learning environments for groups of learners face a difficult challenge to ensure that learning resources are optimally designed so as to be responsive to individual needs.

(e) *Learning and living are integrated*

In today's society it is important not only to 'know' a subject area, such as 'managing the implementation of change', and even being able to undertake the activities involved in 'managing the implementation of change'; it is also important to be able to learn 'how' to learn. Rote and procedural learning are no longer sufficient. We need to understand what we are doing and why we are doing it, and to be able to change what we are doing to help us become more effective in our sphere of operations. To enable this type of learning, identifying how we can become a more effective learner is paramount.

REFLECTION

What are your strengths and weaknesses when it comes to learning? How can you improve the process? In what ways might you reconsider your ways of thinking about and viewing the world? Where do you hold incorrect assumptions? Do you know your abilities as a learner? Have you thought about ways in which you might improve how you learn?

In the next section we introduce you to some theories about how we learn and some ideas about how we might improve our learning. The focus is not on learning for its own sake, but, as we mentioned above, on the learning process as the means by which we can more effectively manage the implementation of change in organizations. Because change is 'messy', and managing change in organizations cannot be prescribed, we need to find out what works and what does not, and how these different outcomes relate to situational factors. The interaction of theory and practice through learning can help us refine our own practical models.

Theories of learning

Experiential learning theory

A very influential model of how we learn has been developed by David Kolb, an American psychologist (Kolb, 1984). His theory has its origins in the works of earlier well-known writers, namely, John Dewey, Kurt Lewin and Jean Piaget. Whereas other theories of learning give emphasis to behaviours (e.g. reinforcement theory) or the manipulation of abstract symbols (Brewer and Nakamura, 1984) this theory, while acknowledging the importance of experience in its name, actually seeks to combine, in a holistic way, experience, perception, cognition and behaviour. David Kolb provides a working definition of learning as 'the process whereby knowledge is created through the transformation of experience' (Kolb, 1984, p. 38).

The experiential learning process (see Figure 2.1) is seen as a four-stage cycle: (1) concrete experience is followed by (2) observation and reflection. This tends to lead to (3) the formation of abstract concepts and generalizations, which lead to (4) hypotheses to be tested in future action, which in turn lead to new experiences. This cycle is seen to be continuously happening as we operate in the world. Our experience of the world is generally felt in terms of continuity because our expectations about how the world operates are usually met.

FIGURE 2.1: The basic Kolb cycle based on Lewin's experiential learning model (from Kolb (1984); reprinted by permission of Pearson Education, Inc., Upper Saddle River, NJ)

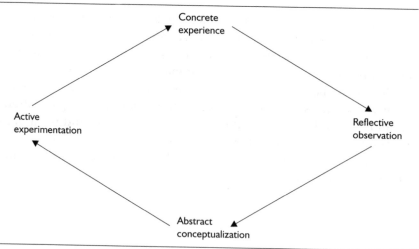

Sometimes, however, when we enter new situations or meet new people, we find our expectations are not met and we are stopped short. Kolb asserts that it is in this interaction between expectation and experience that learning happens. We become 'aware' during moments of discrepancy. We experience 'surprise'.

For Kolb, because people enter a situation or read a book with preformed ideas about it (some of us have more sophisticated or more 'correct' preconceptions than others), all learning is actually 're-learning'. Can you recall any recent event when your attention was suddenly drawn to something in a situation or to a sudden thought that was unexpected and which caused you 'to ponder'? At that point you experienced something and moved on to the observing/reflecting point of the learning cycle, but to learn from the experience you would need to continue around and complete the cycle, i.e. develop a different understanding as a result of what is seen to be a 'transformation'.

We are thought to be continually testing and modifying our concepts through experience, observation and redefinition. This has important implications, because it means that people not only need to develop more refined ideas, but also need to reject aspects of what has already been learnt. Yet, as many of us know, some conceptualizations are more difficult to change than others.

Argyris and Schon's (1978) work on professional learning and practice showed how this can occur when espoused theories (theories that professionals use to describe and justify behaviours) are incongruent with theories-in-use (operational theories of action), i.e. when words and actions are discrepant. For example, managers who have in the past operated in the workplace by using an authoritarian style with their staff may wish, because of changing circumstances or re-education, to adopt a more participative style. Although these managers appreciate and listen and encourage their staff, and state that this is what they do, it is likely that, at times, they will catch themselves 'telling' rather than 'suggesting'. 'Old habits die hard', as we say.

Another aspect of this theory, already touched on above, is the view that learning is directed by our own needs and goals. In some situations we are very clear about our objectives – we know what we want to gain from the experience; in others our objectives might be hazy. For example, if we have particular questions we want addressed in this chapter we will be reading this material in a different way from someone who is just browsing. At a different level of importance, a person who wants to learn how to defeat alcoholism has to be very strongly driven by this objective and very clear about how to maintain this learning over their lifetime.

REFLECTION

What do you see to be the value of experiential theory and its associated ideas when thinking about implementing change and actually implementing change?

Action learning theory

In the field of management, the term *action learning* is synonymous with the name of Reg Revans, who applied the approach to managerial learning. The central belief is that a linkage between acting and thinking is necessary for learning to occur. There are a number of alternative structures and designs that action learning theory can work through (Easterby-Smith and Burgoyne, 1983). Because of this, action learning has been described and viewed in different ways. Reg Revans (1983, p. 22) saw it as an approach that:

> ...demands that each participant attacks a real-life problem (or opportunity) for which no course of action has yet been suggested, even although attempts have been made do so. The problem may or may not be in the organisation in which the participant is at the time employed... the programme is to help the manager develop as a manager, not as a business analyst, a staff advisor, an expert nor as academic. He is to observe himself in action .... Managers are not employed to describe, nor even to recommend: they are employed to act... each manager needs the support, not of confident experts, but of those who are themselves going through the same tricky apprenticeship. To provide such support and to encourage him further to learn by offering the same support in return for what he has received is another aim of action learning. The primary market for these exchanges is the small and stable set of comrades in adversity, regularly disciplining themselves in their problems and progress, more realistically appraising and more effectively applying the vast store of their lived experience.

McGill and Beaty (1992) define action learning as 'a continuous process of learning and reflection supported by colleagues, with an intention of getting things done'. They detail some of the key characteristics of their approach to action learning as follows:

(a) Action learning is based on the relationship between reflection and action. The focus, i.e. action, is a 'project', which can be specific issues or problems. The process enables people to reflect on past action and attempt to produce more effective action in the future (as in Kolb's stages).

(b) Action learning involves a group of people, termed a set, who work together for concentrated periods of time.

(c) Each member reflects on their experiences while others engage them in dialogue. That is, the aim is not to discuss the problem and 'tell' each other what to do, but, through active listening, to help the speaker's thinking process so that as they reflect, they can reformulate their understanding of an event, and revise their hypotheses and generalizations, and so make their own way towards formulating the next actions to try out and experience based on their revised understanding of 'them acting in the world'. Supporting members, through open questioning and the reflecting back of what is being said, help make underlying values and assumptions overt to the speaker. As the saying goes: 'How do I know what I think if I don't hear what I say?'. In the action learning set, people can reflect on both aspects of their 'espoused theories and theories-in-use'. Through this, people can change, i.e. transform their thinking and acting, rather than merely repeat past patterns of behaviour.

The belief is that no member can be more expert on the issue being presented than that individual: 'The information the individual has about the issue made up from his own view of the situation, his feelings about it and his knowledge of its context, is fuller and more complex than any other individual could possibly have' (McGill and Beaty, 1992, p. 30). It is viewed as an empowering approach because it enables people to take responsibility for changing themselves and their situation.

REFLECTION

What do you see as the value of the action learning approach when thinking about implementing change and actually implementing change?

The third framework we are going to introduce is that of action research, but before this we are going to address the issue of ways of knowing and forms of knowledge.

Ways of knowing, forms of knowledge, and 'valid' knowledge

It has been observed that each part of the experiential learning cycle – experiencing, reflecting, abstract theorizing and testing/experimenting – can be viewed as a distinct method of generating knowledge and a different way of 'knowing' (Payne, 1982).

'Experiencing' depends on our sensation and perception, and gives us an awareness, or 'knowledge-of' an event, which is personal and known only to the individual. 'Reflecting' is when we compare a current awareness with past experience. Here we are drawing on 'knowledge-that', which is factual knowledge and which can be built from our past experiences or from other sources such as books and other people. By comparing the two different kinds of knowing, 'knowledge-of' and 'knowledge-that', Payne suggests that we 'build ideas about how situations like this might be more generally explained ... [also] ... We begin to build prepositional knowledge about similar situations and phenomena'. This leads to the process of abstract reasoning. The next step is that the propositions need to be tested and evaluated. George Kelly's notion of people as 'intuitive scientists' suggests that we use a naïve 'scientific know-how' to remodel our knowledge and understanding of the world (including us in the world) (Kelly, 1955). We can then take this revised model and test it in experience through 'practical know-how'. Here, the notion of competencies (e.g. Boyatzis, 1982), as the ability to apply valid practical models through action in an effective way, comes into play. And so we go around the circle.

The process of 'enquiring' in the world, particularly as it relates to managing organizational change, is conducted in a formalized way through social science research. As academics we are concerned with the notion of 'valid knowledge', so we ask what evidence can be used to corroborate claims to knowledge?

Traditional science requires a particular methodology for generating knowledge, including objectivity and empirical experimentalism so that laws for prediction and control can be 'discovered'. As Chris Argyris and Donald Schon (1989) observe, this creates a tension between rigour and relevance. What happens is that in an enquiry (i.e. learning about phenomena in the world) the researcher tries to control the investigation to ensure that postulated relationships between independent and dependent variables are not compromised by extraneous factors. However, the greater the control, the less is the generalizability of the findings. Similarly, the need for precision can reduce the richness of an experience or phenomenon; or there is an imbalance between 'elegant' theory that is found not to be 'applicable' in local contexts, i.e. 'fit' or 'work' (Glaser and Strauss, 1967).

In response to these difficulties a number of other methods of enquiry have come into being, some of which have different underlying paradigms (i.e. the set of beliefs that guide everyday action or disciplined enquiry). Space precludes us from detailing these, but since we seek to improve practice, we are adopting an integration of rationalism and pragmatism as our philosophical basis (Pepper, 1942). Hence in writing this book and suggesting ways in which it might be used we aim to link thinking with practice; definitions with results; logic with feedback; and structural with multiplicative corroboration.

Action research

This side-tracking has set the scene for introducing our next approach to learning and enquiry. Managing change can take place at a number of different levels: the individual, the group, the business unit, and the organization. We looked at the learning process from the perspective of the individual via experiential learning, and we saw how the process can be facilitated through the structured group learning experience of action learning. We are now moving to the level of the organization in considering action research.

Rapoport's definition manages to encapsulate the essence of this approach. It is research that '...aims to contribute both to practical concerns of people in an immediate problematic situation and to the goals of social science by joint collaboration within a mutually acceptable ethical framework' (Rapoport, 1970, p. 499). This form of enquiry has its roots in work by Kurt Lewin (as did the experiential learning model). It is about generating knowledge about a social system (the organization) while, at the same time, seeking to change it. Hence the similarities between the two theories, although at different levels of analysis.

Kurt Lewin (1946) identified six distinguishing features of action research; namely, that it is client-centred; is problem-driven; challenges the status quo; produces usable theory; produces empirically disconfirmable propositions; and produces propositions that can be developed into theory. The purpose of action research is to bring about action or change. This has implications because of the difficulties in attaining a balance between research (inquiry) and action (implementation). There seems to be agreement that the best way of dealing with this problem is by participatory action research. This means that researchers and practitioners jointly addressing practical concerns in organizational contexts provide rich insights unobtainable by other means (White et al., 1991). Both are addressing different aspects of the enquiry/learning cycle.

Argyris and Schon acknowledge additional difficulties in their approach to action research, which they term action science. They think the focus should be one that is able to overcome some of the difficulties of generating valid information because people often erect barriers to learning and change. For them, action research:

...places central emphasis on spontaneous tacit theories-in-use that participants bring to practice and research... [including]... strategies of unilateral control, unilateral self-protection, defensiveness, smoothing-over and covering up, of which their users tend to be largely unaware... (Argyris and Schon, 1989, p. 613)

Because of the difficulties in generating valid knowledge, Eden and Huxham (1996), among others, have produced a number of criteria for judging the validity of knowledge. They produced 12 contentions that they regard as standards against which action research outcomes and processes can be assessed. Outcome contentions focus on issues of generality and theory generations, the type of theory development appropriate for action research and the pragmatic focus of action research. Process contentions relate to design issues and issues of external validity. The first eight of their contentions relate to issues of internal validity, i.e. that a piece of action research qualifies as 'research'. The remaining four contentions are concerned with external validity, i.e. the degree to which the results can be viewed as represen-tative and generalizable to other situations.

Internal validity is measured against such standards as the production of implications beyond those derived for the particular situ-ation; an explicit concern with theory; adherence to the incremental nature of the theory-building process; and a high degree of method and orderliness throughout the process. External validity is measured against standards such as the extent to which the project focuses on aspects of the situation that cannot be captured by other methods; the skills and procedural knowledge required to undertake this approach; and the extent to which triangulation is used as a device to build theory.

Conclusions so far

All of the models we have presented have focused on improving action: all share the underlying framework of building knowledge (personal or social science) through the process of enquiry and accomplishing change in individuals and organizations through the learning cycle. Some practical knowledge about managing change has been codified, while other practical knowledge remains tacit.

Because of their histories, and increasing change and uncer-tainty, organizational environments share some aspects (i.e. some factors are generalizable), but many aspects are in unique configura-tions. This means that professionals, of whatever kind (managers, occu-pational psychologists, information specialists), need to be able to connect theory and practice. This happens, not through technical ratio-nality (Schon, 1983), where problems are presented and rules for solving them are applied, but through experimentation and improvisa-tion (Vaill, 1989) where diagnosis of problems and praxis are key abili-ties to be developed.

Practitioners can use existing theory about managing change to develop 'sensitizing concepts' for use in diagnosing their own partic-ular case. These can then be tested out and the results experienced as individuals iterate through their learning cycle. While learning through acting in the workplace generates particular and local knowl-edge, discussion of particular perceptions and understanding, in struc-tured situations, can help to generate theory that has its basis in grounded research. This book has been written to enable you to increase understanding and insights through your own actions, through reading about others' actions and practice theories, and through social science theories, particularly in the area of psychology.

Enquiry as undertaken by practitioners and by researchers/scientists differs in the kinds of knowing and knowledge generated, but through collaboration 'practical' theories and 'formal' theories can help refine each other.

Thomas (1993) sees the difference between these two types of theory in terms of maps. He suggest that both the scientist and the prac-titioner are 'engaged in a form of map making':

> The scientist judges maps according to scientific criteria such as parsi-mony, comprehensiveness and empirical relevance with the aim of advancing knowledge... practitioners judge maps according to their practical interest in acting within the world to attain certain ends, and use a narrower set of everyday methods to develop their understanding of the world around them.

REFLECTION

You may have found parts of this section on learning theories difficult to understand or perhaps not sure as to their relevance to your learning objectives. This is a situation you will often face when reading about theo-ries being put forward by social scientists. When faced with such a situa-tion, how can you ensure that you are not missing something that may be useful to you now or in the future?

The role of mental models in learning

Learning has been defined in a variety of ways. A typical definition is: 'a process in which relatively stable changes are brought about in the way we see things and behave in pursuit of our goals' (Williams, 2001, p. 68). This definition incorporates the notion that learning is goal-directed, that it affects behaviour as well as cognitive properties, and that the changes brought about are relatively stable. The construct of 'memory' enables us to explain how individuals come to store images, words, knowledge, skills and experiences in such a way that they can be drawn upon when needed in the future. It is this function of memory that enables us to reproduce the way we see things and behave from one situation to another, and from one time to the next.

However, we know that memory is not just a simple copy of what the person has seen: it is the symbolic representation or schema of the external world (Bartlett, 1933). These schemata, mind-sets, or mental models are formed through our experiences. They come to our aid when we find ourselves having to understand or to interpret complex, ambiguous, incomplete and uncertain situations. Since they are the result of our experiences or learning, and most of these take place in a social context, we find that the mental models of individuals who belong to the same social groups as ourselves will have much in common. Our use of the term 'culture' recognizes the similarities and differences between the mental models of those sharing the same culture and those having different cultures.

You will notice that the construct of 'mental models' is compatible with, and indeed readily emerges from, our earlier account of the nature of learning and of experiential and action learning theories.

The benefit of the construct of 'mental models' is that it enables us to understand and explain why some people see things and behave in certain ways and others see things and behave in different ways. Their stability, naturalness, and ability to help us to make sense of the world are their strengths. Ironically, these are also their weakness. The fact that they are mainly the product of experiential learning, and that their stability provides us with a certain amount of emotional security, means that they are relatively easy to reinforce but very difficult to change (Vosniadou, 1992). There is risk of us getting locked into particular mental models when changed circumstances require new responses.

> **REFLECTION**
>
> We have given a particular definition of learning above. Does this fit with your understanding of learning? If not, why not?

Eliciting mental models

In the process of implementing change one is inevitably concerned with changing the mental models of oneself and others – in order to see and do things that are more appropriate for new situations and more compatible with new knowledge. Therefore it is not enough to understand the function of mental models; one must also find ways of gaining insight into one's own mental models, of expressing them in a form that is communicable to others, and of learning how to change them. This presents a problem. We cannot have direct access to another's cognitive structures. The best we can do is to sample those beliefs that a person holds toward given objects, issues or people. The assumption made is that, given a particular set of beliefs, there is a high probability that compatible behaviour will follow. A variety of methods can be used for eliciting mental models through the medium of assessing belief systems. Criteria for evaluating these methods include their reliability (i.e. we get the same result on repeating the measure), validity (i.e. the result is meaningful in that it can be shown to relate to some external criterion such as behaviour), and acceptability (i.e. in terms of costs, ethical considerations, etc.).

We are using the term 'beliefs' in its most general sense to cover knowledge assumptions or cause–effect beliefs (e.g. 'resistance to change will be reduced if the implementers of change are consulted at every stage of decision making'); attitudinal beliefs (e.g. 'I would not want to change my job even if I was offered considerably more money elsewhere'); and value beliefs (e.g. 'respect for the individual should dominate our thinking').

Although we are proposing that we can obtain some idea of an individual's mental models by sampling their belief systems, we are not suggesting a simple one-to-one correspondence between their beliefs and their behaviour. The fact that you are reading this sentence at the moment (your behaviour) may be the function of a whole gamut of beliefs. You may believe that you will learn something useful that can be applied back at work, you may believe that the topic will be the basis for an examination question, you may believe that your tutor expects you to read it before joining a group discussion, and so on. Our behaviour is not just influenced by our beliefs about what is good and bad, pleasant and unpleasant, cause and effect; it is also influenced by our beliefs with respect to various situational contingencies. In other words, if we go and have a game of tennis rather than finish reading this chapter, what are the consequences likely to be for us? What are the rewards and costs? You may decide to finish reading this chapter because the important thing for you at the moment is to hold your own in discussion with your peers; but others with a high degree of self-confidence and self-efficacy may opt for tennis, because they believe they can hold their own in any discussion with the minimum of preparation.

A great deal of research has been and is carried out on the impact of beliefs – particularly of those reflecting our attitudes – on behaviour (Petty *et al.*, 1997). Thus there is support for the proposition that attitude strength moderates the attitude–behaviour consistency (i.e. the stronger the attitude, the greater will be the attitude–behaviour consistency), as do certain personality factors (e.g. individuals relying more on internal cues, such as attitudes, as a guide to behaviour will show more attitude–behaviour consistency than those relying more on situational cues).

As discussed previously, Chris Argyris (1992) has highlighted the gap between what managers say they believe in (espoused theories) and what they actually do (theories-in-use). There are several possible explanations for this phenomenon. They may genuinely believe that subordinates should be consulted on how to implement change, but because of various contingencies operating on a specific occasion they fail to put this into practice. Alternatively, various defence mechanisms may be operating to make them think they believe in this principle, but deep down they do not.

The term 'cognitive mapping' has come to be used in the management literature to describe the different methods for eliciting mental models. The different methods will reflect the theories and experiences of their users. One of the best-known techniques is the repertory grid. The father of this technique is George Kelly (1955), who proposed a theory of personal constructs and devised the repertory grid for assessing them. His theory saw each individual as his or her own scientist. We strive to make sense of our world, and invent an implicit theoretical framework that is our personal construct system. It is in terms of this system that we anticipate events and behave toward objects and other people. As 'scientists' we are continually re-evaluating and modifying our hypotheses (i.e. expectations based on our theories or personal constructs) as a result of the outcomes of our experiences. The repertory grid technique is based on Kelly's definition of a construct as a way in which two or more things are alike and thereby different from a third or more things. The traditional method of applying it is to present the subject with three concepts, objects or people and to ask in which way two of them are similar and differ from the third. Thus when presented with the names of IBM, Microsoft and Hewlett-Packard, and asked in what way two of these companies were similar and differed from the third, a manager may express his belief by responding with the construct of 'innovation'. The presentation of the results of a repertory grid analysis will be in terms of a matrix of correlations, and these in turn can then be plotted in a diagram or map to show the relationships in a more user-friendly form (Fransella and Bannister, 1977).

Kelly's personal construct theory and its method of eliciting beliefs embedded in mental models is presented here because of its compatibility with our discussion earlier in this chapter, its scientific underpinning and its use over many years. Its main advantage is claimed to be that the constructs identified are those that will influence an individual's perceptions and behaviour rather than being the result of the methodology used or the suggestions implied in a direct line of questioning. However, it has not been shown to be superior in terms of the criteria of reliability, validity and acceptability. Moreover, in the work situation, as opposed to the clinical situation, its laborious and time-consuming nature puts it at a distinct disadvantage over alternative approaches.

The repertory grid is one of the more sophisticated and scientifically developed techniques for arriving at features of mental models likely to influence our thinking and behaviour. A more recent approach has been that of 'cognitive mapping', as developed by researchers working in the business strategy area (Eden, 1989). Research techniques have been developed for eliciting key factors influencing the strategic thinking of managers. The problem of analyzing data based on a multitude of factors and their interrelationships has been tackled by the development of appropriate software. The end result is diagram or cognitive map that identifies the dominant factors and the relationships between them. Tools are therefore available for organizing the complexity of an individual's experiences into a meaningful and coherent picture that can be shared with others.

Eliciting mental models for the purpose of individual learning rather than research allows us to be much more adventurous. Visual models have become popular because of their ability to improve the communication of complex issues, and the ease of generating attractive diagrams with the aid of the computer. The attractions of 'visiospatial' layouts for representing mental models are considerable (Worren *et al.*, 2000). Almost every page of management textbooks contains a diagram of one sort or another. While some will be based on quantitative research, the majority will reflect the reasoned attempts of authors to convey their ideas and theories to readers. These qualitatively based diagrams will also be expressing cause–effect beliefs, and they will invariably do so through a framework 'borrowed' from a discipline.

Figures 2.2–2.5 illustrate the basic elements of four such frameworks. These have been chosen to illustrate the diversity of choice available; there are many other visual vehicles underpinned by different theoretical assumptions (Sparrow, 1998). Figure 2.2 illustrates the 'systems' framework, and incorporates the messages of interdependence of elements, sequential arrangements and feedback pathways (Katz and Kahn, 1978; Senge, 1990). In this particular diagram we are trying to get across the idea that when we express our beliefs about implementing change to others, these will reflect what we have learned (a) through observation and studying, and (b) through direct personal experience. In keeping with the literature on experiential learning we are differentiating between these two modes of learning because our mental models, from which our beliefs are derived, are more likely to be affected by the latter than the former. The process of testing our beliefs on others provides the feedback for us to check that the beliefs we are communicating are those we intend to communicate, and to help us to further validate our beliefs against the beliefs of others.

The 'experimental' framework (Figure 2.3) exemplifies the scientific paradigm by differentiating between the independent, moderating and dependent variables (Likert, 1967). In our example we are proposing that any changes in a manager's beliefs will be a function of

FIGURE 2.2: A 'systems' framework for communicating various beliefs relating to key variables and relationships

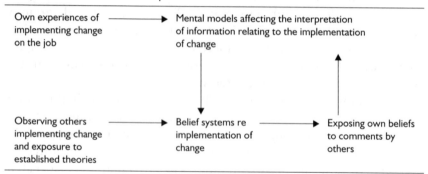

FIGURE 2.3: An 'experimental' framework for communicating various beliefs relating to key variables and relationships

Independent variables	Moderating variable	Dependent variable
	Strength and compatibility of the manager's relevant mental models	
• Learning experiences through simulations		Changes in the manager's beliefs relating to implementation of change
• Learning experiences by studying the established theories		

their learning experiences through simulations and/or by studying established theories. But we are qualifying this hypothesis by saying that the relationship is only likely to hold if the beliefs to be acquired are compatible with the strong beliefs characteristic of the manager's relevant mental models. Or to put it in another way, the new beliefs will be acquired if the manager has only developed weak beliefs relating to implementing change – a likely outcome if he or she has had little relevant experience. The attractiveness of the experimental framework is that it expresses specific hypotheses that can be tested against the experience of others, established theories and planned experimentation. The disadvantages are that a very limited number of variables can be included for the very good reason that it is more research-oriented (i.e. controllable and generalizable) than practitioner-oriented (i.e. helps solve an immediate managerial problem).

The opposite can be said in the case of the 'mind map' framework (Figure 2.4) – it conveys the uncertainty, complexity and organic growth of the reality that faces the practitioner manager (Buzan, 2000). In the example given we have tried to show how an individual's beliefs relating to the implementation of change can be organized around main issues such as 'contextual', 'managerial style' and 'learning experiences'. The strength of mind maps is that they help us to identify the main variables interacting with our beliefs, and they clarify the links that exist according to our knowledge of the literature and our personal experiences.

The 'fishbone' framework (Figure 2.5) is a simple diagrammatic approach to identifying various factors that have a causal relationship with an issue or phenomenon.

In selecting a suitable framework for communicating, for instance how to implement change beliefs, a number of criteria should be considered:

FIGURE 2.4: A 'mind map' framework for communicating various beliefs relating to key variables and relationships

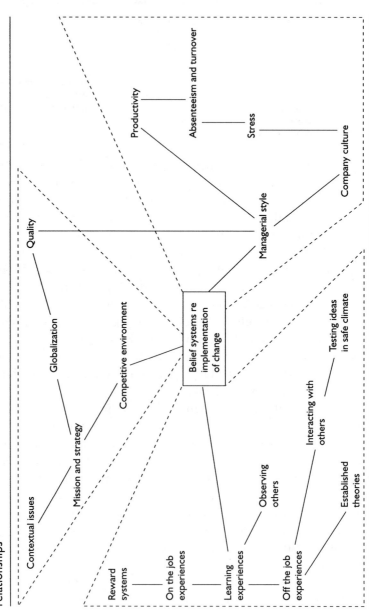

FIGURE 2.5: A 'fishbone' framework for communicating various beliefs relating to key variables and relationships

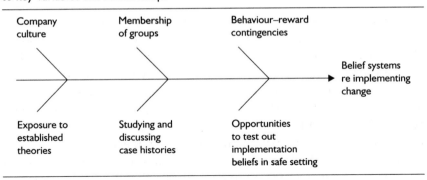

1   We should be clear as to why we are trying to communicate. In the present context it is to encourage us to generate certain guidelines from our experiences and those of others that will prove useful when implementing change.

2   We should be clear as to who is our target. The fact that you are reading this book suggests that you are (or soon will be) involved in the process of implementing change, and therefore we can assume that you already have some relevant background knowledge on which to build.

3   We must be clear about what we are trying to communicate. For instance, are we trying to highlight critical causal variables, paint a comprehensive picture of variables involved, help ourselves to understand a particular theory, and/or describe a dynamic and interactive system?

Answers to these questions will affect the sort of framework we shall employ and the balance we are trying to achieve between comprehensiveness and usefulness. While there is no 'right' visual representation for expressing beliefs, some will be more appropriate than others according to what we are trying to achieve.

REFLECTION

We have given four examples of visual frameworks that are frequently found in the literature. Are there any others that you have found useful when trying to make sense of a complex situation or problem?

Learning from case histories

Case histories enrich the research literature and learning resources. In the former context the information gathered needs to be in considerable depth, and from several perspectives, if the research is to result in any significant contribution to knowledge. Where case histories are being used for learning, other criteria are legitimate. They include: the learner can identify with the events being described; the learner accepts that a real life as opposed to a fictitious story is being told; the material is readily understood; and the material is directly relevant to the objectives of the learning situation, and appropriate lessons and insights can be gained from their study and the ensuing discussions. The cases gathered for this book fall within the learning context.

Within the learning context, case histories may take various forms. The famous Harvard Business School case study method of learning usually presents a complex problem and the learner has to analyze the case and recommend and defend a solution. The pedagogical value comes mainly from the ensuing discussion that takes place between the students and the instructor, i.e. the active learning element (Christensen, 1987). As will be shown below, the cases presented in this volume are being used in a different way, albeit involving active learning. The term 'case history' rather than 'case study' will be employed so as to emphasize the distinction.

Whatever the purpose of case histories the methods of gathering the data are important. In our study we designed a semi-structured schedule that enabled us to cover the ground in a two-hour interview. The trigger questions were carefully thought out, and took into account current knowledge relating to the implementation of change. The guiding questions relating to the change project being studied are presented in Table 2.1. The selection of the case histories to be studied was not random. We wanted a broad spread of cases so that we had a very diverse set of situations. Thus we have examples from financial institutions, manufacturing, the oil industry, retailing, law partnerships, local government, central government, professional institutions, consultancies and charities. We also wanted to focus on the process of implementing change rather than formulating change. This meant that our respondents were more likely to be middle to senior managers rather than top management or professional change agents.

We were not after 'good practice' cases. The literature is replete with these, and some organizations, such as the Advisory, Conciliation and Arbitration Service in the UK, have made it part of their mission to

TABLE 2.1: Outline of interview schedule for collecting case history material

Introduction
We have obtained funding from an educational trust to develop a learning programme for middle managers to enhance their understanding and abilities to manage change. As part of the programme we are interviewing a number of managers to obtain in-depth case histories about managing change.

The interview is in two parts. First we ask questions about your experiences in managing a specific change project so we can build up a description of what happened. Then we ask you to think about competencies involved in managing change that are likely to be critical for success.

Part I
1   How did this change project come into being?
    – history including source of ideas and support for it
    – stakeholders involved
    – key objectives
    – kind of change involved: Big Bang or incremental; perceived centrality of change to the primary task of the organisation (i.e., what it has to do in order to survive); predicted or unforeseen; novel or familiar; complex or relatively simple; extent or scale of change; pace of change; time frame involved; any other relevant factors about the kind of change involved?
    – your responsibilities and accountabilities; others involved

2   Can you tell me how this project unfolded over time, particularly focusing on what went to plan and what did not, and why? (Probe about events not going to plan in three stages.)
    2.1   Triggers: detailed descriptions (concrete and specific) of events that you experienced during this project that placed unforeseen or unexpected demands on you or that caused you problems or difficulties.
    2.2   Behaviours: specific behaviours when confronted with each event. If no action was taken were there internal responses, i.e. ideas about future and/or revised actions, thoughts, plans? Did others respond to the event confronting you – i.e. support or add to problems?
    2.3   Consequences/outcomes: what happened as a result of what you did? Can you tell us about how you felt about what happened, i.e. the outcome/consequences?

3   Can we just touch on.............. (to include here any topic areas not covered in answers to the above questions):
    – who planned the changes and how?
    – implementation of change?
    – support for the change (e.g. training, engineering, finance, consultants)?
    – attempts (if any) to gain commitment of those involved with or affected by the change. If so, how? If not, why not?
    – emotional consequences of change? How were these handled?

TABLE 2.1 (continued)

- any mechanisms in place to monitor the effectiveness of change? If so, what mechanisms were used? If not, why not?
- how effective was the change from your viewpoint, e.g. were the objectives achieved? If not, why not? Which aspects of the change were most effective and why? Which aspects of change were least effective and why?
- reviewing the whole change process which aspects, on reflection, would you improve, and why?

Part 2

4   In thinking about what happened in this change project, what do you see as being the key competencies that were critical to success and why?

collect and disseminate information relating to 'successful' change attempts within companies. Good practice cases tend to be unbalanced in their reporting, for obvious reasons (e.g. no company wants to publicize its failures, particularly if they have not yet been corrected). Since our case histories were to be used to learn about implementing change in general rather than how to manage a specific change, it was important that our cases were not selected on the basis of their favourable publicity. We were interested in collecting data about the problems that ordinary managers encountered in implementing change, warts and all. In order to highlight situational differences, some of these managers were at a more senior level than others.

How can one best use these case histories for learning how to implement successful change? Earlier in this chapter we indicated that an active strategy (i.e. one that requires directed and explicit responses from the reader) was more likely to result in effective learning. Each of the 15 cases (Table 2.2) describes a focused set of experiences and beliefs of a particular individual. Each story is told in the respondent's own words, but the broad structure has been influenced by the semi-structured interview schedule outlined in Table 2.1. We need to recognize that the account is told from the perspective of one individual (two in two of the cases). They are interpreting what happened in terms of their own mental models. Given the learning purposes for which we have researched these cases this is not important. What is important is that readers feel able to identify with some of the respondents and the situations they found themselves in.

TABLE 2.2: The organization of the 15 case histories.

___

CHAPTER 3: FUNDAMENTAL ORGANIZATIONAL CHANGE
Planned organization-wide change in an office equipment manufacturer.
Major changes in structure and culture initiated by the American parent
company in order to generate growth in an increasingly competitive market.
Implementing strategic change in a charity. Major changes introduced by a
newly appointed CEO.

CHAPTER 4: DEVELOPING A MARKETING ORIENTATION
Market testing in central government. Implementation of market testing
approach in a central government agency service department. **Compulsive
competitive tendering (CCT) in the housing department of a local authority.**
A local authority's first attempt to subject white-collar services to the market.

CHAPTER 5: DOWNSIZING AND OUTSOURCING
Downsizing and outsourcing in an oil refinery. Site-wide and radical
changes introduced to reduce costs. **Restructuring in a processing plant.**
Parent company introduces changes in an attempt to increase profits from
its investment in a declining industry.

CHAPTER 6: REORGANIZATION OF SUPPORT SERVICES
Restructuring support services in a partnership. Changes introduced in a
personnel department providing support services to professional lawyers.
Work reorganization in the back office of an insurance broker. Change
involved functions being split on two sites, but success was not sustained.
Strategy for a professional body. Redefinition of roles of part-time volunteers and paid staff in a small professional institute.

CHAPTER 7: MERGING ORGANIZATIONS
Integration following a takeover in the retail industry. Two head offices of
previously competing companies are brought together into one location.
Merging two management consultancy units. Two companies belonging to
the same parent group are brought together to create greater value-added
services. **Merger and reorganization in a health authority.** Further savings
are sought following a merger of two health authorities by creating a single
management team and reducing the number of sites involved.

CHAPTER 8: INTEGRATING IT INTO THE BUSINESS
Helping the IT function adopt a customer focus. Newly appointed head of
IT attempts to change the culture by getting IT to take on a partnering role
to support the business. **Re-engineering global custody operations in a
bank.** The use of leading edge technology to try and turn the business
around within a short time frame.

CHAPTER 9: UNPLANNED CHANGE
Unplanned change in a market research agency. *Ad hoc* changes introduced
to cope with a massive growth in business.

In Chapter 10 we shall be illustrating this process of learning by following through the progressive development involved in eliciting the 'implementing change' mental model of one of the authors. The iterations of arriving at a model in trying to make sense of the information in the 15 cases are described. We suggest that this chapter is read only after readers have tackled this task for themselves.

Of course one can always argue that the dangers of students or managers learning from each other is that they may be reinforcing invalid as well as valid beliefs. This is where the learning process needs to be tempered by other 'experts' steeped in the results of scientific studies – studies designed to discover and to disseminate 'valid' knowledge – hence Chapters 11–14. It is only when we interact with the scientific literature, or its interpreters, that we are likely to become confident that we are finding the answers to the 'why' questions in this difficult area of knowledge. Formal learning programmes should be designed to facilitate learning from a range of resources.

EXERCISE: INITIAL MODEL FOR IMPLEMENTING CHANGE

A suggested process for using the cases as a resource for learning to implement successful change is the following:

1   Identify what you believe to be the most useful guiding principles for implementing successful change.

2   On the basis of Table 2.2 and the introduction at the beginning of each of Chapters 3–9, select and read those cases which come closest to the situations with which you are most familiar, likely to be managing or most interested in.

3   In studying the cases you should analyze them in terms of three questions: (a) What factors (variables, concepts) should be considered as part of the explanation of successfully managing the implementation of change? (Have you considered all key factors, i.e. those that facilitate as well as inhibit change? Can you delete or subsume any because they add little?); (b) How are these factors related?; and (c) What are the underlying dynamics (e.g. psychological, economic, social) that justify inclusion in this description of factors and relationships? In other words, why select these particular factors and relationships?

The first two questions cover the subject of successfully managing the implementation of change by describing relevant elements and events. The third question covers explanation and prediction. This third question should help to make clear the underlying assumptions that have been made. These can be considered in terms of another question – do they connect together in a logical way and provide a cogent and plausible explanation as to why we should expect certain relationships in the data?

4   On the basis of the beliefs stemming from (a) your own experiences, (b) the experiences of experts, and (c) the experiences described in the cases, develop a preliminary model incorporating your beliefs for implementing successful change. The purpose of the model is to arrive at a meaningful visual vehicle that incorporates cause–effect relationships which you feel are critical for managers to learn given your understanding about change. Figures 2.2–2.5 provide examples of some of the formats (but not the contents) that may meet your requirements.

5   Test out your model in discussion with others with the same learning objectives. Modify your model in the light of any new insights you develop. This part of the exercise will be most constructive if the others are also seeking to validate their own model. A mutual learning situation of this nature is more likely to avoid dysfunctional defensive behaviours, and to stimulate functional supportive behaviours. Ultimately the beliefs stemming from your model will be tested through your own personal experiences; as we have already pointed out, it is this form of active learning that is most likely to lead to reviewing and changing your mental models.

One cannot overemphasize the need for incorporating social interaction with others in the process of testing out your model for implementing change. Reasons include:

■ You will be able to differentiate between those beliefs incorporated in your model that are shared by others, and those that are not. You will then be more motivated to review the latter with the expectation of enhancing your learning.

■ Others will come to the learning situation with different personal experiences and may have focused on different cases. They will therefore be able to bring to the discussion a fresh perspective, thus creating conditions for new insights. One of the outcomes of diversity may very well be the significance of situational variables in determining which approach will lead to successful implementation. Thus the most appropriate approach may differ according to whether the changes involved introducing a new IT system or a new managerial structure, a profit or a non-profit organization, a manufacturing or a professional organization, delayering or merging, an American or a British company, and so on.

■ Identifying similarities in beliefs about the implementation of change is as important as identifying differences. Any actions that reduce common problems in the implementation of change need to be identified and the reasons for their success understood.

■ **PART TWO** ■

Cases

Classes

CHAPTER THREE

Fundamental organizational change

These two cases are concerned with what Beckhard and Pritchard (1992) label *fundamental* as opposed to *incremental* organizational change. The account of the first case is given by a middle manager in an international company that produces office equipment and services. Major changes with respect to structure and culture were initiated by the American parent company in order to generate growth in an increasingly competitive market. It was characterized by changes that had a strategic base, were planned and were organization-wide. The changes flowed from the realization that business equipment was not the business that they were in any more, but that they were in anything that had structured information which helps people to communicate. The case illustrates that at the end of the day it is the behaviours and attitudes of individuals in the organization which need to change, and shows how the use of a relatively sophisticated organization development approach (including systematic use of workshops) is perceived by someone who was both a receiver and an implementer of the changes. It is interesting to note that although these changes were motivated by building for the future rather than reacting to a crisis, and an exemplary approach to change was adopted, there were still many instances of resistance to change, some of which could have been avoided with hindsight.

The second case was recalled independently by two key players, and it is therefore in two sections. The first section is the account given by the chief executive officer, and the second account is that of a line manager who was a member of the client–consultant working party of five given the task of consulting members throughout the UK before the final consultants' report went to the Trustees of this very large charity. The chief executive officer had been head-hunted from another charity. He faced a major management challenge, the Trustees having sacked all the management team bar one. Fundamental change was provided by strong leadership at the top, and incorporated contingency measures to ensure that the approach used would be successful in a predominantly voluntary organization. It is worth noting the key role played by the CEO in structuring the general approach used in the early (and probably most difficult) stages of implementation.

Planned organization-wide change in an office equipment manufacturer

Background

This case history is told by a manager in an international company which produces office equipment and services. It has recently undergone radical changes initiated by the American parent company and intended to ensure the organization meets the challenge of a highly competitive market.

Part 1: the change

The organization as a whole has been going through a massive change over the past 18 months in terms of changing our structure and changing our culture: a total organizational change.

How did the change come about?

Going back in terms of the company's history, up through the seventies we were riding high, very successful, had the patents on several types of office equipment. In the eighties we were on the brink of bankruptcy, going out of business, and the Japanese had moved in. Through the eighties, through our Total Quality Management change, we had actually recovered in some ways. In the late eighties and early nineties we realized that we had been sort-of surviving (it was called The Crisis of Survival). We said 'OK – we've survived – but where do we go from here?'. It was really looking at where we go in the future that started this change.

So a task force, for want of a better word, was set up in the States that called upon academics, economic analysts, and all sorts of different people to analyze the market-place, review what was happening in other parts of the world, in globalization, what was happening in terms of the speed of change, etc., and then where does the company have to change to meet that?

So early in the nineties the strategic group created a plan that became known as our 200X Vision. That was what initiated the change.

Alongside that we realized we also had to change the image of the company. It meant recognizing that the office equipment business is not what we're in anymore, and not where we are going to be in the year 200X. Instead it's anything that has structured information which helps people to communicate. We realized that was the core of our business.

Instead of the Crisis of Survival, we then had the Crisis of Opportunity. We could just have plodded along probably for another five, six, seven years, and then we'd have been in trouble again because we wouldn't have identified how to meet future demands. Since the strategic group was set up we have been communicating the change to our employees, to our customers, and also changing things internally to make it happen.

The overall change plan
It's rather complicated. We have three main elements in this change. We have the organizational structure, which we call the 'hardware'. We have the cultural elements, which are what we call the 'software'. Then the big piece overlapping the other two is the 'people'.

In each of these areas we have made a lot of changes. The most visible ones are obviously in the 'hardware' because they are easy. You can draw an organizational chart and put different people's names in different boxes. And we made a good many changes in that area relatively quickly and easily. Our whole structure has changed in the last two years.

The piece that we're obviously struggling with, and still changing, is the cultural aspect, although we are making progress.

Key objectives
The key objective was growth. We translated the vision, the 200X Vision, into a very specific growth target. We said by 200X we want to be a Billion Dollar Company. The Breakthrough Case is what we call all the things that are going to get us there. We have achieved about four-fifths at the moment.

So we translated that strategic vision into something much more tangible. It's about becoming the most productive company, and helping our customers to become productive. It is all about growth, looking forwards, new technologies, new customers, and everything that goes with it. I would say the key piece about it is the different sense of productivity. It used to be about things like volume, and to some extent speed – productivity was about efficiency. It's now about different things like quality, the value that somebody adds. We recognize those changes that are happening around us and how we as a company have to change to meet them. It's about having equipment and services that help customers become more productive, which is a totally different way of thinking.

Restructuring
We used to have functional alignment. So you had sales, service, marketing, finance, etc. and HR, which I was part of. Within that we also had five, six or seven regions. So, for example, sales had five geographical regions. In the old structure you would have had West London sales, West London service, West London administration unit. There were some advantages because you get your expertise pretty strongly honed. But of course the customer doesn't actually see us that way. They see the company name, whether it's a sales person or a service engineer or a query with their invoice.

We've set up our organization now into Customer Business Units (CBUs), which are small, not exactly companies, but small units of no more than about 400 people, who are focused on the customer. Within that they probably have sales, service, administration, etc., but they are responsible as a business, with a profit and loss account. So you now have a West London Customer Business Unit. We have six of those.

Then there are Business Division Units. These were created because we realized it was a long way from the business in the States to the local customer in terms of the number of layers of management, and employees, that they had to go through. For instance, on product development the information from a customer back to your research and development team never quite made it. It was such a complicated route to go with so many layers.

These Business Division Units, which are worldwide, are actually focused on a broad product range. It's complicated, which is one of the downers of all of this. We then have a Managing Director over all that lot (the Business Divisions) and what we call core enterprises, which in essence provide support and a bit of governance, e.g. legal services. Then there are Group Resources which encompass Corporate Communications, and Corporate Policies, that sort of thing.

The Business Division Units are running a business, so to some extent they could buy in or not buy into the corporate policy, within limits of course.

All these different groupings have to contract for business with each other, so all the lines of communication and authority are criss-crossing.

In line with that structural change, we decentralized the HR department. At the time I was an HR manager and I went into a group, in essence a Unit, and not only reported to the General Manager of that Unit but was paid for, and made accountable to, that Unit. For me, this meant I had to, for example, negotiate for any training I wanted to provide, and take responsibility for it.

That change in the HR function was quite substantial in terms of how we had to work. One of the things we did was to set up networks of people with similar remits within the company. So we have an HR Network with all the HR people from all these CBUs getting together about once a month. Although we discuss policy and strategy, in relation to whatever the core enterprise is saying, each of these Units could, to a large extent, do whatever they want.

What have the effects been on your role, responsibilities, accountabilities?
I'm actually going to go back a bit, to my previous role as an HR manager because there was a massive change in how I had to operate.

Specifically, I was much more empowered. Previously, if we wanted to change our organization slightly, e.g. close down one unit in Manchester and move the people to Birmingham, that would all have to have been centrally signed off. After the change I would put the plans together, submit them to the General Manager, possibly call on some central resource to support us, if it meant redundancies for example, but in essence the decision making was down to me and my General Manager. Which is very different from having to go to the Centre and get everything signed off.

That's a relatively small example. But you can actually change things now without having to go through lots of hierarchy.

The level of empowerment varies depending on the individual and the Unit they are part of, and how much they have made the transition. Individuals do have both authority and responsibility. If it goes wrong you are the person who is going to answer for it. There's a lot of talk about empowerment, but actually there are a lot of people who are scared of being empowered.

Some people really struggled with that. They were still going back to the Director to get approval for everything. That's not how it works. You have to learn to do a contract, you have to learn to do a training plan. You have to learn all these other things.

Another role change is that we had to develop a contracting relationship with various people. So for instance we used to send people on training courses to the training centre we had at Basingstoke. You just booked them, then sent them. You didn't really think about it. There was a course there, so people went on it. Now you have to sit down at the beginning of the year and contract X number of training days, say what the sorts of courses we want delivered are, and they will say how much it's going to cost. That makes you think about what we really need. Is this the best way to deliver it? So it does affect the way you work.

You have to become business people, and realize the true value of some of these things.

It's been a hard process for people to go through, this contracting. And we contract across the whole organization. I've described only a minute example of what we do at a much larger level where a Customer Business Unit has to contract with each of the Business Development Units as to how much business they can deliver, and in a sense agree their plan for the year. Eventually that all gets rolled up to where hopefully we will be a Billion Dollar Company by 200X.

Most important tasks in the change process
First, it's getting the right structure in place. I think the next big step is getting the right people in the right structure. I'm not sure we still have it right. Some people in the new structure are still working in the old paradigm.

They are still sending things to people to get signed off and not making decisions. Not looking across the Network. They are always looking to the top of the triangle rather than across. So you have to have the right sort of people in place.

The other big task is engaging the people who are involved in the change and also are affected by the change.

How was that done?
A lot of it was very structured. In terms of the overall organization, we had a little booklet which says 'This is our change'. But that won't really engage you. It gives you the basics, it gives you the understanding. A lot of the engagement overall I would say in the organization is just happening now through workshops, through activities the General Manager or Managing Director take on, that show there is a change going on. Sometimes it's very subtle. It's about how people talk to other people, the sorts of questions they ask. Rather than telling you about something, it's bringing you in to understand what's going on.

We have a Foundation Workshop, which in essence is re-inducting every employee. One of the exercises we do is give everybody an overhead projector slide, an acetate, and some pens, and we say OK, draw a picture of how you see the company at the moment. And you get all sorts of awful things, from we're not customer-focused, all the infighting, all these competitors – all sorts of different pictures. And then you say OK draw where you want the company to be. Everybody says, facing in the same direction. And you see some wonderful pictures! It's a very simple exercise but it's the one that sticks in people's minds. They say, right, so what we are trying to do is getting everybody to work forward, and we are doing it because of all these competitors that are out there, and we put this structure in place so that we can look after our customers and slowly but surely the cogs start turning and it starts sinking in.

What other strategies are there for getting commitment?
It happens at all sorts of levels, so it's hard to know which level to pitch it at. We seek a lot of feedback from our employees. And based on that feedback come improvement projects.

So, for example, I am in a group called Empowerment. We are going to be instigating a thing called X-teams which are high-performing, high-powered teams. On the project team to set that up we have employee representatives who give us feedback.

Sometimes there are *ad hoc* groups, sometimes an informal structure for getting feedback. So there are loads of different levels. I mentioned that we are re-inducting every single employee in the Foundation Workshop. In essence it is explaining to people what the company is all about – what it means to them, what it means to where we are going, etc.

Then we have what we call a policy deployment process, which every year, from Managing Director down, states what our goals are, what our vision is. Then we get down to what we see as our vital core programmes. So this year we have eight programmes this organization is committed to. They include empowerment, improving our skills – there are eight of them that we are just about to launch into our next policy deployment cycle. And every single employee gets taken through this every year. We've been doing that for four years or so. Obviously the detail changes, although the goals and the vision don't and there are opportunities to reiterate them again and again.

That's two formal things. The third big formal thing is what we call our Management Model. Basically, we defined what the 40 or so areas that as a company we are looking at are, so it includes management leadership, human resource management, our processes, our quality tools, the customer – which is obviously right in the centre – and things like business results.

This is our model, which comes from the top. From this model, every year, we assess every unit in the business. Employees all over get involved in the assessment. So it's not just the senior manager getting down as an examiner saying what's wrong. Instead he says 'Tell me what you do. Tell me how it fits into achieving our common goals. How do you think we are doing on communication? How do you think we are doing about this?' And that happens at every Unit once a year. In a sense it's our assessment process, which then builds into what we should be doing next. It's a continuous cycle.

Those are some of the more formal things. We also have a massive feedback loop in terms of our employee motivation/satisfaction survey. That's one of the things we've changed in line with the organization. We've done a survey for numerous years, but it tends to be much more focused on traditional things like pay, benefits, that sort of thing. No one is ever going to be totally satisfied with their pay, so it's almost like 'Why do we keep asking the same question?'. What we have done is actually created a survey to look at the 'software' elements. It looks at things like valuing people, trust, learning, direction, communication – all those sorts of things. Then it examines the issues in two different ways: one within the workgroup, and one within the manager. So you get a sense of the manager as a leader in his or her role, and how the manager and the group work together. The group takes the findings and says 'Well we actually don't treat each other with respect' or 'our manager creates the direction for us, but we don't actually work with it in any way as a group'. The results have just come in, and they are quite positive, which is encouraging.

The survey was a tangible way to start looking at that 'software' thing. Because it's so difficult. What do you do? The structure has been easy and it's had a massive impact across the board. People say there's a lot more conflict. I'm not surprised, with all these lines going all over the place. I would say that's the one negative. But there's a lot of positive outcomes – the customer is much closer, contact is much more direct, people are more responsible, in terms of profit and loss, and can see much more clearly how they, as individuals, can affect that profit and loss. We are expecting more of our employees in terms of being business people, because in a small company of 400 they have to be.

So there are lots of things we've done here structurally, and some of the more difficult ones are where we really start engaging people, like the Foundation Workshop, the satisfaction survey – it's on-line.

Are objectives being achieved?

Absolutely. There are two or three things that show me. First of all, our customer satisfaction ratings have gone way up over the last couple of years. That's one of our key measures. Our employee satisfaction ratings, even on the old survey, have jumped considerably and at a period of time when externally the norms for the UK are going downwards. Our return on assets, which at various points was not what we would have liked and our shareholders wouldn't have liked, is climbing year on year. We are in something like 20 per cent growth, year on year now. It's not good enough for us, because our plan was 30 per cent, but the fact that we have grown 20 per cent is pretty incredible. I don't think we make enough of it. Our year ends in a few weeks time and people are beating their heads against the wall because we haven't hit plan. But at the same time we've achieved enormous growth in very competitive markets. If you think of our market-place, in things like laser printers there is an enormous amount of competitiveness. But a few things we do now are very distinct, which nobody has come close to imitating yet, which of course brings in a lot of money.

But it's fascinating that we are actually growing so much on all measures.

Part 2: experiences in managing change

Have there been any critical incidents or events which have made the change successful?

It's a good question, but it's very hard to answer. Because it's been such a big change it's hard to pinpoint one. The one thing that seems to be having a massive effect is our Foundation Workshop. At the moment it's mainly gone to middle and senior management, and now this coming year it will be cascading to everybody. But all the managers come out of that and say 'That's really good'.

Factors which promote changes or inhibit change

As far as promoting change is concerned, as an organization we have always been very change-oriented, at least since the eighties, and tend to hire people who are that way focused. We are probably ahead of other companies in terms of our attitude to change. Much as we all whinge about it, you don't hear the phrase 'It's not my job'. You hear a bit of sentimentality about the old days, but no one would prefer to return to the old days. It's very strange, but I think we are unrepresentative of British culture at large. People here do generally tend to accept change as inevitable and there are some things that are not so good. I guess when it gets personal and affects them, they can get a little bitter, but generally you actually don't find that.

Something came home to me the other day when we were working on something to do with team working for engineers. They have all gone to self-managed work groups without managers. Someone said recently, 'What the engineers want to know is what does the company expect an engineer to look like in three years time?'. Because they want to be that engineer. So they have recognized things are changing, they recognize they have to change along with it, but at the same time they want the company to provide them with the answer as to what's expected. Then they will hopefully get some support to help them with that change.

In terms of inhibitors, 99 per cent of it comes down to behaviours and attitudes. We, as a company, are very results-orientated, very competitive by nature in terms of our people, because that is what we have bred over the last 40 years. So there's still very much an attitude of 'How many boxes can you sell?'. That's actually not the way the market is going and it's not going to get us to the future because you need to be selling the service that box provides, because quite honestly, one piece of machinery is very much similar to another, although they may have different bells and whistles! It's all about selling services. Yet that attitude about selling boxes still pervades a large proportion of the organization.

This whole idea of results means that people don't necessarily focus on how they do things, but just the ends. So a lot of it is about means to achieve the ends. We could go out there and sell loads more, but basically alienate every customer we have. And that's not the organization we want to be. So a lot of that's about attitudes.

Does the company give support when it's needed?

Yes, loads. When we went to self-managed workgroups all the engineers went through loads of training on how to manage themselves as a group. Each of the groups has support people who provide them with hardware information, like what is their response rate, and how many customer calls there are – those sorts of things. But also in terms of group development they run their own meetings, they decide how they are going to handle the workload – whether they are all going to come in early tomorrow because tomorrow is going to be a busy day. They are actually at a point where they are doing their own appraisals. There are some groups who have agreed their own pay reviews. They were given a pot of money and told 'You distribute it amongst yourselves as you see fit. Here are some guidelines, here is some support, here is some administration process, but in terms of the decision-making – over to you'.

Looking back, do you think anything could have been done differently?

If it was up to me, I would have done the Foundation Workshop much sooner – after a number of years we are only just beginning to get to some employees. OK, you need to see the overall picture, but I think we could have done that much faster and been much slicker and acknowledge this 'software' piece even before we made some of the organizational changes.

We put it in place almost two years ago, even though it seems like yesterday, and we sort of muddled along. People have adapted and come up with ways of working and vaguely understand why we are doing it all, but I think we could have done something much sooner by saying 'This is what it's all about'. That would have made a big difference. I think we would have been able to move faster then. A lot of employees probably still aren't on board. If you ask them 'Tell me about X and what it means', I wouldn't be surprised if you got an incoherent answer from them. That's the big thing I would do differently.

The other thing I would do differently is not necessarily to change the people at the top of the organization, but I would have forced the change on them first. Because I actually think that a lot of the reason we are still not where we want to be is because of the influence of the people at the top of the organization who have basically been there all the time.

They have grown up in this company and they have become successful because of a certain type of behaviour in the last 20 years. And I can understand why it would be difficult for them to change. But you almost need some sort of external view that says 'No – you need to handle that one differently next time' and not to continue behaving in the same way. A lot of it is very subtle. Sometimes I feel like a fly on the wall and I feel a lot of the unwritten behaviours, and unwritten rules that we work to, are actually preventing us moving as fast and as significantly as we want to, particularly on things like empowerment.

We might have got away from the fact that we needed to get three signatures at the bottom of a page, but are people really empowered to make a decision? I'm not convinced they are. That's because, if they do make a decision, and it goes wrong, nobody says 'OK – I understand why you made that decision. Let's learn from it'. Instead of that it's 'You made the wrong decision', which actually is a very different way of dealing with it. Doing anything in this company that's a 'failure' is just not acceptable. But you have to have failures in order to learn. So there are some subtle things like that – I don't know how I would have done it differently, but I think I would have focused more on that senior management team, first of all.

Is there anything you think it's important for managers to learn about, in terms of managing change?

One of the things that has come to mind over the last few months is that we actually don't have, as far as I am aware, a model for change management – which is fascinating when we are in the leading edge of change and having been the leaders in Total Quality Management and all the rest. I have never actually seen anywhere a model of change management. I think it would be very useful if someone could come up with a simple model for change management, like what are the key things to consider, what are the key building blocks you need to have in place. Not something like 'improve communications'. Then, before you start thinking of major change, you would have to make sure your employees understand what model you are using, so that they can actually get involved in helping you manage that change. So it has to be a model with two sides to it almost – this is how I am going to do it from the management side, but also what the employees see and get involved in.

My current manager thinks that if you take the story of Moses leading the Jews out of Egypt that actually gives you a change management model. He did a presentation on this and we're working on it! If you look at what Moses had to deal with – resistance, they fell back a bit, you've got to pull them up again – all those sorts of things, it seems to fit.

How would you say management itself has changed in the last decade?

It's very hard to be a manager nowadays. In many places the manager is seen as next to God almost, leading the way and all the rest. I think we put an incredible pressure on being a manager and we keep changing the goalposts to a certain extent. Now you have to be a leader, now you have to empower your employees. But what does that mean for me as a manager? What role do I have to play? So there are a lot of changes we have imposed on management without actually giving them the support they need in changing their role.

One change is that we no longer want managers who control, who tell people what to do, who are authoritarian. But a lot of managers have grown up in that sort of style, either as a manager or an employee working for a manager. And that's who they use as a role model. So even the people who are coming through don't actually have a role model to measure themselves against.

We have managers who manage 110 people with no supervisors in between. That is a totally different role from when they had four or six managers or supervisors they were managing. It's had a massive impact. It's impacted career development and all the rest, and I don't think we'll ever get back to that stage where we all had hierarchies, and the way you moved forward, and got more money and more status was when you moved to the next level.

I think there is even more pressure at management levels than at employee levels. We have always had employees who are, for example, engineers who are happy being engineers, who have been engineers for 20 years and will always be engineers. OK – they will have to keep up-to-date, but it's the managers who have lost their career structure, not the employees. Yet we always focus on the employees not having this career structure. It's actually the managers who don't.

Expectations of a manager are also that a manager will be a font of all knowledge. There is so much information now that they have to try to keep up-to-date on, there's no way they can be a font of all knowledge. Even if you spent all day accumulating knowledge, you still couldn't fulfil that role, and you certainly wouldn't have to put it into practice.

Who knows where it's going. It's very difficult for people, especially when they get to line managers. More and more and more is constantly being pushed on them without letting anything drop off the other side. That's maybe where I would do things differently. It's almost saying 'We're now doing this – but it replaces X, Y and Z, so forget about that'. But instead we just keep adding and adding and don't drop anything. it will be interesting to see how it develops in the next few years. There will be a lot of stressed out people.

Implementing strategic change in a charity

Background

It's a fascinating experience when headhunters ring you up. I was changing the structure of another charity. It was a bit like this charity, on a downward spiral, it had lost its way. It was like a big sleeping giant. It was the biggest agency for that disability, but not really sure what its role was. I was there for nearly five years. They had said 'Come in and sort it out. Increase morale and give it a proper sense of direction'.

My predecessor had been sacked there, as he had been here. So I went and did it for that charity. It went from four and a half to fourteen and a half million pounds annually. It was very influential politically. Trying to get new services for these disabled people, new legislation, that kind of thing. So it increased the profile.

Anyway, the headhunters chased me for a couple of months, they were very persistent. So then out of sheer frustration I said I'd come and talk to them if they promised to let me alone afterwards. By this time I was talking to the top man at the headhunters – posh office, nice bottle of wine – and ten minutes later I was on the shortlist.

They had done their homework (at the interview). They asked me questions about articles I had written years ago.

The next thing is, I found myself here. The thing that sold it to me was that it was a real management challenge. It needed a major change process. They (the Trustees) had sacked the whole of the management team, bar one person, so we had to recruit a new team.

Recruited ahead of me was a part-time UK Personnel Director who, interestingly enough, had been to see me at the previous charity looking for a job. I'd interviewed him for two hours – I got on really well with him – I hadn't got anything for him. So it was good to get here and find somebody that I knew.

We then appointed a new team, worked out the change of direction, where we were going. First there was the strategic plan.

Did you know where you were going before you appointed your new team?
No. I arrived early January and eight days later I was hit by a war abroad, so we had to mobilize here and in the region affected. So I didn't know what had hit me. We had a major fund-raising campaign, I'd got a team manager there, I'd got every branch on standby. So all that was going on while I was trying to set a strategic direction.

The strategic plan
The strategic plan was produced as a fixed five-year plan – very much top down. I said 'You've got to do it this way. I know you are all very competent Directors but this is the way you are going to do it. I know it works. I'm sure you have got better ideas than I have, but we haven't got the time'. So I gave them the model, a set of papers setting out what I wanted to do.

I said 'You've got three months to get back to me and tell me how you are going to do it. I want some information about who the main customers are, I want your strategic priorities in your division for the next five years based on the knowledge you've got. You can do it any way you like, but follow this model. You can do it as a group, you can put a wet towel over your head, whatever you like, but by early April I want the result'.

They each came back – we obviously had discussions and meetings in between. The problem was we didn't have any systems here to find out anything I needed to know. Finance systems weren't in place. When I wanted to know how much money there was, how many buildings we had, it just wasn't available. They could just say 'There's a lot of this'.

They all put something in to me, as best they could. Then I took three months. I recruited a volunteer for strategic planning meetings, an ex-Personnel Director, and he came and worked for me for three months as an assistant, on secondment. We just paid his expenses.

His job was to work with me, read through all the plans, see where the commonalities were, see where the conflicts were, begin to knock it into some shape so that it would read like one document and then do the external environmental reviews. We worked on that for three months.

Then we took the team away for three days, just the Directors. I said 'This is the document. This is the first draft of the plan'. I said this wasn't the normal way I would do it, but everyone was very busy with the war. Then we had the cyclones and a crisis in Africa, so we were trying to do all of that at the same time.

We went down to our training centre. I said 'Look, we're not leaving here until we've got this done. It may be all day, all night, but we're staying here till we've finished.'

And we sweated over this damned document. We changed it and moved things around. We argued over the tensions and strains and so on.

So we revised the document and then did seven or eight roadshows around the country. There were two Directors at each. The audience was anybody from the membership, the Branch Directors, Presidents, etc.

In the UK we have around 100 000 unpaid, active, trained volunteers. We have around 3000 paid staff. They had never had a roadshow until then where they had been consulted, so again it was a first. Basically we did a presentation, everyone gave the same presentation. And we listened to what they had to say. There was anger, there was frustration, there was pleasure that we were actually doing something. Some very useful comments came back.

As a result we made some changes to the Plan. We then put it to our Council on October 23rd. Nine months after I joined. And we got it through. It was hard work. They had never had to work like this. It was driven from the top, no question about that. But frankly, if we'd gone out for lengthy consultation and all the rest of it we'd never have got anywhere. I'd still be doing it.

I made the point that it needed to be fixed term because it was the first plan and they weren't used to it and also they needed to see some progress a year or two into the plan. I wanted to have at the end of the five years something clearly measurable that could show progress. So we set very, very aggressive targets for our income.

We had five strategic priorities in the Plan:

1   Raise the profile
2   Raise more income
3   Improve and develop the support services
4   Start to improve and develop the quality of our programmes
5   Research the programmes to see if we are doing the right programmes for the right people in line with our mission.

Two years before I came, my predecessor had actually looked at what they termed the 'long-term mission statement', which was a bit outdated and old-fashioned but was workable. So I decided to take that for the time being and said OK, we won't change that. We'll accept that for now and develop the strategy along those lines.

I felt we needed a bit more time to review our programmes of work, because we had 65 different programmes of work. For example, I commissioned some market research within the first months. The title they came up with was 'Best Known, Least Understood'! That said it all. So we had a lot of information there that was useful.

I knew the structure was a mess, it was almost unworkable. I know a lot of Chief Execs come in and make a lot of structural changes to make a big impact – change the names of Directors and give them different responsibilities. I didn't want to do any of that because we didn't know yet what we would be restructuring for.

It was a risky strategy, raising the profile, because if we put our head above the parapet and said 'Aren't we brilliant?' the media might say 'Well actually, in this area, you are not brilliant'. But we had an opportunistic view of profile raising to start with because we had the war, and we were active there. I took every opportunity to get on TV. It didn't matter. I would be there, trying to create an impression of being Mr Charity. And we wrote a newsletter. And it worked. Of course you can only do that for so long before you need a proper strategy behind it.

So all that was going on while we were reviewing the services. The sixth strategy or strategic priority, was to commit ourselves, or recommit ourselves to being a volunteer organization that worked primarily using volunteers, both here at home and overseas, and the paid staff were there to support the volunteer workforce.

Which meant we had to look at our volunteer force, and when we looked at it we realized it was dwindling. For 10 years we had been losing 4 per cent of our volunteers. But no one had noticed mainly because no one had bothered to count them before. I said 'Did you know you were losing volunteers?'. They didn't, although it was difficult to do the counting because the systems were not in place.

So we then developed a volunteer policy, a contract for volunteers, a recruitment policy and a maintenance policy. Basically we started at the top, invested heavily in fund-raising and profile raising for a year or two. Then we started the systems – the computer system, finance systems, personnel systems, all of that.

So from an organization which was headquartered here, there were 40 people here when I arrived; there are now 300-plus posts. There were three fund raisers – two were ex-journalists. We now have a public relations division with 85 staff. That's a hell of a commitment. We now know we have around 3000 staff, not the 1500 I was told we had. We have created a lot of new jobs out in the regions. We had 35 staff overseas; we now have at any one time over 100 staff overseas, which means two or three hundred missions a year. That's mega growth.

Income has doubled. We haven't touched our reserves to do any of this growth and development. We have more than reached the aggressive income target we set ourselves. We have tracked our PR. The market research that was done two years ago showed we were 17th in a list of charities. The Foreign Office did some work, unbeknown to us recently, and found that we were now in the top 10. The income speaks for itself.

By bringing all those people in, and being more aggressive in fund-raising, it's put strains on people. We've recruited people who were aggressive and wanted to grow with us.

I think the next five-year period is going to be a bit different and we are going to have to create an environment which recognizes that change is healthy and part of the ethos of this place. So the next plan, which we've deferred writing to the end of this year, (this is the fifth year) will look at the organization bottom-up.

The idea originally was to start the process of rewriting the plan at the end of last year and work on it throughout this year, and phase it into our budget. But last year was a major birthday, so we had a heavy year last year. I wanted to get that out of the way. In fact, two paragraphs in my strategic plan of five years ago referred to the structure, saying it's a mess. It's not a very effective structure. It's bureaucratic, it's wasteful of resources, and we must do something about it.

Well I think it was about two years ago I pulled these two paragraphs out, photocopied them, and showed them to the Trustees. I said 'Do you remember we said this, and we agreed this? Well it's time. We must do this now'. And they were very nervous about it but they agreed in the end to go through a very long-winded process and bring in another volunteer, a lawyer, who was seconded to us for six months.

I said to him, go out into the UK, and talk to the members and find out from them what the structural issues are which are causing them problems. What the blockages to progress are as far as the structures are concerned. And he came back with this really emotive report. I sat down with him and with a few other people and we hacked it to death and got it down to the bare essentials. I don't think he liked it. But we ended up with something that was very useful.

It said basically that there were eight problems with the structure and you must do a review. Which is what I wanted it to say.

We went to five consultancies, including Coopers and Lybrand, and Compass, who work exclusively with charities, but we chose McWilliams Consultants, who work a bit with charities as well as the commercial sector. They are a fairly small outfit. We chose McWilliams on the basis of price and sensitivity to the volunteer system, and also I leaned hard on them. I didn't want Coopers coming in and giving us a typical Coopers review. I'd been burnt by McKinsey so I didn't want someone coming in doing a typical job. Instead, I said 'This is the way you are going to do it. There is going to be a lot of consultation, it's an 18 month job, the process of change has to be part of your work. By the time you get to make your report to the Trustees, everyone will know what the recommendations are, and will more or less have accepted them'. That's the process you've got to follow. 'And, I'm going to second to your team of consultants a full-time Branch Director'. Coopers didn't like that idea at all, but McWilliams did. They said 'You're the client'. So I seconded Peter, who you're going to see. He worked full time with the McWilliams team. We also had two volunteers from our charity, typical, elderly, from Liverpool or somewhere like that. And a guy from Harrogate who was an accountant. They were all volunteers and offered their services to do this.

The other feature of the consultants' work was that they did not report to me, or to the Board of Trustees. Instead, we brought in an independent Chairman. He had been the Chairman of a pharmaceutical retail firm. If they had been working to me, people would have believed the team were in my pocket. Some people thought I should do the review. 'If you're so bloody good – you've been to Henley – you should be able to do it'. I said well of course I could do it, I could do it standing on my head, but if I do it you are not going to accept my recommendations.

I said we can't work with the current Board, because they are part of the problem. You're the wrong people doing the wrong job in the wrong place. So we can't work to you. You'd put a gloss on things and be defensive. So we have to find a neutral body.

A neutral body has to be an independent team, that you have given authority to, to go and do the job. We have consultants, and we'll pay them. I went to the Charity Commissioners about that because I didn't want them to think we were using the money inappropriately, I had several members who threatened to report me to the Charity Commissioners for spending all that money. But the Charity Commissioners were happy with what we were doing.

So the steering committee for this exercise consisted of Sir Chrystal Butt, Chairman – at the time Chairman of three major companies; so quite a good guy. That would be his contribution to the Charity for two years. There were several internal people, including Branch representatives, one was a Director. There were two working volunteers, a user of our services – she was severely disabled – and one member of my senior management team. Then there was the MD of a retail clothing company, the head of social services for a county in the South; and the Chief Executive of another large retail organization, he's a good guy.

So they were all neutral. Their brief was to produce a structural report which would bring about some changes. They did. They did it in three phases. First there was a report which said 'This is what we think. Does it sound right?'. They did roadshows all over the country – the consultants and some of the steering team. Sir Chrystal Butt started by saying he only had limited time, but then found himself going out to the branches and getting more and more involved. They held big meetings for anyone who wanted to help or take part.

They produced another report. And on the basis of that they said these are the issues and these are possible solutions. What do you think? Finally they produced a report which went straight to the Board.

They had it in December last year, and they spent three hours considering it, including presentations from the steering committee. They had a chance to ask questions; they got things off their chest.

I stayed in the background, but of course they had been reporting to me all the time. I was paying their bills but I wasn't formally part of their process.

They made no decision at that meeting, but they said on January 15th, this year, we'll have a special meeting of the council devoted to this topic and we're going to make some decisions. There were ninety-odd recommendations in the report, but they boiled down to five things I would have to insist on with the Board.

In other words, if they didn't go through, I would have to go. The rest of the items flowed from these key decisions.

So we set them in the form of resolutions and made them debate the resolutions, but they were being forced to make decisions. They were voting on them. They voted on the resolutions one by one and we took them in the order which we thought they would find easiest to understand. I'm sure they all understood the seriousness of what they were doing. We got something like votes of 22 to 6 for each one.

The consultants were at that meeting and during the meeting they were preparing a composite resolution based on the reactions to each of the resolutions. That was put to the meeting at the end, and it was unanimous. So we had a unanimous meeting of the Board to reduce themselves from 33 to 12. To get rid of all our separate charities – we had more than a hundred separate charitable bodies as part of the group. All the local county Branches were independent charities – that had been forced upon us by the Charities Commission in 1963. We created a tier of regional middle management; what the regions felt like and looked like was yet to be agreed. But there will be some regional directors with teams. There will be a branch council, a regional council, a national council. The regional directors will report to a UK Director who will report to me.

So there's a consultation line for users, members, donors, people we contract, bringing in a lot of people, even on the international side. Obviously we're hopeful there will be crossovers in discussion, but there's a very clear line authority and management chain. Because that's a very important feature when you have to respond quickly to an emergency to a particular quality standard. And I've insisted that people work to quality standards. And if they won't work to quality standards I don't want them.

We have a massive training programme. We have a fast track management training programme as well.

So where are we now? The final resolution was that we would have an implementation group established to see the whole thing through.

I would have argued very strongly that we needed a Chief Executive and a management team to implement the change, but I would not have got away with that. So what we have is an implementation group chaired by the Chairman of our finance committee. He's an ex-PWC partner and a great guy. He fully understands executive and Board relationships and so on. We've got four Presidents representing different aspects of the organization, a Branch Director, a Regional officer, and three senior management people, including myself.

I have an inner group, Dave is my executive assistant, and we are driving this. I am actually leading from the front and driving this one. My five directors and myself, in terms of implementation, are working in pairs on six of these 90 recommendations, which have become 124 issues requiring action. Many of them have project teams falling into six strategic groupings. So there are six directors including me. We are working in different pairs leading these six strategic groups. There is a senior coordinating project group and nothing goes to the group without first going through the senior management team for coordination.

The implementation group has authority to make whatever decisions they like in order to start to make things happen. There are one or two decisions they can't take, however. Like one of the recommendations was that three branches should disappear. They will debate it, and I have commissioned the research. It doesn't matter to me whether they go or not. But that decision will have to go back to the main council and one or two things like that will go back.

If the Chairman of the group – the Vice Chairman of the Society is on the group – and one other Trustee, feel we are pushing things too hard and they want to refer it back to council, they have the power to say it's got to be referred back to council. So far they haven't done that, but it gives the council some comfort.

I'm assuming that implementation will take about 18 months. I've been out and done a whole series of roadshows, me and the Chairman together, just to show it isn't just me pushing but that it's a joint thing, and we have now done the whole country. We've explained the whole implementation process and explained what it means for them. We've been up-front and given them as much information as we can and saying this is the way it's going to be and asking 'Are there any problems?'.

Scotland was a bit difficult. They wanted to hang on to their structure.

The message now is get on with it. We've been through all this. Some of us have lost and some of us have won. That's where we are.

What's been the reaction to the plan at the lower end of the organization? Broadly favourable I think. There's a lot of nervousness around now, uncertainty. But I can't really help that other than just keep feeding information out. So after each implementation group meeting we have a structure update. It will be written by five o'clock this afternoon and it will be out on the multifax overnight.

So if anyone has any questions there is an emergency phone line, post mailbox – they can leave it anonymously or they can give their name; that is trawled daily, it's written up, it's monitored. We can reply to many of them because the person who manages the communication is so involved. Letters all get channelled into him and get monitored. This includes letters from staff or members. I'm trying to be as open with everybody as I can.

I think there is between two and four million pounds to be saved from this exercise, and getting rid of the duplication of bureaucracy and economies of scale. That can be ploughed back into services, so why not do it?

It means that about 50 headquarters staff will have to go, so we are working on redundancy policies and relocation policies and so on. They will be offered jobs in regional offices. It they don't want to take them they will have to go. Some people will be sucked up from the branches into the regional offices.

The new structure must not cost more than what we have at present. There will be some one-off costs – we estimate about a million pounds – but we are saving several million pounds a year, so that's got to be good news.

I've done change management before, but nothing quite like this, due to the size and complexity of the organization. It's an international organization and we have legislation that directs what we have to do.

Our governing instruments have to be rewritten. We have to satisfy the Charity Commissioners and the Privy Council. The last time our governing instruments went before the Privy Council was in the 1970s. So our lawyers have been involved in this from day one. They seconded an articled clerk to us to help with the change process. So when it comes to rewriting the governing instruments he knows the nuances. So we have to see everything up to the Privy Council by the end of the year.

There will be some pilot changes. We already have some people bidding to become pilot regions. There will be some benefits – like we'll invest some cash, properties, computerization. It's going to be a big, big implementation process.

But I think it's going to work. It could affect our income, our drive, and our sense of direction. We've gone through a process of being clear what our purpose is, a refocusing exercise. That we have to complete six months ahead of the structure review because the consultants had to know what they were restructuring for. We have produced a video which explains this new focus and goes out to all our branches. We have written it all down, but now the video brings it to life.

There is a bit of confusion in members' minds about the focus – we now have a new National Focus Strategy. We have to keep driving the Focus forward as well as the new structural review coming in on its coat-tails.

Before you came in, what prompted the Trustees to recognize change was necessary?

They sacked the Director General. They had an attempted coup on the Board with the Chairman. He had to be re-elected for five years in the October before I came and there was an attempt to oust him. The senior management team was disintegrating. There were people on the Board who were unhappy. Clearly it was on a downward spiral.

I was invited in to change the organization. It had lost its sense of direction, which is perhaps not surprising because no one had produced a strategic plan. There had been some attempts before I came to look at a long-term strategy but they didn't seem to worry about what was going on out there in the branches. Policies would be created by the Board here, sent out to the branches, and that would be the end of it. Nine times out of ten the branches would just ignore them.

When I came in I had no idea that was how they did it. So when we issued a policy I'd go out and monitor it. That sent pulses racing in a few places.

What I was trying to do was to get to grips with the whole organization, to pull it all together, to understand it so that I knew what I was managing. And now because I can do that I can devolve authority to the regions; I can get the management authority nearer to where the action is. So we now do have a sense of direction. We certainly have a higher profile and the money's coming in.

It's not without its problems sometimes. But the systems are in place. I can ask the Financial Director a question and in 10 minutes I've got the answer. If we had carried on as we were we would have been heading for a deficit by now, rather than a surplus.

When I arrived in 199X I was the only one in here. The guy across the corridor at the time happened to be on the finance team and sat at the computer, and I said to him 'How much money is there in the Charity?' He said 'I don't know. How accurate do you want the answer to be? I can give you to the nearest million for two years ago'. Now we have daily cash measurement.

Is it possible for other voluntary organizations to achieve the same results, without you?

Yes I'm sure it is. I do a presentation to the NCVO conference so I know there are 15 to 20 other organizations which have a similar structure to ours. Charity B won't change, but they have the same problems. It needs someone who understands change management, or if they don't, are prepared to get help from somewhere. There are plenty of people around, even here.

We have consultants working behind me, in a sense keeping an eye on what we are doing. Giving us comfort. And I need that too because this is a massive job.

I've now got three consultants. One is from the Base who is doing the handover exercise. One of the strategic groups is called Hearts and Minds. I'm the leader of that group with a new Director I've just recruited. That's a group to ensure everyone feels part of this new Society – they understand the principles that we are all moving toward together. It's in here [touching his chest over his heart] and not just an intellectual exercise.

One of our new corporate sponsors has given us, free of charge, access to as much time as we want from their Board Director who is responsible for strategic planning, a French guy from a FTSE 100 company. So he is coming in to help. The implementation group is headed by an ex-PWC partner, and we have some good project managers, change managers from PWC. There's an expert who has been here several times before just to be working with us to make sure we are not going off track anywhere.

I'm not an expert on critical path analysis, but we have a program here we use and the whole thing is on computer. Dave is learning rapidly now to make Microsoft Project work. The PWC guy can do this so we are paying him a retainer of something like three days a month to be on the end of the phone, or pop in and see me about something at a moment's notice. He's there in the background saying 'Hey you've gone askew a bit'. I need to be reassured and so do the Trustees. Because this is big money. We're investing a million pounds.

I went to see the Charity Commissioners before the Council took their decision, to give them some reassurance that everything was OK. I now meet regularly with the Charity Commissioners to report back to them. They have put together a group of 10 people, senior folk, to work with us because we of course have immediately to get rid of our excess charities. Each of those sets of Trustees – well it means work for the Charity Commissioners. The organizations will lose their independent charitable status and just become a branch of the main charity. It has put a lot of noses out of joint, a lot of fiefdoms being defended.

There's a lot we haven't got right but it's not through want of trying. We try to be straight and honest with them. Where people have something to say we listen.

I had a blazing row with someone at one of the roadshows in Scotland. They were quite rude to us. He was shaking with rage. Accused us of being arrogant, centralizing, and various other things. It was very hurtful. Who knows? It may not work and I may be looking for another job at the end of the year! But it feels as if it's going in the right direction. The Chief Executive is often the last to know what's going on. I do try to get about the organization. In fact, I'm missing the travelling at the moment and feel the lack of a trip to Africa! But this has got to be my priority for a while.

It will be interesting to hear what story you get from Dave. He is very committed to it and has had some problems of his own. He was directing the Canterbury branch and one of the recommendations of the report was that Canterbury should take over Kent. Someone said to him 'You've been trying to do that for the past five years'.

Part 2: second interview

How long have you been here?
I've been with the Charity for four years. I've been involved in this process for just under two. I think the CE had something going for quite a while, but from my point of view I was involved when the working group was set up to actually go out and consult with the members in the branches in order to produce the final report which went to the Trustees last December.

I was based in Canterbury but I lived in Maidstone. But it was a national brief so it was a consultation across the country. Working with two consultants and a couple of volunteers from within the organization. So it was a working group of five, established about 18 months ago. Then last year we did a lot of the ground work and produced the report in December.

Did you hear about what was going on before you were actually involved?
Yes. Because my previous existence was as a Branch Director, so when Jim, who was one of the original consultants, came to do an initial look at the Society, and produced his report, I knew that was going on. But I

wasn't otherwise involved until the establishment of the working group which required an internal member of staff, and I was seconded onto it.

Has it been an interesting experience?
It has. It's been very interesting, and very eye-opening. In many, many respects. It's certainly not the job I envisaged. Working much more closely with national and headquarters staff you begin to see things from a different perspective as well. Because of course I had come from a branch perspective, so I had only seen it from that direction. Obviously I felt there were things that needed to be changed, otherwise I wouldn't have agreed to do the job. But you begin to see the bigger picture when you work for national headquarters.

Do you think the organization would have survived if these changes had not been made?
It's an interesting question. Long term, I don't. Not without the changes. That seems quite a dramatic statement, but I don't think it would have survived in its current form. For example, the age profile of the volunteers, and a lot of the giving is in legacy form from people who remember the Second World War. Without being too blunt – that's a dying breed. It had to change. Those two things, especially the age profile of the volunteers, is still a significant external force. That is, it's forcing change. The age profile is still far too high, but we are trying to do something about that.

The reasons for it are mixed and varied. But in answer to your question, the organization could not continue as it was. It would have struggled on. It wouldn't have died and disappeared and gone overnight, but it would have dwindled rapidly.

If you look at the statistics over the last 10 years the number of volunteers, if you want to use that as a rule of thumb, is constantly falling. In the last two or three years it has levelled off. You could argue that that is because there is a more accurate measure now of volunteers, but I'm certain in my own mind that it's because people are leaving, or dying off. So it's a factor that has to be taken into account.

Was the change predicted or unforeseen? Could you see it coming or was it thrust upon you?
Having had experience of being a Branch Director for two to two and a half years, I could see things that were very wrong and I knew that something had to change. Which is why I was quite keen to be involved

in the change process – not only for the benefit of the organization but also for the benefit of the users of the organization.

I have had a career that goes back in the voluntary sector. I have been overseas. I've seen the international side of the work. And I've been with various charities in this country, disability charities. There were things this charity was doing which didn't feel quite right. And the primary one was that it was focused on its members, not on the service users. That was the culture and that was one of the really difficult ones to shift.

To change structures is relatively easy. To change cultures is far more complicated. That process is on the road now.

So again, in answer to your question, yes I could see something was wrong and I was quite keen to be involved.

How has your actual role changed?
It's changed! When I was recruited full time onto the process it was very much to work with the consultants to bring out an internal viewpoint to the deliberations – someone who knew how it worked in the branches and who had experiences of working in the branches themselves at the point of delivery. It was also to work through with the consultants to see what the best structures were and to have ownership from inside as well as from outside.

Since the report was written, and accepted in January, this role has become very unclear. It's much busier. In the sense that OK we have the report, we have the recommendations, we have to implement them. But the report itself stops short of recommending a definitive structure. It says you need to change certain key things, one of which is the governance, one of which is the line management structure. But it didn't lay down how those things should be implemented. So we are currently in a three-stage process. We have to define what the actual structure, what the actual model is. The 'we' in this case is the Charity, from the centre. The CE is very keen to involve as many people as possible in the process. For example. One of the recommendations was regionalization. So in terms of defining where the regional boundaries actually are, and which branches are in, we have to consult widely and involve many people. In that sense there are things which are open to negotiation. But it's being led by the executive with an implementation team in a steering capacity.

So my role is rapidly becoming a link between various groups working on various issues. There's one group looking at what the structure of the branch should look like, what staff there should be, and who reports to whom. There are other groups looking at what the structure of the region should look like, what the financial model should look like, ways to generate income, and the job itself is acting very much as a link between all three, and indeed the other groups as well.

The job will eventually discontinue. There's no doubt about that. When, depends on the CE. He keeps changing his mind. He tends not to see the detail sometimes. So he says 'Oh, we'll only need that post for another six months', and actually there's a tremendous amount more to do. So I guess by the end of the year most of the work will be done.

What about other people's roles? Have they changed?

They will do. We are trying to work out what the structure actually is. One of the shifts is going to be to focus much more on service delivery, and it looks like the branch model (each branch is a county, so the staff within a county is what we refer to as a branch), so the branch itself is going to be much more service delivery orientated. At the moment each county branch is autonomous in its own right, so it has to generate enough income, it has to service a Trustee Committee, it has to do all the personnel issues, as well as provide services and look after the volunteers. Each branch is a charity in its own right.

So the difference in role of the staff at the branch will be much more focused on service delivery rather than on worker support functions, which can easily happen. These could happen at a regional level, so the branch could be left to get on with the services and let the support functions happen behind it.

Is there going to be any reduction in the number of people employed?

In terms of headcount probably not. But in terms of staffing at the regions there will be posts moved from the county branch up to a region, and from national headquarters down to a region. So headcount will stay roughly the same, but if people don't want to move then there will be a personnel issue there. And of course headcount doesn't take account of salary levels and things like that sometimes. So there will be quite significant change for some of them.

Do people feel unsettled?

Extremely. Extremely unsettled. Part of it is the strategy the CE has adopted. I think it is him. He's adopted a very 'go slow, take it easy, consult everyone, let's not rush this through' type of strategy. And so people have known what's going on. They have been consulted. They have raised issues. Problems have been aired. All of this has exaggerated the feeling that something is not quite right. It's encouraged feelings of insecurity. The alternative would have been the 'Big Bang' way, but I don't think that would have achieved what he was aiming to achieve.

Have there been any effects of changes yet, or have none of them been implemented?

No. I think we are in the stage where a lot of people know what the changes will be. The pilot regions will be up and running mid-year. So the actual impact is not yet.

What are the most important tasks in managing change?

What is important is that we have achieved an agreement to change. And that was far from easy. Just a brief explanation. We have a structure currently where each county branch is autonomous, and therefore the national trustees are made up of representatives from this federal structure. Now if you think that through, to get the national Trustees to vote to abolish the status of branches the phrase 'turkeys voting for Christmas' comes to mind. So to get that one through was quite significant. And that was really a key issue in how to write the report, how to present it, and what to get agreed when it went to the Trustees for agreement, because it was a report with 130 recommendations.

In the end it turned out that only three significant resolutions were passed. They were the broad brushstroke resolutions, one of which was to abolish the charities. So we are moving from a status where there were more than 100 registered charities down to one.

So the Trustees had a lot to lose in that decision. They didn't have a salary, and a mortgage, and a career to think of, but they had other things: status, kudos, power, authority, standing in the local community, those sorts of things.

What were the most difficult tasks?

Last year, when I was working with the consultants, the most difficult one was to get through what I've just described. That was to lobby the Trustees, to explain to them why these recommendations were being put forward. A lot of them couldn't see why we shouldn't just continue the way we were. We had to get to the position where the people in authority could understand the issues about seeing further down the line.

Currently, when we are trying to implement the changes, the most difficult task is probably managing the senior managers. The CE manages the senior managers and I suppose technically the National Board manages him. But there are a number of individuals in the organization who can see the issues at grass roots level, which senior managers are too far removed to see, and that's difficult.

Senior managers, including the CE, want to get things done. And I would support that. They want to get things done, they want to get things moving and they want to do it at certain times. But there are some very difficult decisions that have to be thought through very carefully; for example, to try to define what staff positions and what functions exist at a county level, at a regional level and at a national level. One of the things the Charity does is training. And that's a very complex issue because it involves training staff internally, training members of the public, and commercial training, which is an income-generating activity. So there are different aspects to it. And it's very easy, just sitting at a desk, with a piece of paper in front of you, to put 'Training' in a box in a structure. But until you appreciate the diversity of what that means, it's not quite as simple.

What attempts were made to try to get commitment to the changes?
A lot of that was done last year in the sense that we started off with a lot of people who would make the final decision not being convinced it was necessary.

I suppose the obvious one is the length of time taken to consult over 12 months actually going round the country talking to people – talking to groups, talking to individuals, having the phone line answering queries. There was a long time span where people could actually raise issues and have answers, and actually voice concerns. So it wasn't a case of 'If you don't tell me by Thursday your concerns will be ignored'. That was all part of the process whereby people felt they were being listened to and involved – helping to gain that level of commitment.

How did people seem to react at the meetings?
It was mixed. We started off by saying what the positive and negative concerns to do with the organization were. The very nature of those sorts of meetings mean that people will come out with the problems. But some were thinking very clearly that change was needed. Others were very parochial and saying, 'We're quite happy. What happens over the other side of the country is nothing to do with us'. It was difficult to get them to see that it was one society. Their charitable status encouraged them to think that way, as well as the history of how they have been dealt with. They have been given a lot of autonomy. So it's hard to tell them that they don't actually have it, legally.

They have a lot to lose. It's not just the Trustees. It's the Branch Directors who are the senior executives in the branch. At the moment they are managed by their own Board of Trustees. The proposal is to get them line-managed from London. They do have a lot to lose. So they are your key players trying to undermine the process.

How do people feel about all this? You mentioned insecurity?
A few individuals have a lot of anger. So in that sense it's an emotional reaction without thinking the reasons through or the logical pros and cons. It's just a knee-jerk emotional reaction.

What is the anger directed towards?
They are angry at the perceived centralization. What springs to mind is the anger in Scotland. The Charity has its headquarters in London. A number of the Scots feel that this is England taking over Scotland. So you have that aspect of it. It's a nationalistic problem.

There is also anger at there being no answers. People are very annoyed at the fact that these are radical changes yet there are no answers. For example, branches would ring up and say 'We have a vacancy for such and such. Can we reappoint?'. And the answer is 'Well we're not quite sure yet because we haven't finally decided'.

And that again is a function of the process that has been adopted. Because of the strategy of going out for consultation, and asking for opinions, involving as many people as possible, that tends to slow things down. It becomes very bureaucratic by the very nature of the process, whereas a dictatorial decision could easily have been implemented – yesterday – and you know you have to put up with the consequences. But that was not the decision that was taken.

But for a Branch organization with thousands of volunteers, I think probably the approach has been the right one. So there is concern over that. And even now, in the process of implementation, the CE wants to involve as many people as possible and has given various tasks out far and wide to try to get many people involved in discussing what the answer should be.

I'm not sure about the boundaries between the voluntary and the paid staff?
It's historical. Not that long ago you would find that most people in the organization, including staff in the branch would be volunteers. And that's not long ago – say 10, 15 years. So the line is a movable one. And that's emphasized by the fact that if you go to Scotland they will have a lot of the branches with volunteer directors. And yet in London, which

is a branch, at a Centre level, which is the level below Branch, they have paid staff managing the centres. So in Scotland you have a volunteer director, while in London you have a paid centre manager.

It reflects the level of work, but it does not reflect the position of the job. So the boundary between the paid and volunteer staff is up for grabs. We are trying to define that now. We are trying to equalize things by defining what a branch is and what a centre is.

Is there any anger from people who have given their services voluntarily and may feel they have not been appreciated?

Yes. But it's not from the structural review. The implementation of paid staff in the branches has been ongoing as and when a branch needed it. So it wasn't a function of the review of structure. But you are absolutely right to say that one of the key problems a branch director has is the balance between the volunteers on the one hand, criticizing the paid staff, primarily because they are getting paid, and the paid staff criticizing the volunteers because they are not there nine-to-five and they are not as efficient as they would like. So that's the nature of the beast, given a branch organization with that number of volunteers. That tension between paid staff and volunteers has to be managed. But the anger from the volunteers, yes it's about the staff being paid, and yes it's about them being treated as second class citizens, at times. But it's not about the restructuring.

It is relevant to point out that six months ahead of the restructuring went an initiative that was looking at the mission of the organization. The focus has caused far more anger among the volunteers than the structure has. This is because the focus touches on services. The focus initiative says what is and what is not a legitimate service of the Charity. But the implication is that the volunteers who have been giving a particular service for the last 10 years shouldn't be doing it because it's not a service the Charity exists to provide. Of course they are very angry. You know: 'We give our time voluntarily. We are providing a service. It meets a need. There are people who need the service'. No one is arguing that.

So the focus initiative affects the lives of the volunteers far more than the structure ever will. The structure affects the staff and they are concerned about jobs and mortgages and the rest of it.

Who decided what the mission was?

It was a consultation. Staff in National headquarters beginning to realize there was this one charity that provided 57 different services. What was it that linked a picture library in one part of the country with a trolley shop in another? And how did they link with the Charity's brand in an international context?

So there was a misunderstanding about what the Charity stood for. It's very difficult to run the organization when it's doing a multitude of different things. But also financial pressures mean that you have to look at what you are doing.

Also there was a whole confusion because the branches were going off in all different directions. So there was no uniformity and no unity. And that all led to the process of looking at it again.

Have you any systems for monitoring the effectiveness of any changes you are going to introduce?

Yes, we will have systems. At the top level we will have systems for measuring income, for example. One of the objectives for restructuring was to get a better return, so that's an easy one. Volunteer membership, that's an easy one. So those are the two top level measurements that are being introduced.

There's the other one about staff morale. Staff morale is low at the moment. The CE might disagree with me on that one, but I think it is. So I think there has to be a system for measuring staff morale. Again I don't know how accurate it would be, but you could measure turnover. It's awful at the moment. We've got more than 50 branches in England and the average turnover is about 12 a year among the directors. So that's significant. And that needs to slow down.

Also, if you are talking about morale, you could look at how many people use the restaurant, how many people ring in sick; so those measures need to be observed now, and later, to test that sort of feeling.

Do you think the objectives are being achieved? Or will be achieved?

Yes. I do. But I often wonder whether we are taking too long about it. I have to counter that with the fact that you have to judge by outcomes. And if the outcomes are working then it probably doesn't matter how long it takes. We got the Trustees to approve the abolition of all the charities across the country. That was a major achievement. We got the Trustees to agree to direct line management from London so that the branch directors are accountable. Yes. We are achieving that. The next big one will be can we actually make a pilot region work, because we don't have any effective regional staff at the moment.

How long are you going to give them to set up and evaluate a pilot region?

I'd be very surprised if it would be less than 12 months. That's the argument about not having a pilot because it will take too long. But it may be appropriate to have one region running six months ahead of the others and learn lessons from them. Have one out front and make all the mistakes with the first one. Especially when you are talking about financial systems and things like that. We shall probably have two pilot regions. Because of the national problem, one might be in Scotland or Northern Ireland.

Were there any incidents you consider to have been key, or critical to the change?

The key incident was the voting on the report at the end of last year. That was the big hurdle. So for us it was how to write it, how to present it to them, and before that, how to lobby them. They were lobbied in a number of ways. They were all involved in the consultation process, so probably a good three-quarters of them were actually interviewed by the consultants (I was present too) and asked about their views. So they felt they were being listened to. Then of course we had a new Chairman of Council, Chairman of the Board of Trustees, who played a significant role because he was behind it. That's what swung the doubters. The Chairman of Finance was behind it. That helped. And then the individuals themselves were spoken to by individuals on the Committee.

But as well as that, when we were working as a group, the two consultants, me and the two volunteers, we didn't report to the staff at national headquarters, we reported to a committee, and that committee consisted of a number of key senior Trustees, so from Day 1 we had the senior Trustees involved as part of the process. By the end of that process, not only were they convinced they understood the issues, but they were able to talk to their peer group about it. Whereas if any of us had talked about it, we would have been dismissed as insignificant. But with the senior Trustees on board that was very powerful.

What do you think are the factors which promote change?

I think one of the key factors is strong leadership – strong leadership that is able to explain the issues. Other people are very stuck in their own world or their own job, and getting along nicely, but don't see the overall picture. So for the key individual at the top to be able to stand back and communicate the issues: 'Look we're losing members, and this is why we are losing members'; 'Look, these are external changes. You may not understand about contracting out certain services, and you may not think it affects you, but this is what's happening, and these are the knock-on effects for us'. So it's the ability to stand back and say why. Not just that we need to do it, and we are going to because I'm in charge, but this is why we need to do it. And that's the selling process which gets people behind you.

Which factors inhibit change?

There's the fear of change that is natural in everybody. And the fear that change will mean you are worse off. Whereas the reality of it is that there are also opportunities and some people could be better off. And the organization as a whole certainly has to be viewed as being better off, otherwise they wouldn't do it.

So the key is to focus on what you are going to do and say 'This is why the organization exists. And if we change we are going to be able to do it better, more efficiently, in larger quantities'. But to focus on the *raison d'être* of the organization helps to pull people in behind you, because theoretically everyone has joined the organization understanding what the mission of the organization is. So it they can see that mission being improved they have to be for it.

I'm not sure how well we did that because the mission exercise only ran six months ahead of it, which is too close. Yes, defining your mission has to lead the structure, but not by six months. About two years I would say. The problem was, they confused the two initiatives. I had volunteers ringing me up and saying 'Why can't I do the hospital service?'. And I would have to say I'm sorry, but that's not an issue for me. I sympathize, and all the rest of it, but that's an issue for the services, which is an issue for the focus of the whole organization.

The volunteers especially got the two mixed up. But the staff did as well. So we have been getting a lot of flak for stopping the volunteers doing things when it's nothing to do with us (i.e. the structure and implementation group). But I do believe the *raison d'être* of the organization has to come first. If you are not clear about that, the rest of it is in a very grey area.

Is the mission statement tightly worded, or is it extensive?

It's extensive. The mission statement is about responding to the needy. So all the services the Charity offers should train volunteers to respond as needed.

So I don't think the mission statement is tight enough. But of course we're trying to bring it in from out here [gestured with arms wide apart] and trying to narrow the vision.

Is there anything you think you would have done differently?

I may be contradicting myself here, but I do think we have taken too long and are taking too long. And although people are getting used to it and falling in behind it, they are becoming very nervous and threatened and morale is low. You can only sustain that for so long in a change process, and I think we are taking too long about it.

At the moment, what happened was external consultants were recruited to go out and talk to the members and staff and come up with recommendations as to what to do. But that report was very top level. In other words, when it was presented to the Trustees, it didn't say 'This is what a branch should look like'. It said you've got to do away with the charities. You've got to have line management from London. You've got to change your governing structure and have a different Council. It was those broadbrush recommendations. I would have liked it to have gone on to say 'This is a model of a Branch. This is a model of a region. Here are the functions which should be at each level'. The argument that I subscribed to at that time was 'Let's get it through'. But now the CE has said to his senior managers 'Come on, let's do it together'. For a number of reasons I think that should have gone out to external consultants as well – probably the same team who did the initial report.

Because they know the organization. They have got the time. They have the objectivity. If you introduce the senior managers to this process they are removed from the branch level. They don't understand some of the issues. They also have their own operational plans they want to continue alongside the change process. They have their own personal agendas. They are only human. So when you start looking at restructuring national headquarters it's difficult. And that's why at this stage I would have kept on the external consultants – told them to come up with some details. And that would have solved some of the problems I'm right in the middle of at this moment. Some people are digging themselves in. We need the objectivity.

REFLECTION

These two cases have similarities and differences. The most obvious difference is that one is a profit-oriented organization, and the other a not-for-profit organization that depends a great deal upon the voluntary contribution of its members. In fundamental change, should the implementation process be different in each case, and if so, why?

■ CHAPTER FOUR ■

Developing a marketing orientation

For many years there has been a feeling that the public sector could make significant efficiencies if they had to compete with the private sector. The assumption was that competition would lead the public sector to adopt some of the best practices of private industry. The first case in this chapter tells the story of such a change as seen by the head of a central government agency service department. His department was seen by the chief executive as a nice discrete unit that could be compared with the private sector, and therefore was a prime candidate for being subjected to market testing. The chief executive's agenda was for the in-house team to win, so with this pressure on him, the departmental head devised and implemented a strategy to bring about the desired results. This exercise placed him in a very difficult position because, whereas previously he had been heading the department, his role changed to one of client–purchaser and the departmental staff (who previously were his 'colleagues') had to organize themselves to submit to the test, and if successful, would become contractors. From the point of view of the teller the change achieved its objectives. What stands out are the subtle political manoeuvrings which took place, a readiness to take advantage of opportunities, the importance of good working relationships and open communications with one's staff, and a readiness to cope with the stress generated by conflicting ethical values (i.e. civil service culture versus business culture).

The second case describes a local authority equivalent of central government's market testing – compulsive competitive tendering (CCT) in the housing department. It is told by the assistant housing manager. The authority had already gained experience of competition in its blue-collar work, and this was its first experience of subjecting white-collar services to the market. An interesting situational factor in this case was the need to consult three groups of stakeholders (the elected council members, the residents renting the accommodation and the staff of the department).

Other things to notice include the careful preparation, planning and structuring of the changes; the open and fair procedure adopted in determining
who would have a job after the changes; and difficulties in getting the
message over to staff that the culture had to change to a business culture
where one had to survive within a given budget. The change was a very
costly exercise in management time and effort, and as with the previous
case very stressful for those whose jobs were threatened.

Market testing in central government

What is market testing? When and why was it introduced?
Market testing was brought about by government policy, the aim being
that private sector practices should be applied to the public sector. The
belief is that competition between the private and public sector is a
good thing and that no work should be sacrosanct.

Market testing came about in the early 1990s – this is when the
germs of the idea were beginning to come through. Formally we came
to hear about it through a letter from the Treasury which pointed the
way ahead. Prior to that Michael Heseltine in [the Department of the]
Environment and later Board of Trade pushed the idea and sold it,
although there were ears in the cabinet that were ready to take it on
board. John Redwood was possibly one of the originators of the idea
when he was working in the think tank. The official publication that set
out the way for market testing is 'Competing for Quality'.

The Treasury put out an invitation to Departments to take part in
a programme of market testing. At this time, this Agency put forward its
first tranche for market testing and we were in that tranche. In common
with a number of other units in other government departments we were
seen as a nice discrete unit that could be compared with the private
sector and therefore a prime candidate for being subjected to the market.

The management of change process
The Agency, in the form of the chief executive and senior management
group, set up a steering committee (SC) which was tasked to deal with
market testing issues. Proposals for units to be market tested were put
forward by the SC to the senior management group.

The Agency is quite small, around a few thousand persons, and
at my level and above there are fewer than 50. It's possible to have a
fairly close working knowledge of everything that goes on in the
Agency. The SC thought it was a good idea for us to be market tested.
This was not my view, obviously, nor that of the unit members.

So, my strategy was that rather than put the whole of the unit out in the first tranche we said we would do it in three parts. We decided we would put our Northampton work out first, then the IT work and finally the remaining business area, which was dealing with Bristol.

Once we were 'in the frame' so to speak, we went at it pretty quickly because we didn't want to agonize over the issue longer than we really had to. So I think we were the first market test to complete within the Agency. Others who were also being market tested included office services and supplies, e.g. messenger services and catering services. The distinction that was being made was between core and non-core activities. Since we were not seen as an Executive function we were seen, to a degree, as non-core.

Gratifyingly in some respects, but not in others, the chief executive and management group thought we would be a good unit to put out because they 'knew' that we would win! But that did not help unit morale. The senior management's way of thinking was, 'Let's put something out for market testing that we know will win. We will satisfy the Treasury that we have done the market test and not lose our staff'.

This is fine when you are dealing with it at arm's length, but... we were pushed 'screaming and struggling' down this road, because I protested and said we shouldn't do it, that it wasn't appropriate, but for the reasons given above it went ahead.

So we did it in three parts. My rationale for doing the Northampton part first was that we did not have any staff doing that work anyway – we had three vacancies – so even if we had lost the market test we would not have lost any staff from our current numbers.

What I had done earlier, going back to when we were hearing about the germs of market testing, I immediately called in the Staff Inspectors. We spoke to them and gave them our job descriptions and various numbers and volumes of work that we should be doing with the result that they recommended we should have three additional staff, which I never recruited, but I kept the three 'up my sleeve' for market testing. Funds would have been available for the three staff, but I didn't actually take them on.

[Note: Staff Inspection is a function of most government departments. It is a central initiative, again from the Treasury and is there to make sure that jobs and grades are reviewed on a cyclical basis to ensure that government departments are not getting too 'fat'. Each department generally has their own unit.]

The usual recommendation from Staff Inspection is that they will recommend cuts, so it was quite an achievement to have additional staff recommended. This was because we 'sold' it well.

How did we do this? Because we are professionals there was a little bit of fear on the part of the staff inspectors in the first place. With specialist and technical matters they tend to keep a bit of a distance. So we played on that. We produced our own audit needs assessment, which is a statement of our requirement in staffing terms and details of our work. We were able to show, by converting the work into man-days, that we had insufficient staff. The inspectors were not sufficiently technically adept to contest that. What we did at the time was legitimate because we had a lot of turnover of staff, so when we were putting our figures forward it was on the basis that we had over 50 per cent of trainees. When the time came these people were not trainees, so they were doing more work than they would have done otherwise. They were about 16–17 weeks out of circulation through studying at university and taking study leave, etc. So you only have to multiply that by about six people and that is the three staff that you are short.

We were successful with Northampton, and the work is serviced from Bristol. In the next stage of the process we come on to the IT aspect. But when it came to it we decided not to do that any more because that would mean breaking up the unit that we have in Bristol. So we said, 'We'll merge IT with the rest of the work'.

The original reason for deciding to have three tranches was that if you 'salami slice' unit work so that it was so small, the work would not interest anyone from outside, so our competition would be negligible.

The factors that came into the reconsideration of the first decision were that, because the work was so integrated, it would be very difficult to practically undertake the separation of IT from others. Also, to a degree, on the IT side we would have been vulnerable. We could well have lost any bid on that if it was put out on its own.

The in-house team thought we had a better chance if it was combined, so I went along with that. Note here also that some of those who were servicing the Northampton work also were coming under the Bristol market test as well. So, how did they convince me of the need to change the strategy?

We had several meetings. A senior unit manager was appointed to lead the in-house bid and he selected a small team to work with him that represented all unit interests. The appointment came about almost naturally because the bulk of the work was in this particular individual's area, so he was the main stakeholder.

We were talking to each other all the time. Market testing was the number one issue, so we were talking informally about it – every conversation had some aspect of it. I was aware of the misgivings and could sympathize with them. I said, 'Let's put the reasons forward', and this is what they did.

I put the case forward to the SC and the finance director and said 'I am convinced this is what we should do and this is in accord with what the in-house team would like to do'. My case then went, in writing, to the chief executive, who agreed. This of course was preceded by a lot of face-to-face contact with members of SC, the finance director and the chief executive. Although none of them are in this building, the strategy is that you go to speak with them on a technical issue and once that is cleared you say '...and can I also speak with you about...'. I have got a good relationship with them so it wasn't as if I had to knock at the door and make an appointment for a fortnight's time and produce a briefing paper in advance.

The current chief executive is retiring this year, but has been with the Agency for 10 years, which virtually coincided with my taking over this function. I took over about a year before he arrived. Prior to that the function had been 'the pits'. It was the worst area in the Agency. Anyone who was no good was moved there. I didn't know about this until I arrived, because I had come from a different department. But we turned it around to the point where we are probably rated as one of the best outfits in the Agency. This was largely because the chief executive found by our work, and what we were saying and doing, that we were giving him good support. Even though we were challenged on what we did, one of the quotes I use from him, is 'I'll back you because it has been proved that 99 times out of a hundred you are right.' So, when you have that sort of relationship with him you can discuss various issues on market testing.

We put the two parts together *but* there was then a third dimension! The British Standards Institution (BSI) has the quality standard BS 5750. About three years ago the chief executive and Agency embraced this because it was good and would provide them with kudos. This was adopted for the IT work within the Agency. After getting off to a reasonable start, primarily through the use of consultants costing hundreds of thousands a year, the BSI inspections (of which there are two a year) threatened certification might be removed from the Agency because the Agency was not carrying out quality audits properly. Senior managers were in a bit of a dilemma, at which point I jumped in and said 'we'll take over quality auditing for you'. It was in the remit of two members of the computer services staff, although consultants were doing the audits. I put a case to the senior management group and this was accepted, saving the Agency a considerable amount of money.

We then added that dimension on to the market test. It was now a diverse bundle of services, with the result that the more you put in the more difficult it is for an effective challenge to be mounted against you. Most firms in the market are ones like the big 'five' and IT firms who can do several of the tasks, but very few can encompass the three areas. They have been speculatively dipping into market tests, thinking they could put everything under the umbrella of accountancy and consultancy, but they are not really plugged into the quality audit world. We knew, via the government grapevine and heads of our network, that this was a weakness in the opposition camp. We were monitoring others' experiences, what the best tactics were, discussing how we might play this. These are the sorts of activities that the private sector do and we in the public sector are having to develop some of the same ways of thinking. This is part of the change process.

Another benefit of this strategy was that the in-house team had been making tentative stabs at saying how many staff we need to do this work, and prior to the quality audit work they were constantly in fear that they were overstaffed. I said that if we take on quality audit work that will soak up any last bits of fat that we have got in the unit. They said 'Yes, that will be fine. Can you get the chief to buy it?', and he did, as detailed above. This then meant that they knew the whole in-house team was going in together into market testing, there wasn't a risk of the in-house team leader saying to a few people 'there isn't a place for you in this'. It created a certain amount of unity, which was at risk at the very beginning even though they had confidence after having won the Northampton work, but Bristol was the big one. Northampton was only three posts, whereas Bristol involved 16 posts. Most of the quality audit work has been absorbed into the unit, although we took on one extra person who came across from computer services. Twelve of the unit went on a two-day course – an introduction to quality audit – and one person went on a two-week course and obtained a relevant qualification.

While this change was under way there were other changes, and there is yet further change. Setting this change into context we need to look at changes – past, current and future – that are relevant to this case. First, around 10 years ago we were one of the first government bodies to become an Agency. Part of that, the 'deal' of being an agency, means that every five years the Agency has to undertake a fundamental review to see if it should stay under its existing status or whether it should be privatized. That dimension affects everyone in the Agency, but adds on to what we have got – the need to make a case to the Treasury for Agency status. This happened several years back. It is not a rubber stamping job. But what we thought was the basis for a strong case for remaining as an Agency is not strong when set against the political momentum for privatization.

Recently they have been talking about the future of the civil service and what comes out of that is they are looking for greater efficiencies, and there are ways of achieving this other than by market testing – such as benchmarking and business process re-engineering. We now have a number of initiatives hitting the Agency, one after another – anything new that the government has got behind. At senior management level, down to me and my people, we are always having to battle with these; because our unit is so close to the management of the Agency, we are consulted on everything: first on what we think of the idea on its own merits, and second on how it will actually affect the areas we are looking at. Change is almost becoming a piece of the wallpaper now. I think it is fair to say that over the last 10 years we have known nothing but change.

My job is not technical anymore, it's just trying to get things done. Hence you notice people. When asked what proportion of my time is split between professional/technical duties and managerial duties I don't think I can make a distinction. Even when I am dealing with Agency-wide initiatives, my advice is still being sought with my specialist hat on, so it is still professional involvement.

As a result of market testing the unit is becoming more efficient and is cutting back on things that have a knock-on effect of people having to make good those deficiencies. We are all subject to this. It all adds to the work and to the feeling that I am having to do more work where this is really someone else's responsibility. It is causing a lot of bad feeling within the Agency generally. For example, tasks that used to be done centrally are now being imposed on managers. Central personnel used to check travel claims, but this has been given to managers, who say they have enough to do without being given someone else's tasks.

When I first arrived at the Agency, my task was to make the unit professional. This came as a result of a report following the critical review of the service. Resulting from this was a totally new culture developing, with training and accreditation by the professional body. Hence I was tasked to change what I termed earlier as 'the pits' to a professional unit that could conform to government expectations to get civil servants of a traditional mentality (don't want to do exams or leave home) to go and undertake full-time studying. And also to manage the effect this was having on the rest of the Agency staff who saw 'These real young upstarts telling us what to do, and just because they have passed a few examinations who do they think they are?'. Amongst the old guard there was a lot of resentment, particularly when the success in getting qualifications resulted in them getting more pay. So it was not just a question of my people telling others to do things in a way that could be done better, but they were also younger, had not been in the service as long and were getting more money than us, so our unit was becoming the route for promotion. People had only been in the grade for three years and they were being promoted. We had a lot of very rapid promotion at that early stage. This was quite difficult for the individuals because they were having to wrestle with the professional status and the old timers. This is where my role came in to a degree, because I saw myself as being the bridge between the two. Where there were disputes (although first of all you try to avoid the disputes) I was in the middle of it.

Then there came another change. When the recession set in, training virtually stopped and staff didn't move on, so you had a group of people that got quick promotion who then had nowhere to go. I could always get people and keep people prior to that because they knew this was a path to bigger and better things. But that stopped – and then it started again as we have lost people to the private sector. It's turning full cycle.

Another change that has come about in the Agency is that of having to implement its own pay and grading. This involved virtually everyone in the Agency completing a lengthy questionnaire and having interviews that formed the basis for the pay and grading team to determine where that job sits in the hierarchy of agency work. That process brings a lot of pressure with it because instead of all Higher Executive Officers and Senior Executive Officers being paid the same, there will now be four different bands. You can now be Higher Executive Officer Band 1, 2, 3 or 4. That will have its effect on what you are getting paid. In the sample that was taken, we were included and came out the highest. This was quite a pleasant surprise to our people, who have been given the perception by others that 'You are only specialists, you don't know what it is like to run an operational division'. My answer to that is 'Of course they do, because you run an operational branch running one scheme which you do year after year'. My people look at different schemes so they have to get to grips with several different areas each year. That then has another knock-on effect in terms of the resentment of the rest of the agency towards us when they see their own preconceived views of what is a good job and what is a bad job turned on its head.

Initially, after the sample, the findings came out in this way, and there was a felt fair panel set up to ensure that the output from this scientific formulation stood up to further investigation. There was a lot of unrest on this felt fair panel, with our work being cast as 1.1, and it was said the grade should be 1.4. I had to put the case that what they were saying was totally wrong, but in a nice way so they were not alienated. But that did not work, so I had to come in hard and say that I think there was a lot of bias there, they were being very subjective, the anti-unit feeling should not be allowed to carry on. This was a scientific method, this is what it had proved and as far as I was concerned it was right. So the finance director and the chief executive endorsed it. Funnily enough, it is having the effect at the Agency that now we are starting to advertise posts again – people want to come and join us. So there is good and bad in every issue that arises.

I've always given my staff status by speaking very highly of my people wherever I've gone. A lot of managers refer to their staff in derogatory terms. I've never done that; I say they are professional, well trained and work hard, and if they put a finding forward then it's valid and I tell them that as well. This tends to build up a bit of esteem for themselves, particularly where they are subject to criticism from what they have said or done I take the line that the heavier and louder the criticism and shouting then the more likely you have got to the nub of the issue.

In market testing it's all been designed to ensure that we win it and my people keep their jobs. The computer services head has taken the opposite view. He doesn't want the in-house team to win it, he wants everyone to go. That's almost been running in parallel with our market test and this has had a good knock-on effect with my staff, because they can see that I am gunning for them whereas the other head is wanting to get shot of his staff – and he has, with the result that we are getting applications from his staff to come and join us.

Basically, in trying to ensure we win the market, I've pulled off a few tricks and that has got out, but it's not something that I have been marked down for. All I'm saying is that these are the kinds of things the private sector will do – they are ruthless, they will do what they can, they will twist circumstances to their advantage. It's not telling lies or being unfair, but you just twist it to the benefit of what you want to achieve.

Probably the biggest problem I had on market testing was deciding whether I was going to be heading up the in-house team or whether I was going to be the client, and I raised this with the finance director. He said, 'No you are the client. You shouldn't head up the team'. I said this is going to cause all sorts of problems. He replied that if I didn't it could cause all sorts of problems for the organization, because if I wasn't the client and if I headed up the in-house team and lost, the organization wouldn't have anyone who would know how well the service was functioning. So I said fine, but what happened was in effect I got cold shouldered and was perceived as the rat running from the sinking ship. What I knew in my mind was that by being the client I could decide what was in the specification, I could make the selection of people that we would interview and I would be doing the evaluation. Hence I would be doing more good to the in-house team because the prime user would be rooting for them.

But that was very difficult over a period of about six months. I was made to feel bad because other heads headed up their teams and I was one of the few that was going to be on the client's side. The in-house team said 'Look, everyone else is doing it, why are you separating yourself from us? Market testing doesn't affect you because your job is safe'. This caused me all sorts of dilemmas because, yes, my job was safe, but so were their jobs going to be safe, because they were not going to be made redundant, they would have been moved elsewhere. But that was the perception at that time, faced with market testing all their legs were going to be stripped from under them, but here was I sitting OK. It was only as a result of what they actually saw happen as a result of that first market test that they realized their bread was buttered on the right side, and I didn't get any of that hostility when it came to the Bristol market test. They knew by then that these Chinese walls that are supposed to exist didn't exist. I told them everything that I was going to put into the specification, even asking their suggestions, such as what is in this spec. that will be difficult for you? What can I put in the evaluation criteria that will make it easy for you to win it or the other people to lose it? What do you know about these firms? The other thing which we did was to buy off firms to act as consultants for us where we thought they were competition. This last time round we had six interested firms. One was bought off at the very beginning. We visited two others and talked them out of it, and have put the promise of work to two others so the competition was cut down to one. I had managed to secure a budget for the use of consultants, which I used, but not in the way that it was probably intended to be used. I think they saw as well that by doing that if I wanted to I could write things in ways that would suit consultants in the private sector. I think market testing has become more of a partnership rather than client–server relationship.

So it's a game and you have got to play that game... because a couple of the firms, it didn't take long to read what they were after... they wanted some sort of compensation before pulling out.

Their brinkmanship made me see what business is like outside. It is a horrible feeling. You know you are not going to like doing it, you're twisting, your integrity is going. Particularly in the civil service. You have always had the public service ethic and you know it doesn't matter what money is involved, you have always got to do what is right. So when it has been put onto you that you have got to do some of these things then you think well, it's not right, but I then think the right thing is that the in-house team wins and how I achieve that is no one else's business but mine. Because whatever the government says about privatization and market testing, the right result or the best people to do the job are these and I know if the consultants come in they can't do the job, they have not had the same training, they have not got the same commitment so that all other niceties were subordinated to ensuring the workers won here.

I found it very interesting, but I always felt that if something went wrong, if someone I had offended blew the lid on this and said the reason they won was because I did not maintain these Chinese walls and secrecy, then I could be in trouble. I felt that I was the one that was going over the wall in effect, because the project board took its lead from what I told them and the steering group took its lead from what I was telling them, so I was in the middle hoping that nothing was going to blow up in my face. If it was seen that there was a bit of 'jiggery pokery' then the chief executive would have been forced to disown me and I would have been in a far more vulnerable position as head of the unit than I would have been working in any other part of the Agency. I did nothing illegal or immoral, but I just felt it was wrong. Probably in the private sector you would just see that as normal behaviour, but to me it was not normal behaviour. Ethically I felt myself being compromised on quite a few occasions. Even the staff said to me 'How can you live with yourself during this?', and I said 'Well I'm living to make sure you win'. They weren't saying it nastily, they were recognizing the situation that was being created and that in our part of the public sector we had not come across this before.

It has brought about stress for the team leaders and for myself. I think I have coped with it reasonably well because at the bottom of it is the thought that whatever happens I am not going to be losing my job. Even if it did reach the stage where I might lose my job, I am coming to the age where I can get early retirement terms and it wouldn't be the end of the world. But for the two team leaders, first Northampton and then Bristol, both of them suffered as a result – physical and mental strain. I told one of them to take a fortnight off, which was recorded as out of the office time. It was between the two of them. This again is not something that you would do in the civil service. If you take a day's leave it has to be signed and accounted for. But circumstances drive you into dealing with things differently now. They worked so hard and it was taking so much out of them – they were carrying the responsibility for so many people on their backs in making those decisions they were living with it for over nine months; it was a terrible strain.

At the end of the day you say 'What for?'. We'd have made 10 per cent savings through market testing. If the government had turned round and said you don't have to market test as long as you make 10 per cent savings we could have done that ourselves without the anguish that goes with being under threat, because we had those savings lined up already (via the quality audit). Those were the two best decisions I have ever made since I've been here; that is, the staff inspection and the quality audit. Those two decisions won the market test for us. It's never a nice time when market testing is going on, but one interesting effect was that it attracted a much greater degree of sympathy from the rest of the Agency – a lot of the aggro which my people faced went when the rest of the Agency were faced with the prospect of having the private sector specialists in. When the rest of the Agency realized what the impact could be, they felt a lot more kindly towards us, which prompted me to feel confident enough to put out a customer satisfaction survey to the Directors, which in all bar one case were favourable. That helped the in-house team a lot, because they felt they were not battling on their own, and that there was support within the Agency.

One thing it has done is to destroy some of the factions that existed within the unit. They were not large factions, just a bit of 'We're better than you', a bit of animosity. When it came to market testing everyone had to get together and work as a unit and that has made for much better working relationships. One thing which helped this process was their training – because they are qualified, their professionalism came through in their approach to things. They researched everything involved in the subject. They knew market testing inside out. They also dealt with a government department that had been subject to the same process. They were also knowledgeable about interpersonal factors and realized these conflicts were there. One part of the unit is 'old school' – taken a long time to get promoted, nothing much ahead and the new youngsters at their heels. Classic confrontation material. There was a large element of this, and I found it difficult to keep them all together, but it has been a lot easier since market testing.

During the market testing period I spoke with them a lot. I would bring them into meetings together. I would not try something on in secret. I did it openly so they would all be aware of it. One advantage is that they are practical jokers and wind-up merchants, and I delight in being wound up and having practical jokes played on me. I have always tried to encourage the fun element in work to the point where I can say something to them, and they will say something to me and we will not take offence. So when we did have these meetings I will tell someone 'You are being bloody minded. What are you playing at?'. And they would say 'Yer'.

Market testing is usually on a one-year or three-year cycle. I managed to swing it that we would go on a five-year cycle. How did I do that? Well, I convinced the director of purchasing and the chief executive that it would not be sensible to do otherwise because we work on a long cycle. So to my mind the logical thing was to put out to market test so that one cycle could be completed. They all argued that this was most irregular, since the usual term was three years. But I argued that was ridiculous, and that we must be able to make these rules a bit elastic, and in the end they said yes. They had to go and speak with the Treasury and among themselves. They'd come back to me and raise questions, quite amicably, but this was outside their normal guidelines. I took the position that if you want to be seen as pioneering this then you have got to do something that is reasonable. I'm not prepared to go along with something that is only for three years. And in effect, the chief executive's heart was with us winning, so he felt that if we could put up a case to the Treasury that sounded reasonable, and which could be sustained, then he would go with it. The director of procurement was not with us to the same degree, as he had his commitment to the centre – he was more of a centre man than an agency man – but he knew where his bread and butter lay with regards to the chief.

So the whole crunch really comes from the support we got from the chief. And the chief conveyed that to me fairly early on and that was the message I passed on down to my staff. There was a meeting between the three of us – the chief, me and the MD – and they both told me 'The in-house team is going to win, isn't it?'. In some respects I felt under more pressure then because, although I was the client, I still had to get involved in the in-house team's bid to make sure that they were doing things the right way. It would have been extremely difficult if they had put up something which would have been a loser. So I had to advise them... surprisingly it wasn't in the way you might think. The main thrust for people under market testing was that you must get the costs down to the bare bones, and that is what they were doing and they were cutting the flesh back so much; I said, 'No you can't, you have got to sustain a certain level of service and that requires a certain number of people, and this is what you must do, and if you put in anything under that I am not going to accept it'. They said, 'What if another bid comes in under that?'. I said, 'Well you have got to trust me'. That was difficult. I had virtually promised them that if they came in with that number of staff, and that price, then they would win the bid. If they hadn't won, and there might have been redundancies, then.... I had sleepless nights at that stage. Because I knew whatever the chief and the finance director said I would still be the one floating on the water and everyone else would be floating on their islands. I didn't like that; that was not a nice period. But I still felt we had the trial run at Northampton and that gave us a lot of confidence to know what the market would come up with, and I was pretty well tuned in with what was happening elsewhere in government. I received confidential copies of bids put in by other bodies to see what sort of pricing we were talking about, because the line I would have taken would be that even if the other ones had come in under price I was looking for a certain degree of quality, and that is what I would have justified it on, but it's a lot more difficult to justify things in those terms if the in-house team is significantly undercut.

Another change is the way in which the Agency runs itself finan-cially, in that you have got cost centre managers, so we are all now heavily constrained by budget recognition. Before, you never knew what your budget was: you just have x number of staff, travel and subsistence allowance, and spent what you wanted. Now there is regular monthly monitoring and you have to report to the finance director if you are under or over. You must make a case for more money; if underspending occurs you need to give money up, so it's a totally different way of thinking, managing the financial side as well as the business. The culture changed. In some respects this has been good because the Agency has been among one of the first to do this – my people experience these things before their peers in other government departments. So they tend to feel 'We've cracked this already', so they can give advice to everyone else, so there is an element of having been there. Within the unit there has always been the line that if there is anything to be done we will not hang back, we will do it. It's always been a reflection of our practice, because we review our work every so often, and people are fairly open and good at saying their piece. If there are things wrong, changes can be made. The climate is such that they feel they can put forward suggestions, and provided they have done their research properly and got their background information right and there is substance in what they are saying, then we will go with it. But, to say the least, there has been an 'initiative overload'.

Compulsory competitive tendering in the housing department of a local authority

Background

The main change affecting the department is the preparation for CCT (compulsory competitive tendering). This is the major issue that is facing the department and it has been for the last two years. We will have to subject most of our housing management service to competition this year, with the view of letting the contract as from the 1st of April next year. There has been a lot of preparatory work going on for the last three years – preparing the department for competition.

This is a government-inspired initiative. It's a policy of the government to subject local authority services to competition. It began with the civil service and then was extended into local government. It started with the blue-collar work, like the refuse collection, grounds maintenance and street sweeping. Now it is being extended into white-collar work. Housing management is one of the first white-collar services to be exposed. There are other services within local government which are to be exposed, but we are one of the first within this authority. CCT is not having the effect here that it is probably having in other local authorities. There are various reasons for that.

We are very far advanced in preparing for competition and there is a lot of work to be done between now and January when the contract will be awarded.

When the legislation was being developed to expose housing to competition there were various bodies involved in discussing the proposals with the government. that ranged from the professional body – The Chartered Institute of Housing – to the local authority associations like the AMA or the London Boroughs Association (as it used to be known). There was a joint working party between civil servants and local authority representatives to discuss the proposals and look at the details and point out to the civil servants where things were not going to work. There was a quite a bit of success in that respect, in that the original proposals were changed dramatically as a result of the discussions that took place between the Local Authority Associations (LAA) and civil servants. We were involved on the working group – either my boss or myself went along to the meetings – and LAAs wanted experts in housing to put the housing perspective.

There are three main groups of people who have been involved in this process: the management, the staff and the residents who receive the service. They have been heavily involved, kept up to date, and are becoming increasingly involved as we get down to the crucial process of selecting who is going to be awarded the contract. Members, i.e. councillors, have also been involved. The key stakeholders in this process are residents who receive the service, the staff who are going to have to deliver it (or who are already delivering it) and members who we have to report to.

This change is not 'Big Bang' – we knew it was coming so we had to prepare for it and we have had time to prepare. But often, you think it's a long way off and then you find yourself with not much time to go. But there has been a lot of preparation and one of the major changes we have had to do is to restructure the department in readiness for competition. Ultimately, if the in-house team are not awarded the contract, then potentially we are into a situation where a number of staff will lose their jobs.

How the project unfolded over time

The restructuring was done in two phases. The first phase, which was completed in the mid-1990s, involved senior management, so that was the first three tiers of management. That involved reducing the number of divisions from seven to five and allocating the areas of work accordingly. That was achieved relatively painlessly because we had two people who retired, so although the staff had to compete for their jobs it was relatively painless. Obviously people who have to compete perhaps wouldn't say it was painless. But it was compared with the second phase.

The second phase was undertaken in 199X and was completed in 199Y. That involved the other levels of management and the rest of the staff here in the Town Hall. We have a total staff complement within the department of around 100. About 30 are based here and the rest are based on the estates. Some of them actually live and work on the estates – they are in tied accommodation. So we were talking about reorganizing and restructuring the rest of the department based here.

As we had reduced the number of sections from seven to five that meant we had staff who were previously working in one section uncertain about which section they were now working in. They may have been doing a job that straddled two sections. So, we had to create new jobs, many of which were almost identical to some already in existence. The post-holders in those particular jobs, if their job description had varied very little, were assimilated into the new post.

Those whose jobs changed significantly had to compete for the revised jobs. That meant we had to advertise the jobs within the ring fence of the department so that we could have a situation where several people were applying for the same position. At the end of the day we had all of the jobs evaluated – we have a corporate job evaluation scheme. So all of the new posts were evaluated and graded accordingly. The job descriptions and person specifications were produced. This whole process took some considerable time and a lot of planning. It involved a lot of meetings with personnel specialists from central personnel and our employment legal advisor. It also involved staff briefings and staff communications about what was going on and why it was necessary. These were held fairly regularly, updating people. We then went through the process of advertising the job. We then interviewed and staff were selected.

At the end of this process there were four people who were made redundant. Two were fairly happy about that arrangement. Two were not. That was a traumatic time. It was stressful, particularly for the people who had to compete for the jobs. Their future was uncertain – they were asking themselves 'Am I going to have a job at the end of this process?'. It was pretty stressful and traumatic for the managers as well, particularly having to deal with two staff who at the end of the day were without jobs and had to be made redundant. Fortunately, things worked out reasonably well. It was unknown territory because we couldn't see how it was going to work out. You couldn't say who was going to be without jobs. You knew how many jobs were available, but it wasn't always the case of there are 15 jobs and 15 staff so everyone will have a job. It didn't work out like that because some staff were not suitable for the posts that remained. Those staff had to go. Making people redundant has not been common to local government. It is becoming increasingly common. That's part of the change, and it's not very pleasant.

This change was very complex. It was a case of 'We have to do this to survive'. Some may not agree with that. It was necessary to go through this pain to get ourselves in a better structure to give the in-house team the best possible chance of winning the contract when it is on offer. I think it is part of the overall picture that we are now in a climate of trying to get more for less. We have to get leaner ('Get better or get beaten' is a saying I have upon my wall). This sums it up nicely – we are living and having to work in a very competitive environment.

During this process it seemed as if a lot of things were happening because this had to be done on top of your daily work. There was the planning process, the briefings, the information to be disseminated, individual meetings with staff, job descriptions and person specs to be produced, there was the need to evaluate these new jobs – that involved a certain procedure to have the gradings and then the advertising and interviewing of staff. It took about six to eight months, phase two reorganization in particular. Phase one was shorter.

This is an ongoing change, with the departmental restructuring being part of the overall change. The overall change is trying to change the culture of the organization: to get the department into more of a business frame of mind. I think there was a perception amongst all staff, myself included, that 'Oh well, competition – that doesn't apply to us. Don't worry about it. It'll go away'. But it doesn't. And competition is just one aspect. Financially, like all local authorities, we are under pressure from the government where funds are being withdrawn. So there is greater pressure to put rents up. If you put rents up then tenants naturally expect better services. To get better services, sometimes – not always – you have to employ more staff, which puts costs up. So you have this sort of difficulty where expectations were rising as rents were rising. You were trying to improve the standard of service, often with fewer resources – it was like a squeeze, and that squeeze is continuing now because we are restricted by how much we can put rents up. It is a case of getting more for less.

Local government is coming into this arena late. What is difficult is to achieve a business-like approach when you are working in an organization like this. I think it's fair to say we are recognized as being a rather bureaucratic organization. We have a structure of committees – a whole raft of procedures to go through. This militates against increased efficiency in our department. To try to square the circle is that you still have to work within this organization, which is bureaucratic.

Getting the message across to the staff was important. We said, 'Gone are the days when we can afford to carry people. It is about maximizing the output from the resources that we have got'. Someone commented about the culture now being about the survival of the fittest, and I think that is an appropriate observation. Where you have a high unemployment market outside you need to get across to staff that they are in this environment where increasing demands will be placed upon them. Unless they are able to perform we would have to look to the market to provide someone who can. That's the name of the game today. What it does is to expose weaknesses. You could hide them before. You can't now. That is weaknesses in procedure, in staffing. One of the ways we have tried to tackle this is something which is very common amongst other organizations, but hasn't been long here, and that is why we have delegated financial budgets to divisional heads, even large ones like staffing budgets. Divisional heads now have to work within their budget. They are given a little extra to provide for overtime and agency staff, but this year is the first we are doing this, and they have to work within that. We have had to cut our financial budget for staffing to keep the rents low. We could not increase the rents without incurring certain penalties from central government.

People on low income get rent rebates and housing benefit. Basically, with the housing benefit scheme, if you put the rent up by more than a certain percentage then those on housing benefits are fully protected. Their housing benefit title will increase by the required amount. For this year the government has said, we will not change that rule, but we are going to say that if you increase the rent over a certain threshold (which is extremely low – between one and two per cent) you will not be able to claim subsidy. In effect, the local authority would have to find the difference.

That was quite a penalty, and meant that realistically we couldn't increase rents by more than 1.2 per cent. With inflation running at 2.5 per cent that was a reduction in real terms. They also reduced the amount of subsidy which they gave us. This is a trend that has been operating for a number of years now. So we either had to increase income – we couldn't do this because we weren't able to put rents up – or we had to reduce expenditure. We chose the latter. One of the items we cut back on was staff salaries and wages, which meant there is enough money to pay people here in the Town Hall, but there is only a limited amount to pay for extra working hours, i.e. overtime and temporary staff. That puts pressure on management to keep sickness down. Because if you have someone who is long-term sick the job still has to be done. So either the existing staff do it on overtime or we get someone in. Hence we come back to survival of the fittest – can you as a manager afford to have people on your books who are sick? It puts pressures on managers to deal with sickness absence, and we have almost a vicious circle. As the pressure increases, staff are suffering. We have looked at our sickness statistics and there is no doubt that there is an increase through stress. Stress management comes into play, counselling. We can no longer carry staff.

Once we were preparing for CCT, which involves a number of staff, I did a calculation on how much our preparations for CCT had cost. To date, the department over the three years has spent £328,000 on the exercise. This is a considerable sum of money. A lot of it, because we have a time recording system, is fairly accurate. Most of this is not additional cost – it is more lost opportunity. This means that staff have been preparing for CCT rather than undertaking other work. Consequently that has meant that standards have suffered because often senior staff who have been preparing for CCT have had to reduce the amount of supervision. We measure our performance (we have been doing this for four years now) against targets – common ones like rent arrears collection, housing benefit calculation and repair service satisfaction; a whole raft of performance indicators. What we have found we noted in a quarterly report, which we produce for a committee. This report records our performance in various activities in the department against targets which we have set ourselves, and in many areas we haven't hit the target for the whole financial year. You can see a gradual deterioration in standards, with the performance tailing off. We think this is probably an inevitable knock-on effect. If key members of the department are spending a third or half of their time on preparing for CCT then other areas must suffer. That puts increased pressure on us because members are dissatisfied that performance is falling. Tenants (our customers) who pay the rent are dissatisfied. We are working in a climate where (I don't think it is any secret) the vast majority of tenants don't want CCT; certainly our members don't want CCT, and I imagine many of our staff don't want it, because their future is on the line. It is difficult to perceive where the benefits are for CCT in a small department such as ours (100 staff and less than 5000 properties to manage). The difficulty is thinking where are we going to recoup that three hundred-plus thousand pounds? And another one hundred thousand pounds we will be spending this year. Where are the savings going to come from, since it is basically the residents that are having to pay for that? So that is one consequence.

I have mentioned about the change in culture and trying to get that across. That is quite a long process. We have staff briefings and an internal staff newsletter for the department. Obviously the performance culture where we measure our performance against targets. That tends to instil a culture that performance does matter. The old culture of 'Not to worry, the money will be found' is going. The housing department unfortunately is not rich, and staff must realize that the money isn't going to be necessarily there; and the same message has to be got across to residents as well. There seems to be a belief among residents that the Authority is rich and if they wanted anything done we would find the money. But it isn't there, we cannot get our hands on it – that is the trouble.

I talked about stress. We are finding the emotional consequences difficult to handle. We have even set ourselves targets for sickness absence for the department. We have got near that target, but more recently, our sickness absence has gone up. We have this slight conflict because it is local government, and local government has always been recognized as providing safe jobs, safe professions and a safe environment in which to work. We still have various procedures that have to be gone through when dealing with sickness absence; these don't always occur in the private sector. Sickness pay and other arrangements are often more generous than in the private sector, and you have this conflict between the expense of keeping a person who is consistently sick on the books and dispensing with their services. What are they going to do? Where are they going to go? They are colleagues. So we have this difficult balancing act.

Interestingly, in phase two we found that some of the staff who were successful in getting a post felt guilty because they had got the job. They knew that because they had got the job some other people that had applied obviously did not. Were these people going to end up with or without any form of job? It's difficult times.

The Authority has a staff welfare officer and an outside stress counsellor was engaged for any member of staff who is still on the books but who is potentially facing unemployment. What we don't seem to have, apart from the welfare officer and perhaps the occupational health service, is stress counselling for staff who are in a job but are just finding it increasingly difficult to cope. Having to be more task-oriented has consequences for me and other managers. We are not perhaps managing as we would like to manage because of the limitation of resources. It is often the case that the job will not be done unless I do it. It's all very well to try to delegate, but when you are trying to delegate to staff who are fully occupied, it's difficult. This is part of the government's approach and it is working because productivity has had to increase. The work has not decreased – in fact it has increased, but we have had no increase in the resources to do the work.

There have been spin-off benefits from competition. It has made us look at and document what we do. Like many local authorities there were no detailed procedure notes for housing management so there were no standards of service that the customer could expect. It has had those positive outcomes. But going back to my earlier point, it is trying to get the in-house team to think like a business. For example, if I don't collect the rent and my arrears are above the target, what is the consequence of that? The consequence will possibly be there will be a penalty because they haven't performed. So we will not pay the in-house team or the contractor all of the money. As the purchaser I am able to do that if targets are not achieved. There will be a framework for monitoring the performance of the contractor, regardless of whether one is in-house or external. If certain targets are not met there are financial penalties incurred.

Experience in managing change

I think the outcome of phase 2 reorganization was quite an achievement to go through. We were aiming to achieve the completion of the reorganization by a particular date and we didn't quite hit it, but we got very near to it. I think that was good and primarily down to proper planning. It took a lot of time. What I don't think we did very well, on such an important issue as staff reorganization, was our communications with staff. We did staff briefing and letters, but with hindsight it could have been better. I think that is indicative of the situation we are in when you have so many tasks to do that something as simple as staff communications tends to be put to one side. It's not right but it does happen, and this is one of the reasons we looked recently into how we might improve communications. One of the views was to introduce a staff newsletter. We have done briefing sheets, but now we are going to have an internal newsletter for staff. One of the problems we have is the geography, in that 70 per cent are out of this office at any one time – some as much as seven miles away. Even to do a single briefing (we have a lecture theatre) is difficult because half of the staff have to be on duty. You can't shut down the service. Another area we might improve is communications with residents as well. This newsletter is primarily focused at the residents, but all of our staff read it. It has got items of information relating to staff. This is produced quarterly.

REFLECTION

Preparing for compulsory open competition is an effective method for bringing about changes leading to greater efficiency. In this process, to what extent is it desirable that the dice should be loaded in favour of the in-house team? What implications does this issue have for the implementation of change?

■ CHAPTER FIVE ■

Downsizing and outsourcing

Two cases fall within this category. It so happens that they were both in processing plants: one in the oil industry and the other in the chemical industry. Given the nature of the strategic changes to be brought about in the oil refinery, it is no surprise to find that an authoritarian but carefully planned approach was adopted. The case is recounted by the engineering manager of one site of a refinery that is owned by an international oil company. The parent company had reviewed its strategy and decided that if it were to remain in the refining business, costs had to be reduced to ensure survival. The interviewee was one of a team of three people tasked with designing and implementing the site-wide change. The design involved a bundle of changes, some which were new to the parent company and therefore carried considerable risk. Some of the changes were surprisingly smooth, e.g. de-unionization. Others were troublesome. Thus there was disappointment in the contractor selected to meet the refinery's needs. This meant that a number of corrective steps had to be taken during the process of change, and the engineering manager recognized that he should have been more thorough in the process of appointing the contractor. The story takes place over a period of 18 months or so.

The situation in the chemical plant was quite different. It was losing money in a declining industry, and the parent company attempted to make it more cost-effective since this was seen as the only way to increase the profits from its investment. Changes made were in accord with theories relating to empowerment, flat structures and internally led work teams. Unforeseen problems arose because those given more responsibility had not been adequately prepared for it. Certain changes had to be reversed, and the plant was subsequently sold to a competitor. This case highlights the dangers of rushing through changes without adequately learning from the experiences of others, and without appropriate training for the new organization – both at the top and bottom of the organization. Information was obtained from a line manager involved in the changes.

Downsizing and outsourcing in an oil refinery

How did this change come about?

In the 1990s the parent company reviewed its strategy on whether to stay in the refining business, which is a costly, low return effort. If it were to stay in the business, what changes were needed to ensure survival for the foreseeable future?

At regular intervals, organizations working in the oil industry cooperate and produce aggregated results on a number of measures. These are used by individual companies to compare their performance against others in the sector – a form of benchmarking. The parent Board looked at the figures, decided the refinery business was overmanned and that in order to remain in this business productivity needed to be improved. A team of three people, including the engineering manager, was tasked with designing the change, which was a plan for reducing numbers across one site of the refinery business.

A bundle of changes?

Some delay occurred between the decision to reduce overmanning and the task of designing the plan. During this time a decision was taken to reduce the total headcount at the refinery site, including contractors. There were a number of contractors from a variety of contracting companies and it was decided that this situation would change. Rather than continue with the current process of competitive bidding for work, the refinery would move into a partnering relationship with one contractor.

Other changes were introduced as part of the effort to remove overmanning. These included decisions to de-recognize the unions; reduce the amount of supervision by cutting two layers out of management and introduce performance-related pay for everyone.

The change process

The first task of the design team was to undertake a core/non-core business analysis. The core business would remain in-house and other activities would be taken on by the contractor regardless of the current position. This meant that people employed by the refinery would need to apply for a core job (with many of them applying for the job they were currently doing). Where successful, each would be given a new terms and conditions of employment contract to agree to. As part of the introduction of performance-related pay for all, previously hourly paid people were given staff status.

Type of change involved

The engineering manager described this case as an example of a 'Big Bang' change, with a lot of changes taking place at the same time across the whole site. The change of reducing overmanning would not have been as central to the primary task of the organization had it not been bundled up with the additional changes. Rather than just reduce headcount, this was seized as an opportunity to make additional changes which were deemed likely to introduce much greater profitability.

In terms of predictability there was obviously a certain inevitability that there was a need for change because of the pressures on the market. Any visit to a local supermarket in one of the group that are providing own-brand petrol on their forecourts demonstrates this. The unforeseen aspect was the sheer size of the change to be attempted. For example, within the engineering department half of the people went either in voluntary severance or in compulsory redundancy. There was an expectation that change was coming, but no one foresaw the extent.

The novel aspects of the change were that this was the first occasion on which they and the parent company had:

- undertaken de-recognition of the unions
- introduced staff status for all
- experienced such a high level of redundancy
- adopted the partnership approach to contracting

Familiar aspects of the change were:

- reducing layers
- contracting out activities
- a low level of redundancy

The scale of change was perceived as vast: no one expected so much to be achieved at one point – i.e. the design stage. From the start of the design stage to full implementation took only six months. All those who were going to leave (employees and contractors) left by the last day of the fifth month; and the new contractor firm and its staff, together with the new ways of working, started on the first of the following month. Additionally, by bringing in one contractor, the exit of existing contractors needed to be planned and undertaken during this five-month period.

What are the effects of this change?

Since this time there have been two additional initiatives, building on this one: the first has been an investigation to determine if and how the company can get synergy between different refinery sites. This led into a drive to get better alignment in hardware, software and information and communication systems generally, which further turned into a full business process re-engineering effort. The root of these changes lay in an outcome of the sweeping changes at this site. This was that the company developed the confidence to undertake large-scale change. The engineering manager viewed this as a process of evolution within the company and can see a path back from the present to this point of change.

In terms of effects on the site, there was an increase in workload during the period of changing and subsequently. Additionally, there was an increase in most people's responsibilities: for people, and for budgets and other financial resources. It was interesting that, virtually across the board, everyone responded positively, and in some areas the response was outstanding.

In the engineering department, the technicians (who previously were described in terms of their trade – fitters, welders, etc.) were given financial responsibilities and the responsibility for organizing their day, spares, materials and support. Each autonomous group of technicians now reported to a chartered engineer. Both foreman and supervisory levels were removed. The technicians now organized themselves.

The engineering manager gave an illustration of differences in working practices. 'The prior way of working was that management would set up a maintenance plan, and during operational periods overnight and at weekends things would break and need repair. Management would have to schedule this into the plan and this process took up a lot of management resources. The technicians originated a different, more effective process. They appointed one person from each of the four groups to ring an operative who was working on the night or weekend shift to find out if anything had happened. If so, for a minor problem he would fix it, or if it was more serious then he'd call the engineer. In this way things were sorted in a much more timely manner by those who needed to know.'

The people who suffered most during this period of change were those who could not handle the uncertainty. Many were happy to work out what needed to be done and then went ahead and did it; some had to be told what to do rather than take the initiative. The latter group felt very uncomfortable and asked, 'How do I know that I have got the authority?' and 'What happens to me if something goes wrong?'. They still needed written or spoken instructions to feel sure of their actions.

What were the most critical tasks in managing this change?

The design task was key. There were four key design elements of change. Behind the need to reduce numbers was the objective of reducing costs, and this was achieved. However, it was also important to maintain the reliability of the kit, since this has cost implications. So the team chose to design-in a condition where there were no industrial relations disputes or loss of morale, as the knock-on effects would be that the refinery suffered in changing levels of reliability.

Ways of promoting change

The engineering manager and his team had the task of convincing people that change was needed and that their solution to the problem was the right one. The refinery manager and managing director were both very supportive of the design team. These people were only interested in the results, not the mechanics, and the design team members had been able to convince them that the required results could be delivered by this means.

The task of getting their design adopted involved getting others to buy-in at very early stages of a selling process. The engineering manager identified those who were not 'coming to the party' and used a variety of techniques to 'neutralize' them (e.g. move to another site, transfer to a non-influential position or tie them down in some other way). Early on, he identified someone who could have been a key driver, as on opinion maker, but he was not 'for the plan', so that problem was addressed in one of the ways described above. Conversely, he identified those who would help with the change, who saw the need and, in some cases, who saw some advantage to them of helping introduce change.

Factors inhibiting change

One of the factors that might have inhibited change and that was difficult to manage was how (or even whether) to act when so much change was going on? This led some people to hold a perspective with a greater degree of short-termism and yet also a reluctance to deal with the issues of today. There could be a tendency to sit down and do nothing because of a belief that there was no point in doing anything, since tomorrow another person will come along and want to do something else that will negate or interfere with what you have done today! This combination of factors meant that it was very easy to become effectively paralyzed in terms of acting: 'I don't know what's expected of me, things are always changing' and inertia resulting from the view that 'Today I'm being asked to go uphill while tomorrow they will want me to go downhill'.

Another inhibitor related to organizational politics: many will not choose to get on the change management bandwagon until they see it's successful, because, if it goes wrong, they and their career might suffer in the process.

A third inhibitor that the engineering manager identified he termed 'corporate arrogance'. This was where a large organization thinks 'they know best', and it seems the stronger the corporate culture the stronger the arrogance. The prevalent view was that if an idea has come from outside then it won't be good for the organization when compared against 'tried and tested methods'. An example he quoted was that of contracting. The company was very sophisticated in this area and had refined ways of operating in the inviting bids process – evaluating, awarding and managing how the work is done – but he found a lot of resistance to the idea of contract partnering.

The engineering manager also thought that another aspect involved in this task of convincing others was the importance of first convincing yourself. In his view, it was crucial to understand what was being proposed by the plan that they had largely drawn up: 'You need to be able to look people squarely in the eyes and say 'This is what to do', and then be able to take the questioning and demonstrate through your answers that you can make the plan work, because you have a full understanding of the proposed solution together with convincing answers to the implications that questioners draw to your attention'.

He said 'They have to have confidence that you can achieve what you have said you will do. They want to hear that you have thought through all the difficulties. They will not contemplate failure going in, although they will face it as an outcome. But obviously organizations can't contemplate a plan that won't succeed... they will not give you authority to go ahead and fail'.

The second key task was telling the union officials that the company was going to de-recognize the unions. He had difficulty in keeping a deadpan face, not because he was anti-union *per se*, but because he had a lot of experience with shop stewards in the past and had taken a lot of stick. In this particular situation it was not a question of who was going to win and who was going to lose – the traditional adversarial combat situation. Instead, it was a case of telling them he (and the company) were 'no longer going to play the game, and the unions could go and play bat and ball at another wicket elsewhere'. In this company he had his best-laid plans messed about; in his view the unions had been a big event for many years and lots of people had spent hours and been in jobs trying to manage the unions. Now the company was saying it would not have them anymore. It was a very significant moment. When he told them there was some bad language, some blustering and then they disappeared; nothing happened subsequently and it was a glorious anti-climax. There was no reaction on the part of the workforce, since they were concerned about getting one of the remaining jobs. This is what the process was intended to do. The timing of events – what was said, what was said to whom and when bits of information went out – was carefully thought through.

A most satisfying outcome of this event was the ability to talk with individuals as members of the company and not in roles as 'a member of management' and 'a member of xyz union'. He encouraged his engineers to talk to the technicians on a one-to-one basis and not to involve the stewards, so the unions were cut out completely.

The next task was telling people they had not got jobs. Everyone, including himself, was interviewed for their job. Each person had to apply for a job against a written set of criteria so that in cases of de-selection it could be demonstrated that the process of decision making had been fair and equitable. There was a selection panel of four engineers (who had in turn been selected to stay). They were divided into two groups and interviewed prospective technicians. After this selection exercise, each person that had been interviewed was informed by their boss, on a one-to-one basis, if they had been selected or not.

The four engineers that sat on the selection team were not chosen particularly for this task. They were identified as being people who would be capable of leading the organization in the future; were flexible and could manage change; could achieve standing when dealing with technicians and their opposite operating numbers; and would be fairly outgoing and could do lots of facing up to people plus be technically sound. They managed to handle this process well.

Around three-quarters of those who had been made redundant left on the same day. It was an emotional experience for everyone. He was very surprised by the lack of acrimony. Indeed, a large number of them shook his hand, which he interpreted as giving a message 'We are making the best of it; you may have sacked us but you can't beat us'. One of the leavers was the convenor of the shop stewards and he said 'I don't like what you have done but I don't dislike you for doing it'. He seemed to have accepted that someone had to do it. Interestingly, most of those leaving were able to recognize the difference between him as a person and his actions in a company role. He said, 'People are surprisingly able to differentiate between the two once the chips are down... in the final analysis I could deal with the union people as individuals within a normal personal relationship that is built up naturally'.

The engineering manager was very unhappy about the poor performance of the contractor's site manager. Three months after the change had been instituted he decided enough was enough! Having spoken with different people from the contracting firm and meeting nothing but platitudes, he resorted to ringing the Chairman and said that 'If after [a specific date the next month] this site manager has not been removed, as Engineering Manager I am no longer prepared to pay for this person since he is spoiling the process'. He felt this was a significant point in the partnership relationship, since it showed that the company was still in control. Although the contractor's people and his own people were in this partnership, providing operations and the company with a satisfactory service, it was still, through him, the company's responsibility. This was an important and critical message to get across to the contractor.

Problematic areas

The choice of the contractor was one of the areas in this change that did not work out as well as anticipated. For example, it took the contractors nearly eight months to find a suitable replacement for the site manager. The engineering manager had chosen the contracting firm because they were 'lean and mean, cheap and cheerful'. However, he had not thought through the full implications of this, as this episode shows. The person who is site manager now is of the required capability, but unfortunately has 12 months of previous failure to live down.

The type of relationship between the company and the partnering contractor is very important. The engineering manager explained: 'I kept very tight control of the selection process. I wanted someone who can understand me and my team's way of operating. Generally, we interact three times a week on a formal basis, but of course there are many more contacts made on an informal basis. It is very important to develop a relationship of trust and candour where either party can pick up the phone and say for example, "I've dropped a whatsit, can you see if it can be fixed before things get too difficult?".' He feels this type of process also needs to take place at key points in both organizations. People chosen for this role need to have authority, ability and nous, each person needs to know how to operate in both organizations to fix things so they stop developing into formal issues. Often 'fixing' can simply be giving the problem to someone else, as it's a long-time problem.

They and the contractor bought up this issue of relationship management very early on in the selection and contracting process. The contractor nominated people they thought would operate well in his company. The engineering manager felt that it is very important to have appropriate persons working together. In order to make the relationships work each needs to believe that this is the right way to operate in order to cope with the thousands of problems that could otherwise override and overcome them. There is always a solution, even where you cannot solve it and can only manage or contain it.

The engineering manager measured the effectiveness of the contractor by setting a number of performance indicators and a period of time in which to get up to speed. When this time-point was reached the contractor's profit was dependent upon meeting these indicators.

Other measures of effectiveness, those more people-related, included the standard absence, sickness and turnover measures. The company did start to institute a series of opinion polls to measure trends over time, but these were not continued because of lack of support from the senior management team.

In retrospect what might have been done differently?

While the response of the technicians to the change was the most effective and satisfactory outcome, the least effective was the ability of the contract partner to manage the non-core activities. In retrospect, the choice of partner is something he would have done differently. He would have put in a lot more upfront effort before appointing a contractor and he would also, during implementation, ensure that the contractor had enough people with the required skills. In choosing a contractor to work with in a partnering relationship he thought he should have borne in mind the old adage 'You get what you pay for'. In choosing the cheapest he felt, in retrospect, that he was naïve in thinking he could have the cheapest and the best! By adopting a cost focus he ignored the fact that the firm was running with a minimum number of people, and in times of need it would go to the market and recruit at a low rate. Engineering and allied trades are a competitive market and in many cases the larger firms are willing to pay more and can recruit better people.

A second action he would change, in retrospect, was the process of managing the capability gap. In many operations, managers try to keep two systems running in parallel: the old system and then bringing on line the replacement. This allows time for the replacement system to learn and come up to the required standard. Often in his experience this system encourages exceptional time lapses before handover. Hence he decided that all non-core posts would fall vacant on the evening prior to the contractor taking over. This meant there was no overlap between incoming and outgoing staff. It took him three months to put in satisfactory people and systems; hence a three month backlog built up which meant that the contractor was pushing a large bow wave ahead of him for a long time. Decisions about whether to implement in series or parallel have no easy answer.

Because he had pushed for a partnering relationship, his decision was made more difficult to justify because of the poor performance of the contractor who had been taken on. They had created high expectations to get a high level of enthusiasm for the change. These expectations could not be met. Even today, with satisfactory current performance, there are disappointed people because they are not solving all of the problems that exist. With the strong selling process, the contractor took over problems that the company had lived with for a number of years, with many in the company expecting that these would be resolved although they may acknowledge this was unrealistic. He still doesn't know, even with hindsight, if expectations could have been managed better.

Lots of organizations have old lingering problems that have not been resolved and when these are thrown to the contractor there is the expectation that he will do better. If the contractor does not do better, why is he brought on board? There is the expectation he will bring along something special – like a new insight or new way of doing things.

He is convinced of the merits of adopting the partnering approach. He had worked for many years with the adversarial approach: 'Partnering works well if you are both going towards the same goals. Unfortunately, many in this company had worked for a long time under the old adversarial style and can hear what you say but still think that their way is best. In situations where this is the case, people spend time trying to undermine what you are trying to do; I can only deal with this slowly and with patience and by not flinching'. He rewards good performers and realizes it is not possible to change old habits quickly. It's a long process, with him recognizing the right ways of doing things and punishing those who do not adopt new ways. It's a form of shaping behaviour in the desired direction. Unfortunately, people are often being given conflicting messages and getting different slants on things, so many go along ostensibly with the corporate line through conforming, but given a chance they'll revert to what they have done previously. This chipping away will always happen and at the same time the organization will be moving along, and as long as it is going in the same direction or an appropriate one, change to what has been done before will go on.

Reviewing the whole change process therefore, he would choose: to improve choosing the contractor – preferably one with more depth; he would also manage expectations better and acknowledge that people are optimistic and hope that all the problems of the last 20 years would be 'changed at a stroke'.

Thirdly, he would keep going. Before he left, he took his feet off the pedals and he thinks 'It needs for you to constantly keep going, else you start going backwards. There is no position of rest. Managers need to keep the flywheel going ever faster and faster'.

What are the key competencies required in managing change?

An initial proposal for change was put together on how to reduce numbers, how to effect cost savings, the implications and time span. The refinery management team obviously had to get high-level approval of the plan. This was done in two stages: the first involved the general informal selling and persuading approach described earlier. This was done in conjunction with making two separate proposals to the Tender Board to get their approval. The second proposal was to clarify and expand on the idea of introduce a partnering relationship vis-à-vis the contractor. These were 20–30 minute sessions. The second stage involved making a formal proposal of what was involved to the Board of Directors of the parent company. This was done by the management team: himself, the operations manager and the managing director during a two-hour session.

In this process, talking to people is what it is all about. The whole process was about convincing people that this was the way to go. Part of this task was to convince his operations counterparts that by introducing this contracting relationship with engineering would be able to provide them with a first-rate service. Another part of this task was to convince those who were identified as 'stayers' to indeed stay. The leavers he just 'told' because, in his view, it suited them not to hear. They preferred being 'done to' rather than seeking to understand where they needed to take responsibility for the decision.

During the process the management team and his team had a lot of support from the personnel department of the parent. They helped him to handle the contractual and social side of the redundancy and to draw up new contracts. They also helped in the process of managing the stayers and the emotional consequences of managing the leavers. His team were given two sets of counselling courses and they all did a lot of counselling.

He concluded: 'People trying to make change happen need to have a good understanding of how things work, i.e. business processes not only in their own narrow field, but also have an understanding of how their field impacts on other people. The engineering department came out well in this exercise in terms of service to its customers. It did not come out so well on the financial side because some of the key players did not understand some of the financial implications of certain decisions and hence mistakes were made for a longer period of time than should have happened.

'It is also important that people can manage uncertainty. When starting a process of change, many things are unknown. It is impossible to work out all of the implications, so that people working need to be able to work in that uncertainty. They need to be optimistic and think they can solve unforeseen problems that arise; they need to believe in themselves and the process they are using so they are problem solvers not problem staters.

'People managing change need to know when to use their own initiative and when to be a team player. This works both ways – to know when to stand back and when to give support to other members of the team is a key competency.'

Restructuring in a processing plant

Background

They've been managing change for the last 10 to 12 years since I've been here. But we'll talk about the most recent series of changes because it's the freshest and it's affected me. And because it typifies the death wish of British industry.

My company was formed in Norwich in 1936. It was then Brutex Wraps (BW). It was always part of a larger chemical company.

Product X was an innovative wrapping material and formed the basis of a big and expanding business until the late seventies. Since then the company has been in decline. In order to keep the business viable we have had to go for what the market wants. We have been very successful at that. But also you want to reduce numbers and make the place more efficient and always be looking at ways and means of making the place more cost-effective, which is the reason for the change I'm talking to you about which was instigated before the parent company finally sold the business.

So we were part of a big group which was not particularly interested in making Product X or developing the business. It was just milking the business and ploughing the profits into other parts of the larger group, which means that we had to run the business on a shoestring; cut maintenance costs to a minimum; and not replace equipment, struggle along with kit that was wearing out and wasn't being replaced, whereas in the days when we could sell everything we made it was quite different. Not any more. The main objective in life, up until the early part of this year, when we were bought out by a direct competitor, was to run the business so as to squeeze the last ounce of profit out of it and pay it to the parent company.

That's the background against which the latest phases of changes were instituted. This is before the takeover – I think before we even realized we were going to be taken over, and probably even before the parent company realized it.

So the objective of the last changes was to make the place more efficient, reduce numbers and keep squeezing the maximum amount out of the people and the plant. Back in the sixties we could employ 2500 people and made about 600 tons a week. Currently we employ about 600 people and produce 540 tons a week.

What changes have taken place since you've been taken over?
Very little has happened since we were taken over. The changes I am describing are what we were doing starting in March 199X, but we weren't taken over until January 199Y. So it's a year's management of change I'm describing, which, hindsight being the best science in the world, had we realized we were going to be taken over, we would never have started.

Despite assurances that this plan was going to cause no disruption at all, it was painfully obvious to anybody who had their feet on the ground that it was going to cause disruption. If you spoke to anybody else who has put in the same sort of changes, which is very common in British industry as I understand it, they would have told you it was going to cause chaos. And it has.

Big Bang or incremental?
The changes were put in pretty rapidly. It was presented to us as a plan then implemented pretty rapidly. And that was a major mistake, without a doubt.

What changes were made?
We took out two layers of supervision. The management structure at that time was of departmental managers, of whom I was one, who were mainly responsible for the kit, the plant and perhaps a few people. There was a shift manager who was responsible for the men in the whole factory, and under him was a supervisor or foreman, or a number of foremen scattered through the various departments.

What was done was to remove the shift manager, who was responsible for the men, remove the foremen, who were the people who really made the place work, and also remove the plant manager, who was the person who made the kit work and maintained the continuity of the place.

Instead, they appointed, in each of the five departments of the factory, a business manager. That business manager was responsible for the men, the equipment and all the things the previous team of three managers had done.

Remember we are talking about a process that runs 24 hours a day for 365 days of the year. It's not the sort of process you can shut down. It takes up two days to shut the process down, so we must keep running.

The supervisor was replaced by dividing the people up on the factory floor into teams. Team working became the buzzword.

Everybody went away on training courses. Building cardboard aeroplanes, in woods and suchlike exercises. In the last 10 years I've been to more presentations, to more training courses – to all sorts of what I see as ridiculous time wasters that are decreed by our parent company.

Would the organization have survived without the changes?
Long term it would have been important to make changes to reduce numbers. The change was designed to get the man on the factory floor more involved in the business, more involved in the decisions, more involved with the actual nuts and bolts of running the place. And that was essentially the correct way to go.

What impact did the changes have?
What I don't understand is how we got it so wrong. It's as if it's the 'in thing'. Ten years ago the 'in thing' was to get away from your traditional-style manager who was there during office hours, and to put a shift manager there instead. A lot of companies put shift managers in. They drew their shift managers from the day managers, and having done that they then discovered that because they had put the day managers on shifts, the things that day managers had been doing were no longer getting done. So the poor old shift managers then found themselves doing extra-long hours to do the things that weren't getting done. So they weren't working very efficiently and used to get pulled in. They held lots of meetings to try to organize themselves better.

I have heard the story so many times. Day managers were suddenly put on shifts. 'Right. You're the shift manager. Run the factory.' And all of a sudden the things like taking lorries to get their MOTs, or putting out the essential paperwork, weren't getting done, because there was no one organized to do that. So you either had to find somebody else to do it, or employ the bloke who used to do it, and understood it. In other words, the change always happened too quickly.

In our recent change, removing shift managers and supervisors and dividing the workforce up into teams, that was done too quickly as well.

The difference between a day manager and a shift manager is that they work different hours. You are talking about a 24 hour continuous process. So there will be three shift managers within a 24 hour period. The shift manager is responsible for his shift. For the men and the plant.

It's not just this company that had problems moving to shift managers from day managers. I have spoken to lots of companies who followed this pattern and experienced the same difficulties. It seems as though the people who plan these things don't really understand what is going on.

Who planned this change?
The senior management of the company. The factory manager and his subordinates. Very often they are not involved in the day management because it is not part of their work.

I have spoken to other factory managers who had done this previously and they said you need to retain your supervisors for well over a year alongside the new team leaders so that they are gently introduced to the things that need to be done.

So the aim was to get people to manage themselves, and also to reduce numbers of staff. In the end, the object was to reduce costs. But as the pressure has intensified within industry in this country, management has ended up working longer and longer hours, but the bloke out on the factory floor is still sitting down watching the machine and twiddling his thumbs. He's not taking the responsibility. So the management team, very often the foreman or supervisor, was working harder and harder and were under much greater pressure than the blokes on the factory floor.

So the change was partly an attempt to get them on board to the same extent as the rest of the company.

What have been the effects of the change?
It happened so quickly. We were told about it in March 199X – that is when the plan was presented to us – and everything had to be in place by September. Broadly that was achieved, but suddenly the whole

factory performance started to fall apart. We have got a very good factory information system, so it's instantly known to people now much waste we make. Everything is graded, how much grade one we make, the tonnage in and the tonnage out. It's all there, shift by shift. Rejects started to increase dramatically. The performance of the place just fell apart and it's still falling apart. We are not making anything like our budget profit.

Does that mean further decline?

It could do. In some respects the takeover this year means there is more money to spend on the business. Our capital budget for last year was £0.9 million. This year it is £4.5 million. Something like that. So there are chances to invest more money in the business, but if we don't start getting the place performing like it used to do under the old management structures, I think our new owners are going to come down and start moving the managers about. We've been a declining industry for a long time and when you are a declining industry you're always cutting costs and cutting numbers, so everyone's jobs theoretically are on the line. But its interesting that the situation has changed somewhat. It's the Production Director's job which is on the line. If it doesn't come right this time, his job is as much under threat as ours is, lower down the line.

Over the last 10 years, when we've been reorganizing, it has always been the people from middle management down that have suffered.

Has anything been done well?

Having said that I think there are some things we have done well. Commercially we have done well. We have increased our market share from the companies that have closed, gone for the specialist part of the market that is likely to keep Product X manufacturing going in Norwich for a long time. I shouldn't be sitting here being totally negative about the organization. We've done some things well. But the major thing we've done wrong is managing change too quickly, and not listening and taking heed of the experience of others.

People have gone out and talked to other companies. But I don't think they have listened. I went to a seminar in Gloucestershire and spoke to a manufacturer from Bristol. They said they had gone into this team working. They said they had done it four times, and still hadn't got it right now.

When I told a friend of mine who worked in a company in Lincoln what we were doing, she said you had to leave the supervisors there for twelve months.

But even when those kinds of views were brought back, the senior managers said 'This is the plan. The reduction in performance is not going to happen. We are going to be better than everybody else'. But it hasn't happened.

What was the effect on your role and responsibilities?
My job was going. I was a plant manager. The thing that was stressed categorically at the time was that there were going to be no compulsory redundancies. Any redundancies that occurred were going to be on a voluntary basis. So you weren't afraid of being thrown out of the gate.

But you suddenly found the job you were doing was not going to exist any more. At that point in time they didn't know what job I was going to do. For five or six years previously I had worked for nine or ten hours a day doing my job. At the time of the reorganization I was working 12 hours a day and I didn't have any spare time at work or at home – and there were other things going on in my personal life – and all of a sudden I found myself, with three or four days' notice, having to apply for a new job in the structure: write a CV and make a presentation. The pressure was absolutely enormous. It was not something I shall ever forget easily.

Now I belong to the Operations Improvement Team, which means that I have the time to do properly the jobs in my old department that I didn't have time to do before. Basically I carry on doing a lot of useful and interesting jobs that I now have the time to do. And I don't necessarily have to work the very long hours any more.

How did you feel about that?
Initially I felt very aggrieved. There I'd been doing my best, working long hours, to run the department I'd been in charge of for six years. And all of a sudden they didn't want me to do it any more.

And some of the things that happened were ridiculous, I thought. Obviously I went for one of the business manager's jobs. I had to make a presentation with a slide show under very strict time constraints to get this presentation organized. But really at the end of the day they were just going to enormous lengths to demonstrate they were being fair. At the end of the day the people they put into the business managers jobs were the people that had been earning the best money: surprise, surprise, the old shift managers. They picked the three shift managers who worked well together and were being paid the most money. It was the obvious choice. Yet we had to go through this stupid rigmarole, and I still find it incredible that it was done that way.

Another ridiculous thing: when there was the next stage of jobs, for example for support technicians to the business manager – the number twos in the various departments – you found yourself in an interview situation where the interviewer was reading questions off a card. So everybody was asked the same questions and you were marked on your response.

At one point I found myself being interviewed by two people, a bloke I had known for 25 years and that I had skittled with every week for 20 years. The other one I had worked alongside on the factory floor 20 years ago. So they were people I really knew very, very well. It was obvious they were embarrassed at having to sit down and ask me these stylized questions.

What do other people think about this?
The same as I do. The people who are involved in the company reorganization always stick to the company line.

When the process of managing the change came about, what were the most difficult activities?
It's always difficult to get people to accept change. In some cases it was persuading the men on the factory floor to become team leaders. In one particular group, even now, the people on one particular shift will not have team leaders, to the extent that no one will come forward to be a team leader and they are even talking about spreading the extra money, because the money was a very small increment for the Team Leader. In all fairness they work quite well together anyway. They say: 'We'll carry on. We'll do the job'.

At the end of the day the things that don't get done are the legal requirements like 'Care of Substances Hazardous to Health' checks. Basically, if you've got a pipeline carrying concentrated sulphuric acid, which we certainly have, then that pipeline has to be inspected once a week to make sure it isn't going to spring a leak, or hasn't any signs of leakage. And that check has to be recorded. But that sort of thing, in that particular department, won't be getting done because nobody will step up for the team leader's job.

What were the most important things that had to be done to manage the change?
The most important thing was trying to get people to support the new structure. Actually believing it was going to work.

It is working in some areas. About half I would say. You still find people reacting to instructions from three or four different sources.

That is because the line of authority is not always clear. I could quote instances where people who were, say, specialist electricians, technicians in certain areas, they are still being used for that skill, five or six years after their original job title had gone. But because we failed to recognize their expertise, or train anybody to replace it, they are still being used.

The man I was working with today is one of our best instrument technicians. He's taken part in Open University courses. He has been made a plant engineer in one particular part of the plant, but today he was working with me, in another area, because he was the only bloke who could do the job.

We have failed to appreciate what is wrong, so we have done nothing about it. People tend to say 'Oh it'll be all right. So and so is the expert in this. We'll find someone else some other time'. But no one gets it organized.

Is this because a layer of management was taken away?
I think the people who are making the decisions are too far removed from the realities of life. Also, if people have a little bit of expertise in an area they tend to hang on to it anyway. It's difficult to get them to impart it.

About eight years ago we were undergoing tremendous change in Norwich. It was a pretty unpleasant time, but I was very fortunate. I got transferred to our American factory for three months. There, they had the old-style traditional management. It was absolutely marvellous. You knew exactly who to go to see, there was only one person who could have made a decision in a particular area. People working in this factory were complete strangers to me, but I found it dead easy to find my way around, find out who was responsible. The structure was obvious. It was a typical downward pyramid. And it doesn't always happen like that these days.

Have there been any attempts to get people committed to the new structure?
Oh yes. Quite a lot. In the way of training courses, management consultants, endless streams of management consultants. It did us a lot of good. It made everybody think about the right way of doing things by throwing up the objectives on the wall before you set out to do a task. Good managers did this anyway. It was the poor managers who didn't have clear objectives.

One of the most ridiculous things I ever went to was a so-called 'Helping Others to Succeed' programme which we all have to go through. We all spent enormous amounts of time, usually your own time, because you are busy running a factory anyway, and then you have to prepare for courses and cope with worksheets beforehand. This was a parent company inspired thing where every month you are supposed to sit down and have a formal interview with your immediate subordinates and come up with the things you said you'd do for them in the previous month. Then you have objectives, and they're all very stylized.

I was very lucky: when I first started here I had some good people I worked for. Every so often they would say 'Have you done that job yet? Do you understand what you are doing?'. They would take you aside and explain things because they were just naturally good at it. They didn't need to be told to help others succeed. I've had lots of young people working with me, or alongside me, over the years and I remembered how I was treated as a young lad and I reckon I managed to help them as I had been. It's ridiculous how many courses and things there have been. Some have been useful.

If you installed a new piece of plant you had to make sure that the piece of plant was designed and operated in a safe manner. In the old days, in any normal company, a couple of blokes would sit down and go through it themselves. They would ask the 'What if?' question a few times. The company's way is that you have to set a team up to do it. And you have to follow a computer program with set answers and action points, as a result of which it takes four times as long. So if you get someone in charge of that operation who likes that sort of thing, they can't see the short cuts.

What have people's emotional reactions been to the changes?
They have been rather poor in some cases. People have become ill. It made me ill because of the stress. I was totally committed in my working life, then suddenly they throw something else at you which is going to affect your future and your job. I got shingles. Other basically fit competent people have got things like Bell's Palsy, psychosomatic diseases; there was quite a bit of that.

The whole culture of the company has been to push people as hard as possible. I'm not against that because if we hadn't done it we would have been out of business and closed down by now. I worked for a company in Lancashire which was just like that, and did close down. But we push people to beyond their limit.

Have the objectives been achieved?
No. Not in anything like the time-scale. If we survive long enough, another year or so, then the objectives will be achieved. But they will be

achieved in a modified form, in as much as we have had to put people back into their old jobs to help the team leaders. I have had team leaders actually coming to me to ask for help. Either they didn't have the technical knowledge, or they didn't have the time to do what had to be done. So they have had to reverse the changes in some cases. This is a good thing. Because if we just kept rigidly to the plan the performance would have fallen off even more. What has happened is that the change was too great; then they had to put certain aspects back again and reverse the process. You've got a job, say, that's being done by 20 blokes, and you look at it and think 'That could be done by 12'. But in actual fact the real answer is that the job could be done by sixteen. On the other hand, you could only have found that out by trying it.

In managing the change, were there any key or critical incidents which made the change more or less successful?
The thing that went particularly well was the reaction of some of the young team leaders who did take on the responsibilities. But there were other disasters that occurred in the plant because the right people were not there at the right time – incidents of breakdowns and faults that were never corrected. Under the old system they would have been put right quickly, but after the change they took 10 times longer to correct.

What kind of qualities do managers need to manage change successfully?
You have to be able to delegate. I think that's the most important one. You have to recognize people's strengths and weaknesses and not gloss over them, but take positive steps to assist or help. That's what managing change is all about.

What are the factors which inhibit change?
People don't want to change. You don't want to change do you? Nobody wants to change. If someone said to you 'Come and change your car' you'd say 'No. Go away. I like my car'.

What would you have done differently?
It was done too quickly. The changes were implemented quicker than the people were willing to accept. I still don't understand why we got into such a mess when the actual information and advice was there. Part of the Improvements Team I now belong to have ended up going to visit other companies and seeing now they do things. But this is after the event. It is plain that the people who planned the change went to talk to people about best practice before they instituted the change, but

I don't think they listened. Or they thought we were better than other people. That was probably the biggest mistake.

REFLECTION

These two cases are good examples of downsizing. What guidelines can we formulate from them that will be useful to other managers having to implement a change programme where downsizing is a significant element?

■ CHAPTER SIX ■

Reorganizing support services

The three cases in this chapter were concerned with improving the efficiency of in-firm service. Cultural barriers to change are a feature of all three. The first case is told by a personnel manager of a large firm of City lawyers. On joining the firm he was tasked to set up a personnel department, but he soon discovered the inefficiencies present in the existing structure of support services to the professional lawyers. He recounts his efforts to initiate and implement an improved structure in a climate of conservatism. A significant factor in this case was that the organization was a partnership, and this meant he had to build up credibility and support among the partners before he could implement plans to achieve the changes he saw as necessary.

The second case involves a change at team level. It is told by an insurance manager who had been involved in shaping and implementing the changes before he left the firm a year ago. The broking process for a personal insurance business was split between staff at two sites. The London office undertook bringing in the business and programme design and the East Anglia office provided the back office support. For various reasons this split of function was not operating and a number of changes had to be made. The work reorganization took place and began to bear fruit. However, changes were not sustained, and this may have been due to achieved cultural changes being too superficial to overcome the changes in the personalities of some of the incumbents.

The third case is told by the chief executive officer of a small professional institution. Work pressure meant that the professional members could not devote enough time to dealing with matters relating to the institute. The result was that certain important issues, including future strategy, were apt to be neglected. The chief executive officer saw that a change of culture was needed so that it became more legitimate for the paid staff to be involved in decision-making committees, normally the preserve of the voluntary professional members.

A similarity with the first case is worth noting – the limited power both managers had because they were essentially in a servicing role to others with considerable power. This meant that an incremental (almost covert) approach to change was adopted by the chief executive officer.

Restructuring support services in a partnership

Background

This interviewee is personnel manager for a large firm of City lawyers. He trained as an engineer then entered the Army on a short-term commission. In this capacity he feels he started his line management experience, which was later consolidated within an engineering company. After an MBA he joined his current firm to start up a new personnel department. It is this change, together with the reorganization of the firm's support services, which forms the subject of the case study.

The change

I joined the firm three and a half years ago. I was recruited to set up a new personnel department, but really my brief was quite wide – not just pure personnel and training. One of the elements of the brief was to take a complete look at the level of service that was being given to fee earners in terms of secretarial and other support, such as photocopying, fax, post and all of the day-to-day services.

   Whilst everything was essentially in place, we had got to a situation where the number of fee earners had grown quite dramatically. The litigation business was doing very well, despite the recession. However, the increase in the level of fee earners had not been matched by an increase in the level, and indeed quality of the support services, be it finance, personnel, marketing, or indeed other support elements such as photocopying.

   I have been responsible for many other changes which have mainly been initiated by bringing in new people, such as a director of finance and a marketing manager, and by setting up an IT department. But the area that's best to centre on is how I went about changing the organizational structure of what I call Support Services into a more logical and service-orientated unit.

Who initiated the project?

The project was front-end driven I suppose by me. When I arrived, it immediately became very apparent that the level of services was highly unsatisfactory. Take photocopying for example. We had one person in a room which was actually doubled up with the post room. In terms of equipment and staffing the level of service was completely below that which was needed for the size of practice and the level of fee service required. We were short staffed, and we didn't have the right type of staff. People had the wrong skills, they were not particularly motivated and they didn't know what their jobs were or what was expected of them.

The level of photocopying was such that people would invariably have to send their work out to external contractors who charged a fortune for it, or they were doing it themselves because there weren't skilled staff or people to do the work. I can remember people having to put stamps on their own post, and these are fee earners who are being charged out at hundreds of pounds an hour, wasting time copying a document or finding out where the document exchange number is. They rang couriers themselves because there wasn't someone there who could ring the courier. They sent faxes themselves. The list is endless.

The change wasn't written in stone in my job spec. – but I could see it was an area where I could make a big impact because I was also responsible for recruitment. I could see that I would have to take the opportunity to address all the problems across all types of support staff, including secretarial.

In addition, the fee earners were quite clearly not being given the service they needed. So in one way it was my decision to say, 'Right we are going to have to make a few changes here' in structure, staffing, equipment, siting and all the other factors.

Accommodation

Geographically, we are in a situation where we are on four floors of a seven-floor office building. We had had very much piecemeal development. As the firm grew rapidly over the past four or five years that has meant we have had to continually revamp and refurbish the office space. The situation when I joined was that we had no structure or logic about the location of the various support functions, and there was no central control. So we had the copying department stuck on the third floor, we had the fax machines stuck away on the fourth floor, we had the switchboard on the fourth floor. And there was no real coordination or efficient use of the staffing and equipment in those services. So this was a very useful opportunity for the whole structure to change, driven by the fact that we were planning to take on an entirely new floor within the building. My proposal to the partnership board was that we should use that opportunity to set up a new Support Services function on that floor which would then be devoted to serving the lawyers on all the other floors.

That was about a year after I joined the firm and was really the opportunity and the vehicle for my change programme.

Did you get the support you needed?

Yes. I was setting up a new department from scratch, and they had never had a personnel function before. It took me several months to sell the whole concept because many partners were not even happy about 'wasting' money on personnel. So firstly what I had to put in was a basic personnel function, including personnel management systems and procedures, whilst at the same time trying to understand the business and work out exactly where we were going wrong in terms of the support service I have already mentioned, and what I needed to do to change things.

So, ownership at the start was very much with myself, because I was still having to sell the whole concept of personnel. But after I established that, then I received enough support from the partnership. They saw that the changes were actually making a difference to the quality of service.

The partnership culture

I think the whole culture of the partnership, the nature of the business, where you have got, if you like, the shareholders actually working here, does create a certain type of culture. The fee earners are given targets. They have to bring in £x a year, or whatever it is, and they are very aware of any extra costs which may influence the money they are bringing into the firm. So it is always very difficult to sell the concept of support services in all its shapes and forms.

People can correctly identify the fact that they need a secretary. But if you are talking about adding say, another person in the photocopying department, or having somebody else involved in delivery of faxes, there's a lot of resistance. What I have had to do is say, 'Well, if we structure it in this way, if we bring the right staff in, then it will eventually benefit you in the end'. Partnerships are naturally reluctant to bring in support staff, whatever they are paid and whatever their function is, and that will probably always be the case.

This floor was obviously designed from scratch, it's very comfortable and air-conditioned. It's the only fully air-conditioned floor in the entire building. One of the biggest things we had to do was to say to the partners: 'Look we're starting from scratch, it's best to have it air-conditioned now. It's going to cost a lot more money'. And to sell this to 25 partners who own the business, all of whom will not be sitting on that air-conditioned floor, was, in the light of the summer, as you can imagine, unbelievably difficult.

We had to say, 'It's no good just spending £50 000 pounds – and doing only half a job. It will benefit the business in the long term – lots of support services are going to have air conditioning and you're not ...'. But if you ask me about the politics of this change, that was the biggest political problem I had. It also gives a flavour of how partnerships work.

Was there any time frame?
There was no immediate time frame because I was doing it in a controlled fashion. I tried not to run before I could walk, but to have the careful planning first: put new people in place and see how things worked out.

What stage are you at now?
The change has come to quite a good point of consolidation. The geographical change occurred last October when this floor was finally fitted out. I was involved in the design of it to suit the new support services.

For example, there is a new photocopying department across the way with new equipment. There is a new accounts department which takes up about a third of this floor. We have a new section where people work on trial preparation rather than being stuck away in a small room. We have got all the various functions set up here – personnel, marketing, the director of finance's areas – and then at the front we have got what I call a 'front of house' reception. Not for clients – it's for anything that comes into the building, i.e. post, faxes, deliveries; everything that is external is concentrated in one area rather than being found on all different floors.

And so we have reached a point now where the floor is fully up and running. I have recruited – I can't remember off the top of my head how many I've recruited – but virtually all the people on this floor are new. So I've been involved in redundancy management, dismissals, assessing people's competence and recruiting a number of new people. For example, we recruited a new copying supervisor from one of our competitors, and she was also involved in the actual planning stages of this floor. I recruited her six months before we took over this floor, and when we were designing the floor she and I worked very closely together on the structure of the copying department. And that was the same for the accounts department and other areas of support services.

The service has now increased in quality, and all the fee earners know exactly where to come and all of the contact numbers. They know that nine times out of ten, if it's to do with any type of support function, it's on this floor, and hopefully they can get any service they need.

It has reached a point where I am quite satisfied that the quality of service has increased quite dramatically, and I suppose now we are going into fine tuning.

I have introduced multi-skilling for a lot of the jobs. For example, the person who works normally at the front of the desk on post is also able to go into photocopying if there is an extra need there. This means we can operate more efficiently and rely less on temporary staff. We don't have problems in the holidays, and that has been a main feature of the change.

I would say that because people are multi-skilled we are now saving lots of money. We are not there yet because the firm is still growing quite quickly.

Did you do any systematic examination of what the needs were?
Yes I did. I did that by firstly looking at what we had got. So an audit in all its shapes and forms: numbers of staff, quality of staff, what skills they had. We had no appraisal system at that time, but I also implemented an appraisal system which has obviously helped to analyze what we've got in terms of staff skills on the career development side. Then, in terms of the planning, I looked at the sort of size we were likely to be over the next four or five years, in terms of sheer floor space and numbers of fee earners, and, for example, what sort of level of copying service we would need, the number and level of people to cope with post, faxes, deliveries, etc., and the size of the accounts department we would possibly be needing if we expanded to a certain degree within the medium term. So I linked it with the business plan as far as I could.

Did the business plan include your objectives?
I had a number of objectives which I actually set myself because, coming into a new personnel function, people were not clear what my objectives should be. So I actually wrote my own personnel strategy and plans and objectives. One of them was to review and change the organizational structure. That was my own objective, and what I was working on.

Will you be monitoring/evaluating the outcome?
I evaluate the outcomes on a day-to-day basis. I am fortunately able to do that because I have made sure that I am here, on the same floor as the various functions I am managing directly. I am managing the personnel and training functions, across both this office and our suburban offices, but I am also managing the administration on this floor, indirectly.

Now I am just doing a continual audit, mainly by asking fee earners, at appraisal time, and at other opportunities, a number of questions about what they think the level of service is. For instance, how long does it take you to get your faxes done, how long does it take you to do your X, Y and Z?

And then I react to the comments made in these various questionnaires.

What changes have you observed in terms of ripple-on effects or knock-on effects?

It's a difficult question to centre on because no day has been the same here since I started, both in terms of my own role and the way in which the firm is moving. The ripple-on effect is a greater degree of accountability and motivation among the staff in support services, but that's because a lot of them are newly recruited people who have been given clear job descriptions and job specifications and they know what is expected of them. Because we have also put in an appraisal process, there is a greater emphasis on individual performance. We have quite a meritocratic style of reward here in terms of salary, bonuses and other non-financial career development incentives.

The bottom line ripple effect is that the lawyers are earning more money, I hope.

And because the whole system is working more efficiently, they have a greater respect for support staff. In a partnership it is always going to be 'them and us' between the lawyers and non-fee earners, but I think I have probably bridged the gap a little bit more, and fee earners are respecting more what support staff can do for them, and their role in contributing to earning fees for the practice.

What do you think have been your most difficult tasks in putting these changes into operation?

The most difficult task for me personally is that I don't particularly enjoy having to move people out of a job, and I have experienced great resistance to that. There used to be quite a paternalistic atmosphere here. Retention was extremely high, and still is to a certain extent, and to 'get rid of people' was very much not the culture in this firm, for fee earners or support staff.

So I found it quite a difficult position especially coming in as a new person and having to tell people, or the management, that some of the staff were not up to the job, that we could do better elsewhere, and that we needed to review the skills of various people. So dismissal and redundancy management was the most difficult area.

What about the most important area?

The most important area is getting ownership from the people who are going to be involved. One of the lessons I have learned is that it makes a lot of difference if you really decentralize and hand down responsibility to the people you will be working with. To use the photocopying example, I recruited the new supervisor before we even designed the floor, and involved her in designing the new copying department. You must give people ownership right from the start: explain what the strategy is, what we are trying to do, what the expectations are going to be.

The other lesson is to make people multi-skilled in this type of organization. It saves a lot of money and essentially is an efficient way of running the business.

Did you have to introduce any training?

Most of the initial training has been done with new staff in the form of induction programmes. So for example if we were recruiting a new person for the post room, the training would be done very much front-end. On the day they come in, from the start, we set down the standards and the whole job specification. So training is done mainly when new staff join, but also there is now on-the-job training for more experienced people working in the various functions.

What about the commitment of everyone involved in the change?

As always, you judge by results. It is very difficult when you can't actually come out with a clear 'If we run this very efficient copying service I reckon we are going to save x amount a year'. You can do it in terms of saying we are probably not going to have to send out £80 000 worth of external copying, but the add-on value of a slick, efficient service, quick turn-around times, good response, accurate photocopying – that's actually very difficult to quantify in terms of the fee earners' billing across the firm.

So in terms of putting forward proposals, it's very much a case of devising the plan, assessing the financial considerations, getting agreement to put the idea into practice, and continually selling it in order to get commitment. Then, as always, the proof of the pudding is in the eating.

Fortunately I don't think there would be many people here who would now say it has been a bad idea.

Would you say there's anything you are proud of having done particularly well, or which has worked particularly well?

I'm pleased that I've managed to decentralize all of the support functions, to the extent that I now really don't have to worry too much about

it. For example, as I've said, I have got a very competent copying supervisor. We work very well together. So essentially it is now largely autonomous – it runs itself, with good people who have a lot of responsibility.
Therefore it has enabled me to concentrate on other things to do with
the business – personnel, strategic management, all the other elements
that I'm involved in. I'm very pleased because it's meant that my job has
changed. A year ago I was running around like a headless chicken
trying to work out where we were going to put this equipment, and that
equipment, and did we need another person here, and so it's very much
moved on to another element of the business.

Is there anything that hasn't gone so well?

I can list endless things that haven't gone as well as they should have
done, but that's always going to occur when you are going through
change. I think that it would have been more helpful to have had a
greater degree of ownership from the partnership. I have had to be very
realistic, and I can live with the fact that there are some partners who
may consider we have too many support staff, that they are not perhaps
working as well as they should do, and that they sit around all day
doing nothing.... That perhaps is an exaggeration, but if anything, I'd
like to be in an organization where I felt people valued support staff a
little bit more. But that's just the structure of partnerships, and lack of
communication, and the problem that some people don't know what
other people are doing in the business.

   In any sort of organizational change within a partnership it
would be better to have top-driven ownership. I feel it has been very
much up to the middle managers, i.e. me, to live and die by what I am
doing. It's great if it's all going well, but if it's not going well people are
quite ready to stand back and wash their hands of it and say 'Well, we
didn't think it was a good idea anyway'.

What factors help to promote change?

I think I can go back to my old MBA theories I have been taught,
although I've forgotten most of them, about 'freezing' and 'unfreezing'.
You do see elements of that, although you don't consciously notice it
when you are going through the change. It's all about attitudes, values
and beliefs in the organizational culture. So, for example, this was an
organization that was quite paternalistic, nowhere near the hire-and-
fire organization it is now. But certainly there was a culture whereby
people expected to stay in their jobs. But more importantly they
weren't given any sort of objectives or any sort of expectations about

what sort of standards were expected. I think that is perhaps an area that inhibits change most of all.

The next point is that it's easier to introduce change by bringing in new brooms, that is, restaffing. That has been a key element in this restructuring.

The other key element in change is knowledge and know-how. That's becoming more and more the case as we become increasingly sophisticated, especially with IT. For instance, I recruited an IT manager quite recently. Overnight things are changing rapidly because he has the know-how and skill which wasn't there before.

So I would probably suggest that the recruitment of new staff, and the know-how that goes with it, are among the biggest enablers of change.

What inhibits change?

People are working very much for themselves, rather than as teams, and what we have tried to do is introduce multi-skilling combined with a team-based element. Before, the inhibitor to change was the fact that people were very much working by themselves and therefore could see no reason why they should change their ways and become more quality-oriented.

Another inhibitor to change, a most important point, is the communication of the requirements for change. For example, if a fee earner thought the service he was getting wasn't good enough, the level of communication to the management of the practice was not there. So one never really found out that the quality of service was not up to what it should be, and indeed, because people had always been used to sending their own faxes, or doing their own copying, the expectation was that that was what they were expected to do. When they had been trainee solicitors here they probably had to do their own photocopying, so when they became solicitors they presumed they still had to do it.

Anything you would have done differently?

If I had to do the thing over again, I would go through even more detailed planning and selling of the whole project. I would look even more carefully at the type of staff we are bringing in, at how we can multi-skill and how we could run the business with the minimum number of people. I would certainly have more confidence and the courage of my convictions.

One example of having the courage of my convictions is this. The culture in this firm has been that if you are a manager or a fee earner, then you sit in a room and your secretary sits outside that room. When I first joined the firm I was eventually given a secretary and I was in an office, and she was placed outside my room. I had to set up a new personnel function where I was trying to work very much hand-in-hand with someone, but we were not geographically in the right situation.

When we designed this floor one of the things I had to do was design the new personnel department, which was essentially for two people, myself and my assistant. And I can remember when we first did the plan for this floor the idea was for a marketing manager with secretary outside, a personnel manager with secretary outside etc. I spent a great deal of time and anguish persuading the partnership that it would be better and more efficient for the practice if my assistant and I were in the same room. It's a small thing, but this caused a real political hoo-ha, the fact that a secretary was going to be sitting in the same room as a manager. They said 'Well what happens if you want to talk privately?'. And I said, well there may be elements of that but in terms of the way that I want to work and the efficient personnel function, we have to be almost in tandem as to the information that's coming into the department, and for X, Y and Z reasons I think it would benefit us if we had this structure.

So I recommended that we had one room for the two of us, and we had an interview room off to the side. I remember the Executive Partner coming back to me having talked to the partners, and saying 'Look – I am very concerned that the partners should feel that we keep to the structure of you in one room and your secretary outside'. And I nearly gave in and said all right – if it's going to be a big issue I'm not going to push it. But then I stopped and I thought, no: it's going to make our lives easier. It's going to make the business more effective, I can do my job more effectively for the business. So I stuck to my convictions. It was very late in the design stage, but in practice it's worked excellently.

That's a good example of having the courage of my convictions. I was doing it for the right reasons and I should have had more confidence in selling the point.

Work reorganization in the back office of an insurance broker

Background
The change I am talking about is a change in the attitudes and culture in a team which backed up the team that I was managing. The history is that in the 1980s my company, an insurance broker, moved the backup

staff out of London because it was much cheaper to have staff based in East Anglia. The company built a large prestigious office building there.

I joined the company in the mid-1980s to do the technical backup in a newly formed department in London. This was an unregarded and unfashionable part of insurance that no one particularly wanted to deal with because there were no big numbers involved (as in volume insurance), so we did not have the pick of the people we could get in East Anglia. We were given two well-regarded but incredibly neurotic technicians and one school leaver to do our backup. One of the technicians left and we then had a succession of school leavers come in: some stayed and others didn't.

Also we were dogged by the attitude of local management that, because our team was unregarded we continued to have a complete lack of support. The technical competence at East Anglia was very poor. They did do the processing. Basically we bought in the business, we handled it, we got all the documentation in order and then sent it to the back office for cover noting, accounting purposes and eventually for filing.

In time I became manager for the London side of things, reporting to the managing director (MD). I came under increasing pressure to sort out the problems of the interface between London and East Anglia. The initial way I worked was to bring people from the back office who knew the system up to London so they could get things more usefully sorted out and packaged for sending to East Anglia. But that backfired on me because the people I brought up were sucked in to do front-end work, so we ended up with exactly the same problems down in East Anglia but without their expertise. So in fact the problem worsened.

We had a succession of very second rate managers and team leaders running the back office team, culminating in one who actually wanted to help and develop the team. But the team leader was a problem. She was very nice, a sweet person, but she looked after her 'brood' like a mother hen and refused to let any additional work or additional responsibility come down to her staff. Any attempt we made to push more responsibility down or more work down was blocked. Tragically, she developed a condition and had to retire on grounds of ill health.

I then got together with the manager of the back office and her number two and we conspired to bring in someone who we knew would be cooperative and who would support the changes that we wanted to put into place. At that point we effectively had a management team which I nicknamed 'the coven', and they adopted this as their corporate identity.

At this time, the pressure to shift work down to East Anglia had spread, so not only were staff down there going to be dealing with more detailed processing, but the idea was that they should actually handle all the small business. This is business with brokerage of less than £6000. This represented about 40 per cent of our cases. The proposal was that all of those would be handled in East Anglia, with the exception of the market broking, which would be handled up in London. But, even here the idea was that eventually that would be handled by people who would come up to London and start to develop relationships with the insurance market.

A key problem we had was that the staff had been recruited just to do processing. They had no idea or ambition that they would handle the business, deal with clients and generally be proactive rather than just handling money and bits of paper as it came in. So their culture was one of stolid bureaucracy, and we had to change that in order to get them to focus on the client; to focus on ideas of developing the business, and ways of growing the business. Because one of the things you do is that if you have a small bit of business then you try to get a big bit of business on the back of it, which we in London had been very effective at doing. In fact, the department had more or less created itself on the back of that process. We couldn't afford to lose that by sending business to the out-of-London group. So the idea was that we should (a) increase the technical ability of the other office, (b) change their attitude towards the clients and the business that they handled, and (c) increase the involvement of them in the London sphere of operations. Instead of having two teams, the London team and the East Anglian team, we should become one team that just happened to be separated by physical distance.

Communication between the two offices was actually first class. We, as a company, have been using email since the early 1980s. We had very efficient communications systems, so there are virtually no problems (unless, at times, when the cable was damaged through building work). Even then we could continue to operate because the infrastructure for doing the coordinated activity was there. It was just that the people, in our case, simply were not up to it.

The role of the East Anglian team was to produce cover notes which were sent up to London for checking before sending out – it was a paper-based system, although most of the communications were electronic. The source document, which is called 'the slip' in insurance terms... the broker has a summary of the business and the particular risk on a piece of paper or a series of sheets which is called the 'slip'. Generally speaking this was created in London and then it was held on the database. In theory, all of the other documentation sprang from the slip. So the communication, effectively, was centred around the electronic documental slip, which in fact was normally broked in hard copy. It is only relatively recently that electronic broking has started to develop. The mode of communication was generally electronic, although there was a passage of paper between the two offices, probably in the proportions of 60:40.

The first thing we felt we had to do was to increase the technical capability. I knew, from experience, that if you sent down things that they did not understand, either they would return it immediately with a query (which was more work for us) or they would try to do it but mess it up and then send it back to us (which meant even more work for us). So I wanted to avoid the problem of (a) queries and (b) cock-ups. The only way to do that was to increase their ability to handle the business; to be able to spot or anticipate the likely problems in the file. The other side of this was to get them to actually 'own' the files and to feel that these were their responsibility. Up to then, they had been London's responsibility while they were in London, and when they were moved down to East Anglia they were seen as nobody's responsibility. Hence there was no one with interest in keeping the quality up.

So, the second stage, the involvement and the technical side, really ran hand in hand, because they couldn't feel involved with the files unless they got the technical training in order to be able to handle the queries and they were not going to get the technical training very easily unless they had the files to work on in the first place.

The way that the changes were implemented was that we recruited a very competent, highly intellectual person who came as a technician but also had a training ability. His brief was to sort out the enormous backlog which we had going back about a large number of years and also to impart his technical knowledge to the people. I started off the training process by having a couple of seminars, ostensibly about redesigning our slips, because we obviously work from pro formas. We don't design each slip from scratch. We were not satisfied with the pro formas, so we decided to use the redesigning process as a training vehicle. We brought all of the East Anglian office people to London for two-hour lunchtime seminars and we went through every aspect of it. By the end of this they knew, more or less, what was going on. That had a very big impact. Coming out of those seminars they did start to feel they could handle more of the technical side. They now understood some of the things which they had probably been working on for three or four years. They started with an element of technical understanding built through the seminars and then that was backed up by further lunchtime seminars by the technician/trainer we brought in.

The process of coordinating the two teams was driven by me, and I was driven by my MD, who is a very charismatic manager. He is extremely good at pushing/motivating people. He also has a tendency to be somewhat volatile. The manager in the other office, my opposite number, was June. Her number two was Anne, and the third member of the coven was the new team leader Margaret.

John, my boss, used to insist on everything to be sent down to East Anglia, and then about three weeks later when there was a problem he'd insist on everything coming back up again. It was incredibly frustrating because we would start doing something and then it was going to be a problem. Someone would mention that it was going to be a problem and then John would say 'Oh no, they can't handle that one. We'll have to have it back here, how are we going to be able to cope with it?'. So June and I would be tearing our hair out, particularly as we had this woman who went off sick who, effectively, with the best of intentions, frustrated every attempt we made to make consistent progress on this.

But we reckoned that from the time we shifted everything down to East Anglia we had six months before the MD changed his mind again. We reckoned we could keep the cap on it and make this a serious initiative and we could actually say at the end of six months: 'It is *more* effort to bring things back up to London than it is to leave it down there, so let them continue the process'. But we wanted to make sure that six months started at the most propitious time, so I was keen to make sure that everyone had their training sorted out. In fact, Greg eventually got extremely impatient and we decided we just had to send everything down. So we said 'OK, from the first of November everything which came up for renewal under £6000 brokerage would be handled down in East Anglia. This was decided in September, so we had a two-month period to get everything sorted out. There was a complete flat panic because the renewal process actually starts about two months before the due date.

So the change, as it was originally conceived, was incremental, but, in fact, the way it was actually implemented was 'Big Bang' with a bit of a lead in. It was quite a culture shock when they eventually got it, and there were problems. There was a lot of disaffection over the New Year renewal period because quite a lot of policies are renewed on the first of January. The people were under severe pressure and there was almost a mutiny down there. They felt they hadn't had the training that they needed. The mutiny was headed off very effectively by June, although it rumbled on for some time. She did this by charm and sweet-talk mostly, which was her particular style. She simply said 'This will work out, don't worry, stay with it. You are getting much better', and basically encouraging them to do it. There was one person who had been the acolyte of 'mother hen', and we knew that if we managed to get her on board then all the others would follow because she was, not a ring leader, but the person from whom others took their stance. Eventually she did come on board.

We got to February and had a meeting about the state of the change and the report was quite positive because people had actually started to think in terms of the files and the problems and anticipate the problems and see and read the file through. One thing we were absolutely horrified to discover, when we were discussing the prospect of changing, with the 'mother hen' (Rhona) was when I said 'When you read the file through do you pick up...?' and she said 'Oh, we don't read the file through'. I said 'How can you possibly know what's going on with the files?' and she responded 'We don't have time to read the file through, we don't want to read the file'. Some of these files are two inches thick, but you still need to read them through.

We did get over that, and they started to take a little more interest in what was going on. Some of the problems in the original conception of the insurance may have gone back four or five years before. I said 'If you want to know what the original intention was then you have to go right back to the beginning of the file. That is the only way of doing it'. So that problem was overcome. They now had the feeling of responsibility for their files and wanted their files to succeed. Some of the more difficult ones they still didn't want to own: those were the ones that came back to London. They had to be physically allocated; someone's name was written onto it so they could not avoid responsibility. My aim was to try to enable East Anglia to absorb as many of those as possible so as not to draw the MD's attention to the fact that all problems had not been resolved. I tried to head off as many problems as possible. I didn't draw a sharp line and say these are our problems and those are yours, because that would have created greater difficulties and political problems. The momentum of the initiative would have been lost.

In retrospect it was quite a difficult balancing act, but at the time it was normal. It was 'just the way things were'. I'd been working with the MD for six or seven years, and knew his style and the way he operated. Also I'd been working for a while with June and we had a good understanding about the way we wanted the change to go. At the time it was just the way the office worked, but it is difficult to work with a prima donna!

There was a point where John said 'OK, this is it, off they go', so, in retrospect, I think that was possibly right. If we had delayed it any longer I think we might have found ourselves faffing around and lost the initiative. I think that was the right thing to do, although I didn't like it at the time. In terms of the type of change, it was pretty central to the effectiveness of how our teams worked. We were getting very bogged down in London, dealing with the nitty gritty, which we shouldn't be doing. We were the producers and the programme designers and to get involved in documentation was really outside our brief. So, it was central to us and the company as a whole because we were a technical resource for the whole company. If we had problems, even though they may be a small part of the overall insurance programme being designed by the company for a client, our problem could affect the whole programme.

We did have one or two occasions when it did and we had some fairly extensive fire fighting to do. But, generally speaking, the level of problem was such that we managed to head it off in time. In most cases we actually managed to improve our relationship with the client by bringing them into the loop of the problem and not trying to solve it all by ourselves. The latter is a very high-risk strategy, because if you don't involve them and make unilateral changes then the client wants to know what is going on and says, 'If you told us earlier we could have helped you'.

It was definitely a predicted change. It was a project which we would have liked to have undertaken earlier had we been able to unblock the process. In fact it was this permanent health problem of the team leader, Rhona, that actually effected the unblocking. If she had remained team leader, I am convinced she would be resisting the change to this day.

It was a familiar task because we were asking them to do more of things that they were already doing, but better. It was participative involvement – we wanted to involve them in what was going on already, we didn't want to change any of the procedures except to make them better and make them more efficient and to make the people more involved and more proactive. It was a complex change because there were a lot of people who had been used to operating as individuals and the files we had were not complicated in themselves, but there were a lot of them and they were all different, which is part of the problem. We hadn't been able to standardize.

One of the other changes we were trying to put into place was to standardize the type of insurance and procedure. We completely failed to do that. As far as I know there are still difficulties in that area. If you have an ordinary standard piece of business you do not come to a high flier London insurance broker to do it. You go to your local market. We are a market of last resort. So we really only deal with difficult insurance, so that each tended to be different. No attempt to standardize the work had been successful.

The scale of the change is difficult to say. It was, for the individuals in East Anglia, extensive. They had to completely rethink the way they operate. As far as the team as a whole was concerned it wasn't extensive. We were simply changing the constitution of the team by upgrading the lower end in East Anglia and bringing them up to the level of the technicians up here in London. We had one or two very high-powered technicians up here in London and we wanted them to be role models for the people down there. That was a good message to put across. It didn't actually work because there was a certain amount of jealousy because people in London were paid so much better. That of course was behind the idea of moving the work down to East Anglia in the first place. But the aim was to bring everyone into one big happy family rather than having two warring factions.

The change was about job enrichment for the East Anglia team. It was almost philanthropic for making the work as interesting as possible. Obviously East Anglia did not see it as that: they saw it as us making them work harder. But, at the end of the day they did end up with the idea that it was more fun being involved in more of the process.

Effectively there were few ripple-on effects from the change. It was fairly self-contained. The main effect was that having upgraded our people in East Anglia we then started to lose them. Other teams poached them. There is a very aggressive internal employment market in the company down in East Anglia because of the difficulties of employing trained people in the local area. There are other insurance organizations, and we had an unofficial salary cartel in operation, so effectively we didn't poach each other's staff. As a result it is incredibly difficult to get trained staff and hence our reliance on school leavers.

The way team leaders managed to get good technicians was to poach them from other teams. You don't wait for people to say 'I want to move' or 'As part of my career structure I want to move on'. Rather, you go out there, take them out to lunch and seduce them to move into your team. The team in East Anglia, on the back of the business success of the London team, became quite a desirable place to work. So we came to the situation where people actually wanted to come and work there. But other teams soon learnt that we had good staff who had been trained and two people left before I did and more people have left since.

There is a ripple-on effect. The London staff were able to deal more with the business; there was a reduction in the documentation load. The change was effective because it took the workload off London. It didn't extend much further than that. The other side of that was that we had to put in a computer-based control system in order to be able to track whereabouts the documents were at any one time. Before, we had done it on little bits of paper, which was hopeless because the East Anglia people did it religiously, but when it came up to London it disappeared. It went into our filing system, but there was no document tracking facility so we had to put in a document tracking system. The risk tracking or the processing of the file – who was handling it, who the initial contacts were, who had to be notified of any changes outside the client – was another system to improve. There was one in place, but we had to sharpen it up and make it much more efficient. So although this was connected to this change it was actually treated as two completely different processes.

The effects on my role were that I wasn't directly involved in the change myself. I was driving it in another team, which is a rather peculiar thing. I was having to push it onto somebody else for whom, in theory, I had no responsibility. June was at the same functional level, although in terms of the organization I was several steps above her in the hierarchy because of the skew in the way the two offices operated. We acted on a direct 1:1 basis. My role was to support and push her changes in the East Anglian culture so that I could put in my changes in the way we did the business in London. These were not cultural changes but were organizational changes, in that we were moving more work in their direction. My responsibility from the London point of view was to make sure that the East Anglian people were able to do the work we were sending down to them.

The effect on our staff was that, in theory, they had more time to deal with what they were meant to be doing, or go out to lunch, or whatever! The effect on my peers was non-existent, because it was self-contained. There were some who were interested in what we were trying to achieve because, if we were successful, then they might be able to do a similar exercise themselves. The problems of small amounts of business are endemic in insurance broking. It's the service costs which are the problem. We had originally been very successful in accommodating these. The team was set up in the mid-1980s to absorb all the theoretically unprofitable personal benefit business that was floating around the company. No one thought anybody could make any money out of it. We did, and that caused a certain amount of interest.

My most important activities were supporting June and acting as a sounding board. Also, to a certain extent keeping up the pressure; support and pressure at the same time. As soon as 'mother hen' retired on the grounds of ill health, the pushing aspect became a lot less problematic. It became more about helping sort out problems. But the main task was supporting not just June, but all the members of the 'coven', because they all needed support. Probably my support was more useful to Margaret, who was brought in as the new team leader, so my support gave her instant credibility, which she wouldn't have had if she had just been appointed by the local management without any support or enthusiasm from me in London. But because they knew we were keen and wanted her, despite the fact that she had some problems to start with, she was able to overcome those.

I probably went down to East Anglia about once a month. It was quite easy for me to get to. It involved sitting around the table and seeing if they needed any help. Sometimes it was technical problems they needed help on, which I was able to sort out with them there and then. Or I was able to despatch London colleagues down to them to help sort out the problems. But we preferred to get them to come up to London because that gave a greater sense of involvement from their point of view.

The changes were not designed or planned. They were treated opportunistically. We knew where we wanted to get to, but the process emerged. As for implementation, it was implemented by the East Anglian people because we said it was their responsibility. In addition to training, we held seminars and the technician was brought in to help with training. Margaret was brought in because she is very good at training. She wasn't that technically competent herself, but she was very good at getting points across. To a certain extent we trained her and she trained the others.

Attempts to obtain commitment were crucial and that was what we were aiming for. The whole idea was to get their commitment to the business and the way it operated, and to the files as being the business. They were already committed to the company, which was, until 18 months ago, a very paternalistic company. There is a lot of identification with the company. There was not a lot of commitment to the work!

The emotional consequence of the change was this 'mutiny', which June handled with considerable tact.

The mechanisms for monitoring the change were the meetings and feedback that we had. The mechanical process was tracked by the computer systems we put in, although it wasn't used for that purpose.

I have to say that we had no idea we were 'managing change' when we were doing this. We were not thinking in terms of change management at all. We were just thinking about operational effectiveness and how we were going to do it. We didn't use any formal ideas found in the literature. I didn't know the management literature. Interestingly, as a result of the change I set up a system of what I now know to be 'quality circles'. Essentially there were teams to look at specific areas of the business to see how they could be improved. I'd never heard of quality circles! And they failed because I couldn't get the MD's commitment to the idea and I didn't have sufficient leverage or time to devote to them, to manage them myself. One or two worked out of six or seven, and two came up with reports for improvements, but, generally speaking, as an initiative it was not successful. I felt that without the MD's support I couldn't give them my wholehearted support.

Were the objectives achieved? This is an interesting question. They continued from the East Anglia point of view, but when I left the London office, the support in London dwindled, so that now there is a gradual process of bringing the work back to London again. The problem is that the culture change had embedded in East Anglia, but what I didn't do was to change the culture sufficiently in London for it to become embedded there as well. It didn't occur to me that I needed to do that. So now the process is starting to unravel.

I still see people from both London and East Anglia socially, from time to time, and I keep tabs on what is going on. The East Anglian people are very fed up because they see all this wonderful system and capability that they have developed is now being wasted. So now there is a process of demotivation. This is probably one of the reasons why people are becoming open to selection by other teams. This is a great pity and waste. There is this person in the London office, an ex-East Anglian person, who doesn't think anything good can come out of the area, who is at the level I am at, and who is undermining it.

On reflection, I should have done more to embed the organizational change in London to try to make the process irreversible. It hadn't occurred to me I would need to do so. And I would put in a more efficient monitoring system than we had. We did try to and there were lots of efforts to put together a very efficient online database that could be accessed by both sites and that was emerging. But the constraints of the technology prevented that from fully happening. We got a system that gave us about 75 per cent of what we wanted to do and the online connectivity between London and East Anglia was seen as low priority, so they thought we could do without that. In retrospect I don't think it was. I think we should have gone for a system that could have delivered less in terms of programming but more in terms of communication. In theory we had the capability to do it, but unfortunately the PC support was very weak because the company had outsourced their IT department and this was a big mainframe operation. The idea was for us to have dumb terminals on all our desks operating off a radial net – the idea was that it should be fairly robust, it shouldn't go down very frequently. Of course it did. In the mid-1990s everyone was moving over to PCs as their terminals, so it became a lot more flexible and efficient. There wasn't enough money in the budget to buy PCs for everybody, so we had a team of 20 people with one PC! It was absolute bedlam. There was another parallel team to us that were on Macs and they decided to move over to PCs, so the Macs had to be scrapped. There was a complete lack of direction. So for several years we were unable to get the support to put in an efficient database to be able to build an online monitoring system between the two offices. And I should have made that a higher priority because I think that the monitoring of change, in retrospect, would have driven it a lot faster and would have helped to embed it at both ends.

The London people would have been very keen to monitor what the East Anglia team were doing and that would have dragged them into monitoring the system, out of disbelief that the Anglian people actually could do it. The Anglian people would have succeeded just to spite London. The competition had started to become constructive, rather than the previous aggressively unconstructive relationship, where everyone was blaming everyone else. It had reached the stage where each team wanted to outdo the other and were making sure that they were in a position to do so.

The main problem was the lack of credibility in London about East Anglia. London simply did not believe it could happen. This was because at the time we had two of the key people from East Anglia moved permanently to London, and they thought that without them East Anglia could not operate. We also had the related problem that East Anglia was seen as a training ground and staging post for careers in London. If you were good, you went to London. There was a constant flow of people starting in East Anglia, proving themselves, and going up to London. But soon it was seen in East Anglia that this was not going to be an option any more. However good you were, you would still stay in East Anglia, you would be appreciated and thought well of, but you would not be going up to London. That could have had an effect, although I don't know if it did. The people we recruited liked to come up to London from time to time, but didn't actually want to stay there.

Factors that promote or inhibit change

The main factor that promoted change was the openness of communication at the management level, which filtered down to the operations level in East Anglia. My relationship with June and the relationship within the 'coven' meant there was a very open flow of information effectively at three levels. That meant that it was easier to push the change down because they could see there was a huge change of attitude at the next level up. So the openness. Also the formation of the coven was the process that unfroze the attitudes down in East Anglia. They were the key. It wasn't a particular vision, it wasn't 'We are going into a bright new dawn and everything is going to be wonderful'. It was the feeling that information could flow around and the feeling that everything was open. And the atmosphere at the top in East Anglia was good.

June was her boss's first appointment when he took over from the previous manager, who was very difficult and had an extremely poor opinion of this particular East Anglia team because, as I mentioned earlier, when it was formed it was a lowly status team and he never revised his view. When he left, his successor didn't hold that view and this facilitated the information flow and had a big influence on relationships at all levels. A lot comes down to personal relationships. Yet in the change management literature that I have read subsequently, personal relationships are hardly mentioned at all. The team-building side of it is, but it's also about do the key people in the change get on together?

Restructuring support services in a professional body

What change will we focus on?

The volunteers work very hard for the Institute on professional issues, such as managing the education process, marking the scripts. So they find it extremely difficult to think about where the Institute is going long-term because they get bogged down with the day-to-day. Perhaps some commercial organizations will have that same problem – I wouldn't know because I have never worked in one.

The difficulty for us is... being managers and trying to manage the various projects we have got, as well as the same time as trying to change hats and think 'Where are we going with this?' How am I going to convince this group of volunteers that we need to sort out what the strategic direction is going to be before we start doing any more?

Otherwise all you're doing is more and more work, and you don't get any further forward. And that certainly, I think, is the crisis that the Institute is facing now. No matter what we do, we've not moved forward. Our membership numbers are dropping instead of increasing, and I suppose, if there's any sort of change happening in this Institute it would be that we have moved through the last two or three years to become more staff-driven.

We've allowed the volunteers the space to think strategically. We haven't convinced them or we haven't allowed them to learn how to do it... because they don't do it in their ordinary jobs, so why should we expect them to suddenly come along and be strategic? They can't.

How did this change come about?
I've been here 10 years now. When I first came the staff were very clearly the people who did what the Executive Committee or Board told them to do. They were not allowed to think, they just did jobs. They were fortunate enough to have two or three people who were actually quite capable of just doing that, but couldn't help but think about what they were doing, so we were making changes to processes and procedures as a matter of course really and then having the competence and courage to go to the volunteers and say 'I do think if you do it like this it will improve this'.

And that was accepted and that is what has happened and we have done more and more of that as time has gone on. And so they have then looked to the staff as people who have perhaps got the ideas of where we can go. And that has been quite difficult to manage, not only from the volunteer point of view but also from the staff point of view, because there are a number of volunteers who will say, 'No, the staff are here to serve. Therefore they can have all the ideas they like but we're not going to take notice'. Or 'OK, up to a point but we really must control this'. And what they really mean by control is they have got to get into the detail and 'I want to see every letter that goes out, to cross-check this with this', which of course makes the managers' jobs that much more difficult, because then they don't feel as if they are managing anything except bits of paper.

From a staff point of view it has been difficult because firstly, we cannot afford to recruit the calibre of manager that we would really like. So you have to take, very often, second best, and I include myself in that, so the sort of people we employ tend to be very good at administration or they have expertise in a particular area and then we have to try to mould the job to fit them rather than mould them to fit the job. It won't work in any other way. Our membership services manager came in with various skills which we thought we were going to be able to use, but what has happened is we have created a job for him and every time we have had a committee chairman change or whatever, we have moved things around so that he can actually perform to an acceptable standard doing the job that we know he is capable of doing, rather than what we might have wanted him to do when he first came. It has gone on down the scale like that, in the sense that the people who he recruits are not going to be of the calibre that he wants.

So it's a matter of settling for what they can achieve in the given time-scale. And what happens is that all the managers have got to be administrators. You have got to be able to shuffle pieces of paper. If you can't do that you are sunk. The type of manager, the style they adopt, is going to be important to us. There are people who would like to come in and say 'Well, I'm the manager. They do, I sit here, and I think and plan'. It is not going to work. There is a little bit of time for that, but not much. You have got to be rolling up your sleeves and digging them out of holes because we are generating so much work that we couldn't cope with it otherwise. It's the only way because you really understand what goes on as well.

How many staff are there?
We've got five main managers at the moment plus myself, and we have a total of a dozen other staff. All the staff are doing key roles. If one is off sick or on holiday, the job does not get done. There is no one to cover.

So what I have done over the past two years is to bring about a change to the committee structure and I have aligned a manager to each of the five main activity areas of the Institute with a team underneath. I've said you have to be responsible for everything that happens in that area. They have had to learn to try to cover for one another as they can.

What are the main areas?
Professional development; training; conferences; marketing; and membership services. And we've developed a business plan for the first time this year (we being the managers). We were supposedly working with the coordinating committees to which these managers were put, and they helped a little bit, but basically we did it ourselves; we looked at these five areas and we said what are the key things we need to achieve this year in order to meet overall objectives of the Institute? And they have been working on those throughout the year.

I think they have been unfortunate in the sense that a lot of their work this year has been market research and it is actually very difficult then to measure your performance against tasks that say go and identify x, y, z.... You either do or you don't! It depends on the staff as to whether you get any decent information. That has been quite tricky for them this year. But it is certainly the way we want to go forward. We want the managers to have much more input into where we are going, what we are trying to achieve.

By 'we' I mean the Institute... I suspect that is quite an interesting point actually, because there is a very thin dividing line between 'we' as the management team and 'we' as the Institute. I think, although we appreciate and respect the volunteers for their input, I do think the managers feel that they actually run the Institute, and they feel that they have got to do that because we can't expect the others to do it. But it does mean that balance between what the volunteers are putting in, what the managers are putting in, and how you deal with people on a personal level is very difficult to achieve.

Although we have divided our activities into five areas, there is so much overlap that the only way we can cope is to have a regular managers meeting. Now there are all sorts of good reasons for having that anyway, but it is our lifeline because we are able to find out what everyone else is doing and work out where the correlation is and say, 'Hang on: I can give you a hand on that because we are doing this', or 'Did you know about this?'. We would be sunk without that, totally. We have brought that in on a regularly monthly basis.

And I also expect managers to meet with their own team on a regular basis too, because it's important that they know what is happening overall. (We are also bringing in a once a month meeting during our dressing down day – an opportunity for staff from one group to meet and tell, on an informal basis, others what the group are doing, over coffee).

Where we fail is really telling the staff right at the very bottom end of the line, so to speak, what is going on in the Institute. We fail, partly because people are very busy and we don't know how much information they really need. We never assess that. What do they really need to know? How do we make them feel part of this without really swamping them with so much information they don't know what to do with it all? That's a real challenge for us in the coming year: to work out how to do that so they feel comfortable and part of us.

Volunteers have less and less time to devote to the Institute. In the past it was fine: employers would give volunteers all the time that was needed. They can't afford that any more – every hour counts because it is looked at from a commercial point of view: 'It's costing us x...'. So there is less and less time available. I think we are all doing more and more work than we used to, so it has been a natural shift in many ways because we couldn't help but go that way.

But I think we have also instigated it as well – we have tried to volunteer for certain tasks where we have really wanted those.

Why you have you sought them?

For a number of reasons. Firstly because the volunteers, however good they are, do have a habit of failing to deliver, and if it is a crucial task to your particular area you do not want to be seen not to have delivered – the excuse of 'Well, I was waiting for so and so' wears thin after a while.

I think the way the team works at the moment is that they are all very committed. They actually want this to work and we have managed to devise not only the tasks they do but also objectives for them, which makes them feel they actually want to achieve these things. It's not just that they've been laid down and here they are... they are so integrated into what they are doing that they are getting a buzz from achieving them and performing well, so there is no problem about people volunteering to do things because they're thinking 'Hang on: this could be really good for me' (and good for the Institute). So I think we've been lucky there. I'm sure that's not normal.

Would you describe this change as incremental or Big Bang?

Definitely incremental. Its been a natural evolution. Certainly not a revolution, we wouldn't have lasted that. I wouldn't have lasted. I make no bones about that. If I had gone in and said 'Right, this is the way we are going to do it', they would have had me out in three years. You have to go in very gently.

I have a feeling about how we should operate as a headquarters, and what the relationship should be between staff and between us and the volunteers. I think I have an understanding of where the Institute ought to be going, but what I am lacking is the support for this. You see, I have come in with relatively little experience, and certainly none in the commercial world, so there is always this ever-nagging doubt 'Am I off my trolley here; do I really believe this?'. I think given my head yes... there's lots of things I would stop, lots of areas where I would cut budgets, because I don't think we're achieving. I think we are convincing ourselves it's all for a good cause, but yes, I'd plough more into marketing certainly, and I'd employ a good corporate planner or a good management consultant to work with us and say let's be revolutionary. Let's have a good look at it and decide what really has got to go because I think we are reaching crisis point within the next three years. If we don't do something radical I don't think we will survive.

What are the effects of this change?

I suppose another factor we haven't talked about is the fact that the volunteers are forever changing, which means that there is no continuity from their point of view. The only continuity is the staff. You can have a new president every year, which means that in essence your strategic direction could change. I think we have managed to get to a position now whereby it's actually quite hard for the president to say 'Right: this is where were going from today', but it is actually possible and it has happened in the past. I think this is very dangerous for the organization. On the other hand, you need that input from the new people coming through because you have got to be prepared to change direction, and that is a problem with the Institute because some of the volunteers have been here so long that they have been doing this forever, so why should they change now? This results in great resistance to change, particularly if it's coming from the new blood so to speak – 'What do they know?'.

I think we have put in more procedures now to try to stop the volunteers taking us down a direction where we know we'll be faced with a problem. We write more guidelines for directors and committee chairmen in-house now (they would never have been written in-house 10 years ago). We actually tell them what we expect of them, subtly. We have stopped staff members being regarded as the secretaries of committees, and in exceptional circumstances we will come and take minutes, but the manager's role is to be part of that committee and not to be merely the scribe, otherwise it's not going to work. So that is quite a difficult change for them to accept, but we are getting there all right.

How did you get that change accepted?

I suppose when we started the structural changes which would have been about three or four years ago; we were looking at what the precise responsibilities of directors should be. We changed the Constitution and suddenly we had to look at the subject of whether directors were pure directors, whether they were shadow directors or really what their responsibilities were. We wrote a number of papers, we talked to the solicitors and got it tight so we all understood what the various responsibilities were, what authority people had; and we included in that the role of the chief executive officer, on the basis that that position was going to have a seat on Council, be a director. That's a major change – I forgot all about that! But it's all part and parcel of what we have been talking about. But we had to be quite careful; we highlighted what the CEO should do, what the President was going to do, what the Secretary was going to do, and because it came as part and parcel of a change to the articles of association it all went through smoothly.

Now that we have got that, nobody is ever going to look at that again, since no one is that interested any more. Clearly if we wrote something totally outrageous it would be spotted, but I have to say that when you work on the principle that nobody actually reads very much the things we churn out, you can do most things like that. But what we are trying to do is to get us into a situation where we think we have got a measure of control, because nobody else seems to have any control. So that's how we have done that.

We have suffered... we lose a lot of staff very frequently, particularly down the lower end of the scale, because there's no real career progression – with 17 people, where are they going to go? So there is always somebody on a learning curve somewhere. It may take about two or three years to get them to the top of that and then they go and you start all over again, so there is always an area somewhere that's still learning. That is actually quite difficult to cope with because you tend to forget that the new person coming in (because they are all coming in so frequently) knows nothing, and you assume that they will pick it up as they go along, which they do most of the time. Then you hit the one area where they really haven't got a clue. That causes us enormous problems.

Can you give an example?
We have just had a new professional development officer join us, with a new manager in that area as well, and she came and was taught the basic administration of how to register people for distance learning – bits of paper needed, etc. And we suddenly came across the revision courses and asked 'Are we prepared for the revision courses?', and the reply was 'Revision courses? What are revision courses?'. This is quite a huge event in the Institute's calendar and nobody had thought to explain it because it is so well known, and nobody thought that the new staff wouldn't have come across reference to these things. So that was a last minute everybody pitch in, get the venues booked, get the people out there. It was fine as it turned out, but that was desperately poor management and should not have happened, and it is always going to be the big areas. The little bits and pieces you can live with, yet we totally overlooked a very big event. We won't do that again!

Also, I think we accept the responsibility as a management team for everything that happens, but we don't always have the authority... now, we can win some of it and we can go and we'll say 'OK, we'll carry this' and if there is any flak we'll just stand it. But there are times when you look at something and you think that's too big. There's no way that I'm going out on my own on that one. But that means it's going to be delayed because you have to wait for two months for the next Council meeting and it is a problem for my relationship with the President. He's in for 12 months and no one has ever defined that. Sometimes it works, and sometimes it doesn't, and its going to be a personality thing to some degree. The only thing I know is that the President is supposed to assess my performance. But he can't possibly know what's going on, and sometimes he is not interested in what's going on. He is interested in his own little corners and the bee in his bonnet about x, y, z, and you have to know when to pull him back and say, 'Hang on a minute; I think that actually belongs to committee x'. I am a master at delaying tactics! Anything that looks as if it is a little bit dangerous you can bog down in a committee forever, and you have to learn how to do that.

Any other critical activities in managing this change?
Well, I think we've covered some of them but I think in managing any sort of change the top people need to know where it is they are going, and if they don't really understand that, and the need to be able to achieve that, then I don't think you're going to get there. Change then becomes a battle, and I think also people don't realize how change is perceived.

I mean, we've got some very young members of staff and you have to be very careful about how you handle change with them. We're putting in a new computer system which is being developed, and a little bit has come along to be tested, and I know the young girl (who is our training administrator) who is testing the machine is thinking to herself 'This is going to mean more work for me'.

I can see this and it's really because she doesn't understand what she is doing. Now it can take you a little while to appreciate that is what is going on. There is nothing wrong with the system. OK, it's got a few bugs, but it will be all right, but actually what is wrong is her attitude and approach to testing, because she feels it is going to be an extra chore. It is a chore at the moment because she is still doing it in the old way and she is having to do this in addition.

Taking time out to sit with these people to try to explain what it is we are trying to achieve, what we think the benefits are going to be, putting them in a position where they can come back and say to you: 'Well, I have tested this now, I have looked at it and I think we have got a problem, a genuine problem and could we please solve it?' rather than thinking 'Oh well, they've told me I've got to do this and I'm stuck with this computer system so what is the point?'. It's actually one tiny thing were doing at the moment. I've spent hours trying to explain, and we are so busy that what you don't get is thinking time. I know all these things should be planned months ahead, and we should be working through the programme and saying 'At this point we should be doing this'... and it's a joke and if you can find me a company that works like that I'd go tomorrow....

There's so little time to do real thinking, any reading.... No time to keep yourself technically up to date... reading on the train or getting up before anyone else and having a few moments to yourself is about all. There isn't time to do team-building work that I want to do. The time is never really there and I think that is sad, because from a professional development point of view we don't give them the opportunities, as managers, that I think we should.

In terms of prioritizing your time and activities, to what extent is it driven by committee work?
Quite a lot of it, without a doubt. In producing the business plan we have actually tried to take over that; because we have highlighted certain tasks, they have all got dates – we all know who is supposed to be doing them. What we have tried to do is say 'OK, now we are going to drive it from the plan', and that gives us a focus for our activities, and everyone knows what we are doing, and that is quite crucial with a volunteer-driven organization. They have got to know what you are doing, otherwise they don't think you are doing anything.

In this job you can get a committee member whom you haven't spoken with for three months suddenly deciding that he had something to do, and knows he has got to report in two weeks and he needs your help! It's drop everything and help him, because if he looks bad at the committee, then the committee looks bad, and you know eventually it is going to bounce back onto you, so you get on with it. You can never tell what is going to happen... the phone rings and someone has got you going off in one direction, and then another direction... and I don't know how you solve that in this sort of organization other than making yourself unavailable, which again won't go down very well.

To what extent do you have to involve people who are affected by change?
Oh, absolutely. They have got to be on the same path, they might diverge from time to time, but you want to try to keep them with you. They have got to know what the goal is. If you haven't got that over then you are going to fail. I'm a great believer in that. I know that I don't always achieve that, but you have got to explain to people from the

outset, they have got to buy into it, and if they don't you have had it; you will be criticized for little things and they will become an irritant, because they are not really important but it is the only thing they can latch onto, since they don't really understand where they are going.

When you don't achieve that, what are the reasons?
Poor communication without a doubt. Assuming that everybody understands everything that comes out of your mouth or a piece of paper and you forget some of the underlying principles and data; to me its like testing the computer system. I understand how the whole system fits together. You can forget that when the operator sees it they've just got boxes on the screen to fill in, so they don't know why they are filling in that box. Unless you have taken trouble to explain what the underlying data is they can't be expected to fill in all the boxes correctly, because they don't know what it's for. For example, when we were running the roadshows, did we really tell our staff why they were important to us? They had a vague idea what we were trying to do, i.e. sell a qualification, but they didn't know why it was so important for us to make a good impression. They didn't realize that it mattered if the admin. was not smooth. For example, a box of brochures didn't turn up in the right place. It was part of a pack, and this pack had a contents page which, if omitted, gave a message of incompetence and non-professionalism. You forget to tell people the little things, and it's the little things that often matter. I also believe it's the little things that grind people down. It's not the big issues. If we have major disasters we cope. It's the little things: people feel they are going to be placed in a position where they can't answer a question and will be made to look stupid. That's the manager's fault, not theirs.

REFLECTION

It can be said that the changes made to improve internal support services are not significant in themselves, and yet one can learn as much about the factors determining the successful implementation of change from these cases as from the more strategic ones. To what extent do these three cases support this statement?

■ **CHAPTER SEVEN** ■

Merging organizations

We have three different mergers here – a major takeover of a Do-It-Yourself company, a parent IT consultancy deciding to bring two of its independent units together to form a single management consultancy, and the merger of two health authorities. The first case is told by the finance manager who was involved in the process of merging the financial and accounting systems and the relevant personnel from two distant head offices into one location. The overall merger was managed by a senior management team who were being advised throughout by external consultants. Things to note here are the planned approach used in bringing together two different systems and cultures, the emergent problems of uncertainty and stress among those being taken over (some would lose their jobs, and the rest would have to move to the head office of those taking over), and the role of external consultants.

The second case was less complex in terms of logistics, but its strategy underlying the merger was quite different. The strategy in the first case was to take over a poorly performing competitor and to improve its performance, and thereby the performance of the parent company. The strategy in the second case was to bring together a technologically oriented IT consultancy and a creative information design consultancy, with the aim of creating a single management consultancy capable of gaining access to the higher levels of client companies. The bringing together of different skills enabled the emergent organization to provide its clients with greater value-added services – a trend which was being followed by major competitors. Again the changes made were carefully led and designed. Of particular interest here was the ambiguity concerning cultural values, and the approaches used in dealing with resistance to change.

The third case is told by two respondents – the deputy chief executive, who was in effect the project director of the change process, and an individual manager whose job was affected by the change and who was a representative on the change team. The health authorities merged as a result of legislation, but further savings were required from the single management team. This was mainly achieved through downsizing, starting from the upper levels of management. The case gives insight into the benefits of having a change team to coordinate the processes involved, the importance of communications, the value of an external consultant with relevant experience and the drawbacks in having insufficient resources in dealing with the human problems which arise when people are losing their jobs.

Integration following a takeover in the retail industry

Background
The big change that has happened at Actioncraft recently is that it has acquired Docraft; so from having 120 stores, we have now acquired another 130 stores.

The head office of Docraft is at Winchester, about 100 miles from here. Obviously the plan is that the two organizations are put together and run from one head office, here. The implications are that there are going to be 50 per cent more people here – half the Winchester jobs will transfer down here and the other half will be lost.

My job title used to be finance manager of Actioncraft, reporting to the finance director of the company, who in turn reported to a director in the parent company. In future, my job responsibilities will be largely unchanged, except they will additionally embrace 250 stores. At the moment I have got about 16 or 17 people who are by and large qualified accountants, so they are fairly senior within the organization.

This change has been thrust upon us, like it or not. So, rather than needing to generate change it's more a case of needing to live with change or accommodate it and adapting to it. The company has gone out and said, 'Hey, things are going to be different', but middle managers and senior managers have by and large just had to manage that change.

What led to the takeover?
Look at the parent group. They are obviously getting to a situation where it is getting more and more difficult to open new stores in the UK; therefore they have got funds available for investing elsewhere. That puts a little more emphasis on their subsidiaries and where they think there is opportunity, or where they thought there was opportunity, for profitably investing in subsidiaries' business or indeed in new acquisitions. As part of this strategy they had identified that Actioncraft

was a profitable business, and that they would like to invest further in it if the right opportunity arose.

The parent company of Docraft were known to not view this subsidiary as a core business, and therefore it's not entirely surprising that some discussions were initiated, and that is when they finally managed to agree a price and the acquisition came about.

Since mid-March there have been an extra 130 stores to worry about and to be managed and incorporated into the existing Actioncraft business. That's not very long ago – about six months or so. Very topical.

Type of change

It's certainly Big Bang in that, for the bulk of the business, most people in Actioncraft would not have known anything that was going on – although there were some rumours that were rife, obviously, but basically nothing official until Christmas or shortly after. Then come March it was here, so any planning was limited to a matter of say 8–10 weeks, and in sheer scale terms there are as many Docraft as Actioncraft stores, so it's presumably fairly large on the Big Bang scale!

The experience of taking over a company was new to the parent company. Previously they had tended to go into joint ventures.

What ripple effects did the change have?

I think the important thing there is that in a change like this everyone looks at their own little piece and says, 'My goodness, we'll have to do that differently, we'll have to do this differently'. Everyone is facing a colossal series of changes at the same time, and what may be a high priority for me may require the help of someone next door, but it may be a very low priority for them. There are certain areas where every-thing comes together, computer systems for example, in that an awful lot of other changes are dependent on changes to computer systems, and systems resources are finite. Everyone is in the same boat – they have got a pile of their own priorities – but they are also crucial to other people, so that prioritizing assumes huge importance.

What have been the effects on your roles and those of others?

What I think it has actually led to is that, all of a sudden, people have been given more headroom than they had before.

Whereas in the past, perhaps before something was done, my boss would want to have a look at it and perhaps he'd talk to his boss to make sure people were comfortable with that, all of a sudden, because many people are so busy it's not possible to check things, to talk things through. It has meant people are definitely more accountable for things and have more responsibility.

I think what is going to affect me most is actually going to be the movement of the centre of the organization. In the past, Docraft has been run from Winchester; henceforth it will be run from Ware, and we have got to get from A to B. That's probably the most important task I have got, making sure that elements of my area are transferred smoothly.

What about designing the change?

Directors will oversee what is happening, but designing the arrangements for bringing the business to Ware will be at all levels. The process has been threefold: firstly there has been a data gathering exercise, secondly there has been an exercise to identify the way the companies need to be put together, and the third stage will be implementing the outcomes of the second stage.

Effectively, each area of the business came up with a series of questions it felt was going to be relevant to the process of putting the two companies together, the purpose being to make sure that any decisions that were going to be taken were actually based on good information.

The areas which needed to be explored were identified, and then small groups were put together to ask such questions as: 'How does Docraft handle this at the moment?'; 'How does Actioncraft handle it?'; and 'What are the key differences?'. That sort of approach applied across the business; for example, in talking about our sales reporting and sales accounting system we said, 'What sales information is available from Docraft at the moment? How does that compare with the sales information that we use to run Actioncraft's business? Where are there big spaces in terms of information that we use to run the latter that is not available from the former, and vice versa?. What information is there that Docraft are using that currently we are not using at Actioncraft?'.

Basically we took someone who was familiar with what Actioncraft does and sent them to talk to their counterpart at Winchester with the purpose of producing a short report on the previous questions. I wrote the brief for sales accountant and the same team looked at various other elements of the accounting function – a brief for how people account for VAT, how they pay suppliers, how staff are paid, how do we account for fixed assets; and for each one there would be a little write-up. There was a small group of about three Actioncraft people charged with producing short reports.

How well did this approach go?

I think what is important is that people understand what is going on and why. Because obviously what is floating around at Docraft is a huge degree of uncertainty about the extent to which their job would vanish or move. Basically the jobs were going to exist in Ware or they were not going to exist at all.

There was a reason for everything that was being done, and it was important to try to reassure people about what was going on and what the purpose of the exercise was, and obviously keep them informed as to where the process was leading to. It was announced at the start that business would effectively be run from Ware in the future, and that, where possible, existing employees would be relocated. But obviously it is not always possible for existing people to relocate.

I think the most important thing is that you have got a plan in place for what is going to happen – a timetable set for gathering the data and putting it into a usable document that was available as a reference point for any future work. It was actually about getting some reliable data on which to build in the next stage of the process and I think it was important that the whole wider picture was mapped out.

This was overseen by someone in my department pulling the whole thing together and agreeing what the timetable was going to be. There was a process for reporting back to those who were overseeing the process, and their function was to identify anything that was in danger of crossing two task forces; there are times when you can say that is something to do with the buying department, or no that's something to do with the retail department, so there was plenty of scope for things overlapping.

It wasn't too much of a problem for the accountants. Their role was really to identify any of those things and say 'yes' there is a danger that it gets blurred. We don't want to do it twice, so will you agree how you are going to go about it, and if that means two separate groups working together then fine. Similarly, we also charged those overseeing the process that nothing fell down the hole between two groups, because it is equally possible that two groups think the other has dealt with an area, e.g. retailers and buyers. There was a central point where everything came together.

As far as critical incidents and events go I think the most important aspect of it has been making sure people understand what is going on. And that itself gets quite difficult, because the first question that springs to mind if you are working at Winchester is 'Well, how long is my job going to be here and when is it going to move down to Ware and, obviously, am I going with it?' No one has been able to answer that question inside six months. That has been the biggest problem – dealing with the uncertainty that has been around.

How do you manage this uncertainty?
I think all you can try to do is to try to make sure people are as well informed as they can be and to be as honest and open as you are able to be. When the answer is 'I don't know', there is not a lot you can do except say 'Well, I am afraid I don't know, but I think it's likely to be some time between six months or twelve months', or whatever the situation is. It's when things are not communicated well that troubles start, when all of a sudden everybody knows about something unofficially and then you're open to the problem 'Well, no one told us'.

I think the power of the grapevine should not be underestimated. It needs to be appreciated that nothing stays secret for very long. If it is the intention to move this department on such and such a date, then the quicker someone says so the better. The flip side is that you don't want to say something and find you have got it wrong, because everything changes around. There is a very fine balance between being able to say something with a few caveats around it and being able to say nothing at all. When there is such a big change around and feelings of uncertainty, and people's jobs are going to change or disappear, there is a real danger that the simplest things are misinterpreted.

Interestingly, there were also knock-on effects; certainly there were a number of people in this building who felt 'Oh no, my job is going to be at risk', when actually the reverse applied. What was going to happen here was that there was going to be vastly more work to do, and in practice there were not many people transferring, so there was a need to go out and do some recruitment. Perhaps communications needed to be better in this building, even if we were not actually facing the problems of Docraft.

In the managing change process, overseeing of the data gathering was important and that was tied into regular progress reports about what was happening and what the next stage was and so on.

I realized that people in my department had got a lot of questions and I said 'Fine, we'll get together every 4–5 weeks and basically I will tell you what I am able to tell you about what is going on, and if you want to ask me anything you can'. I felt the communication coming out of official channels was less than comprehensive, and I just took it upon myself to sit people down and tell them what I knew, and I think that was worth doing. There was a tendency for more effort to be spent on communicating with Docraft people, who were obviously more affected, but perhaps there was a need to do a little more in this building.

I think another important aspect of it was the need for everyone to appreciate the difficulties that others were facing. The whole organization faced a state of upheaval and because of that it was very easy to jump up and down and say 'I need this change done today' and so on. But of course the person who you were getting cross with may well have had half a dozen other people also seeing their job as very important. The process of prioritizing and working out interdependencies is not easy. Someone may well say 'It's vitally important that I have some information on the profitability of this part of the business'; that's fine, but if the information that the accountants might have needed to do that exercise was just not readily available, then the first thing that had to be done was not to argue about why you aren't doing it but to set someone else running in order to make that information available.

Of course, the natural assumption is that the sorts of information that Actioncraft takes for granted are not necessarily available at Docraft because they have got different systems. The question of how profitable product X is involves the question of how much space you devote to it; whereas Actioncraft stores are by and large the same layout and each one is carefully measured up to determine how much space is allocated to particular products, that information was just not available from Docraft. A fairly simple question to ask, but the information was just not there, full stop. You needed to accept that you are operating against a different backdrop.

I think it's quite important that people went on the data gathering to understand what does happen, and that doesn't involve saying we do better than them... we need to have an open mind. Important rules of engagement were to find out the facts and then to say what we like about this one, what we like about that one. So at the first stage it was all about finding out similarities and differences. After that, the process moved on to designing and drawing up plans for integrating the two businesses, and that was a joint effort between people who knew the Docraft ways of doing things and people who knew the Actioncraft ways. Often the plan was to run the two systems and in time introduce a third that will have some features of both, but which will be better than either. Given the logic behind the acquisition and the fact that the buyer has a reliable profitable business and that the seller's business has not been performing so well, obviously the inclination would be to go with what the buyer had been doing. But it's important not to miss out any good ideas that were there in Docraft.

The next stage of identifying what needed to be in place involved a steep learning curve before you could actually start implementing the change, and that is what has been going on recently: saying 'Well, sure we have a rough timetable, that's got to happen and this has got to happen, and that depends on the systems department delivering this, and these are the training needs, and we will need some extra people down here, and maybe some extra PCs are required'. In other words, identifying what the problems are going to be and how we're going to tackle them, in what sort of time frame, and what the key interdependencies are.

All those have been put together by the steering group overseeing the process, with a view to identifying any conflicts between what different groups are going to do. That coordinating role also ensures nothing has fallen down the big hole in the middle.

I suppose what is very important is the speed at which everything is going to be done. You have got two large businesses, and while they are trundling along as two large businesses that's fine, but actually putting them together is a major task, particularly with different computer systems. One needs to understand what the key time constraints are, and to some extent those are self-imposed. For example, if Actioncraft had said 'We're going to run Docraft as Docraft from Winchester for five years', it would have been possible to manage the change in a different way. Of course, a five-year deadline might have meant everyone switching off, and being more concerned with finding another job elsewhere. So different time-scales bring different approaches and different problems. We found ourselves forced into doing things quickly, but doing things quickly brings its own sets of problems.

Were consultants used?

Coopers and Lybrand provided a facilitating and coordinating role, and I think that role was very important. It meant that someone was actually pulling everything together, making sure the directors set themselves a timetable, reviewing progress against that timetable and adjusting targets as necessary or reallocating resources or whatever. Someone had to make sure that the processes were planned. I think that was one of the reasons it could not have been done internally; it would have been difficult for them to say to the Board 'Do this, do that', and so on. Paying outsiders to come in and say 'You need to do this or that' makes you more inclined to do what they say. Also, an internal might always say 'I'm very busy and I can't do what you need for the moment'.

Merging two management consultancy units

What is the focus of change?

We are focusing down on a change that involved two separate organizations – one was an information design organization, called Credo Associates; the second sat within a larger organization, Knowhow Group – and the emergence of an IT consultancy with a new breed of information knowledge systems strategists joining that group. Thus there were two primary groups that needed to be brought together to form a new organization.

A new managing director was brought on board for the merged organization. People in line for the UK managing director's post were John Brown and at the operating unit level for the consultancy – David Smith. His mandate was to create this single consultancy organization. The challenge he had was to pull together a people-based change organization which, in itself, had already changed out of recognition from its origin (i.e. an information design practice) and fuse that together with a highly technical consultancy.

David commented: the types of people who worked within Credo were highly creative – thrived on design and visual processes – whereas the other group were heavily into technology and had quite a different outlook on life and quite different values. For example, they valued detail, technology and functional aspects of a job. So what we searched for was a common culture they could adhere to: a common set of values and a single point of focus. The point of focus we chose was around a particular service – it was a service that harmonized those disparate groups. We chose that because through that we could define a common purpose for the two groups.

How did this change come about?

The two units were sitting there independently but already owned by the parent group, one operating as a separate plc, but John could identify the opportunity to merge them together to fill his own personal ambition, which was to create a management consultancy within an IT organization. I think a lot of the motivation behind him doing that was based on competitive movements. Most of his competitors were all moving up the value chain and were gaining clearer access to higher levels within client organizations. His ambition was that this consultancy would be able to get the group into a position to protect the business, so that by moving up the value chain entry points were created higher up the organization where core business could be delivered.

What kind of change was involved?
It wasn't strictly Big Bang because it wasn't the creation of something brand new. However, it was a significant change in that the nature of the new organization was quite different from that of the old and the purpose of it was quite different. The old was about providing the support around which IT was implemented. The new focus and new purpose was around pulling together people, processing and technology, and offering a service which was to enable organizations to transform themselves. So it was fundamentally different in its outlook and scope of service in the degree to which it could work with clients.

It was a planned activity, but it was also opportunistic in that two events happened to coincide – the existence of these organizations within the parent group and the fact that competition emerged with similar types of organizations, so it wasn't quite a 'follow me, me too' type activity, but it was spotting the opportunity to get strategic advantage over the competition. These two organizations were already in the group and they could be integrated more easily than other organizations that maybe had to be acquired from outside. It was relatively simple to execute for those reasons. Both parties understood and knew who the key stakeholders were and what they needed to do to be successful within the new structure. The purpose was fairly well articulated within the market, so although it was very challenging for the individuals, at least they understood what had to be done.

The scale of change is obviously fairly large. The purpose had fundamentally changed. The pace of change was fairly rapid. The change actually occurred over a three-year term. The financial results were that we moved from a two million pound turnover business employing around 60 people to a six million pound business employing 80 people. These figures reflect the change in commercial success: increase in staff numbers was around 25 per cent with a 300 per cent increase in turnover. That is largely to do with the fee rates for the individuals employed within the new organization. We moved from employing 2–3 year experienced graduates to hard-hitting, highly paid management consultants. Obviously in order to achieve that there was a high rate of churn, in terms of how many people who are currently with the organization were there in the beginning. We are probably down to the last third; that is, around two-thirds have been replaced by new entrants. However, it is quite an achievement in that those last third of individuals have attained a new and more significant status within the new organization.

This type of change was novel within Knowhow Group. It was not novel in the context of the experience of the people involved in the change. Most of the senior management team have been involved in similar consolidation exercises. Also, in terms of the organizations merging – they were not of the size where it became a major factor. What was novel was probably the characteristics of the two groups. They were quite distinctive and disparate groups of people.

What are the effects of this change?
The ripple effect has probably been two-fold. First, the ambitions of the consultancy were of large-scale growth. Rather than thinking of us increasing by 20 people we embarked on the change thinking of increasing to 250 people and becoming the more significant players in the management consultancy market. We haven't realized that, but what we have realized is that we act almost as a magnet pulling people from within other parts of Knowhow towards a higher value-added status, so we see the emergence of partner consultancies within both our systems and outsourcing businesses.

Knowhow Group have redefined their purpose as being IT consultants. From that standpoint we have had a fairly significant influence over the whole organization. Not only that, but because we had already established how to run a business in the consultancy style, we carried out a lot of investment projects which were imported into that organization. We would regard that as having been a very valuable thing to have done. However, because it is not recognized in monetary terms, and it isn't measured actively, it is perhaps not given the degree of weight that it perhaps deserves.

In the outsourcing business, through understanding what we were doing, we also were able to create our own consultancy, and it is four times the size of Knowhow Group Consultants. This gives you some idea of the scale of activity. I would say there is less of a relationship between ourselves and that organization. It is far more closely aligned to how you deliver technical services and how you refine those to deliver at minimum cost rather than the kind of work we are involved in. However, I think we have defined the style of organization that they have followed.

Outside of the UK we are also the only consultancy that has survived within the rest of Knowhow Group (Europe) as a whole. This is probably to do with the fact that we do have a stronger purpose (i.e. further up the value chain) than a pure technical consultancy, so we were able to survive through having that broader purpose.

What is your place in this and how has it affected your role and responsibilities?

I started out as a chartered accountant and moved in to Credo Associates as Head of their Finance Department in 199X. We went through a change process taking that from an information design business to a change management consultancy between 199Y and 199Z. However, the change we are discussing in this context occurred between 1994 and the current date. Initially my primary role was to manage the strategic planning process and to manage the finance measurement. That was extended to performance measurement as an integral part of the change programme.

The finance role has waned quite significantly over time, but the intermediary step between a strict finance measurement role and my role now was heading up all the internal support services that were there to provide structural and physical support for people who are still going through these changes. So, for quite a significant period, we had to be quite introspective about how we managed the business. Individuals needed to go through quite a significant personal change, and that needed to be actively supported. However, we have been through the more painful and disruptive phase of the change and my role now is externally focused, and acting as a role model in terms of the behaviours we are trying to encourage in a client-facing role.

One of the organizational refinements we have made is to more tightly define the markets we serve through a sector focus. I now have a role in one of those sectors – managing the energy sector. So, I have come from a functional, tightly defined role, enabling and encouraging change through one of the primary support functions for a change through to one of the primary pull activities, the role model activity for taking the change through to being a more commercially successful organization. So it has seen me through three career changes, quite significant changes in personal direction over the term.

My personal role has always been one of enabling others to excel. That is particularly appropriate for the type of organization we are trying to create here and the kind of behaviours we are trying to engender. Consultants have to be self-managing and self-reliant. In order for them to do that they need a certain amount of support at certain stages in their development and also some active encouragement so that they mature sufficiently to be star performers.

What are other key activities in managing change?

There are a number of actual management activities which are more about the relationship and the networks that need to exist to support people through the change. You perhaps need a variety of different mechanisms to help people to bridge the gap between the current state hierarchy or future state matrix organization. What is probably very certain is that the future organization is likely to be more complex, which represents the way in which people have to work in a number of different roles rather than having narrowly defined roles.

Within our own organization we did move towards a matrix style structure. People were confused about which line they reported through. They were not used to the idea that they could have several different roles in a day and several reporting lines according to each role they were playing during that day. So there are a number of different things that we did, but it is more of an attitude of mind of the leading group to say we are jointly speaking the same stories, sending the same messages, adopting the same values, supporting whoever needs help, rather than trying to identify any closer than that.

The particular support mechanisms put in place were first, measurement activities which at least gave people a focus; a series of measurement objectives which, if met, meant they were safe, meant they knew what was expected of them. They knew if they weren't performing to that they had a problem. Second, communicating both on issues of policy and on issues of measurement, and third, living the future-state values. Being the person that we wanted to be, to aspire towards. I think those were, perhaps, the three most important activities that we took.

How were the changes designed?

In terms of the overall decision about what should happen and the need to adhere around a common purpose, that was formed by the executive – the senior management team. But we ensured that we had the buy-in from the UK managing director, so we were sponsored through the change, because inevitably change means a decline in performance and that needs to be accepted and understood by those who, in turn, are measured on their personal performance. We gave some of the bad news to the UK managing director, that performance would decline before it improved. However, within Knowhow Group we were tightly constrained by the need to perform, so although we said we wouldn't be able to perform quite as well as we would hope, we were still expected to make profit and year-on-year improvement through the change. That actually determined the speed of the change.

Who planned the changes?

A lot of them were defined by the executive during the strategic planning process. That was used as the tool around which to string the need for change. We looked at the current state via an audit and then looked at the future state and what was needed to achieve that five years on. That was where we initiated our action plans. We didn't actually have a formal overarching change programme. We tended to do it through (a) having a common purpose and understanding of what we were trying to achieve, and (b) some fairly invasive, individual programmes of activity. Not too many, three or four of them. The first one was to inform the organization that passed down the responsibility to the individual – target them with individual targets, empower them with information so that they felt that they were in control, and that they were actually in control of how much work they did, and the bids they got involved in. So rather than management taking the responsibility for spoon-feeding the individual, it was very much down to the individual to make whatever they might out of the supportive environment that we presented to them. That process was managed internally.

We did, however, go through two activities that were facilitated by externals, where we did buy in external competence and input. One was for ISO accreditation where we needed technical input and also someone to drive the process externally, otherwise it probably would not have happened. That was used to introduce some method and control, because we had devolved power and we were largely relying on the ISO processes to regain some control over some of the critical processes.

Another initiative was to redefine the competencies, the way in which we recognized individuals within the organization and we bought in external consultancy advice for that. Apart from that, I, with the help of my colleagues, had the total responsibility for bringing about the change.

How were the emotional consequences addressed?

The organization was inherently friendly. It did not cast blame, and was very forgiving of people taking risks and making mistakes. It was appreciated that people would make mistakes, they were being challenged. It is purely by recognizing those facts and understanding that failure was, if anything, evidence of trying, rather than evidence of incompetence.

The second structural support put in place was a human resource initiative. This was a mentoring scheme. This meant that people could go outside of the line, even though that was not very distinct, for advice and guidance so they could develop themselves personally. That also incorporated personal development and training, which was channelled through the mentoring activity.

In addition to that there weren't too many formal mechanisms. I think you perhaps can get oversold on the need for lots of mechanisms to understand change. I think we did actually miss out on some of the risk assessment aspects of managing the change. But we were very attuned through some of the more anecdotal information and trying to read into that the state of the nation, rather than have formal attitude surveys or anything like that. So whilst I personally recognized the need for measures outside of strict financial measures to understand the degree and extent of change, I think we were well enough in tune with what was happening, looking at areas where, potentially, we could improve things.

An observation of something fairly recent might disprove what I have said! We were trying to move values without defining, fairly explicitly, what those values were, and through those values, the current culture we were trying to embrace. So the only true reference point that people had were the role models being played by the executive. Probably the figurehead in terms of the role model was the managing director. He was the person who people saw as defining the culture.

When he left it meant there was a significant vacuum in terms of people's understanding of what the culture was they should adopt. Should they adopt the new managing director's explicit values as he would portray them, or should they continue with the existing cultural values? It was almost a sense of betrayal through continuing to follow those values rather than adhering to new values as exhibited by a new managing director. What it meant was that in the absence of a strong culture to follow many of those who came from a strongly defined cultural background tended to revert to that because it was safe and comfortable. So we have potentially lost two years in terms of people now referring back to a time before the change. That has really been very surprising for me. I had not appreciated that until we did a cultural audit, fairly recently, to establish what people really felt about the organization and what cultural values they were ready to adhere to.

Could we focus on some of the problems in managing change?
Just going through my personal experiences of critical incidents during the change programme, it is often difficult to recall exactly what happened at any particular point in time, because at the time you are so engrossed with what is happening and responding to it that it is only after a fair amount of reflection, over a fairly long time-scale that you actually truly understand what was going on at the time. Why there were the emotional outbursts; why there were dysfunctional behaviours

occurring within your own organization. Perhaps you ought to be able to anticipate and predict it. In fact, we have got models that will help us to do that. But, in the heat of the moment and in your own organization it isn't that easy.

We had a significant amount of initial resistance. We were operating from an Oxford site and a London site with two different cultures and we were trying to make them adhere to one purpose and believe they were in one location. So, I think one of the critical incidents was overcoming that resistance. I think that was purely by just being very firm and committed, and convincing that we were not going to revert back to the prior organization; that we were going to move towards a single-culture, single-purpose organization. The resistance wasn't ignored, but it was 'corrected'. It was corrected through face-to-face rather than through any elaborate mechanism. As objections arose, as behaviours which were reverting back to two cultures emerged, they were dealt with.

We were trying to engender an open organization. Communication lines were fairly free. There was a fair amount of resistance which we weren't able to pick up on; that surfaced, was dealt with and through dealing with that which was obvious, that which was not obvious or being suppressed either surfaces because there is a frustration in it not being overt, or it's dissipated because people understand they have got to move on and discover their own path forward – otherwise the 'old school' is not going to remain there.

The second kind of phase or period of time, when I was aware of something different happening, was when people started to resign, disappear out of the door or we would have an acrimonious fall-out with individuals. Perhaps they could fit into two schools. One was those where, although there was overwhelming evidence that we were moving to a new value set, couldn't accept or believe in those values. They were not going to adopt them. They didn't want to fit and had to go. The second group were probably those, of similar type, who had invested a significant stake in the old organization and had lost out because the values they held were no longer valued in the new organization.

High technical competency was not valued; ability to interact with clients was. So, again, through losing significant kudos and status they became dissatisfied and had to leave. We didn't want to provide a dual career path. To do that we would have to accept parallel cultures to support them and the main thing was to drive towards a greater purpose which was to create a management consultancy, and I personally don't see how a technical consultant would fit into a management consultancy.

So those that were able to exhibit strong interpersonal skills stood a chance of becoming a management consultant; those with strong technical skills were probably not remotely interested in business issues and so would not make the more significant transition that we have had to embrace in the greater journey, which is towards management consultancy.

How did we deal with exiters and new entrants? With the exiters it was pragmatic. We had wakes for certain individuals because there was a large amount of emotional commitment between groups that were disbanding. We had to allow certain groups to mourn their leavers during those periods of change. The joiners had to almost find their own way and fight for their own position rather than being presented as the way things were going to be. So they had to establish their own credibility. That was one of the principles that we fully adopt. It is hard work for the first few months. You are not going to be given a lot of support because the best way you are going to establish your own personal credibility is through demonstrating it to your peers within a consultancy organization rather than being presented as someone who has the authority or trying to sell that authority. It is much better if that is demonstrated either through the way in which that individual influences other people or peers or actually out on a project.

The third kind of critical incident was where we began to introduce new people with new value sets imported from other organizations. We began to become more overt in showing the way – being a management consultancy and not even thinking about our origins or where we were aspiring to move from. It was just that we are, *de facto*, a management consultancy, competing against the top five consultancy organizations and not referring to from where we came or how we got there. We brought in role models to reflect that as well.

Note that the two organizations never came to the same site. This was a virtual organization. What we were trying to do was to ensure that we didn't have two groups of people operating independently. They had to work together. The way we could get them to work together was to remind them the organization would represent them as groups not split by site but split by the origins of their skills. Were they heavily people- or process- or technology-oriented – irrespective of where they were coming from (site or new entrant). This is the internal organization. In terms of the projects, this is really defined by the client need. Based on what they wanted, we would select a team from those three resource pools, i.e. people, process and technology.

In terms of a change programme we were applying a very simple model to how the activities that needed to happen, and the impact that we expected to have. It is one that is an amalgam of several models, and one that we have developed within our own practice, which is push–pull support: creating the push through telling them that there are 'Indians coming', that we have to move towards a single organization, that we have to move from their own specialism niche consultancies into a management consultancy and that if they decide to go elsewhere they would be better placed through the experience. If they decide to come along they will have a significant improvement in terms of status within the consultancy community. Provide the vision (why they should do it), identify the advantages of embarking on that journey, and then provide the support mechanisms to ensure that they feel secure. The kinds of support mechanisms being measurement, actively managing the people and putting organizational things in (like a mentoring network) to make sure that there is a safety valve there to pick up anyone who is suffering under the stress.

For every decision we made or every issue we dealt with we tended to refer back to this model as a working framework, so we could understand whether we had catered for each of those domains. If you don't get those in balance then you find the change is impacted.

What were the inhibitors of change?

What initially inhibited change were the current stakeholders. People who had something to lose because they realized they didn't really have a strong purpose in the future organization. They were losing out. I term these as being political resistors. They would always refer back to 'the good old days', there was a sense of retrospect. They also had a committed group of people behind them as well, and if they wanted to they could engage that network to resist change. It was very easy to resist and spoil things.

It is very important to deal with that resistance through identifying those stakeholders who have something to lose and making sure that they either are neutered or completely eradicated! If you want to change something which is fairly challenging, don't rely on consensus all the time and a reasoned approach, because there is too much emotionally at stake to rely on that. You can fool yourself into thinking that you have got a good change model to adopt that is totally invalidated if you then look upon the lines of how people are emotionally committed to an organization. A lot of people care very dearly about what they do and the things they believe in – the values they hold – and as soon as you start to attack those through saying you want to bring about change, then expect extreme emotional reaction; otherwise you will be unprepared for what is going to happen.

What factors helped the promotion of change?

There are those that aspire to gain position through the change. They will be people who have probably been working against the current state. They will be far more objective about the change and promoting the change. You might engage them as change agents. We look towards the next line of command – people with strong potential who might not have all the credentials, but at least have the energy to take the organization through the challenging period.

The other particular promoter is having a strong sense of vision and purpose. Essentially what I'd regard as the most important personal quality that we had to exhibit during the change was going way, way beyond the logical and making people want to do it because they believed in what we wanted them to do. Also they liked us as people, they were coming along with friends, not adversaries. As soon as you create an adversarial relationship between you and those that you want to follow, then it is very difficult to hold them without them feeling that they are being manipulated and being 'done to' and being changed rather than changing themselves. That requires quite a bit of leadership; being very careful about not corrupting those relationships through trying to get something to happen more quickly when people, perhaps, were doing the right thing all along. Some things do take time, some people do take time, so if they are not actively resisting, they are actively trying, and if you believe they have a good chance of success then give them time.

What might have been done differently?

I might have been more explicit about the particular values that we were wanting to establish and make sure they were associated with the organization, rather than a particular individual. But also probably, in our case, to have gained greater commitment up-front from our key sponsor so that we could make the change more quickly and more extremely. Both the scale and pace of change that we could have embraced could have been greater. It would have meant a downturn in profit, but it would also have meant that we would have attained a stronger purpose to take us into the next phase of our development. I feel as if we have allowed people to catch us by not making the change quickly enough. We could have been in a unique position within our market, whereas we are alongside some very strong competition.

With hindsight we would have been more ruthless both in terms of getting people in earlier and dealing with people who were resisters as well. For instance, we allowed someone to stay with us for two years who did not really contribute during the period, and that wasn't an isolated incident. It is very difficult to get rid of people, even those who are impotent and just hanging on there, not really doing anything positive or negative. So it is really dealing with some of those problems and confronting those problems very much earlier. They needed to be dealt with, and all we did was to defer the decision rather than change the situation. Everyone who we thought would not make the transition has not made the transition; even those who we gave a good chance to and supported all the way just didn't make it. Had we come to terms with the fact ourselves, and helped them to come to terms with it, we would not have expended so much unnecessary effort.

Merger and reorganization in a health authority

Respondent A (Deputy Chief Executive)

Background
The history is that three years ago there were three health authorities covering different parts of this area and one Family Service Health Authority (FSHA). Three years ago the three health authorities merged to create a single health authority. As of 1 April this year, that health authority and the FSHA merged.

The management team of the two authorities has been a single one for about the last 18 months, so one management team has been servicing two different authorities. And we have been through a process of bringing the two Health Authority Boards together for joint meetings and what's happened over the last six months in particular has been the final crunch down to creating the new authority.

This was in the context of having to reduce our management costs. So as a result of the process of the former merger we lost something like 40 posts out of the structures which equates to something like 20 per cent of the combined staffing of the two authorities. That's taken something like a million pounds out of our management costs. So it's a fairly major change exercise.

The key objectives were threefold. They were creating the single authority, reducing management costs and creating a new authority which was appropriate for a model of health authority working which was primary care led.

In addition, 18 months ago we were accommodated on five different sites. We brought them down to three and we are within spitting distance of getting our business case through the region for new single-site accommodation. So that's been quite a significant part of the change process and a further objective. It probably won't be accomplished until September.

The time span was over an 18 month period, although much of the detailed work has happened over the last six or seven months. We probably have another month or so to go before the final structures are bedded down and people feel they are back on an even keel.

What was your role in the change?
My role has been as the project director of the change process. The way my role as the Deputy Chief Executive has been focused is that the Chief Executive is doing much of the outwards and upwards work; in another type of organization I might be called Director of Operations. I manage on a day-to-day basis the corporate management functions: building services, administration, secretariat support, personnel. So I manage all those functions and use them really to support the organization in moving forward.

What have been your most important tasks in managing the change?
There are two different aspects. One is more straightforward, which I'd characterize as the technicalities. So actually just making sure that the nuts and bolts of the new structures fitted together, that they did actually release the right amount of management costs, to make sure that the practicalities happened.

But then there's the more difficult and less tangible issue of staff morale, communication, how you take people with you through the change process. People have, overall, responded very well, yet if I'd had a scale of good to bad in terms of how staff might feel it was 'quite bad to very bad'. It was contained towards the 'quite bad' rather than the 'very bad' end, but, as one can imagine, in losing 40 staff, even if it's handled through voluntary redundancies and natural wastage, it still feels a heavy toll.

Were people committed to the change?
A bit more of the history is important here. When we originally went about the exercise, which was a merger of the two authorities, we wanted to try to manage it in a way which was as least disruptive as possible and therefore took a very conservative view at the outset trying to minimize the amount of turbulence within the system.

That meant, in terms of cost savings, looking at bits around the edges. And from some of the communication work we did with staff, what they were saying back to the management was 'Don't fiddle around. We're worried if you fiddle around with the edges, because then things will just drop off the edge unnoticed. We would much rather have a more radical change quickly rather than tinkering at the edges and going on and on'.

So there was a staff meeting where we had all 300-plus staff together. So at the beginning of November the Chief Executive was saying 'We won't have major restructuring', etc., etc., but within three weeks of that we were saying 'Well, we've heard what you are saying and we are'. And we did it very quickly.

We started at the top. From having eight directors we went down to five. I don't believe anyone had thought it would happen and certainly not within 10 days, but it did.

We then went on to the next tier. These were staff working for directors and we went down from 30 to 20. And again we did that within the three-week time span we had set ourselves.

There was a deal of unhappiness. They could see it coming down the line. And they knew that we were taking the brunt of it at the senior levels in the organization, whereas a lot of staff thought we would start at the bottom. We were very clear that if we started at the bottom we would have to lose a lot more staff because they get paid less.

So I think the staff have been committed. They have been very keen to get information and be communicated with and to take opportunities to input into the change process.

Have you put any mechanisms in place for monitoring the changes?
We have something called the Change Team, which is what I would describe in this organization as middle managers. They are third or fourth in line and there are eight people drawn from the eight director-ates we then had. They were seen as a group that could take forward some of the change issues on a practical basis – things like the logo for the new authority, looking at some of our merged HR policies – but also could act as a conduit up and down the organization for sharing infor-mation and communicating about the changes. If they heard a piece of gossip which was wildly inaccurate they were in a position to give a very quick response or if they didn't know the answer they could talk to me or to the Chief Executive and find out what the latest was on that.

So it's a way of trying to prevent some of the wilder gossip that very quickly started to flow around the place.

We have a series of other groups just looking at the accommoda-tion issues: from basic things like how many photocopiers we will need, to looking at how our postal service works and how we can improve it.

Until we get to that point, there is still going to be a degree of scepticism and there is still going to be a problem with communications.

Are the teams representative – from different levels?
Yes. That's right. Another type of group we have is to take kind of diagonal slices of the organization and to work with those groups looking at the ways in which we work with each other. So we talk here a lot about matrix working, or project management, but we don't have very many good examples of it. We are quite good at individual objective setting, but not so good at encouraging teamwork through those objectives. I don't think we have been very good in the past at supporting our middle managers in developing their person management skills, so we tend to find that communication gets so far and doesn't go any further. Or it goes out in a variety of different messages at that point. There isn't a consistent way in which people's individual development is looked at, so access to individual training courses is very variable, depending how good your manager is.

So these diagonal slices are trying to look at those sorts of issues. So we've had some groups looking at the tangible practicalities to do with our accommodation and others looking at the less tangible: 'How are we going to work with each other? How does somebody who is sixth or seventh in line in the organization and who has a bright idea, get that bright idea recognized?'.

Have there been any critical incidents which have been particularly successful or unsuccessful in the process?
I think there's one of each. They are both to do with timetables and hitting timetables. As I've already said, when it came to taking the first step and reducing the numbers of directors, the fact that a decision was made, followed through and delivered within a very short time-scale, was seen as being effective. But in other areas where we have set timetables – for example, production of a staff manual, which set out all the procedures around the change process, including what you would be entitled to, appeals, how you could apply for voluntary redundancy, all those things – we set what we thought was a very realistic time-scale for it and then on the day before it was due to come out the photocopiers burnt out and we couldn't produce them.

It was planned to have them out on a Thursday so that people could have them for the weekend, but we didn't get them out until the next Monday. And we have had two or three occasions where for technical reasons timetables haven't been hit and you feel the organization is poised waiting for it and it doesn't appear.

I think that for every deadline you hit you probably get two or three brownie points. But for every one you miss you probably lose five.

In your experience of managing change, what factors inhibit or enhance change?

Clarity of vision and leadership are very important. In my experience, even if at the end of the day decisions are unpalatable, people want to see that somebody at the top is making decisions and is signposting very clearly where we are going.

The second one is communication. Even though we kept saying 'Communicate, communicate, communicate', it is still not enough. That is incredibly important in just keeping everybody informed, particularly if you are working at split sites as we are. We have a fortnightly news sheet of key points about the change process and try to make sure it hits people's desks in the different sites at the same time, so that one site doesn't think it's being left out. You need clarity in the language you are using in communications so that you are not assuming that people know things. And pitching things at quite a low level so that people understand them.

What communication systems do you have?

We have a fairly standard team briefing system. And then we have the change team which works on an *ad hoc* basis. And we have the newsletter which, apart from giving regular news on the change process, has a comment slip to come back. I respond to those within 24 hours. So they know the point has been taken on board. We also have a very good email system and 99 per cent of staff within the authority have a PC on their desk. And they use it. We use the email system quite a lot to send out messages.

Respondent B (Senior Commissioning Manager)

Background

The commissioning function is at the heart of the Health Authority. Commissioning is the process by which we contract, and determine what services we need to contract for, in terms of service provision, to meet the health needs of local people. We negotiate those contracts, monitor those contacts and evaluate whether they are being met. So it's a cycle of activity.

In the most vivid part of the change, that is during the last three months when we restructured the Health Authority, one of the most dynamic things that was decided was that strategic commissioning would shift from the Commissioning Directorate to Public Health.

My role disappeared. I still have the same title, Senior Commissioning Manager, a senior manager within the Commissioning Directorate, but my brief is changing. So I have been responsible over the last year – it's difficult to put boundaries around jobs in the National Health Service because we've had constant change – but for the last year my responsibility has been for commissioning children's services. Effectively I am moving from strategic commissioning role to an acute commissioning role, including a contract management function.

So the work of myself and a number of colleagues who were all senior managers with what we call 'Care Group' – children, mental health, elderly, women's sexual health, disabilities – most of those functions have now shifted to Public Health.

Does that mean your activities and tasks have changed?
My old activities and tasks disappeared from this part of the organization and went into another part of the organization.

How did people respond to the changes?
This was obviously developing as the change process developed and the focus of people's anxiety and interest also developed. There have been two major drives: one is that we formally merged the two local health authorities; that was a national thing, by statute.

The second is that we tried to cut down on our management costs locally. So those are the two drives. That supplied a lot of change. But also we are a diffuse organization geographically, so there's been a lot of interest in where we are going to go. We said from an early stage we all wanted to go onto one site. That had implications for team-building, for cost and for coherence of working, so there was a lot of interest in where we were going to move to and what that implied. It's an inner city district and people come from a wide area. Would people have to move? It might not be viable for some people to carry on working for us.

There were lots of anxieties about that. Would people still get travel allowances? Do they increase? So there have been a lot of nuts and bolts administration issues.

More recently, as the new structure for the health authority was published and began to be worked through from the top down, obviously the anxieties have focused on 'Am I going to continue to have a job?', 'Are there opportunities for me here?', all those sorts of things.

Do you think the organization has coped well with those anxieties?
I think the organization has coped adequately. I have made my views well known on this. I think the organization was naïve in expecting that process to be managed by one full-time human resources manager. She has a number of junior managers, but in terms of senior management there was only one person, and I think it was quite impossible. She had an impossible task. She did as well as she could have done, but it wasn't feasible.

Also there were a number of people in the organization who felt isolated in this process. Isolated because the amount of support that would have been helpful to them was not there, not available. Because of the nature of the task itself it had to keep being asked for, rather than being offered.

I have been through that myself. I lost my job and have only been confirmed in the new one quite recently. So there have been a lot of complicated personal issues for me. Which is ironic because I was one of the architects of the change. But at least I have been in a position to ask, to know what was available, and to ask for help when I needed it. And I'm aware that other people found that more difficult. So we've done OK but we've not done brilliantly.

Were there any points at which you would say the objectives were not being achieved?
Inevitably, the timetable has slipped. We were supposed to be in new accommodation by June. But we won't be. The structure was in theory supposed to be in place by the end of March; the authority started its new legal existence in April, and it started its new existence with effectively the Board level and the Executive Director level and most of the second level management team in place, but everything else is still trickling down now.

So we missed timetables and I think it's inevitable that we did, but we have lost a certain amount of faith by so doing. Some of those things have been in our power. Some have not.

I think our human resources should have been reinforced. Having said which, we have formally got into union negotiations. We have re-established a staff side. They are a new group, a relatively undereducated group, so they have delayed things. When they had to be consulted formally they took longer than they should have done. It's inevitable, but it's a shame.

What were the most important activities you were involved in, in managing the change?
Well I was the commissioning representative on the change team, so I was the link between the team and the commissioning staff in the

Directorate. So I was feeding back to them what we were discussing, what was happening, and feeding through to the team what the concerns and issues were for individual people or for groups of staff in terms of that process. I tried to manage that relationship, which wasn't easy.

Was anything done particularly well?

The principle of having a Change Team was a very, very sound one. We had an executive team, the management team and the board of the health authority who had to make the decisions. But the Change Team acted as a filter. A number of key policy issues were given to us first for us to say 'This sounds reasonable' or 'This sounds ludicrous'. One or two things were knocked out at a very early stage. I think that saved a lot of valuable time.

I think we've discharged our function reasonably well, although I think we have lost trust recently. Initially there was quite a lot of trust in us. I think people were comfortable with the thought that we did represent all the disparate views within the authority within the various groups reasonably honestly, and we reported back what happened. I think recently it's become more complicated.

The original relationships within the team were very consensual and corporate. And we worked as a team and reported back in a consistent way. What has happened as the anxiety levels have risen over the last few months is that the executive, and possibly the Deputy Chief Executive, who is seen as the major architect of the whole process, and the HR person – the relationships within the change team have changed. It has become more confrontational, a more adversarial thing. When you come with people's anxieties, there is a danger of behaving more defensively. And we have tried to talk that through recently, but it has been less comfortable. I think members of the team have felt on occasions that they were being, to some extent, associated with the views that they were representing. Our job is to represent views, some of which we may agree with, some we may not. I think something is becoming confused and the team has become a less comfortable place. Maybe now we are reasserting ourselves, but when things were at their most anxious the team did not function very well.

We were affected ourselves, we did have personal issues. Nonetheless, there was a defensiveness instead of an understanding, and I think that was a very, very anxious time and a very, very difficult time for everybody. So I'm not sure how we could have done that differently, but it started to work not as well as it had.

Is there anything you would have done differently?
I would have had people working on the change process full time. And I would have been more consistent in the guidance people were given. People's guidance depended to some extent on their access to the people who were in the know. Some people obviously had personal issues and therefore felt less able to go forward. And there were very few alternatives. We didn't offer people many alternatives.

So the Change Team were carrying out their normal jobs in addition to the change process. We were all managers with heavy workloads.

But the last two months has been difficult. Some people were in their new jobs, some in their old jobs; the handover was complicated.

I think that we should also have clarified the role of the other directors – the new and the old directors. I am aware that the Deputy Chief Executive has tried to reinforce this in the management team itself. Some directors have been quite hands-on in the change process, but most have stood significantly away from it: 'It's not my business'. So they have felt unable to support people or thought it would be inappropriate to support people. For most people who have been through a period of change or uncertainty, the only individuals they could turn to, in terms of advice or guidance or briefings or whatever, have been potential job interviewers, or competitors for the posts that remained. That's been very, very complicated.

Another mistake we made is that in cutting down we allowed no slack financially. We lost £700 000 from our costs. I think what we should have done was lose £800 000 and kept £100 000 in our pockets for reviewing some gradings. There are a number of historical incongruities in grading and a number of historical grievances. Also, a number of people have now been slotted into new jobs which are bigger than their old jobs at the same grade, and one or two have actually been slotted into the same job on a lower grade. Now we should have given ourselves the discretion to do something about that, because good people will leave.

Has there been any category of manager which has coped less well than others?
The second-level managers have been the most decimated level. We lost a third of our number, one way or another. Some of us have slotted in sideways. Some have gone half a step down like me. Some people have left. Some have gone on secondments. I think that the next level down, the middle managers, have also had a lot of anxiety because they have had less discretion. There have been some casualties at that level

but there has been no discretion. Some people have actually said 'Well, I would like to do that job', but we wanted to keep the competition for posts to a minimum where we weren't obliged to have competition. At second level, all jobs were open to competition, but at third level they were not. And that was sensible because to open them to full competition would have completely destabilized the organization. It would have prolonged the agony.

Nonetheless, what it has meant is that people have been slotted into posts they didn't necessarily particularly want and they have not been allowed to compete for the posts that they actually want. So they possibly could have done better. It's very difficult to get that balance between competition and actually managing the authority coherently.

Some authorities have actually rewritten every job in the entire authority and gone for open competition. We chose not to do that. We went for limited competition.

Are there further changes still to be made?

There are still some posts unresolved. I think there will be changes, and I think there will inevitably be a number of people, regardless of whether they have jobs or not, who will leave. People who have been so destabilised by the changes they are not going to stick around. That will offer positive options to the people who are still left, and they may then be able to make the changes they wanted to make but have been unable to.

It will mean effectively that the new team, the new authority is not going to be fully functional for another six months or so. Because there will be people leaving. And I think that's difficult, because we have a lot of work to do.

Also there's the problem that we have a huge task to perform, or a series of tasks, and we will be doing it with a much smaller authority. I'm very scared about that. They are all thinking 'Gosh, I was working all hours six months ago. I am now going to be working all hours in a smaller team. It's going to be worse and I'm not going to be paid more'.

Use of consultants

One final thing it might be worth saying is that we had an outside person helping us, a person very well known in the NHS. A consultant in the management of change. She is a human resources person and has advised a number of authorities. In theory she joined the team, and she supported the team, and talked through the agendas. Her experience is elsewhere and she has a certain amount of academic background, including how other authorities have done it, etc.: for example, starting the newsletters. I think that was helpful. I suppose I would say she would almost describe herself today as a professional change management consultant, because that's all she is doing. Just in the NHS.

There is a familiar career path for all former HR directors in the NHS: they all become career consultants and advise individuals and organizations on managing change and on the inheritance of change. And some of these people are highly skilled. We are going to have development programmes for second-level managers to help them re-bond in the new authority. I think that is very sensible.

I have met a number of these consultants in different contexts and I must say sometimes it seems to me that they can be very cynical. They are highly expensive, really big money we are talking about, and in terms of organizational advice it seems to me there is very little they have to say that anybody with a few years' experience could not have said themselves.

There are a lot of them around these days. Public sector change is almost a career option in itself. Some of them seem to have very interesting frameworks, particularly for individual development, and some of them – I fail to see what expertise they have. They talk in truisms. You know, the kind of stuff any group of managers could write on the back of an envelope in five minutes.

So I have a slight cynicism about this because it has become such a big deal.

REFLECTION

To what extent are cultural discrepancies a serious problem when trying to merge two units that have developed independently? What measures should be taken during the process of implementing the merger in order to lessen the adverse effects of this problem?

■ CHAPTER EIGHT ■

Integrating IT into the business

Both these cases fall within the investment and banking industry. The first case is told by someone with a business and finance background who had three months previously been appointed to the role of IT director to bring about what was, ostensibly, a culture change within the IT function. Previously, the function had attracted a lot of discontent from business users because of its technical focus. Few benefits were to be seen, in spite of a huge spend. The new head of IT was expected to improve the image of IT in the business so that relationships could be re-established and developed, and IT could take a partnering role and work to support the business. The case is notable for the interpersonal problems encountered and dealt with by this manager in a highly unfavourable situation.

The second case is about the global custody operations of a company which administered the security portfolios for investing companies who outsourced all their back office processing. It was clear that while the company had a good image among its core customers it was falling behind developing technology. The teller is the IT director who was tasked to drive through a business process re-engineering (BPR) activity to ensure that the business was able to meet the company's criteria for success. The IT function and its relationship to the business was a critical target for this activity. One of the problems encountered in many cases of implementing change is the extent to which an authoritarian as opposed to a consultative approach should be used. This is highlighted by the teller in this case.

Helping the IT function adopt a customer focus

How did the change in your role come about?
I have been here around three years. I expected to go into industry after a period of further study, but I was head-hunted for the City. This is where I didn't want to work, but here I am! I was recruited to work for

the then managing director of the UK business. I worked for him in that role for 10 months. I was working alongside another person who had supported him and I was effectively working with her. She left and he changed roles from being managing director of the UK business to being global head of sales.

For some time the equities business for the bank were all managed out of here, so London became the focal point for all the global equities businesses of the bank. We were taken over in the early 1990s. These bankers are acquisitive: they buy established brokers and then they try to develop a network. That is another horrendous change problem, because all these have got established local unit identities and it's very difficult to get them to pull together to get this global aspect established. We are struggling at the moment.

My boss took over as global head of sales, which was a new position created as a result of expanding the equity side of the business. There was a huge international privatization that we became involved in, and he asked me to coordinate that, on his behalf, from the sales perspective, so I effectively moved with him. I stayed in a support role to him and I moved from the UK side of the business into the international side of the business as he moved.

He then went, after about a year or so, from being global head of sales to being Group Chief Operating Officer for all the equities divisions, and again I moved with him. So we moved from the front office side of the business into the back office side of the business. The many support sides of the business – finance, personnel, IT – came under his remit, and that was my first exposure to operations, other than being a user.

During this time when he was working as the Group Chief Operating Officer the managers in the IT department were people he had brought in. I was instrumental in not bringing in people from outside, but moving people up from the business. The focus was on the equities network, developing IT systems, developing strategy for the equities network as a whole, across the globe. But, they lost focus on what was happening in the business.

We got to a point where the business was being led by IT and certainly that's how the users perceived it: that there were all these nice new technological things coming in and sexy systems. All these IT chaps were wanting to drive forward in the forefront of technology. But that wasn't necessarily what the business needed. They were very much looking at the global strategy, long-term, let's do this, let's do that, not thinking about what was happening here. So they rather took their eye off the ball. They were encouraged to do that initially, but when that encouragement stopped, they weren't very quick to pick that up.

The encouragement came from management of the equities business. But that encouragement stopped as the businesses took a bit of an about turn. Because business was not quite so good, we started thinking we should, perhaps, start by getting our own house in order before we went to 'rule the world' and perhaps this is not the right way to go technological: there are lot of problems, lots of linkage problems. The focus should have switched to looking at what is happening here. They didn't see that, for whatever reason. They were already on the technological train and couldn't get off it.

So there were a lot of problems within London, particularly user perception – an appalling image, appalling PR – and the IT department had grown from about 40 people to around 130 when I took over. Not all permanent, there were quite a lot of contractors in that, but it was two if not three times the size it had been when these guys took over. And from a users' perception, it was just a waste of money, because they weren't seeing any benefit from it. All these people running around, big screens, new technology.

When the new Group Chief Operator Officer took over, one of the things he was concerned about was the IT department. There was a directive which came from the bank that we should look to cut the costs for next year when we were doing the budget. One of the areas that we should cut costs is in the operation side, the back office side, principally within IT, because that would be seen as the most fat: more people to lose and huge cost base. There was a need to look at that very closely.

I was involved in an advisory capacity, if you like, looking at what we could do with IT because I had been involved with it in the past. So I was special projects manager for that.

The person that took over as Group Chief Operating Officer had run the New York business and I worked in New York for him, so he knew me and we had a good, easy relationship, he always had confidence in me and I would do things for him, not necessarily visibly. There were two of us involved in looking at reducing costs. A person who was reporting up through IT and was taken out of IT in his department, the project office, to report straight into the Chief Operating Officer to look at remodelling IT, with input from the then managers of the IT department, so they knew that this was going on. I was just helping the project office because they are a new team. They've not been here very long. I knew the individuals, so I could give them the background and an insight into to how the individuals would fit together and how this would affect the business. Also, as a user, I have got quite a different perspective.

Over a period of three months, the project office developed models as to how IT could be structured, and I was helping to do that. About 10 days before the end of the project, the Chief Operating Officer wanted to see me and he said, 'I've got this job and I'd like you to do it, and I think I can persuade people that you are the person to do it. But I'm not sure and I don't want to tell you and get you excited about it and then have to upset you, but on balance I need to tell you because I need to be certain that if the opportunity arises that you will take it'. So he told me that, on a particular date, in the near future, he wanted me to take over as IT Director.

That would be a huge change for me, from being responsible to one person to being responsible for 130 people. I had 10 days when I couldn't talk to anybody about it because nobody knew what was going on. Within the IT department nobody knew this was going to happen. We also had to decide how we were going to reduce the department, which people were going to go, but without talking to any of the people who would be my managers within IT. So it was very hit and miss, based on the input that we had already got from the then management of the IT department on previous exercises, but knowing that it would have to be refined very quickly as soon as we were in a position to go public with things, so that was a frantic 10 days. Trauma, unbelievable, because we didn't know until 9.30 on D-Day whether I was actually going to be able to do it or not, because we had to get an approval from our parent.

The announcement was made at lunchtime that I was taking over as IT Director, which has caused lots of raised eyebrows; lots of questions like 'What does she know about IT?' and 'Does she have the right experience?'. I'm not technical, I don't have a technology axe to grind and I do have relevant experience, but in a different form of engineering. Also, I've spent three years on the user management side, and before I came here I was used to managing people. Hence from the Chief Operating Officer's perspective he thought, 'The business is the people, and there are a lot of people problems'. I've got very well qualified people reporting to me, who've got the technology knowhow where I haven't. I've been involved in IT for a while now, so I know what's going on in that sense.

I moved into this office two days after the announcement was made, and I came in by train that morning and I remember thinking that I need to get my PC here, because there was just a small one and I like a big screen. I need to get it moved. It actually takes ages to get things moved, I would be a week without it. And then I realized how stupid! They work for me. Of course I can have my PC.

The people who have moved from here had been trying to establish what they were calling a competence centre for IT, to centralize IT within London. They had been working with the head office of our parent, I think with a view to keeping control of what is happening here, but developing this competence centre so that they could sell their services to other parts of the bank, which we don't do at the moment – to other fixed income divisions and to the bank itself. So they've actually been given the opportunity to set this up. But they would be reliant on people, such as ourselves, giving them work. At the moment we don't need to outsource our work – we have enough people here to do what we need to do. So they won't actually take on any staff and will just resource up on a need-to-have basis.

It is not certain if that will take off, and that's just added to the complications of actually running this department now, because some of the projects here had been planned to be rolled out internationally into other divisions; whereas now, the focus for this department is just on the equities division here in London. And anything else that we do has got to be managed through this new group that has been set up. And it's a logistical, bureaucratic nightmare. I'm sure it will settle out eventually, but at the moment, it is just adding to the confusion and it is very unsettling for the people here because there is a certain amount of divided loyalties. Do they want to go and work for the other group of people, which may or may not have work to do? It is very confusing.

It is going to be an internal consultancy. They will be treated like a third-party supplier, but a preferred supplier in that sense. The legal side of it and the setting up, the contractual side of it, hasn't been established yet. They will be a wholly owned subsidiary, whereas at the moment they are still part of us because they haven't set up the legal entity side of it.

This will have an impact on us because, at the moment, we are the only people who have got the resources. If they need to do a project for someone they are coming to us for the resources. I've just downsized, horrendous word, I haven't got the spare resource, but we've all got to work together, we've got to be seen to be positive about all of this, and I don't want anybody to get the impression that I am very anti what they are trying to do. I have a personal relationship with one of these people – our families meet socially. I'm not sure whether that has made it easier on me. Some of the meetings have been more difficult because I don't want to antagonize him, but I had to. At the moment it is working out OK. We are both able to separate the 'This is business; don't take it too personally, however, you're wrong' from our out-of-work relationship.

What type of change is involved?
I think definitely it is Big Bang. From my perspective, it is not something I had intended to do. It was very unforeseen. It was novel in this environment, some of the problems, the people problems, the issues are familiar from what happened in the past in my previous employment experiences. It is complex, very complex. I mean the scale of change from my perspective is very big. And the scale of change from the departmental perspective is also very big, because I am going to change the whole focus of the department.

The department has got to start to realize that it's a service department. We are not leading edge technology, and we are not there to lead the business in technology; rather we are there to support the business and we have got to operate as a service department. That is the mentality that has not been there. I think one particular factor I can add is that I have got quite easy relationships with the business managers in senior positions, because they are the people that I have been working for directly. I know them all very well and we can exploit that. The Chief Executive and the Chief Operating Officer and the Head of Sales, all those people and the Board Members they are all people I have worked with and worked directly for, for more than two years now, and I had a very comfortable relationship with them. I think they trust me and that's good.

I don't think anybody who has been in this position before me has had those kind of relationships, so they haven't exploited them. They haven't had very good communication with the business or with the users, because they haven't had the relationship and there is not really time to develop those relationships. There's a very big front office/back office divide, which I object to very strongly and I don't think there should be. I think the only way that the business can move forward is if everyone realizes that we are a team and that we are all working for the same end. People should stop referring to it as the front office and the back office. I mean call us 'operations division', but to call it back office, it can be very undermining, particularly for the people who are working here. They feel they are second-class citizens. If we are going to establish this team spirit, it has got to come from further up the organization.

My experience of IT is as a user, and the only programming I have ever done was when I was an undergraduate, and that was FORTRAN, which is like using an abacus as a calculator! But I have used the systems a lot. I do communicate with people and I am used to dealing with people. The techie types are much more comfortable with the screen and communication is not good, even between the groups of developers working with the user groups. Communication is not good. The user group will say, 'Does the system do this?' when they are trying to develop functionality, 'Can it do this?'. And if it can't actually do that right at that minute our IT guys will say 'No' and then the users are climbing the walls. Whereas IT people probably mean we are developing that at the moment, or even 'Yes, it can do that, but there's no data on it so I can't show you'. There have been a lot of problems with the IT department in the past due to poor communication.

What are the effects of this change?
Hopefully the changes within IT will improve the image of IT to the business, so we should be able to develop and re-establish the relationship between IT and the business, and get the business to trust us a lot more, and the business to come to us to look for solutions. And also if people within the IT department are often well placed to say that 'If we just twiddle with this bit of kit here, we could automate this particular system', it would make the users' life a lot easier. To get people within IT to do that, and then to get the business to understand that some of these things might cost them money upfront, but long term we can save them money and we are not just doing it for the sake of it. We are not trying to impress people technically. This will improve the business and we are working for the business. Just trying to build up this kind of team spirit. So I think that could have a quite positive effect.

In the next few years different divisions may be moved, as we are all going into one building. When that happens, it is unlikely that they will want more than one 'operations' division. They won't want three IT departments and three personnel departments and three finance departments. There are those kind of changes on the horizon. I think it is up to those individuals involved, like the individual IT directors and the individual finance directors – it is up to us to be proactive rather than reactive. And instead of all going into little corners and saying, 'Well, when I move in there I'm going to take over the world', I think we have got to take it head on between us and say: 'How are we going to address this problem and how can we best work together?' and perhaps there is a role for more than one person at the top and perhaps there isn't, but that's three years away. We could have had another four IT directors in here before then!

We have been looking at re-doing the budgets for next year, sort of 'in the new world' and all the people that have been involved in this are used to traditionally looking three years ahead, looking five years ahead, doing our strategic business plan, as in the textbooks. But, in the real world here, because we are very dependent on the performance of the markets and what's happening at the front end of the business – which is very unpredictable – it's very difficult to predict what is going to happen to a department such as IT.

A couple of years ago the IT department had 40 people and a small budget. At the end of this year it peaked at 130 people with a huge budget. That could not have been predicted two years ago or less. People, perhaps, realized that IT was going to get bigger, but they would not have realized that by the end of this year IT was heading back down again to where it was at two years ago, and things were going to be pulled in and there will be smaller budgets to work with. It is incredibly cyclical.

What were the external factors driving the change?
The IT department grew because they were building a global equities network. It was seen that the operations division would be a global division and that IT, based in London, would develop a strategy for all the equities businesses throughout the global network and that we would be building and developing international systems, and there would be a bond settlement system worldwide. I mean, 'pie in the sky' is the wrong word – there are people who do this – but the cultures are so disparate at the moment within the different entities. They've all got established local identities and to suddenly propose this global blend and this concept of 'Big Brother' sitting in London. I mean, it's bad enough being owned by a national bank, but the fact that you are then managed by a different nationality. The impetus came from the desire to centralize.

What might be the further effects on your roles and responsibilities?
The business managers are desperate for me to give presentations on what we are doing within IT. I have circulated a long memo to everybody in IT and to the business managers, I think it is wrong to send out two different messages. Even if you are saying the same thing, which is written differently, it can be construed quite differently. I had a long memo to explain why the changes have happened, and where the change in emphasis is going to be and to detail the new structure. This is much flatter, fewer divisions between what has previously been called the operations side and the development side, much more one team culture. Everybody has got defined responsibilities. I have got three line managers reporting in to me, and they have got two or three teams each beneath them. So everybody is shown in a little box, everybody has got primary responsibilities, but everybody understands that it is a

team culture that we are trying to build and that we have got to be seen to be working in that way.

I think I have spent the last two months really trying to get the confidence of the IT department – to rebuild their own confidence and to give them confidence in me, because not all of them knew me. Some did, some I had worked with, some of them had seen me around, but a lot of them did not know me.

For me the focus is on developing the people and my relation-ships with the people within IT, because they have got to trust me. I have had a couple of big meetings in the seminar room with them all, to say to them, 'I will be going to a lot of meetings where I am going to get a lot of flak about IT, because there is a lot of history. I will defend IT. If I defend IT, I have got to know that you are all doing what you are supposed to be doing, because I am not going to have time to come out of a meeting and say, 'Excuse me, can you tell me why this didn't happen, or why is this happening?'.

I am just going to defend them knowing that the IT department is working as it should be. So, I have got to trust them. I think my approach has been quite a shock to them because in the past they have not been given any encouragement to think that anything they do has any effect on how the person sitting in this office is conducting them-selves in meetings.

They have not been given very much responsibility or very much sense that they are responsible for the bits that they are managing. And I want them to do that. I think that if they do not adopt a sense of responsibility, they are not going to perform, so I have got to rebuild the department, get them to trust me, get them to get their own self-confi-dence and then to go to the businesses and say, 'Right, I am ready for you now'. But there are problems and it is important to explain to them where I am coming from.

What activities were undertaken in preparation for taking over the running of the department?

It was under cover of darkness really. I spent a couple of days off-site working, because I could not do it in the office. I looked at the structure; agreeing with the head of the project office the post structure and what we were going to do. He provides support to me, and is responsible for providing all the cost analysis and the project breakdowns and to give project managers rigorous project management controls.

We were working on this model, having to do it after hours, all off-site, to develop it because we could not say anything to anybody about it. Also, I was right in the middle of a privatization that went live in the middle of the 10 days. Then I went abroad and spent some time at the parent company. I had to try to keep it in perspective because I didn't know whether it was going to be approved or not. So it was very difficult to strike a balance between there's a lot to do, and I should not be doing all this and thinking why am I doing all this if I am not actually going to be the person doing it? So half of me is saying, 'Well, someone is going to have to do it, so I might as well put some effort in and hand it over to whoever'. The other half is saying 'Do I really want to work to midnight 10 days and sort this out if it is not actually going to be down to me?'. The main tasks were deciding the organization structure and producing an implementation plan for the first 48 hours and what the sequence of events was likely to be, how the meetings were going to pan out, who I had to see first, when memos should start going out, all that sort of thing. But it didn't happen like that!

It didn't happen like that because the people that were managing IT, they weren't sacked. This was the fall-back scenario. They were rescued by the parent and put into different roles. Normally what tends to happen in this kind of environment is that you go and see personnel, and get your marching orders and hand in your security pass and somebody stands behind you while you empty your desk and you leave. That didn't happen, which was good and bad. It was bad in the sense that it did not happen on the day it was announced I would take over, so I could not actually move on to this floor until the Friday morning, because there was nowhere for me to go.

I know there were lots of empty desks, but that wasn't going to give the right impression. I needed to move in, to be seen to be in this office, in control, because these guys were still around as well – it was very disconcerting for the people who were still here, because it is 'I thought you had gone, what are you still doing here and what are you doing and why?'. It was a complete muddle for two days. So, the sequence of events didn't quite happen because I wasn't in a position to have meetings. I was having meetings with people in the meeting rooms on another floor of this building. But it was all a bit still under-hand somewhat, you felt as if you were doing it all behind closed doors and you cannot come out into the open and make a big statement. So a bit of an anticlimax in that sense, and it wasn't really until I got to be able to move into here on Friday morning and people actually saw me here that the penny dropped within the people on this floor.

The IT department is on three floors and we are gradually reducing the number of people that are down on the other floors with more moving here, but there will still be a frontline support presence on the lower floor and a help desk. So I had a department in three places and I could not be in any of them. But after those first few days, I am not sure whether things panned out as I expected or not.

There has been lots of firefighting, lots of people issues. There is one instance: a few weeks ago one particular guy, heavily involved in a development project, got some personal problems. Personal problems not just outside of here, but there is another person involved here as well, and they are just not handling it very well. They are both working on the same project. They have both got problems outside of work anyway, and he has gone completely off the rails. Not sleeping, getting very tired, putting in a lot of hours here, not knowing where to focus his attention and thinking that the time-scale for the development is not achievable. He is really upsetting everything and stirring things up. Telling tales out of school and creating a huge, mega-fuss.

When I was down here, even with the door shut all I could here was this guy outside, just complaining, shouting, moaning, stamping up and down, just like a real drama queen. So my three immediate reports, and myself, spent an hour and a half discussing what we are going to do: shall we approach it this way? I was going to talk to him with his line manager and we are going to say, 'Right we are going to take you off this project because we want you to do a proper handover and we want you to take this week off because you are not doing yourself any good and you are not doing anybody else any good because you are tired: take the week off'.

We were going to have another meeting with the other people just to say this is what we are doing and how we are going to manage it. So, fine, it should have worked out OK, but on the Wednesday morning we had the first meeting and started to say this is what we are going to do and this is why. And he took issue at that. Didn't think it was a valid reason. He felt he was being punished for speaking out, for voicing opinions that he thought other people shared. So I had to come back quite hard with him and say, 'Look it is not that, it is your behaviour. This has been completely unprofessional. You should not be telling tales out of school, anyway: you should come and talk to me about it. You probably don't know me but you should come and talk to me and I want you to take a week off'.

This took about three quarters of an hour. There were three of us and him. Then I said I wanted him to take a week off and he got all choked up and I thought, he is not going to be able to say anything and I didn't think the others had noticed. So I looked at the other two and said, 'Right you have a meeting with him this afternoon, sort out a proper handover plan and I need to talk to him on my own now'. They got the hint and left, looking at me very strange, thinking what's the matter with her. I had to ring up and apologize afterwards.

He was so upset, so wound up about the whole thing, but I think the thing that was upsetting him more than anything was that he didn't think anyone had listened to him. Nobody had ever treated him as a person. So I spent two hours with him and he's had a complete 180 degree turnaround. He has not taken this week off, but he is now a much more integrated team member. All the problems on the project he had, he has addressed. He has managed to talk through with people. His personal problems seem to be a bit more in perspective. He just needed someone to talk to and he hadn't felt in the past that he has been treated as a person. The attitude had been very much 'We are here to run a business and your personal problems are nothing to do with us'. Well, I mean, that's wrong, because if he has got personal problems and he is bringing them to work with him then of course it is our concern, and it is like children at school: it's the people who are with them all the time, it's the teachers who know the child's got a problem. It's the same with me. This guy's sitting right outside my door and I saw he had got a problem. And he was great. I mean he would come in really aggressive and he was a right pussycat when he went out, just because we had given him time.

This is my style. Perhaps that was why he was so confrontational in the past, because he had not been able to articulate how he felt, because he knew he was going to be upset and the natural reaction is to be aggressive. He didn't need to be aggressive with me. I was trying to defuse his aggression. Also there was a comment made by one of the other guys: 'I think you should just take him off the project and just be done with it. He has been carrying on like this for three or four months'.

I said 'Wait. If this has been going on for three or four months somebody should have addressed it sooner, and don't tell me that'. I am prepared to give him a chance because he has only become my responsibility recently. He is my responsibility and it's no good me being heavy and suspending him or sacking him, because how is that going to look to everybody else? I don't work like that, but it seems to have worked so far, thank goodness.

One task that I had to accomplish in my first few weeks was that of making a large number of people redundant. Everybody knew that something was going to happen. They somehow found out it was going to happen and they were all waiting for it. And they were all sitting at their desks, looking glum, because they knew there were some people there that were going to be made redundant. Someone from personnel I already knew and had already spent some time with had a bit of a pep talk with me and produced a script just to make sure that I covered all the points and that I said the right thing. I had to go up to another floor, and the guy from personnel said, 'Right, I'm going to sit round the corner. I'm going to sit round the corner, so that I'm not the first person that they see'. The worst thing was, I'm up on the other floor and I have to ring the individuals down here and say, 'Hello, this is your boss, would you like to pop upstairs?' Well as soon as they pick up the phone and know it's me they know.

That was so difficult. But the advantage for me of doing this so soon was I didn't know the individuals. But because I didn't know them, I'm not likely to ring them, so they pick up the phone and it's me. I mean, it was just horrendous. But I was talking to personnel about it while we were waiting for the first person to come up and he said – what is your biggest concern? I said, 'Apart from I've got to make the phone call, my biggest concern is that I was going to say the wrong thing or I was going to forget to say something'. And he said, 'Well that's why I'm here'. I was sort of speaking and I was wanting to be cool, calm because the people obviously would be emotional. I got very different reactions. I'd never done it before, so I'd never experienced it. I think I got off very lightly because I'd got no adverse, violent or aggressive reaction, not one that was articulated. There were some aggressive reactions but they were not articulated. But because I was looking down at the script, to make sure I got the points, a bit like I'm doing now, I'd hesitate before saying something to make sure I was saying the right thing. I was a bit concerned that it was coming across a bit funny and the personnel person said, 'No, no, it's OK because then they can see that you're not doing this easily. You are concerned about it'. It was not a very nice thing to do and I'm glad I've got my first experience over because I know that I've got more to do.

We were going to phase it across three months and I said 'No way. If they're going, they're all going and I'm not having people hanging around because they'll know. I can't produce an organization chart with people who are only going to be around temporarily. And what kind of three months are you going to have? Trying to manage people who think they are working under a cloud? Not good. So I said 'We'll do it now, otherwise we don't do it'. It means we've got a very reduced team but we were going to be reduced anyway and if we're going to have to manage with 90 people instead of 130 then work it out. At least it's come at a quiet period. Quiet in a sense that it's the middle of the business.

Were there any other important competencies/activities based on your experiences in prior positions?

I think the biggest one is communication. I've got to be able to communicate the change and the need for change, not just impose it. People have got to understand why life is changing. There's all this business about ownership and they've got to take it on board. I don't think you can just impose it in this environment. I've got to be able to communicate that, and if they don't understand that there's a need for change, then that's my problem primarily and I've got to try to articulate it differently and explain it differently. I think it's important for me not to forget that I have been able to assimilate the need for change. I know where we're going, and I've had several months to think about this, albeit from a slightly different perspective. I have been very much on the outside, which perhaps is easier. Perhaps if I knew I was designing all this for me to run I would have done it slightly differently. Like most, I would have started small. I think I have got to be able to communicate.

Also, I think you have got to have a lot of patience with the people. You've got to be tolerant of the people, but not overly tolerant. There is a fine line between being tolerant, letting them have their head, and knowing when to be firmer and saying they've got to toe the line. Obviously we've got a business to support and that's my responsibility. It's my responsibility to make sure that the traders can trade and that they can see the positions. And we've got to make sure that the systems are up and running, so that's my primary business responsibility. But then it's the balance between that and making sure that the people within the department are happy, whatever.

I think I've got to be willing to learn, I've got to stay open-minded. If people have got suggestions, and I do try to encourage people to do that, and if people are not prompted, people tend to be backward in coming forward at this kind of thing, so what I tend to do is to send out alarmist memos – 'I'm going to turn off this system'.

I sent out one last week, saying 'We've had this reported and it's not doing this and not doing that. I'd better turn the system off as a matter of some urgency. Would anyone like to make any comments?'. It was like receiving fan mail which is good. And when people have come back to me I said, 'This is not my choice. Whether we switch this off or not is a decision of the business. But people have just been apathetic about it. Nobody's prepared to come up with any suggestions and I need suggestions and I need someone to sign on the dotted line to pay for it. We can't do it for nothing'. I had to get them to understand that. So I'm open to comments and criticisms and that's when you've got to be careful not to take things too personally.

It will be down to me to drive the change forward. I'm quite comfortable with that. Because I don't have the IT background, the IT experience, I'm relying very much on my immediate three line managers to make sure that technically we are doing what we are supposed to be doing.

I can give a business perspective and I am quite happy to play the go-between between the technical people and the business. Instead of going down and giving senior business staff a technical reason why the system's just fallen over, I'd say 'It's broken, we're going to fix it, but it'll take about ten minutes. It's a real pain'. They haven't got time for long, technical explanations that they don't understand.

I think these three line managers are being very proactive. They're keen to help, they understand the need for change and they are obviously going to be instrumental in introducing the change into their different teams. They are three people with very different management styles and they have three different sets of teams to manage differently.

Because we've had to hit the ground running, I spent the first week in meetings with these three people, individually and collectively, to say this is the structure. First of all, are you happy with this? Can you understand this? Let me explain how we got to this structure.

It was quite sticky because one of them didn't like it, didn't understand the reasoning behind it, didn't really want to know, didn't feel that his role was quite as he thought it ought to be. I thought perhaps I was going to have problems. Everybody has expected me to have problems with him. But they haven't arisen because I could put it in perspective. He might come across as a difficult character to a lot of people here. It might seem that he is going to have a real problem working for somebody that's not technical. But he's not as bad as others I have encountered. Coming from the industry environment that I worked in previously was a foundation for something like this because it keeps things in perspective. I've met him head on and I've been very upfront and said if you've got a problem we'll talk about it. I don't want you sulky and I don't want you behaving badly and I don't want you going to talk to other people about it: talk to me about it. And he's great. We've got a really good rapport now, which has happened very quickly. I think he realizes that I'm not going to muscle in on him technically and I'm not going to impose any technical solution, any technical strategy. I'm quite happy for him to get on with that, since all I'm interested in is the business side of it. Are we getting value for money? Are we doing what the business wants? They will be very instrumental in introducing the change, but I see it chiefly as my responsibility.

There is also the project office function. We have developed this strategy between us and the office is my support department. The head of the project office will obviously be very key in introducing a lot of the change. We've got to look at the way we do the budgets, the way we do the reporting and that's all part of the communication with the business, so that they understand better exactly what they're paying for. It must be difficult for them, because they get this big number: their month end management accounts. Huge sums of money under an IT line. It doesn't mean anything. So he will be the one driving that and driving all the reporting systems and cost control and project bases to feed into the finance department, so that when the results come out, it's hopefully a lot more understandable. So it's change across the board, really.

Were there any mechanisms put in place to monitor change?

I'm setting with the line managers short- and medium-term goals for them to achieve. Some of them are difficult to define because, for example, how do you measure that you've actually built an effective team. I think the biggest mechanism that we've got for measuring whether it's been successful will be the lack of negative comments coming from the business. I won't say they appear as positive comments, because they only ever complain, they don't praise. If we can develop a better relationship with the business, then that will be very visible because they will stop complaining; they'll be much more confident; they will be less reactive and if the system goes down they'll be more understanding. I think that's probably the only and the best way that we are going to be able to manage this.

Anything to add?

I suppose one thing that we haven't touched on is a little bit remote from me in a sense at the moment; but something that certainly has affected me being here, and how I got here in the first place, is the cultural aspect of being owned by a foreign bank. Because the mentality is very different. I'm not sure whether it's national mentality, or banking mentality: it's still in some places very much a job for life and if you've not performing very well where you are, we move you and put you in a different department and you make a complete mess of that as well.

They didn't want these people, i.e. past IT department managers, to be seen to be gone, because they had been very high profile in strategically global things, even though it was misdirected. As technical people we've got a lot to offer; they were just a bit misguided I think, and a bit blinkered in that they didn't see the writing on the wall. There were different forces coming in on us, sort of imposed from on high. You will do this and you will do that. 'Well, you want to do this, well, fine, we don't really care', and once you start to widen the brief and look internationally you've got all the different cultures. I must say my attitude is they're all people and the people problems are much the same; and if you can develop the people side of it, develop the relationship, you can then go from there. It's no good leaping in, appearing like Superman, saying I'm here to change the face of IT, and suddenly imposing completely new systems because they are going to think you're barking mad. So it's the same thing. You've got to work to get the people on your side, but you've just got to work on it differently because the cultural thing is a bit different. I think that's the only thing that we've not really touched upon. But as I say, that's something a little bit remote from me, it's just something that I've always been aware of working in that environment. But it is there.

Having been on the international sales side I know all the heads of equity. Again, this is something that I'm hoping I can exploit, because I do know all the guys that run the local offices at heads of equity level, and I have good relationships with them. The people that I don't know are the heads of my opposite numbers. I know the people above them, but I don't know my opposite numbers. I've got to have some edge. I mean, I'm not an IT professional. I'm an engineer for goodness sake, and I've only been in management a short time. But it's always been like that. I rise to a challenge.

Re-engineering global custody operations in a bank

Background
The background is that we have a business that in the mid-1980s had been quite successful. But during the course of the late 1980s and into the mid-1990s the environment changed.

The global custody operation focuses on the administration of security portfolios for investing companies who don't want to be bothered with all the back office processing. In the 1980s it was fairly common for securities settlement to fail. The back office systems were not particularly good. The custody organization of this company and other custodians were making a lot of free interest income, because people were paying money to settle a trade, the trade would fail, the money would be sat there and the custodian would get the benefit of the interest. During the 1980s, following 'Big Bang', people invested quite heavily in back office systems and after a peak of significant ineffi- ciency it settled down and the process became cleaner: the free balances disappeared. So what we were seeing with our custody operations was a deterioration in the income stream and increasing competition in that line of business.

Custody is a very low capital-intensive business so, for banks that had been sustaining losses in the 1980s, businesses that did not require a lot of capital investment were quite attractive. Hence a lot of people were coming into the custody business. Those who were using custodial services were becoming more sophisticated, and were looking for more services from the custodians, so, if you like, the boundary of the service requirement was moving out all of the time. What had been an added value service last year becomes a *de rigueur* component in your offering this year. The cost to the company and a lot of other custo- dians of servicing that moving business boundary was becoming diffi- cult. The computer systems that we were running were old. They didn't support the full raft of services that the organization felt it needed to provide, so there was a lot of clerical effort being thrown around the computer system to enhance the service offering. So you have got staff costs growing because you are having to throw more people at service provision, deterioration of your income line because there is market competition, fewer free balances.

It is one of those business scenarios when you look at it and say 'Is this a game I want to play? Is there something I can do that will allow me to make a good profit?'. As a company we have some rather strin- gent return on investment criteria. The Divisional Board spent about six months looking at it and had brought consultants in to provide a degree of independence.

The conclusion from the review was that the company was well perceived by core customers, but its technology was felt to be falling behind. The Group Board faced a not unpredictable set of choices: to close the business down, to continue to let it erode until it fell under its own weight, or to begin an investment programme of differing levels of intensity in order to reshape the business.

By and large, this company does not like to invest very heavily in businesses that are not seen as dominant within their niche. So the real question was, 'Could we take this business, which was a significant provider of custody, and re-engineer it in such a way as to provide a viable business against the company's metrics and to create a platform for that niche dominance?'.

The drive to do it was very much within tight cost constraints, so one of the other recommendations made was that if the Board were serious about trying to develop the custody operation then it should be moved into a different division. The reasons for that were twofold: (1) the new division had a tradition of doing its own IT and (2) the business model of custody operations was more closely aligned to the business of the division. So the decision was taken.

I don't think it was a decision that received the wholehearted endorsement of all the directors involved. There were some people that had reservations about custody as a business. But after some debate and discussion the business actually moved divisions.

At that point I joined as the IT director and one of the new divisional managers came in as managing director. Our remit was to drive through a business process re-engineering (BPR) activity that would ensure that the business could, on a sustainable basis, meet the company's hurdle of rate of return but also give the business the capability to deliver a service offering which the market would deem to be acceptable. And, given some of the things that I have already alluded to, what we were recognizing was that this business isn't standing still. During the last few years we have seen quite a lot of consolidation in the custodial operation.

The challenge that we faced was that this business had been left in a sleepy business backwater, it had been moved out of London to two other locations, and a small office was left here in London to deal with the physical aspect of securities settlement. It had not been invested in. It was not really seen as a key element in the bank's portfolio. It had been a site to move staff who were seen as not to be performing in other areas. The business had been left in the backwater, and allowed to deteriorate.

I think we recognized that in order to wreak a change of that magnitude we had to give almost undue focus to the technology. If, in the end, the basic ingredients are a troubled business and, in many instances, a less than fully effective staff, you can't wipe the slate clean and recruit lots of new people overnight. Your challenge is 'How quickly can I turn this business around; how quickly can I change its mechanics so we see a widening gap between the income stream and the cost base?'.

BPR has received some bad press because, quite frankly, people do it very badly. They do it without thinking through, as the Americans would say, 'the soup to nuts issues'. It's all very well to say we are focusing on business processes, and we have, I think, moved very much from seeing businesses as discrete functional components to looking at a business as value streams and processes delivering value to our customers. BPR is simply a set of techniques that say let's look at the business boundary. What are the inputs, what are the outputs and how do you efficiently link the two elements? What is the process that links the two sides?

BPR, as espoused by Hammer, is all about looking, in my view, at what the inputs and outputs are and designing a process that you can hold your hand up and say this is efficient, it is sustainable, it has the characteristics that quality today demands, i.e. reproducibility, consistency, control of errors. What do you do when things go wrong? I happen to believe that it's actually how you deal with errors that distinguishes a merely competent organization from a truly excellent one. A lot of people say get your processes right, and that is absolutely correct, but customers expect you to get the processes right these days. If your process works 90 per cent of the time that's satisfactory. People want to know that your process is going to work. But things go wrong from time to time and it's the processes you put in place to deal with those problems that really distinguish the great from the also rans.

The challenge with BPR is that for many people and for many organizations there is a tremendous gap between the process that you articulate within the BPR exercise and your ability to realize it in the business systems context: not just the computer, but the whole human system (i.e. the human–machine system).

Here we are saying that business process re-engineering is the way forward. Customers want output. They don't care that your interest calculations are the most efficient if your overall service delivery is not up to scratch. So you have got to have a good enough interest rate calculation, you have to have a good enough payment system, you have to have a good enough vault mechanism to allow you to catalogue and manage your physical securities. But the customer expects each of those components to be delivered within the overall process and is really unconcerned that you are excellent in one and deficient in another. All the customer wants is consistency of delivery within the process.

Virtually every system that exists today is functionally oriented. People built systems on the basis that you teach clerks that this happens, then this happens, and at each of those points they may go to one or more computer systems, or filing systems, whatever it is, to execute steps for the transaction, and what you see is that individuals do those steps in different ways, they make mistakes, they access the wrong computer system, they put the wrong information into the wrong screen. We have then a conflict in my view between saying I want to drive my business processes, but what I have actually done is that I have built business mechanisms that are functionally focused.

Look at what was going on in the custody operation at this company, where you have quite complex transaction processing, particularly if you are dealing with overseas securities. What you end up with are control dockets on the front of manilla files, and they might be several pages of tick boxes; and each case that goes through builds up this file of paper. You walk round the office and people have stacks of vanilla folders feet high moving around from desk to desk. If you were to say to the supervisory staff: 'Can you give me now an assessment of the state of all these transactions and how close are you to the business deadlines for given transactions?' they wouldn't have that information. So you had a situation of 'Where was the paper stored?'. It was death 'by a thousand sheets'. And every time, historically, someone had made a mistake, management would apply another control mechanism at that point, so in some instances the same data was, as it moved from department to department or function to function, being checked five or six times by supervisory staff. This was not an efficient way of doing business!

The upshot of all this was that I said 'If we are going to do BPR, we are going to do it quickly, and cost-effectively'.

One of my beliefs has always been that IT is part of the business process. It is not a distinctive department, it shouldn't live under separate rules. It's part of the business. I've been fortunate enough in the time I've been in this company to be part of the revolution where they moved away from the central IT function to a very business unit-focused IT delivery.

The Group were splitting the business down and saying each business must control its own IT, because IT is part of that business delivery. If you believe that IT is part of the business mix you can't, in my view, turn round and say I'm going to re-engineer my business apart from IT. You have to subject IT to the same disciplines and constraints and objectives that you are applying to the whole business.

So we said, when we were driving the BPR exercise for the custody operation: IT is part of the business; hence IT will be subjected to the same process of BPR and we have to take as radical a look at the way we deal with the technology as we do with the way we deal with business.

So the managing director and I came out of that saying 'Right, we will create a technology department that sits with the business people, and the development effort will be a combined exercise'.

How can you, if you are trying to be radical with BPR, go and pick a package that has its design about five to seven years in the past?

The chances that someone five or seven years ago was enlightened enough to deliver a system that is capable of supporting the process nuances that you want today are very slim. The chances that they have designed a system with the right architecture to allow you to modify whatever you want to do today according to future changes in the business opportunity profile are very slim. So we said, 'If we are going to do this properly and deliver a system that meets our needs, then we have to do it ourselves because we wont find a package that will meet our redesign criteria of today'.

We needed to take a radical approach to the way that we develop it so we went for the 'rapid application development' paradigm – iteration, prototyping. If we are dealing with people who aren't that bright then the chances of them being able to visualize and understand the technical specification was very low.

We could sit down with them and show them what we could build; and more than that, build and assemble a project development team that is a heterogeneous mix: development staff alongside business staff. We were able to identify some literate individuals within the business who did understand quite clearly what it was that they needed to do. We were doing this at breakneck speed. We needed to develop a technological capability that has at its heart a process-centric design paradigm, and the obvious way of doing that was to embrace workflow as a technology.

We did BPR and, at the same time, I was trying to get a technology strategy in place, because one of the things that had come out of the consultants' review was a commentary that we really had to do something demonstrable, from a customer perspective, as to our technological competence within 18 months or so time frame. It took the company six months or so to move the business and to make the report, so we were left with a very limited time frame to be able to reassure our customers.

We were saying we wanted to build our own system, that it should have a process centric design. I had made the decision that it had to be a workflow approach, because I wanted to try to get the IT department to mirror the requirements of the business and to marry up to that, whereas the previous IT support that had been provided by the central IT function had been dead clustered, i.e. a mainframe type environment. We said it would be open systems, it would be rapid application development and iterative protocycling.

In a sense we were changing an awful lot. It was an extremely high-risk strategy, because we were saying, 'We are going to change the business radically through business process re-engineering; we are going to set up a new IT department which will embrace rapid application development; it's going to develop its own workflow because we are unsatisfied with the workflow offerings that the market can provide us'. We really set ourselves a huge hill to climb.

When I joined the business unit, because its IT had been provided from the central IT function of the preceding owners, I had no staff, so we were really under pressure in terms of time. So we didn't get everything right, that's for sure. Certainly, looking back, some of the starting decisions I made about building up the department clearly reflected the time pressure. I didn't necessarily get the right people. I got people in because I wanted to do something, but I caused myself some problems down the line by getting in the wrong mix of management. It's certainly something that I will bear very firmly in mind the next time.

But we got to a point where we had decided on our technical strategy. We had done a little bit of proof of concept work to demonstrate the viability of the route we wanted to go down, and in February we went for and got project approval for IT spend to actually develop our new system. We delivered the first working elements of that system six months later. So we were able, in a very short space of time, to assemble an IT department, to grab hold of the rapid application development approach and to deliver, with fairly modest expenditure, a working system – albeit a sub-set of the total functionality that was required.

On the project team, I broke the responsibilities down into four core areas. In traditional terms there was the business analysis element, a communications strand to what we were doing (a custodian has to speak with many different external agencies), there was a focus on customer desktop delivery systems (electronic banking applications) and the basic operational elements of the environment. We adopted a four-schema repository-based rapid applications development tool. It's a very clever piece of technology that does some things extremely well and allows you to rapidly assemble functionality. It has certainly got and continues to get high ratings from the independent analysts. However, our experience, in the heat of battle, so to speak, was that its suitability for large-scale ongoing incremental development was not so good.

Over the period of development my department was growing. We had a mixture of business staff, IT department staff, software house staff and consultants involved. It was very much a question that timing was everything, so we were grabbing whatever resource was available and appropriate to the tasks we were trying to undertake.

It's very typical of the way the company manages things that there was a steering group. One of the big problems we had is that the managing director is a very nice person and extremely consultative in the way he does things. This is fine if you have got a business which is basically stable and is moving forward, but it was very much management by committee. That added to the problems of technology delivery. Each time a decision has to be made it becomes a free for all, and everyone is allowed to discuss it. I think once all the changes have been made the MD will be an ideal candidate to manage the business, but as an ideal character for driving through a vigorous change programme I think he is not the right individual.

If you say 'I want to transform the business and I want to do it in a short space of time and I am going to adopt a number of high-risk strategies to drive this through', the most important thing is the clarity of the vision. By all means discuss up front and, quite frankly, the BPR mechanism should be that discussion point. You can say 'OK, that is what I want to achieve', and then it's about driving vigorously towards that vision.

What happens in these processes is that there is an implied criticism of the historic management. You come in and say 'Sorry, you have got it badly wrong, we are now going to do some radical surgery'. You find some who say, 'Yes, we understand, we were frustrated by the previous top management and we are with you and want to do this'. But there are also others who say 'Well, you know this business has been around for many years. You new guys, what do you know? All we need is to be allowed to do what we think we need to do and the business will recover. This BPR stuff is not really for us'.

Michael Hammer talks about three reasons for doing BPR. You re-engineer because you want to get ahead of your competition; because your competition is re-engineering; or you are re-engineering to catch up. If you are re-engineering to catch up that implies the business has, for whatever reason, got behind. I think it is very difficult to take management who have been responsible for managing a business in such a way that it falls behind and then say to them, 'Come on, take this pill, because tomorrow you are going to be visionary, you are going to have a radical new approach to the way you drive your business forward'. It doesn't work, particularly when you are talking about managers in their late 40s and early 50s. I'm getting ageist there. But what I see within this company is that there is an ossification of people when they get to that stage of their career. More typically they are concerned about preserving the status quo than they are about radical change. That's not always true.

The MD is very keen on making the change within the business, but he keeps coming away from making the hard decisions. If there were hard decisions to be made, then they would be fudged. And so here we are, saying we want a radical approach that will strip the costs out of the business (and for that you can read people). I don't care what people say, BPR is not primarily about making people redundant, it is primarily about making your business processes more efficient. But if you are dealing with a business whose primary costs are staff, then you are talking about taking staff out of the loop. The papers that came out of the consultant's review showed the business was heavily over-managed, and yet there has been no serious attempt to deal with that.

So we certainly had a lot of excitement in the first nine months of our involvement and the delivery of the first wave of the system was seen as quite an achievement. But we discovered a number of things as a result of that. First, if you give the business the opportunity to change their mind and review what they want, they will do that. Because the business had been distributed across a number of sites, each of those sites had their own customs and practices, in many instances, significantly or sufficiently different or divergent, one from another. There was some competition about which was the best way to do things.

So we got ourselves into a situation where there is this very flexible iterative type of technology that allows the user to change his mind and, if you read any of the texts on rapid applications development, the theorists say you need to time box and you say to people: 'There is this much time resource available and you have to get the function right within that time period'. I don't think the people writing that have ever done systems development, because if you sit down with a business user and say we have got a time budget, and within the next day you have got to get this as good as it can be because we need to move on to the next step that doesn't happen. All they will do, and this is perhaps where you need to condition and train your users if they just say 'Well, I've spent the day but it's not what I need to do the business; we must spend more time on it'. And once again, because we were not getting the level of autocratic decision making from the managing director, each of the different streams of business were coming in and saying 'We want it this way'. We were getting a see-saw effect in terms of how we were delivering certain elements of function.

The traditional way of doing systems work is what is described as the Victorian novel or the waterfall approach. What you do is that your systems methodology is all about locking out change and making change very painful for the user. What you say to the user is 'You tell me what you want', and there will be a very highly paid business analyst that will document that. He will write down a summary of what he thinks you have told him and you will sign that off before you move to the next stage, which is to produce a technical specification. The subtext is 'I guarantee you won't understand this, but I won't do the development until you sign it off. And, once I have got your signature on the requirements document and the technical specification, any time you want a change you have to find the budget for it, and when we deliver the system I don't care whether it meets your business requirement or not, what I will do is to point to the specification and prove that I have met the specification'. So, under this model if you don't get that specification right the poor old user suffers. I think that is one of the reasons there is so much dissatisfaction with IT.

You then try a very different approach and say 'This will be business-led. We will give the business the discretion to control the way that the IT evolution works. Users can sit there and look at what is coming out and tell us when it's good enough for their purpose'. Suddenly, you find that everyone is a bloody perfectionist. There is no concept of 'good enough'. Everything they are doing has to be almost perfect and at least as good as the functionality they have already got. There is this mentality that says 'Let's forget about anything other than function, and all I will seek to do by building a new system is to beat the functionality I had in the preceding system.

This is one of the problems with BPR. Your high-level organizational and process design is just that – it's high level. When you come down to the detailed implementation people often lose sight of the high-level design objectives, and so you have this sort of drill down to try to add function, whereas you set off on BPR not for functional excellence but for process excellence.

You don't need the functional components to be excellent. You just need to have an excellent process. I'm not quite sure how in the end you can fix all of these issues. I suspect that systems development will, whatever approach you use, always be an imperfect science.

One of the things that has frustrated me (because I came from the business and it's always appeared to me that IT is a pretty critical ingredient in delivering the business product, service or whatever you are trying to get out to the customer base) are people's attitudes. Many managers are prepared to stand up and say with some degree of pride 'I know nothing about IT'. And I think, 'Here is a resource, a critical resource, a component of your business, and you are proud to say I understand nothing about it'. What does that say about quality of management? If I had my way every manager who stood up and said that would be fired. Unless you are in a business where you don't have to worry about IT, it's like any other resource. You may not be a human resource expert, but you must understand how you are going to manage people. You don't have to be a financial whizz kid, but you have to be able to understand the implications of the financial reports you are getting and you have to deal with the impact of IT.

What we have found in systems development is that there is a lot of 'stones and glasshouses' going on, in the sense that the users complain about lack of control and lack of accountability of IT, and the fact that they don't get what they want from IT. But when you turn around and say, 'Well, fine guys, we're going to change the rules. What we will do is to provide you with the technical services, but you will drive the application development. You will tell us what you want, you will get to see what it is you have told us that you want, you will get the ability to edit and change it. But you have to take responsibility for providing the right people. You have to take responsibility for getting to terms with what this is about. You have to make the intellectual effort'. Suddenly they are not quite so keen. Whereas before it was 'If only I can get control over what was coming out of this everything will be sweetness and light'.

When you move away from the barriers that lock out change to a situation where you say, 'We will not put those barriers in the way. We are going to let the problem be yours and IT becomes truly a business problem. What we are – we are the support infrastructure, the support service to you, but it's your systems, it's realizing your vision of the way you want to do business'. It puts the fear of God into them.

We had all kinds of problems getting the ownership issue sorted out because there were still business managers saying 'I want this and I don't care what the implications are'. If I turned around to them and said 'I want you to double the profit of the business and I don't care what the implications are', they would have turned around and said 'You are talking out of the back of your head. How can we do that?'. They are quite prepared, if the boot's on the other foot to say to IT, 'Well, we agreed with you that we would spend this level of money on systems development and we agreed with you that you would provide this head count and these services to us. Absolutely the IT budget is your problem and the date is on the plan. But we are not prepared to work within those constraints'. We went through all sorts of issues about who should control the project plan, who should control all or parts of the IT budget, which, in itself, is unusual.

In most bureaucratic organizations the IT manager is paid depending on the size of the IT budget he or she controls and the number of staff involved. I tried to turn that around and say, 'Look: I am not really interested in empire building. What I want is recognition for the value-add that we are going to deliver through IT, so if I am coming in and saying I'm going to use low-cost technology and try to deliver things within tightly controlled cost boundaries, then I want recognition on that basis, rather than on the empire'. It certainly created some problems for us, getting the business to accept the limitations that they wanted at macro-level – i.e. budget and head count level – in terms of what then was deliverable to them at micro-level.

I'm not sure that we completed that process and I think to some extent the business is now moving back to a more traditional approach. But I am jumping over a fairly chunky part of the story which is where, having done the first wave implementation of the system, we recognized that some of the things were not as well designed and engineered as they needed to be to sustain the wider business. So we really ended up using our first delivery as a prototype for the second wave. But everyone was sufficiently encouraged by what had happened to believe that 'Yes, the system will be delivered, and it will meet all the requirements'.

Two years after I had joined the division, and into the BPR exercise, they went out and bought another custody business! This was an interesting exercise, because here you are, just over a year into change of division, a radical programme to re-engineer the business, a radical IT change, trying to impose or drive through cultural changes both in the way business is done, trying to get people to come up to speed with technology, and then it's decided to go and buy a business which has got different technology, different working practices and which is actually bigger than our own base business. I think, in retrospect, and I suspect I was part of it at the time, we just didn't really recognize how painful the assimilation of a culturally different unit was going to be.

And of course, because of the managing director's style, it was very much done in the style of a merger rather than an acquisition; with great desire to see harmony and integration. That's a laudable objective, but what that did was to provoke really fierce politics below. As soon as the management which had been bought realized they were not going to be put to the sword, they were going to be offered an opportunity, then wham – you have two sets of management, our side saying 'We bought that business because it wasn't succeeding; we are going through the change programme in our business; they were in much deeper trouble than we were, how can they have a view?'. It comes back to this issue that I mentioned earlier, which is that management who have led a business into trouble don't necessarily have the credibility to lead a business out of trouble. That's not always true, but you understand the sentiment.

So we had a situation where our management may not have been of a particularly high calibre, but some had bought into the change programme that was going on. We managed to get the Group Board to buy into the change programme that was going on with us to the point that they were prepared to fund the acquisition of this business from another player.

The way these things work are that the corporate financiers go out and start making enquiries in the market-place to see who is interested in buying a custody operation. It's pretty hush-hush, because the last thing you want to do is to alert staff to the process going on. During this time I was going to lawyers' offices to read through tomes of documentation to try to understand the systems in place. I couldn't go and walk round the place. The MD became aware that the custody business was up for sale and got his boss involved. He agreed, in principle, to explore it. There was a process of due diligence and at the end we sat round a table and said 'Well, how much is this business worth? What should be our strategy?'.

The initial work was done by the financial controller, the financial director, managing director and myself – all of us trawled through the documentation. If you like you start off and you look at the numbers and try to understand how the business is working. Because systems costs were a significant element and there were all sorts of issues about trying to bring the businesses together with very disparate systems, different infrastructures; I needed to understand what the implications were for the business. But in the end, we decided that we would go for it, but we were also going to try to hold to the overall time frame for the original project. That was just absolutely impossible to achieve.

We spent a period in pilot phase. Some problems came out. We worked on those, and in September we sat down and said 'We have got the next phase of the project to do, let's review where we are with the first release. What do we want to do next?'. And really by November, we had changed some of the team structure, we had brought in some people to help us to do certain things and we were beginning the next wave. But really the acquisition took quite a bit of time and there is no doubt that, for that six to eight week period, there was some uncertainty in my mind as to what we should be doing, because we needed to refocus for the second wave of the application development and I know there was this chance of having a pretty significant change happening to the business within a short space of time, and of course when that came through – again, largely because of the way the managing director likes to run things – the decision was taken that the acquired staff should be heavily involved in the applications development process.

So, not only have we had to contend with three different views within our own business, but we now have people from another organization coming in. That certainly cost us at least three or four months in terms of application development. We really got the second release, with a sustainable architecture to it, last year and we have been building on that ever since.

If you look back at the business today and see the amount of change that has happened over two years – change in ownership; change in technology; change in senior management; buying a business bigger than yourself; trying to integrate it and continuing to try and satisfy the requirements of a very disparate body of users – I think most people believe that good progress has been made.

I think the bottom line is that one of the things with hindsight we could have done better is using the new technology. I am still not sure how we can overcome this conundrum between a traditional methodology-driven development approach (where you are involving the user at the beginning and the end and trying to lock out change) and the model that I was trying to drive through (which was very much to have a very high level of user participation in the systems development process and try to dissolve as far as possible any boundaries between IT and business).

But it is clear that to make the model that I was trying to drive through work, you have got to be pretty persistent at it, because the users are not used to it. Philosophically it's quite different from the traditional methods. There's the joke about a guy walking through Ireland who finds he is lost and turns to a potato farmer and says 'How do I get to Dublin?' and the farmer says 'If I were trying to get to Dublin sir, I wouldn't start from this point'.

There is no doubt that if I had had more control over things then the business would have had a lot more authoritarian managing director. We lost time, and too many decisions were fudged, because there was a lack of true vision. For a long time I was seen as the person behind the managing director in terms of driving the business forward. I had a reputation for being a young Turk within the company, driving the vision, and I think that is desperately important. You must have someone who really clearly understands where you want to get to and they are very focused on doing that. You don't have to be a complete barbarian and slash and burn all those who don't adhere to that, but if you start to sort of waver when you are trying to do radical change then what it does is to destroy the confidence of those around you.

If you are in a situation where you think there is agreement about the direction that is trying to be achieved, and you heard a very firm assurance from the managing director that that is what was going to happen, and then the next thing you heard was that someone else has been to talk to him and there is a shift, it makes other people's (including mine) lives more difficult. You agree what is going to be done and then you're told: 'So and so has spoken to me and I understand their concerns'.... In the end you have to decide what you are going to do and just drive it through.

The truth is that things do happen to cause you to change your strategy or to modify the objective you are trying to get to, but I still believe that the most successful projects I have seen are those where there is somebody who has a very clear idea of what he is trying to achieve and the task or concept is sufficiently discrete that they can wrap their arms around it. Where you have a set of ideas that are embodied and understood by a number of people, where there is no single focus, it is very difficult to drive that through. If you were going to say that 'In 18 months I will put this business back on the map, I will change the technology, I will change the management, I will change the culture and at the same time I will double in size through acquisition' and you lack clarity in what you are doing, God help you.

I think there has been a lot of reasonable luck in the way that the programme has progressed. It sounds a bit negative, and it's not intended to be, it's more reflecting my frustration at some of the detours we have gone down. The business today is well positioned for where it wants to move to. We are through the worst of the merger issues. The technology development will be ongoing.

If you accept technology is part of the business then it is wrong to think of technology in project terms; you need to think of it in terms of an ongoing expense. It is really part of the infrastructure you need to continue investing in.

We met probably 70 to 80 per cent of the objectives that we set out to meet. We have certainly convinced the customer base that we are serious about the business, both in the technology investment and the acquisition of the other business. We are certainly well positioned to be a very significant force in the custody market.

I am not sure that we got the cultural change firmly embedded. I think the problem is that it really does require commitment from the business to deal with issues of IT, to be on terms with those issues. If they don't make that commitment to understanding those issues then you have problems. I think also people understand the more traditional developmental approaches. If you went and spoke to the managing director I am pretty certain he'd say we are into rapid application development, he'll talk about open systems and Oracle, Unix and all of those good things. But I don't believe I was fully successful at driving in the culture that I wanted within the IT department, which was to say, 'We are very much part of and a service to the business, and what we want is for the business to take control and ownership'.

There are things that only an IT department can do. But an IT department should not, in my view, be making business decisions, which is typically what happens with traditional applications development. The analysts and the programmer will believe they understand the issues better than the business person, and if I am brutally honest, often they do. IT seems to attract, by and large, reasonably intelligent people. The problem is not that their logic is weaker than the business person's, because often it is not, but it is not them that will be operating the system to be delivering the business service. It is quite hard to get the IT staff to accept that it is not their responsibility to make those decisions for the business person. By all means tell them where you think it should be better, but in the end it is the business person that has to operate the system. If he wants to do things in a particular way, it really isn't appropriate for IT to tell them otherwise. And that was a very difficult message to get to stick within the IT department.

The better analysts and programmers are very prone to dismissing business people, especially where they are less lucid or less intellectually gifted than they are. The business people do find dealing with some of the IT staff clearly makes their head hurt. They also found that this authority/responsibility issue is a difficult one, because they very much want the authority to tell IT what to do, but they don't want responsibility for the consequences of those decisions. They want someone else to hold it, so they are absolved from those decisions. The person who has been brought in to replace me has come from a traditional structured environment.

What factors helped you, or prevented you, in trying to get across your message to the IT staff?
While we were doing BPR, while we were trying to get the thing to stick, it was driving us nuts because you'd call the development team together and you would explain what was going to happen. And it wasn't me just standing up and lecturing. There were a number of people involved in saying 'This is what we want to happen'. You would get everyone to agree 'Yes, being able to sit down with a user and show him/her what you are building and get him/her to critique it was the best communication medium'. But, as soon as you turned your back, IT people were making design decisions without reference to the users. And it didn't matter that you could sit there with them and you knew that intellectually they had bought into the fact that yes, the very best

thing to do was to show the user what they are building; I could guarantee to you that we'd have 10 people in there, and that afternoon you could walk around and you would say to them 'Why have you done that?' Old habits die hard.

When I was trying to drive this I said something to the managing director along the lines of 'We are trying to radically change the way we build systems. The business has been focused on the waterfall approach; we are trying to pick up rapid application development technology, building workflow. We are doing lots of things that haven't been done before in the company. Therefore what we want are people who are coming to this without too many preconceptions'. My view, at that point, was that youngsters and people who had done a computer science degree would be the right people to move it forward. Funnily enough, some of the biggest problems we have had have been with people who are computer science graduates, who spent three years learning an academic way of viewing things or developing a view.

I don't know why it took some people so long to get on terms with it. I don't know how you can go from a situation where there is certainly academic agreement that rapid application, iterative protocycling is a good thing, and yes, we want user buying and yes, we want to deliver something that the user wants, and in a very short space of time it's 'Yes but *I* thought it would be better this way'. Great, I love the fact that you are using your mind, but come on: have you asked the user? And so many times we would see this blow up, where the user who had been involved in the particular development section would be presented with the 'improved' version that hadn't been referred to him and he'd say 'I don't want it that way, I want it the way I said I wanted it'. And the developer would say 'I thought this would be better' and then the user would say, 'Well, yes, but the problem is... I get this instruction in from the customer and this is what I need to do'.

We had a project manager in from a software house, and after he left the project we never really replaced him, so I ended up with the fairly peculiar situation that I didn't actually have a technical project manager. What I had were a number of sub-sets, each with their own team leader or manager, but nobody between me and the project who had overall responsibility. In a sense we should have filled that gap, and again events intruded, because I resigned but agreed I would remain with the division until they found a replacement.

Once I had resigned it clearly changed the complexion of my relationship with the organization, notwithstanding that I was doing the same role. And although I asked for it, because they were looking for my replacement and they thought it would not take the time it did, they never got round to filling the post of project manager. Obviously my replacement would like to select that person. So that caused some particular problems.

The previous project manager had been very good at communicating the rapid applications development message. He was very messianic about the way to do it. One of the contractors on the project came to the fore somewhat at that point and we started to use him almost as a project office role. His background was in traditional IT methodology and he and I had quite a few fairly heated discussions, but I said to him eventually, 'If you want to try to traditionalize this you have a go'. He had three months when he tried to do that, and he came back and said, 'You are absolutely right: we need to go back to your model – let's bring together the business and the IT, let's go through the iterative protocycle'. To some extent I think that process was more effective in driving through change in culture within IT, allowing them to try to go back for a while. But the situation that they have reached now is that they have certainly brought in someone with a more traditional view of IT development than myself. And the superstructure they are putting round IT is making it much more a discrete entity rather than a business department. But they are still using the same technology; the principles of building teams and involving representatives from the business are still in place, and who knows, maybe that is a better mechanism? What is certain is that we made very rapid progress in terms of application development.

With hindsight what would you have done differently?
I'd certainly spend more time looking for people. I think in the end, in my desperation to get resource in, to get the project going, I made some very weak decisions in terms of the managers I brought on board. The overall effect of that was to lose time for the project.

You need to have a group of people who will play as a team, and I didn't pick individuals who were team players – not true team players in a management sense. The reason I say that is that if you are trying to move things forward really quickly then you have to have people who will play to and with each other and will essentially stand guard, guard each other's backs. You are taking a lot of risks, you are trying a lot of different things to find which way works. So I think the team characteristic is very important in terms of the management group. The flexibility of approach is absolutely vital.

What I found with this almost experimental approach, where we were trying to find out 'How do you make these technologies such as "rapid applications development", an effective methodology? How do you deal with workflow? How do you really address client–server development?' is that you need to get people who enjoy dealing with that, for whom trying something is exciting, not people who are scared of the consequences. The team I put together had typical banking people characteristics. It was the attitude 'It's not my fault'. I brought in a senior manager from the business to run the business analysis side and he was quite older than the other managers, and his focus was 'All I want to do is get to 50 – to make sure that I won't do anything that will prejudice my getting to 50, because if get to that then I can get an early pension'. I brought in a young guy who had worked as a team leader on a project I'd managed some time ago and he just didn't make the transition to management. His forte was to be sat at a PC playing, and if that happened to coincide with a delivery the bank required then that was great, but the guy was unmanageable: refused to accept direction, really wasn't effective in managing other people, let alone maintaining focus on what he did. And yet I had great hopes because he had been a great asset on the previous project. And it's quite pleasant to see guys that you have worked with developing and coming through. The final person I recruited I pretty well lost from the project, because I looked round to see who do I trust that I could put into the acquired business to keep an eye on their technology while we are trying to get the project here sorted out, so he came in and went out. But he has actually proved to be about the most effective of the management team.

But I would forgive them all their faults if they'd actually fought together as a team, but what they have done mostly is to spend their time making life difficult for each other. So I think John Donovan talks about the need to deal with the culture change issues when you are trying to change your technology development, in 'Re-engineering the business with IT'. But in it he talks about the fact that there is a cultural dimension to this. If I were going to do this again I would love to have a proven team that I could bring in rather than abstract individuals that I am trying to force in against all the other aspects. I think it is very hard when you are trying to break new ground with technology to bring people in and force them to operate as a team. Sometimes it works, but not as well as I would have liked in this instance.

If you have got a team that have got the right technical credentials and have that flexibility of approach and preparedness to make things work. I think this is an empirical approach to applications development. People want applications development to be a science, particularly in the business: they want it to be absolutely bloody predictable. This money, this time, defined output – and it just isn't. It's only going to be that if all the components you are using are prefabricated. People talk about how quickly technology is changing and it is. It's come on leaps and bounds since I entered the technology arena. And yet people don't realize that has an impact in terms of the way you plan things, so there is a very wide margin of error in the planning you do for this process.

I still believe that overall there are significant business benefits from 'rapid applications development'. One is that you get component deliveries from the process, so you are not waiting until you have built pretty much the whole system. You can actually chunk it up into quite small pieces. There is much greater sense of ownership from business users in terms of what comes out. I think that part of my frustration with this is that initially we made such good progress so quickly that you start to think 'We can drive this onward and onward'. I guess I wish I'd had a little bit more time to get on terms with the technology before we started the project. But these are all luxuries, you never have that.

Every time in the future when new technologies come out you have to make the decision: 'Do I go with the old trusty proven technology or do I take a gamble and go with something which is going to yield me the greatest chances of success?'. But even then that's not a truly fair analysis. We were aware that a competitor had put a package in to support their custody and securities operation. Before they had completed implementation, they had spend tens of millions of pounds putting a system in. There was also some publicity given to another company's abandoned attempt to build a custody system at millions of dollars and two years of effort. Even where people are using traditional approaches and packages there are still risks in systems development. I keep coming back to the view that I think there is the need for focus on change within the business: how do you successfully manage the change within the business? I think also you need to have that same focus when you are involved in applications development. You must have a consistent view of what you are trying to achieve. Clearly the constancy is improved if you can deliver quickly. If you are talking about a five-year project, then the chances that any one individual will remain will be quite low. The chances the vision will remain constant in that period are very small.

REFLECTION

Different structures and different approaches can be used in the process of trying to ensure that a company's IT capability is used for servicing the business. When trying to implement significant change as to how IT is organized, what guidelines can be extracted from these two cases?

■ CHAPTER NINE ■

Unplanned change in a market research agency

The respondent for this case was an account manager in a large market research organization with a parent company in the USA. The changes brought about in her place of work were the result of an attempt to meet a rapid growth in the business. The picture painted by this individual was of a relatively unplanned series of 'coping' changes. This perceived fragmentation of changes is in marked contrast to the other cases presented.

Background

When I first joined, three years ago, it was obvious we were just starting to go through an enormous period of growth. I've got a chart here which shows you that back in 199X our turnover was £3.8m – that was just our division of the company – and this year's latest estimate is £6.2m. So to us it's been a massive increase in turnover in the last three years basically. That's had implications for us, so I thought it would be a good thing to talk about.

All the subsequent changes we have had to make have been driven by growth. It certainly wasn't planned. We have what's called an Order Book where we record all sorts of client enquiries, and the Order Book just grew. We just found we were getting more and more enquiries, with more and more clients wanting to do market research.

I don't think it was really predictable, although maybe senior management here might not agree. Maybe companies were facing greater competition – I don't know – but it suddenly just took off. I don't know that it was anything to do with the success of our company – we weren't doing anything different. It was almost like a market change that we had to respond to.

At that point we had about thirty-odd staff, which wasn't enough to get the job done. So that first year we all worked very long hours, particularly in the first two months, trying to cope with the volume coming through. It wasn't just getting the jobs done. It was constant enquiries, and having to write proposals, and do that at the same time as getting the business done. There are now 90 people in this division alone.

How would you categorize the change? As Big Bang or as incremental?

Big Bang, in the sense that it seemed to start all of a sudden. But we didn't know how long it would last so we didn't stop and think 'OK – it looks like we are going to have to deal very differently with this and we're going to have to put a lot of change in place.' In fact, for many months we weren't quite convinced it would last, although the pattern was very different from previous years. We didn't stop at that point and say let's make all these plans for managing this huge growth. It wasn't until it plateaued out a bit that we were finally convinced that it might be going to last. It has just been enormously difficult to cope with.

Of course our targets are set by our parent company and our senior management here has certainly tried to get more realistic targets set for us so that we don't have to cope with so much business as we did three years ago. And to take it a bit more easily, because it did mean all sorts of changes. There was a massive intake of new staff; having to change systems and the way we do things. A whole range of different things. We were trying to implement those changes, but cope with the running of the business at the same time. There were an awful lot of frayed tempers that year!

Our business is to make money for our parent company, and this was seen as making an enormous amount of money for them – more than we had ever done before. So they were very keen on pursuing this.

What were the knock-on effects?

It has raised some questions about how that change has affected us. Has the company changed in such a way that our clients might not want to do business with us because we've become huge and impersonal? It was fairly cosy before, very friendly, everyone knew everyone. Now it's not really like that. Our division occupies two floors and there are so many people around you don't have a clue what their names are.

This is the sort of thing staff have found very difficult to cope with. Another important factor is bringing our suppliers in on all of this. Because we had such a great increase in business it had a huge impact on the people who supply our fieldwork and data processing. And to be honest they haven't really shown the commitment we have. We've had massive problems, and that's impacted on every single person in the company at all levels. Because we all deal with suppliers and have to get them to do what we want them to do. It's been an enormous uphill battle this year – a lot of conflict with our suppliers. It's a morale issue too, because people got fed up because our suppliers weren't necessarily moving in the same direction. Even our research executives were having to hit their heads against the wall to try to get the standard of work out of our suppliers that we expected, and timing.

It's an ongoing problem. Our staff were getting so frustrated, and of course we're the ones who have to get on the phone to the client. You have to take ownership of the problem. You can't just say 'Well, our suppliers let us down'. We were always having to ring the client and say 'I'm really sorry – we've not met this deadline', and staff were feeling 'It's not my fault'. So that's been a huge issue here really.

During this period of rapid growth we have had two changes in managing director in our own division. So that's a further change on top of everything else.

It has added complications I think. The first managing director that we lost was transferred to the US part of our business. The second one was with us for about two years and she got promoted, so she is now running all the divisions. Then one of the directors was promoted to take over her role. It's been fascinating for us to watch because they had three completely different styles.

I guess that's been difficult to cope with. One gripe that's going round the company, and the directors admit this quite openly, is that over the last two to three years it's been like a boat. You know how it tilts to one side and everyone runs across that way. So the managing director says 'Right, we need everyone over on that side'. So everyone runs over and then they go 'Oops! that isn't working. Quick, back on the other side'. And that's something that everyone is quite open about. And that's come about through the changing managing directors, because they all have very different ideas, so when we get a new one we all have to run over to the other side.

Yes, very different styles in terms of commercial outlook and things. Our current managing director is very commercially aware. She is getting a lot tougher with us really. She has very high standards and expects people to be very business-focused. A few years ago it was just like working at a business school, or a University, it was like a University of Market Research – all very informal and pally. Now it's run much more like a business and everyone is aware of targets and there are no excuses.

Another thing that happened at the same time is that we got BS 5750. And that has meant putting an enormous kind of structure in place, so that probably hasn't helped things. So we were going through this enormous growth in business and having to deal with BS 5750.

What effects have these changes had on your role?

In some ways, on the surface of it, you could say it hasn't really changed my own responsibilities, because you are just expected to manage your team, and manage your clients, as you were doing before. But it's become more difficult, and a lot more thought has had to go into it.

The difficulty is that staff have constantly had to adapt to new ways of doing things. Certainly we have had to become much more efficient to get through all this work, and it's meant a lot of IT implementation and – I don't mean this in the negative sense – a lot more bureaucracy.

Whether people would say all this anguish is due to BS 5750 or it's all due to the rapid growth, I don't know. I think it's a bit of both really. And I'm sure senior management here would say that BS 5750 has helped us to cope with that enormous growth, because it means there is a common system that everyone works to. We are all busy, but we all do things in a certain way, which means someone else can step in and figure out, on a certain job, what is going on because everything is recorded, filed in a similar way, and so on.

What impact have the changes had on other staff?

Over the last two years we've constantly been asking staff to adapt to new ways of doing things, and every month there is something new we have to cope with. So it has been very difficult. There have been ripples of dissatisfaction at various times and a loss of familiarity by staff with their own company. Before this change happened it was more typical for young people to join as graduate trainees and work their way up, so we have people who had been here for some time. Once the change happened we had to bring people in at all the various levels from other companies. So staff had to cope with that as well.

I don't think people would admit it, but there is more perceived competition for promotion and things, and also the company seemed different – less personal. I wouldn't say less caring, but if management has got 90 people to cope with it's a bit different than if they've got 30, where everyone is very visible and managers are walking round every day, and they know what is happening. They know what your interests are. But if it's 90 people senior management certainly has to step back.

So there have been lots of staff implications, but luckily open communication is encouraged here and I think there is confidence that if an issue is raised, something will be done about it. So that's a very good, positive thing. We have a lot of structure in place to do that.

How has the divisional structure changed?

There are 90 of us. Not all of those are 'execs'. There are probably about 60 or 70 who work on projects on behalf of clients. It's a very American-sounding system. It's called a 'gang' system. We're broken up into these gangs and we have a gang director, who is a senior manager, and a gang leader. That's the level I'm at and you do the day-to-day management of your gang – typically a team of about eight people.

It's a bit of a weird structure, because you sit physically in your gang, and your gang leader or your director, depending on your level, looks after your well-being basically. They will do your appraisal, set pay, morale issues, that kind of thing.

But apart from that you also work in project teams which are very fluid. And you might not work on projects with anyone in your gang. You might work with outside people from other gangs. So you're not only managing people in your gang, you are also managing people in project teams. You might not actually have any people on project teams from your own gang.

The gang system is a very good way of feeding information down from on high, explaining the reasons for things, and what direction we are going to be moving in. It's also a good way of feeding the information up, and we're encouraged to do that a lot. We collect views and information and feed it upwards. So if issues are raised they do get fed into director level, and issues are dealt with in the most appropriate fashion.

We also have what's called 'State of the Nation' meetings, where our whole division gets together once a quarter and our managing director speaks to us about the last quarter and what our plans are for the next quarter. And it's often in that forum where new ideas are introduced.

The way it works here is that divisions are very autonomous. Working in specialist units almost feels like working in a separate company because we don't have that much to do with the other divisions at all.

The company has different research sectors. For example, we have automotive, IT, finance, health care, etc. But that's very fluid too. At the moment we don't really have people who sit in one sector and only do jobs in that sector. But that's increasingly the way. We feel that's what clients want – sector specialists. They want to come into this company and have someone who knows every in and out about, say, financial research, and have a great deal of experience. We do have that, but we haven't focused it into the sectors at present. So particularly at junior level you tend to work in all the different sectors. You might have six different jobs at one time. You might have an automotive job, an IT job, a health care job, a great mix of different types of work. It's only when you get to my level that you're expected to specialize in one sector or another. If you didn't want to, it wouldn't be forced upon you. But there is a view here that we are going to have to maybe start to divide ourselves up more rigidly into sectors and stick to them more than we do at present.

What other related events have taken place?
One of the things here was recognizing that we had to become better at managing projects to get through all this work. So we brought in a consultancy to do some quite intensive training in project management.

Everyone went through that – it wasn't something that managers at my level decided they should do – everyone went on that. It was two days' training. Everyone went on it because some people were not far from becoming project managers and whole project teams needed to understand the fundamentals of project management to be a good team member. It was seen as a good investment for the future really. We may have gone overboard – I don't know.

But the great thing here is that it creates a positive feeling of democracy, that things aren't just being restricted to certain levels. Everyone was encouraged to do the training.

My role, at this level, was more about explaining the need for change to staff, convincing them, encouraging them, finding out what their reactions have been.

The main objective is just convincing staff to stay in there when the going gets rough. They have been quite resistant to all these new systems.

We have had to employ a logistics manager to actually oversee our functional-type roles like typing and charting and IT/IS and the accounting part of things, and he is very good, but the only thing is he has so many ideas. It means he is constantly developing spreadsheets for us to fill in. So it has meant we now, on a weekly basis, have a work-load spreadsheet where you have to say what jobs you are on, what date you can take on more work, that type of thing. It seems like we have a new one of those at least once a month. Staff are resistant because they are busy, and they feel their priority is to give good service to our clients. You could easily spend seven or eight hours a day doing that, and it's felt that these admin tasks that we have to do – and everyone can see that at the end of the day it's for the good of the company and will mean that things do run smoothly – but you could easily spend at least another two hours a day doing spreadsheets, making sure your BS 5750 is up to date as well.

The other thing too is we have a 'recovery rate' which means you have to spend a certain number of hours on work which the company gets money for. And you are expected to recover at 100 per cent (set at five and a quarter hours a day). The feeling is that to do that you really have to concentrate on jobs, but the trouble is there are all these other systems – bureaucracy and paperwork and things that you have to do that takes you away from that. So there is a bit of conflict, to be honest, at the moment, over that issue. People over-recover, which means they only have a little tiny space in their day to get all the other things done.

That's the kind of thing that has been difficult. The logistics manager is right. We do need all these things, but it means that by Thursday lunch you've got to remember to fill in your workload sheet. By Friday you've got to have done something else. You are meant to fill in what time has been spent on each job, each day. Trying to get staff to fill that in is a problem – they leave it till the end of the month and they still haven't done it.

So that's a big issue. Trying to explain the need for systems, and convince them that it's good for the company to keep this stuff up to date.

You do that basically by talking to staff. In my own team I've got a couple of really bad offenders. They are excellent people who make a very valuable contribution, so you have to decide how tough you are going to get with them. Because you know they are very good workers and if you get too tough with them they are just as likely to say 'I'm fed up with all this bureaucracy, I'm going somewhere else'. So it's a bit of a fine balance, and sometimes I think it's better to air the issue in gang meetings and not point the finger at anyone. I just say that I have to go to directors meetings and present what our team is doing in terms of their workloads and they will see the information isn't quite up to date and I'll get a rap over the knuckles. That's been a useful way of explaining to staff, too, although maybe that's not the right way to do it. I tend to say 'Look, I've got into trouble because of this and I'm not impressed, so I need you to keep everything up to date'.

I probably agree with a lot of other staff that the priority has to be the clients. That's what we are here for so I won't let those managers draw me away from that too much. They can't see the extent of your workload all the time. You've got to be careful – this will sound critical – but we do have very different directors in this company. Some are much more internally focused than others. And some are more externally focused and see all the internal stuff as – not rubbish – but that we spend too much time on internal issues. So you've got to be a bit careful. You've got to use your judgement. I tend to think 'Is this one of those internally focused people?'. If so, I'll whip upstairs very quickly and I won't spend more time than 10 minutes – and I'll get myself out.

You certainly have to manage them. That was a real point of conflict here earlier this year, because there was a definite division between people who, some felt, were too internally focused and wanted to get all the systems right within the company, and others felt that it was taking too much time away which should have been spent with clients. There was a bit of a watershed over that one, and the people who were externally focused had their way pretty much, and it came down from on high that all of us had to withdraw slightly from an internal focus.

What more can you say about the management structure?
I have a manager who is a director, and he sits in the gang too. He's great, and we spend quite a lot of time talking about things. It can be difficult in that you've got *that* manager, who's responsible for your appraisal and so on, but you've also got, on the projects you work on for clients, project directors. Sometimes you feel like you've got seven different bosses, because you've got your gang boss but you've also got seven project directors who you're answerable to. Often it's difficult because everyone is making different demands on you and your time, and you're having to figure out who has got priority and so on. But people are fairly understanding.

To cope with the changes, several of us had taken initiatives in our sectors. For instance, to help us cope with the health care work coming in, and to put a good sector team together, we had to educate ourselves about the kind of issues within our sector and so on. That meant meeting together, so we decided we were going meet once a month and spend an hour and a half doing that. Well, it was a bit of a problem because people in all the other sectors felt they should meet as well, so all senior managers could see was a whole series of internal meetings. There were even examples where staff said they couldn't go to a client meeting because they had one of these internal sector meetings. So the externally focused people here were just horrified and really fought very strongly for staff to be withdrawn somewhat from those internally focused activities.

It hurt, because we all thought it was a good initiative. Many of us had been struggling in our sectors anyway because we weren't very sector-focused, so the meetings were very helpful. Suddenly we felt we knew what we were doing. Next minute we were being told 'Sorry, you can't meet monthly, you will have to meet every second month'.

This leads onto another responsibility at my level. It's up to us a lot of the time to explain those decisions and justify them. But it's very difficult because half the time I identify with the people below. I've only been a people manager since March, so I'm still quite fresh, I'm still thinking of managers as them rather than us. It's pretty good here, but there is a feeling that directors take the decisions which just get passed down to us. We are the ones who have to implement them, and explain it to everyone, without having been consulted.

But generally it's pretty good. We get a bit stroppy if that happens and tell them that we expect to be involved.

And there is the feeling too that we could be trusted a little more. That there are decisions which could be delegated to our level – that managers at my level could decide and take care of.

It's become a lot more formal since we've got bigger. The hierarchy has become more entrenched. Whether that's a good thing, I don't know.

Before the change it all worked quite well. There were very good relationships between the gang leader and the gang director, and we were all just managing the gang between us. But it was decided that this two-level division should be rigidly enforced, so you could only really manage people who were two levels or more below you. That caused a fair bit of friction too. Something so formal – even a lot of the gang directors resisted that. It had been working fine, and apart from appraisals and setting pay, everything else could be done flexibly.

Because you are dealing with clients a lot of the time it was important to staff to feel they had someone they could go to. Although I must admit, in our gang, and certainly in a few others, everything apart from appraisals and pay is pretty much my responsibility because the gang director doesn't really want to get involved in day-to-day issues.

He's very good, even with someone who is at the same level. If there is a major crisis he will consult me and keep me informed, which the managing director probably wouldn't be happy about.

Another problem which occurred earlier in the year was over these 'State of the Nation' meetings we have once a quarter. What had been happening was that all the directors – we have eight or nine of them – would all get up and say their piece. The problem was that staff were getting conflicting messages and the staff below us were saying 'What on earth are we meant to be doing?'.

So we were feeding this confusion back and it was decided then that just one person would make a presentation. So the managing director now has decided she will present 'State of the Nation' and there will only be one clear message.

What key competences and personal qualities were needed during these changes?

We need to be as open as we can be with staff. They are bright people who are not going to be fobbed off very easily. I have tried to respect that as much as possible and give them a full explanation rather saying 'This is what we are going to be doing'.

We are probably not building as much consensus as we should. I don't know whether there ought to be this very strong direction from the top, or whether we should all agree on a course of action.

My own philosophy has been to keep staff informed, to try to prepare them and to take note of their fears and worries. The guy I manage the gang with is very good at that and we have tried to build up a very good relationship with staff so that they trust us and could come to us with any kind of concern. We go to great lengths to have gang meetings. They are very much an open, sharing, type of situation where people don't fear something will be held against them, or that we will immediately go and run and tell someone what they have said.

Meetings are once a month, although we do it more often if there is something that needs to be discussed. What most gangs do is just come into the director's office and sit there. But it feels so formal, and what we were finding is that staff would sit there and not say anything. So in our gang we take them outside the company. During the summer we used to go to the park with a couple of bottles of champagne. That's a great way of learning how staff really feel – after they have had a couple of drinks! So we always have alcohol involved. They relax and feel they can start to talk. Maybe that's being manipulative, but I do feel they need to be in a relaxed environment if they're going to be open and honest about their feelings.

Also, because I am relatively new to them as well, I had to build up trust, and I hope I have achieved that now. We have a good relationship, very open.

How can managers promote or inhibit change?

Example helps. You really have to be careful about that. Even though you may not be enthusiastic about half of the changes, you have to be seen to be doing them. So obviously you have to be completely up to date, and meticulous in your own efforts, and make sure you are keeping to BS 5750, because you can hardly ask your staff to make sure they have everything up to date if you don't yourself.

Perhaps I haven't done that well enough. I have had this difficulty, and still have, of identifying very strongly with the people beneath me and not always being convinced of the need for some of these changes. I probably haven't been as good as I should have been at hiding my own views on things and pushing the company line as well as I could have. But then, because they are such good people in the team, they would spot that a mile off anyway.

There's not a great love of BS 5750 in the company, certainly at our level. We can see the justification for bits of it, but other bits, no.

The other thing to do is get advice. There have been situations where I have felt out of my depth and it's important to get some advice and talk it through before you actually do something. So I would always encourage people to do that.

The other thing I haven't done enough of this year is to interrogate senior management – to ask more questions about why procedures are necessary. You could do a better job then of selling to the staff. Senior management isn't always right either, and perhaps there isn't enough consultation among people at our level before things are decided upon. Asking more questions would mean I could do a better job, because I would understand why change was necessary and could convince staff it was a good thing.

I have been struggling a bit this year in seeing what the benefits for the business really are and being able to clearly communicate those to staff. Maybe I'll go for that next year!

Is there anything you would have done differently?
I would definitely have spent more time with the staff. And maybe pushed for more structured implementation of the changes. Maybe if we had a more formal timetable and a clear strategy for staff to understand. 'This year we are going to focus on IT... and these are the changes that will be involved'.

For example, a formal manual for managing staff has just come out – all these things have just landed on people's desks – this huge manual of rules about how much leave you can take, and so on, and no one has really read it yet because no one has had the time. If they had been able to say, at the start of the year 'There will be a Personnel Manual issued in June' and put a timetable together, we would be expecting it.

If there were more planned implementation of these changes, then you would have more time to prepare staff, and they would know what is ahead of them. For all we know, there could be all kinds of changes planned for the next month that we have no idea about at the moment. A contributory problem here is that within the company we have function groups, called something like People/Personnel. They just take decisions on issues. They decided they were going to put this manual together, but it wasn't until they had almost completed it that anyone knew they were even bringing it out.

So a master-plan of change, and better communications about what people are doing, are examples of ways change could have been carried out differently.

It could then perhaps be fitted in with workflow a bit more. We definitely do have busy periods, and perhaps implementation of any change could be avoided during those periods. Typically the first quarter is more relaxed, so that would be an ideal time to give staff a chance to get used to doing new things.

If we had a plan at least a month in advance, we could start to prepare staff and explain a bit about it.

The other thing we probably don't do enough of is convincing them that it will make their working day easier. It's never really sold to them like that. We say it's for the good of the company so that we can have more management information and manage the company more effectively. It should be sold as a benefit to them.

The other thing we haven't probably done enough of is to talk to outside people. All of the solutions have been developed in-house and we haven't gone outside to see if it really is the best way of doing things.

How do staff respond to change?

Better now than they did. About three months ago there was a dip in morale and we were picking up from everywhere that people were not happy. They couldn't really articulate what the problem was; there was just a lot of dissatisfaction. I think part of it was this constantly having to cope with BS 5750, very long hours, and always new systems. Also our logistics manager is fairly unforgiving of anyone who misses deadlines. Even if you have clients who have deadlines and you have to deliver a presentation, we have our internal people saying 'but you haven't filled in that form'. But I'm thinking 'Look my presentation is a priority here'. I think that was causing a lot of problems for people – that internal issues were seeming to have priority. They were thinking 'No – that's wrong. It's my clients who have priority'.

There's a whole lot of issues tied up in that but it came to a bit of a head. I think that's when senior management started communicating a bit more clearly, and feeling that they had to justify things. The staff were saying 'Enough is enough. We don't know what's going on. We can't cope with any more. Just give us a little bit of breathing space'. It seems to have settled down certainly.

But they are very good. The staff are great. They accept it all although you can tell they are not completely happy about it and just don't know when they are going to get the time to learn all these new things, or to go on the training. But basically they accept it and see that it would not need to be done unless it was really necessary. We probably could do more in terms of reassuring them that there is a good reason for things and that there is an overall strategy behind it – and that it is going to get us somewhere really positive.

What other matters would you like to raise regarding change?
We haven't been managing it in a formal way. Because I know when I was at business school, as part of a course we had a little bit on change management and it seemed be that great planning went into it. It was implemented over time and they had teams that were responsible for implementing this change.

That's not something we've done here. Part of the problem was that we weren't even sure if we were in change and whether it was going to last. But maybe we should have stepped back after three months and said 'Right – we have got a situation here that is going to require lots of changes – staff changes, new systems in place – what's the best way of doing this?'. Instead, we have really tackled it on a task-by-task basis and haven't put all these things together to make sure they are really getting us to where we want to be.

And the responsibility for getting these changes implemented has been so fragmented as well. No one person has had overall responsibility. I suppose ultimately it was the managing director, but we will have a director here who is responsible for deciding what we are going to do in the personnel area; we will have a director over there who is managing what's happening in the IT side of things. I'm not even sure that they even come together. So I still don't think we are getting it right to be honest.

Our managing director before last was struggling. She openly admitted 'What do I do? How do I cope with this?'. We have a newsletter that goes out to clients we put a little bit in the newsletter saying we are undergoing quite considerable change and growth. Are there any client companies out there who have been through the same thing who can help us? Well, no one actually got in touch, but it was a little bit of a cry for help.

I don't know how much support our senior management here got – probably not enough, from our parent company even. We were very much left to our own devices.

Whose responsibility should it be?
The Managing Director's ultimately. Obviously they can't do it all themselves, but if they had a clear idea of how it was going to be managed and who would be involved and how it was going to be communicated to

staff. And if they could identify what kind of external assistance is needed to do that.... Someone should have had a master plan in mind really. Maybe I'm being unfair, but I think it would be openly admitted here that we did struggle with it and still struggling now.

Any difference in attitudes between people who had been here for a while and newcomers?

I think it's been most difficult for the people who've been here a long time. Because when you move to a new company you know you are going to have to cope with an enormous amount of change. Things are going to be done differently. A lot of people who came in thought that was what it was going to be like from day one – a bit chaotic – very long hours. They just thought that was the kind of the company they had joined. And they were all warned at their interviews that there would be long hours and we expected total commitment.... But for the people who had been here for ages it was a bit of a rude shock, because they kept thinking back to the more relaxed, personal, friendly, almost university-type days, and they just couldn't believe it – hours increased, new systems, the people, where were all these people coming from? That was quite an issue – part of the crisis in morale. The people who had been here for some time resented all this stuff and wanted to get back to the good old days.

They have gone through that now, and have had to accept it. And the new managing director wouldn't take any silliness over anything. They have realized they have to get on with it or they have to get out. So that's helped as well.

In your experience, has the task of management changed in recent years?

Companies are aware that they really have to compete very strongly, so you need to be open to new ideas constantly and new ways of doing things, and you need to be able to move fast and react fast. Also, customers are becoming more demanding, so you have to react in a different way. So it means managing differently and more effectively. I think the management task is becoming more difficult over time, more complex.

It's odd that when you contacted me and said this was about change management, I thought 'Change? What change have we had here?'.

REFLECTION

What lessons can you learn from this case relating to the implementation of change?

PART THREE

Conceptualizing experiences of self and others

CHAPTER TEN

Developing a personal model for implementing change

This chapter presents a developmental process leading to a model that reflects the critical beliefs of one of the authors with respect to implementing successful change. It is the result of an exercise making sense of four sources of information: the knowledge embedded in the experiences recounted in the 15 preceding case histories; knowledge derived from personal experiences accumulated over many years; knowledge acquired from a study of the relevant literature; and knowledge gained from discussions with co-authors at various stages in the development of the model. An analytical outline of model building is followed by a more dynamic examination in terms of two of the cases.

You may recall that in Chapter 2 we outlined a procedure for using the case histories in this volume for learning to implement successful change. This process of active learning will have made you more aware of the mental models that are likely to influence your thinking and behaviour. The exercise in model building is a way of getting you to draw together, and to assimilate, four sources of knowledge with the intention of modifying and refining some of the beliefs underlying your mental models. The four sources of knowledge are:

1 Experiences of other managers (via the cases) in implementing change
2 Your own experiences in implementing change
3 Your knowledge of the relevant literature
4 Experiences and comments of others (e.g. fellow learners) with whom you exchange ideas

In this chapter we outline an example of the process of active learning we recommended others to follow. It is based on the 'diary' of one of the authors. The resulting model is elaborated and justified. The need to explore further some of the topics identified is highlighted. Two of the cases will then be compared and contrasted in terms of the model in order to gauge its usefulness.

How did we build an explicit personal model?

Three distinct stages can be identified.

Stage 1

A qualitative analysis of each of the first nine case histories completed was carried out. This involved asking oneself three questions:

- What is the primary challenge that the changes were intended to meet?
- What challenges were encountered in implementing change (i.e. the things that had to be done which were difficult)?
- What were the responses made to these challenges and the assumptions underlying these responses?

As a result of this analysis the researcher arrived at five sets of interdependent variables that promised to serve as a fruitful framework for drawing out the insights to be learnt from the cases, and for relating these to available knowledge. The results were summarized in a five-sided figure, and a brief explanatory text. This 'output' was circulated to the other two co-author researchers before a meeting at which the independent efforts of all three were to be discussed.

Stage 2

At the meeting a number of insights were gained as a result of the constructive and critical comments made. They included: the key points were not successfully being made by the model; one of the sets of factors was being given equal weight to others when in fact it was less relevant, and indeed was in danger of being a distraction; and another set of factors was the main finding of the analysis, and therefore should be given more prominence. The researcher re-examined the model in the light of the interactions which had taken place in time for a further meeting a few days later at which a fourth member of the team was also present. The interactions that took place at this meeting helped to strengthen the model as a learning tool.

FIGURE 10.1: A model for understanding the dynamics of implementing change.

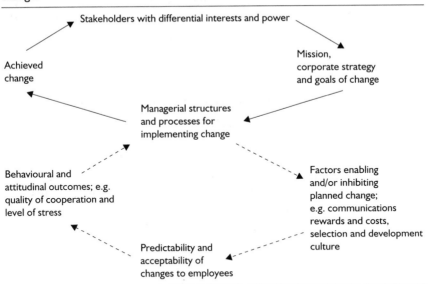

Stage 3

In the light of Stage 2 learning, and the analysis of a further six completed case histories, the main features of the model in Figure 10.1 were arrived at. This is the model that we feel answers the questions posed toward the end of Chapter 2, is consistent with the personal experiences of most managers, reflects the information contained in the cases, and is likely to receive strong support from the relevant literature.

This iterative process of model development is one which we are advocating for incorporating into programmes aimed at helping managers and potential managers to learn about implementing change. It involves the critical steps of making sense of the experiences of others as well as your own, of testing the results out with a peer group, and of revising your conceptual model in the light of new learning. This learning process is one that individuals will undergo anyway. The approach we are proposing is more planned, systematic and concentrated. Important elements in this approach to learning have already been covered, e.g. active learning, feedback, new ideas and different ways of looking at the same phenomena, and so on. The elegance or completeness of the final model is not the most valuable outcome. The real value comes from the learning involved in arriving at this end result, i.e. an understanding of the reasons why some factors are more important than others, why some relationships are more likely to hold than others, and why some factors appear to be important in some situations but not others. The visual model helps to facilitate and to consolidate learning by forcing one to identify key variables and to make explicit the relationships between the variables.

A proposed model for understanding the dynamics of implementing successful change

A wealth of ideas and beliefs are embedded in this model. Its seven elements and relationships require elaboration. The first thing to note is the differentiation between the upper and lower sets of elements. The upper set represents our beliefs about the context in which organizational change takes place. The lower set is a representation of our beliefs about the consequences of using different structures and processes in implementing change.

Stakeholders with differential interests and power

The idea that one needs to recognize the interests of multiple stakeholders in an organization is now generally accepted (Mitchell *et al.*, 1997; Royal Society of Arts, 1995). They may include parent companies, shareholders, employees, suppliers, customers, the local community and so on. However, some stakeholders will have greater interest in an organization than others, and some may have more power to determine what happens to the organization. The power of stakeholders becomes very visible in organizational change. Thus in the case 'Restructuring in a processing plant' the parent company determined that certain changes had to be introduced in order to squeeze more profits out of a product in a declining market. Similarly, in 'Downsizing and outsourcing in an oil refinery' the parent company had decided that if they were to remain in the refinery business then costs had to be reduced. The forces for change were somewhat less decisive and powerful in 'Restructuring support services in a partnership', where much of the initiative rested with the new role of the personnel manager, rather than the majority of partners who held the reins of power. In 'Implementing strategic change in a charity' the impetus for change was even more dependent upon the initiative of the newly appointed CEO. A programme of major change requires powerful sponsors, and this almost certainly means that it will be initiated by the owners or those acting on behalf of the owners (e.g. CEO and top management team).

Employee stakeholders (all those on the company payroll) are the group we are focusing on in this model. It is probably true to say that in all 15 cases the general body of employees were not seeking change – at any rate not the changes that the top management team saw as necessary. This observation is true for most major changes being introduced today, and has important consequences for certain other elements in the model, particularly for 'Managerial structures and processes for implementing change'.

Mission, corporate strategy and goals of change

This is the element that provides the *raison d'être* for change within the organization. The actual changes an organization attempts to introduce are a consequence of the agreed mission and the preferred strategy for achieving it. The adjective 'agreed' is used purposefully, because a mission that is not approved, at least by those with power, has little significance. The adjective 'preferred' is also used intentionally, because there is always a choice in the way in which a mission is achieved. In our 15 cases the mission element was more likely to surface at interview if the respondent was a senior rather than a middle manager. Thus it was highlighted in 'Merger and reorganization in a health authority', where the project director for the change process was being interviewed, and in 'Implementing strategic change in a charity', where the CEO was the respondent. It was not mentioned in most of the other cases, e.g. 'Restructuring support services in a partnership', where the respondent was the personnel manager, and 'Unplanned change in a market research agency', where an account manager in a market research organization was the respondent. Corporate strategy, on the other hand, was mentioned by all respondents, as were the targets of change, since they were involved in the process of implementation. Targets of change included: the organizational mission and strategy (e.g. 'Implementing strategic change in a charity'), structure (e.g. 'Downsizing and outsourcing in an oil refinery'), culture (e.g. 'Helping the IT function adopt a customer focus'), people (e.g. 'Work reorganization in the back office of an insurance broker'), and technology covering both management techniques and equipment such as computers (e.g. 'Compulsory competitive tendering in the housing department of a local authority').

Although the primary target of change may be strategy, structure, technology or culture, in reality a change to any of these factors has repercussions on all the others. This finding is encapsulated in the systems frameworks made popular by various students of organizations; e.g. Leavitt (1965), Katz and Kahn (1978) and Senge (1990).

Managerial structures and processes for implementing change

In the 15 cases a wide variety of structures and processes were present. These were more obvious where the change process was carefully planned, managed and controlled (i.e. clear targets and methods, and clear criteria for evaluating change). Falling in this category was the case 'Downsizing and outsourcing in an oil refinery', where a three-person team was formed to design and implement a programme that would meet the set objectives. A similar planned approach is evident in 'Integration following a takeover in the retail industry', 'Merging two management consultancy units', 'Planned organization-wide change in an office equipment manufacturer', and 'Implementing strategic change in a charity'. In the cases where planning was less pronounced the goals of change were less well defined, and therefore the process outputs less measurable (e.g. 'Unplanned change in a market research agency'), and also an appropriate sequence of activities was less likely to be followed. An example of the latter was 'Restructuring in a processing plant', where changes were rushed through without training individuals for the skills they would be needing in their new role. The result was that some of the changes had to be temporarily reversed.

Achieved change

All major stakeholders in an organization are interested in what changes have taken place or are taking place, and whether these changes are functional or dysfunctional to their interests. Those that perceive the changes to be functional to their interests will wield what power they have to reinforce the changes. Those who perceive the changes to be dysfunctional to their interests will resist the changes or introduce counter changes if they feel they have the necessary power. So the iterative process continues with consequences for other elements in the model.

The most challenging problem in managing change

Most managers and consultants will agree with the statement that deciding why changes need to be made, and what needs to be changed, are not the worrying problems; the worrying problem lies in the implementation of change. There are two good reasons for this:

1   Implementation is a process that spreads out over time. Even when there are visible signs that change is occurring, such as in 'Downsizing and outsourcing in an oil refinery', where a partnering relationship with a single contractor was entered into, there is still a long delay before one can ascertain whether these changes are resulting in the anticipated efficiency. Delayed feedback of this nature, which is common in complex social systems, puts additional pressure on powerful stakeholders to continue convincing other stakeholders that the right path has been followed and that the predicted rewards are about to be realized. Also, successful implementation requires the continual sponsorship of a powerful stakeholder so that the barriers that inevitably do occur can be removed or lowered. The difficulty is that individuals are relocated or resign, or their priorities change as they adapt to new circumstances. The longer implementation takes the greater the probability that something like this will happen! A good example of this is 'Work reorganization in the back office of an insurance broker', where there was a return to the original structure once the sponsoring manager had left.

2   The stakeholders who initiate or plan major changes are rarely those whose jobs are affected by these changes. Thus in 'Market testing in central government' the head of a central government agency service department had to introduce changes to compete for work against the private sector because it was government policy to do so, and because the discrete nature of his department lent itself to this experiment. In 'Unplanned change in a market research agency' the account manager who was having to change the way in which her team operated, was required to do so because of the phenomenal growth in client business which had been approved by top management. In 'Merger and reorganization in a health authority' the changes were largely imposed by government legislation. In contrast, we find that in 'Implementing strategic change in a charity', although the new CEO was recruited in order to give direction to the charity (he had already proved himself in this task in another setting) the power and authority invested in his role allowed him a fairly free hand in giving direction and in determining how change should be implemented.

It is because of this differentiation of roles (i.e. the changer and the changee) that many difficulties arise in implementing change. Those who are in a position to let changes pass them by, or who have the power to manipulate the changes to enhance and to protect their interests, are less worried by change. The difficulties surface among those who have something to lose (e.g. status, pay, job), and/or something to give (e.g. expert knowledge based on practical experience), but little power and control over what they lose or what they give. This is made worse when they do not understand the reasons for the change and are not 'in on the plans' for change. Such circumstances lead to a climate of uncertainty and low self-esteem, resistance to change and low commitment.

These observations are the context for the lower set of four elements in Figure 10.1. This part of the model is reflecting our belief that employee stakeholders who perceive the changes to be 'predictable' and 'acceptable' will have a higher positive attitude toward the changes than those who do not. This positive attitude will show itself in better cooperation and commitment (and thus lower resistance to change) and lower levels of stress. Despite the extensive literature on the enabling and inhibiting factors in organizational change, there are still too many examples where uncooperative attitudes and behaviours have prevented the intended consequences of change being achieved. The adverse emotional effects of stress may not be so obvious, partly because individuals differ in their ability to cope with stressful situations. But in general the costs can be high in terms of quality of decision making, errors, absenteeism and sick leave (see Chapter 13).

The critical question we must now pose is what features of 'Managerial structures and processes for implementing change' will result in a more favourable sequence of events?

Behavioural and attitudinal outcomes

The managerial structures and processes adopted are intended to lead to cooperative behaviours and attitudes necessary for successful implementation to occur, and to limit the levels of employee stress. We shall see in Chapters 12 and 13 that 'cooperation' and 'stress' are two concepts that can be considerably enriched by the theoretical literature; their multiple meanings will be further explored in these chapters.

Predictability and acceptability of changes to employees

Individuals who understand the why, what, when and how of changes to be made will feel more confident in predicting the consequences of change. The positive effect of this will be a reduction in the level of uncertainty, but may have limited impact on the acceptability of the change. The main vehicles for influencing the predictability factor are learning opportunities, advanced planning and clear goals. This high-lights the importance of good communications. The very minimum and least effective are such one-way media as memoranda and company newsletters. More effective will be the face-to-face briefing meetings that allow questions and answers. The most effective is to allow direct participation (of those likely to be affected by change) in the decision-making processes accompanying change – it is only here that a deeper understanding of the changes and their consequences are likely to be learned. Unfortunately, given the size, the hierarchical structure, the multiple stakeholders and the strategy behind many change programmes, the participative pathway is an ideal rather than reality. The compromise solutions available in helping employees learn about impending change mean that significant care has to be devoted to this activity. A very good example where this was done was in the case 'Implementing strategic change in a charity', where multiple channels of communication were used including the CEO and the Council Chairman touring the various locations to speak to staff and to answer their questions.

In planning how to go about creating learning opportunities it should be born in mind that the principles of adult learning outlined in Chapters 1 and 2 apply just as much in this context as in 'classroom' learning.

'Acceptability' refers to the motivational consequences of the changes. Clearly, if the consequences of change are seen as promotion and the opportunity to earn a higher salary, the chances are that the acceptability factor will be high. Note we say 'the chances are' rather than 'will be' in order to cater for the existence of individual differences. Some individuals may have a high need to achieve that is compatible with a more responsible and challenging job; for others, job security or social relationships at work may be paramount. The latter may value belonging to a closely knit team, and may not welcome any change (such as the implementation of an individually based performance-related pay scheme) that threatens its unity.

It is an individual's perception of the balance between the rewards and costs (in their broadest sense) of change that will determine their level of acceptability. There are situations where the consequences of change are predictable and initially unacceptable, such as when individuals face redundancy. Good employers will try to sweeten the redundancy package by offering counselling, an attractive financial settlement and help in finding another job. Such 'caring' measures not only sweeten the pill of redundancy, but also they have a positive effect on the morale and stress levels of those who remain in employment. It would seem that the latter group may experience guilt at being treated more favourably than some of their colleagues.

Chapter 13 will elaborate the rewards and costs that accompany change. Suffice it to say here that there are a wide variety of situations that employees can experience as rewarding. Some are under the control of individuals, such as when we satisfactorily complete a task set by ourselves. Others are very much under the control of their managers, such as when they recommend us for a pay increase following outstanding performance. Rewards and costs are potentially powerful tools for influencing behaviour in times of change. Whether they act as such in a given situation will depend upon how closely they are related in the minds of employees to targeted behaviours. So this is another area where knowledge of learning comes to be extremely useful.

Individuals differ in terms of competencies and abilities as well as motivations. Any significant change will involve the movement of individuals up, sideways and down as well as out of the organization. When implementing change successfully it is important that those who are promoted should be for reasons of ability, competence and their potential role in modelling. The relevance of modelling derives from our discussion of it in Chapter 2 – it is one of the more powerful methods through which people learn in social situations. Careful selection needs to be accompanied by appropriate development when individuals are experiencing role transition. Over time, individuals develop beliefs about their self-efficacy. The foremost authority in this area of knowledge defines the concept as: 'People guide their lives by their beliefs of personal efficacy. Perceived self-efficacy refers to beliefs in one's capabilities to organize and execute the courses of action required to produce given attainments' (Bandura, 1997, p. 3). Self-efficacy beliefs can be changed through appropriate learning methods; this is fortunate given research findings that individuals high in self-efficacy will produce superior performance on a range of criteria (e.g. stress, absenteeism, innovation, level of aspiration). In the interest of developing and maintaining high self-efficacy it is important that relevant development programmes are in place for those whose new jobs will require different competencies from their old jobs. Individuals are more likely to react positively to change when their self-efficacy beliefs are enhanced rather than deflated. Those low in self-efficacy will find it very unsettling to operate in a climate of uncertainty because they may not feel that they have the competencies required to affect outcomes. Those high in self-efficacy, on the other hand, are better able to predict how they will perform under changed circumstances, and predictability aids adaptiveness (Bandura, 1997, p. 2).

'Culture' in Figure 10.1 refers to those shared beliefs and practices that have developed within the organization. Any attempt in a social system to bring about change that contravenes formal or informal norms, and disrupts well-established relationships, will arouse resistance and negative attitudes. This is a well-understood phenomenon (Lawrence, 1954). Inevitably, in any major change there will be disruptions to the existing culture. But appropriate leadership in managing the implementation process will help in minimizing the adverse effects.

The model in Figure 10.1 is intended to incorporate the critical factors and relationships that should be influencing the thinking and actions of someone leading and managing the process of implementing change. There are many theories of leadership. The functional or situational approaches are particularly helpful in implementing change. These are not arguing for an ideal style of leadership, such as autocratic or democratic. Rather, they are suggesting that leaders need to adapt their behaviours according to the needs of the situation they are managing. Within the context of our model this translates into fulfilling the following functions:

1 *Contributing positively toward the goals of change (e.g. cost savings) by implementing appropriate changes (e.g. outsourcing).* It should be noted that in the situation we are exploring the leader may or may not have been involved in the process of setting the overall goal of change (e.g. cost saving by outsourcing as in the case of 'Downsizing and outsourcing in an oil refinery'). However, the leader will almost certainly be involved in planning what needs to be done in order for the goals to be achieved and for managing the subsequent process within their area of authority. Specific change goals will vary according to the level and function in which the leader is located in the organization. Consistency of purpose is brought about by their contributions to the over-arching goals of top management.

2 *Gaining the commitment (or at least the cooperation) of individual employees for achieving the appropriate change goals.* Many will say that success in this area differentiates the run-of-the-mill manager from the leader. Whereas the former may rely on the authority invested in their role to get others to perform satisfactorily, the latter demonstrates through their behaviour that they understand the needs of others and strives to meet their needs in the process of meeting those of the employer. Under the climate of uncertainty that accompanies change the effective leader will devote considerable effort to the 'predictability' factor by creating and using learning opportunities to enable employees to understand the why, what, when and

how of change. The effective leader will similarly devote the necessary effort to the 'acceptability' factor by incorporating rewards
into the change process, and ensuring that employees are aware of
all incentives (e.g. greater job autonomy for those who remain;
generous terms and professional career guidance and training for
those being made redundant); by recognizing, and as far as possible
respecting, existing norms and relationships (i.e. conforming to
cultural knowhow); and to be sufficiently adaptive to accommodate the individual differences of employees with respect to
rewards, level of knowledge and skill, and the ability to learn.

3 *Minimizing the negative impacts of change.* Those who have experienced
change, both as an initiator and as a receiver, will know that some will
perceive themselves as winners and others as losers – regardless of the
skills of the leader. Similarly, there will always be those who find it
difficult to cope in a constructive manner with the stress generated by
the uncertainties and threats of change. As far as possible the effective
leader will take a proactive and sensitive approach to such problems
so as to minimize their negative impact in achieving the goals of
change. Thus priority may be given to attending to the predictability/
acceptability factors in relation to key employees (e.g. those in
powerful positions). Also, due sensitivity and adaptability will be
shown toward those experiencing excessive levels of stress, and
appropriate effort made to create and preserve a climate of support.

By now it will be obvious that situational or functional leadership
requires the individual to be knowledgeable and skilled in organizational behaviour (e.g. context of change), group behaviour (e.g. norms),
and individual behaviour (e.g. motivation). In order to make this vast
area of knowledge more manageable we shall turn our attention in the
next chapter to the 'competencies' managers require to implement
successful change in the light of our research and the relevant literature.

Certain key concepts we have been using in discussing this
model require a more in-depth treatment if they are to be of practical
value to the implementers of change. They include: power; individual
differences; norms and values; motivation; stress; and competencies.
We shall return to these in the following chapters.

REFLECTION

To what extent do you share the belief that the assumptions underlying the
concepts of predictability and acceptability are useful when formulating a
plan for implementing change?

The dynamics of the model

So far we have focused on the elements of the model rather than on the model as a whole. We shall now make up for this deficiency by reviewing two contrasting cases in terms of the model, and assessing the extent to which the model demonstrates its usefulness in facilitating relevant learning. Both cases have already been described in more detail in Part 2.

Implementing strategic change in a charity

The council of this charity head-hunted the present CEO because they felt that someone was needed who was able to give direction and to increase the morale in the organization. The style of this individual was to adopt a top-down approach combined with as much consultations and briefings as possible. His strong leadership was characterized by a colleague as 'Not, this is what we shall do, but this is why we need to make changes'. At an early stage he gave the directors of the divisions a framework for developing a five-year strategic plan. They were asked to come back after three months with the results of their efforts. He then spent another three months with the help of a colleague to bring these plans together into a single draft plan. This draft was finalized in a three-day workshop. Promulgation and consultation followed on a wider front through a number of roadshows to explain and listen. The strategic plans determined the main goals of change, for example: to develop systems for improving the quality of information (including finance and numbers of volunteers); recruiting people who were sufficiently aggressive and achievement oriented; developing a less bureaucratic structure so that resources were more efficiently used.

As already indicated, part of the process made use of existing structures (i.e. directors of divisions). This was soon supplemented by bringing in a seconded lawyer to help find out what the structural issues causing problems were. The result of this preliminary study was that a more thorough review was recommended to study the problems which had been identified. Independent consultants were then brought in to carry this out. Two interesting conditions were imposed. First, one internal member was included in the team so as to facilitate the review and to share ownership in it. Second, the consultants had to report to a prestigious and neutral steering committee that included several captains of industry. This second condition meant that recommendations for change would emerge from the steering committee and not from the CEO. This turned out to be important, since some of the changes recommended meant that council members had to vote themselves out of being a member of a body which brought them status in the community! Again, once the steering committee produced their report concerning structural changes this was followed up by a series of consultation roadshows in which staff and volunteers were told this is what we think the problems are, these are the possible solutions, what do you think? The report then went to the Council who were required to vote on appropriate resolutions.

Following agreement that changes were to be introduced to the structure, an implementation group was set up with an overall coordinator. Several project groups were formed. The implementation group had the authority to take decisions except for those resulting in the closing down of branches – these had to be referred to the Council. In order to allay as much uncertainty and anxiety as possible various processes were brought into play to facilitate open communication. Thus more roadshows followed, in which the CEO and the Chairman addressed various groups, informing them of the process of change and what it is likely to mean for them, and invited them to help identify problems not foreseen. A video was made and disseminated. Staff were assured that, as far as possible, relocation rather than redundancy was the policy to be followed.

This was a major change programme and large sums of money were involved. Both the Trustees and the Charity Commissioners needed to be reassured that money was being well spent. In this context the consultants played an important role. They were able to provide the reassurance required to all concerned that what was being done was right.

In this case history the person who was the internal member on the consultancy team was also interviewed. A number of observations were made that are worth highlighting because they contribute to the further understanding of the dynamics underlying the model we are presenting. Incorporating the consultants in the managerial structures and process was invaluable since the charity was able to draw on their experience of similar assignments elsewhere. Many of the potential problems were minimized because of the care which was taken to consult staff. They felt they were being listened to and involved. On the other hand this slowed the process of change and some people felt unsettled and insecure for a longer period than was perhaps necessary.

The CEO had focused attention on the mission about six months before the restructuring exercise began, but formulating the mission caused more problems between staff and volunteers than re-structuring. Volunteers were more concerned with the mission, whereas staff were more concerned with restructuring because this could affect their ability to keep their jobs and to pay the mortgage. The most difficult hurdle to get over was when the Council was being asked to vote on the report's recommendations – many had a lot to lose in the decisions they were being asked to make. That they did make these difficult decisions was put down to their involvement in the consultation process. They had been interviewed by the consultants, they felt listened to, those trustees who were on the Steering Committee understood the need for the changes and helped their peers to understand the need, and key individuals (e.g. the Chairman of Council, the Finance Director) supported the recommendations. Another factor supporting change was the redefined mission. Once the change in the mission had been agreed the rationale for certain changes became self-evident.

Looking at the model with this case in mind, a number of observations can be made to refine and enhance the value of the model:

- Stakeholders in change will each have their own agenda, and the extent to which these are similar or different from each other will have implications for the managerial structures and processes for implementing change. Two of the main stakeholders in this case were the voluntary staff and the paid staff. Proposed changes meant different things to these groups, and the structures and processes employed to implement change had to take this into account. In this case history the amount of consultation which took place, coupled with the formal review by consultants, ensured that these differences were catered for.

- The two main factors affecting a stakeholder's emotional, attitudinal and behavioural responses to change, i.e. the constructs of predictability and acceptability, probably have a compensating influence on each other. Thus in terms of both paid and voluntary staff the fact that the managerial structures and processes enabled them to experience a high level of predictability helped them to cope with the negative effects where a lower level of acceptability existed.

- The development of 'mission, corporate strategy and goals of change' and of 'managerial structures and processes for implementing change' are ongoing processes. They change as the power and insights of stakeholders change, and as the outcomes of 'achieved change' are felt. Because of this it is not easy to separate out the development of strategic change and the process of implementing change. It is certainly not easy to successfully manage the process of implementing change if one has an inadequate understand of the historical context (i.e. the preceding and current influences of different groups of stakeholders, the factors determining the chosen strategy and the goals of change).

■ Related to the previous observations that one is dealing with in a dynamic system is the variable of time. Organizations that are decentralized with respect to both geography and management are going to require more time to implement change if only for logistic reasons. But the time variable is heavily affected when it is important to introduce changes in a particular sequence. Thus acceptance of the mission is necessary before decisions are made as to choice of strategy, and it may take months to achieve the former. Introducing the various mechanisms and structures for implementation may also spread over several months. The often prolonged time dimension does mean that management has to be confident as to what it is about, have a plan, and receive sufficient positive feedback to continue to support the change. It is in this context that previous experience of managing change and of project management can count for so much. An important, but often unrecognized role of management consultants, is the reassurance they can provide to clients that overall progress is being made despite the setbacks.

Unplanned change in a market research agency

This case history is from the perspective of a middle manager. Growth in market opportunities and the promise of enhanced profits for the parent company led to an expansion of the business. The market research division, of which the respondent is a member, expanded from 30 to 90 to meet client demands for market research services in a very short space of time. Problems of quality and the meeting of deadlines arose, increasing the conflict with suppliers of fieldwork and data processing services. This forced them to review the way things were done, and the climate changed from a friendly, cosy organization to becoming bureaucratic, impersonal and more dependent upon IT. During this period the managing director changed twice. Before, young graduates were brought in, trained and promoted; now external recruits were brought in at all levels, and the competition for promotion had increased.

The research executives were divided up into teams of eight, each team being led by an account manager who reported to a director. In order to increase productivity consultants were brought in to run intensive two-day courses in project and team management. A logistics manager was appointed to oversee their functional type roles (e.g.

typing, charting, data processing), and he was constantly introducing spreadsheets for them to complete. Staff were generally resistant to these changes because they were being diverted from what they saw as their primary role, which was to service their clients. The respondent had to try to explain to her team why these changes were needed and to act as a communication channel for their responses. A complicating factor was that some directors were externally focused and others internally focused. Recently the former had increased their influence and the message came down from on high that people should withdraw from the internal focus. A consequence of this was that the series of meetings that her team had organized to help develop their understanding of particular client sectors (e.g. finance, health) had to be terminated. The current managing director was business-like and forceful; the directors made the decisions and the team leaders were required to implemented them.

This manager was able to list several reasons why she felt changes in her organization left much to be desired:

- The changes that took place seemed to have been unplanned and uncoordinated. There was no team responsible for the change. Change was so fragmented that at one stage clients were asked through the newsletter whether they had any knowhow for coping with sudden growth.
- There was no attempt to prepare staff for changes being introduced.
- Changes were not sold as benefits to staff.
- All solutions appear to have come from within the organization; no one went out to study good practice elsewhere.
- In her team there were two cases of stress-induced illnesses.

The picture painted is in marked contrast to the previous case. True, we need to bear in mind that the respondent was not part of the top management team, and therefore what she perceived as unplanned change was from her perspective. However, in terms of our model it is clear that the emotional, attitudinal and behavioural responses of staff at a particular level are going to be determined by their own perception of events. In this instance morale was low because the acceptability factor was low (e.g. the career progression pathway had changed, the new managing director's approach was saying to difficult staff 'you either get on with operating the new systems or you get out', relations with clients and suppliers had changed), and the predictability factor was almost non-existent.

EXERCISE (continuation; see pp. 40–41)

The model presented in this chapter is one of many ways in which the lessons learnt from the case histories, and one's own experiences, can be encapsulated. In the light of new insights gained, revisit your own model and modify it to reflect your current understanding of the factors involved in implementing successful change.

■ **CHAPTER ELEVEN** ■

Critical management competencies

In collecting information for the case studies we asked interviewees what they saw as being the key competencies that were critical to success in managing change and why (readers are invited in this chapter to complete a similar exercise). The results are presented and discussed. The concept of competencies is clarified and three generic frameworks presented. The value of focusing on the concept of competencies lies in any additional insight it gives us into models for implementing change.

Introduction

In Chapter 10 we described the developmental process that one of the authors experienced in arriving at a model for implementing successful organizational change. We then provided arguments, justifications and illustrations for the developed model, and applied it to two of the case histories. The chapter focused on examining implementation of change from an organizational level of analysis. In this chapter we move to looking at managing change from the perspective of the individual manager, and focus on identifying critical management competencies required.

The overall aim of the managers we interviewed was to bring about the required changes (most often in a planned way) by creating situations and circumstances whereby desired changes could occur and be sustained. This involved taking action, as individuals or groups, to alter existing practices. Managers were key players in change management and, in some cases, they were assisted by internal advisers and external consultants. Managers, during the change process, needed to plan and think about change (particularly when designing the implementation process), they had to sell the idea of changing and influence others to see the benefits. Modelling required behaviours was also a key requirement, as was actual project managing the 'changing' of situation and people. What therefore are the critical management competencies in managing change as seen by our interviewees? What are the special skills, knowledge and attitudes they feel are needed in order to manage change successfully? Before providing respondents' answers to these questions we recommend that you should tackle the same task that our interviewees were required to do. You will then be in a better position to agree or disagree with their perceptions, and to explore the reasons for any similarities and differences.

The latter part of this chapter will clarify the concept of 'competencies', and describe some of the models that have popularized the use of the term in management selection and development. The purpose of this chapter will be to help you gain a better understanding as to how the concept of competencies and its associated models can facilitate the process of learning to manage and implement change.

EXERCISE: MANAGEMENT COMPETENCIES

You should complete the form in Table 11.1 before reading the next section. This is very similar to the task given to the respondents in collecting the data for the case histories (the only differences is that a self-completion format has replaced the interview). They were asked to consider their experiences in managing change, not only in the project they had just recounted, but also across other changes they had been involved in. They were asked to sort out a pack of 13 cards (each carrying one of the 13 competencies) into three piles according to whether they were perceived as being critical, important or desirable in successfully managing a change project. Managers were also asked to identify any critical competencies that were missing from the selection, and any additional key competencies that may emerge as critical in the future management of change because of changing circumstances for the organization or sector worked in. They were also asked to give reasons for their choice. You will need to record in writing the reasons why you think a competency is critical, important or merely desirable. Compare and contrast your thinking with those of others. In what ways are they different, and why?

TABLE 11.1: Change management competency questionnaire

Consider your experiences of managing change. Below are 13 competencies that have been put forward as being characteristic of the behaviours required by managers in carrying out their normal job. Considering your experiences and knowledge of managing change (including implementing change) how would you rate each of these competencies? Tick the first column if you feel that a competency is critical to managing a change project. Tick the second column if you feel that the competency is important, but not critical, to successfully managing a change project. Tick the third column if you feel that the competency is desirable, but not critical nor important, to successfully managing a change project.

Competency	Critical	Important	Desirable
Showing concern for excellence			
Showing sensitivity to the needs of others			
Showing confidence and personal drive			
Collecting and organizing information			
Setting and prioritizing objectives			
Relating to others			
Managing personal emotions and stress			
Identifying and applying concepts			
Monitoring and responding to actual against planned activities			
Obtaining the commitment of others			
Managing personal learning and development			
Taking decisions			
Presenting oneself positively to others			

Empirical findings

Table 11.2 indicates the rankings made by 15 interviewees. In many cases managers gave explanations about what these competencies meant to them and reasons for their ratings. These are detailed below.

TABLE 11.2: Ranking of competencies needed for successfully managing change

Competencies	Critical	Important	Desirable
Obtains commitment of others	11	4	0
Setting and prioritizing objectives	11	3	1
Relating to others	9	6	0
Showing personal drive and self-confidence	9	6	0
Takes decisions	9	4	2
Managing personal emotions and stress	7	8	0
Presenting oneself positively to others	7	6	2
Showing concern for excellence	6	7	2
Showing sensitivity to the needs of others	6	5	4
Managing personal learning and development	4	7	4
Monitoring and responding to actual against planned objectives	3	9	3
Identifies and applies concepts	3	7	5
Collecting and organizing information	3	6	6

Obtaining the commitment of others

The table shows that most managers saw this to be 'critical' to successfully managing a change project. Consensus was that change would not be achieved if this competency or competence was lacking. Comments revealed that there were a variety of 'others' to consider, including those affected by change, the management team, senior management and the 'right' people (i.e. those who can block the change). One manager described the process he used in detail. Comments included:

> There is no point going for change if you haven't got anyone on board and convinced them that this is the right way to go. That's been a critical issue for us.

> It's no use having the right answer if everyone thinks you are wrong!

> Once the reorganization decision had been taken we needed the backing and commitment of the management team to push that on. In the wider context we needed, and we still need, the commitment of the departmental members to accept these changes.

> We found that it is critical to get the 'right' people to commit, and one of the most important analyses we did was to sit down and look at whose commitment we needed to obtain. We asked: 'What do we need to achieve? Who can block it? How do we get their buy-in? Who can help me to do it more easily?'. So there was a commitment-building process with some of the senior management within the company. Then we looked sideways and downwards and said 'Who can block me there?'. In some instances you get to a point when you acknowledge that there are actually some individuals whose commitment you cannot obtain, whatever the reason. Then you ask 'If I think their commitment is vital and I can't get it do I proceed?'. Luckily, in this case we didn't get to that point. None of the individuals who wouldn't commit were in positions to have a critical impact on the project. Where there were blockers we asked: 'What do we have to do to get him to play with us? If we can't get his support, what can we do to neutralize him? Can we take him out of this equation?'.

One manager explained the role of internal advisers in the context of 'obtaining the commitment of others' as follows:

> Our major function was to inform the management team how the change process was developing and what people's concerns were. We found that change management is complicated in terms of leadership. It should democratically be an open process, but in practice, of course, it is not. Difficult decisions had to be made. Our job was to explain why difficult decisions had to be made and why they had to be made in that way. Why a certain amount of radical change was necessary, and why other types of change were not a good idea. So that people understand. They may not like it but they won't think that it's random, or motivated by favouritism or politics.

'Obtaining the commitment of others' can be achieved through a manager's personal competency, and through competence which can be found in managers' roles and internal advisers' roles at both individual and group levels.

Setting and prioritizing objectives

This was also rated a critical competency by most managers, because the process of managing change involves careful forethought and planning to ensure that potential problems are identified, time and other resources are utilized effectively, attention is given to critical issues, and staff are given guidance and direction. For example:

> If you haven't set out what you are going to do, and how you are going to achieve it, then you can guarantee you are going to have a very difficult time of it.

> It's about establishing the overall framework, and you need to start here so it's critical.

> To achieve this part of the overall change we had to plan, set targets, prioritize tasks that needed to be done, and decide on how we were going to go about doing them.

> I needed more of this because often you have three or four things you have to introduce to staff and I didn't always think through what's the best order to do it in.

For one manager this was not critical to success because he believed that change can be achieved if you 'just muddle through'. Although it might take longer, he felt, it can be done.

For another manager this was a critical role of the external consultants. Their task was to make sure there was a timetable, that conflicting requests on resources were resolved and things were prioritized.

These first two competencies/competences received the most 'critical' ratings, but were closely followed by the next three competencies: 'relating to others', 'showing confidence and personal drive' and 'takes decisions'. They were rated 'critical' by three in five of the managers, and 'important' in nearly all other cases.

Relating to others

Managers saw this as 'critical' and 'important' for a number of reasons: because it is part of the process of obtaining commitment; part of helping to link different groups in the organization; and an aspect of managers helping others under pressure. For example:

> This is about *how* you are actually getting others involved and committed.

> It's all about bringing people with you.

> There's no way that change is going to be managed successfully if you can't relate to other people and get them on board. That's a big part of what we have done this year in trying to get them to talk, to build commitment, being able to influence them, and certainly resolving conflict. We've done a lot of that.

> To some extent this is a summation of what the change team was all about. Our role was that of helping the management team, and communicating the change process, as well as reflecting the interests of all the staff.

> It is important to understand others at times of change, the difficulties people are facing, and their feelings, fears and apprehensions. It is also an important part of the manager's role to encourage others to feel that they can express those fears and apprehensions and difficulties and that they can't cope anymore.

Showing self-confidence and personal drive

This was rated as 'critical' and 'important' because of the way managers' actions are evaluated by others, both staff and managers.

> At a time when things are changing if people's own managers – be they senior, junior or what – are not showing they are committed to making things happen then everything comes to a full stop. The behaviour of individual managers is enormously important, and more so in times of uncertainty and when there are pressures on everyone. I would say that everyone in this building is having to work harder than they had to previously, and that's not to say they were not working hard beforehand. At such times it is up to everyone who is in a position of authority to give the lead.

> If you are not confident in yourself, and not confident of your vision, and you are not prepared to drive for that, then the chances that you are going to get other people to buy this is very limited. I have certainly seen that where people lose confidence in a particular decision that they are trying to push, then it spreads very quickly to the people around them.

This is critical and similar to taking decisions. Someone has got to drive this change. Someone has got to show confidence that 'Yes, we can win through'. That it is not all doom and gloom. I and my management team need to show that we can win, and that we are confident, so we have to drive this process.

Managers need to be dedicated and committed to see the job through, particularly when implementing hard decisions like redundancy.

Some saw this as part of their personal style applied not only when dealing with change, but as part of the way they always operate. Several saw this as overlapping with 'Presenting oneself positively to others' and felt it needed to be handled carefully. Also, if a person is too forceful or unhesitating then they may be seen as not being 'responsive to other people's needs'.

You need to be seen as reflecting the party line, so you have to be clear and articulate but not too forceful.

This could be seen as a double-edged sword that can be seen as arrogance if you overstep the line – arrogance as 'I know best and I'm not going to listen to anyone's view'.

Taking decisions

Whilst this was rated as a 'critical' or 'important' competency for managing change, comments revealed that it is also seen as a generic executive/management function, and one that can be fraught with difficulties.

In change management situations it worries me that there are so many things to be decided that there is actually a danger that you take a decision rather than take a right decision.

Another commented that making a decision is important because otherwise the whole change process 'gums up'. Taking decisions is needed to keep up the momentum of change. This was commented on by another:

There are two sides to taking decisions. First actually being able to make decisions at all because it's very easy when there are so many discontinuities and uncertainties around to say 'I can't decide that until I know this' and you end up analyzing for 18 months, at which point it's too late anyway. Second, in addition to being able to take decisions, you need to take the right ones.

One manager's approach to taking decisions involved him in looking at the decisions he was making to decide if they were strategic or not. 'Strategic' was defined as outcomes which are impossible or exceedingly difficult to unwind down the road of change, and are likely to be significant. He then gave a lot of thought to decisions he had to live with, but with decisions that can be reversed or where there is not a big penalty he makes the best decision available within tight time constraints. He commented:

> It's clearly not a scientific process, and you don't sit there and say 'this decision is worth 30 seconds consideration', but there is something like that going on where you are saying 'It really isn't worth spending a day thinking about this. I need to decide one of these two paths. If I make a decision and I want to change it weeks later because I'm not happy at the way it's working out, then that's fine'.

Under strong time pressures, and with the high levels of uncertainty often experienced in change programmes, and more generally, there is a sense of relief when decisions are taken:

> Something that intensely irritates me is people who sit and have meetings for hours, prevaricate, and nobody is prepared to make a decision. It's much better to make a decision, even if you find out eventually it's the wrong one – at least someone has made a decision.

> You have to say at some point, 'Enough is enough, let's do something'.

Several managers commented that whilst during change projects they 'try to sit down with people who can add something to the process', such as through discussion and debate to identify a variety of views, and options for action, it is not always possible to achieve consensus. So having consulted and involved people the manager is left to make the final decision.

Managers were pretty evenly divided in their rankings of 'critical' and 'important' for the next three competencies: managing personal emotion and stress, presenting oneself positively to others, and showing concern for excellence.

Managing personal emotions and stress

This competency was rated as 'critical' or 'important' for a variety of reasons including it being seen as part of managing *per se*, or as part of leadership (an aspect of this being the importance of acting as a role model). It also was a result of the nature of the change situation and its effects on people, and was seen by others to relate to the role of external consultants.

> We certainly know as managers that this is important. We've had to help our staff manage their own personal emotions and stress. We've had a couple of stress-related illness in my own team, so that is very much part of what we have had to do.

> This is very important, especially in this stressful time we are going through. If I don't remain cool, and sometimes that is difficult, and if I am unable to cope how can I expect my staff to be able to cope? It's a stressful environment and I think it is important to be a role model in this area, I have to reflect what I hope other staff would be.

> This has got to be critical. If you lose control, or buckle under stress, or start to get angry, you lose the whole leadership issue, which is so important.

> This is very important, because if I can't manage me, I can't manage anybody else. It's important to remain cool and not retaliate. In my position I've got to be seen to be able to do that because I should behave as I expect others to behave. But there are going to be times when I do retaliate, but I hope I retaliate positively, and be proactive rather than reactive.

> I was surprised at how tired I was last week after dealing with all the emotional people problems, and there were a couple of nights when I got on the train absolutely exhausted. I think it was just all the emotion and all the concentration used to deal with the people. Dealing like that, on a one-to-one basis, is much more draining and you have got to be much more focused, and it's not like writing memos or sitting in meetings when your mind can wander. You can't do that when you are talking with staff.

> This is essential during change because it is not a controlled activity. It is not something where you are always going to be able to predict the outcomes. You are going to be getting some radical and unusual responses in getting people to change, so you must be able to cope and deal with emotions and stress because it is common within the change process.

> When there is so much change around it is easy to lose sight of the fact that everyone else is under lots of pressure as well, and that therefore requests which might have been received in one way previously – all of a sudden there is a potential for people to take offence, when they might not have done so before. You have to be conscious of your own behaviour

and what other people might be expecting so that [competency] is critical.

We used a number of consultancy groups and firms so that most people who have been threatened with redundancy have had access to some kind of support like that.

Presenting oneself positively to others

Managers linked this competency to the manager or leadership role, and to communication generally.

This is needed in the leadership role.

If you can't express your ideas effectively you can't be a good manager.

This is critical, because if you don't have credibility, if you haven't got a positive view of what you are trying to do, then the chances of you carrying people with you are very limited.

One manager pointed out this is important in the context of getting the go-ahead from your senior managers:

You need to identify who it is you have got to influence. They have got to have a reasonably positive view of your competencies, certainly in the context of what you are proposing to do. If you are going in and saying 'I am going to slim this business unit down, I am going to fire 30 per cent of the staff', then they have got to believe you can do that, that you have got the right credentials.

Several managers saw 'Presenting oneself positively to others' as an aspect of getting the organization's message across in a positive way:

I can't go around weeping, saying 'Oh dear we are going to lose. The future doesn't look bright'. You might think it sometimes. This is about presenting ideas clearly so staff understand and, hopefully, we do that through staff briefings where I try to get the message across in a positive way, not a negative, depressive way.

People who participated in the change team were chosen for various attributes... also they were people who were good actors, reasonable advocates for the process.

But, as another revealed, this can be problematic if the message is not actually believed:

Staff will see through this if it's just a persona which is not genuine.

One reason for not rating this competency as critical or important was:

> The scale of change we have been looking at has been such that if one particular manager doesn't come across in the best light its effects are negligible.

Showing concern for excellence

Several managers saw this linked to their business unit or organization's reputation. It can be an additional pressure to consider during change, because it provides an existing standard that must not drop or be disregarded during change.

> I certainly feel this is something that underpins what we do in our units. We have a fairly high opinion of who we are, and what we do, and of being the best, in some respects, in the industry. That is something that has had to continue through all of the change and we have had to be careful that it hasn't been compromised in any way.

> It is key that during change we try to maintain that high quality of service we are renowned for, and look to ways of improving the service through innovation and efficiency. My saying of 'Get better or get beaten' is relevant here'.

It can also be used as a directional, or motivational ideal:

> I think this is a lot about getting the commitment of others. It's all about success. I believe success, or the image of success, breeds success. If you are positive, if you firmly believe we are going to be successful, and are striving for excellence, then you actually give off positive vibes. Then other people want to get on the bandwagon and think 'I am going to go for excellence as well'.

> An achievement orientation is certainly critical in structured change, while 'showing concern for excellence' is important in terms of driving forward the boundaries.

Others took an alternative view of its role in managing change:

> This took a back seat. I'm sure we shouldn't have been, but I rather suspect that our drivers were pragmatic rather than ideal. We have talked about all this kind of stuff, and we have had a few idealistic stabs at how we would do it. If you want to give people an opportunity to create new working cultures I suppose that has to come first, and the structures then have to reflect the cultures. Inevitably we created the structure before

creating the culture. So I think this concern for excellence, and doing things better, was tagged on.

I'm fairly pragmatic in that the important thing is that we actually identify what we want to do, and go about doing it. Wanting to do things better, improving, commitment to quality, are all desirable, but not critical.

Remaining items

There was no consensus by managers on the remaining five items, with more than a quarter rating these as 'desirable', but neither 'critical' nor 'important' for successfully managing change. These items are 'showing sensitivity to the needs of others', 'managing personal learning and development', 'monitoring and responding to actual against planned objectives', 'identifies and applies concepts', and 'collecting and organizing information'.

Those who rated 'showing sensitivity to the needs of others' as 'critical' or important' argued for this because they believed: in times of change, with uncertainty and discontinuities you cannot take anything for granted; middle managers need to let senior managers become aware of problems their staff are facing; or managing change is all about people. Those who rated this as merely desirable did so because they found that time constraints meant they were not available for their staff so they were unable to do this; or they believed that if you are going to drive through change it's like the old adage 'You can't make an omelette without breaking eggs' or that with radical change this is not appropriate.

Ratings of 'managing personal learning and development' as 'critical' or 'important' were made because: this links to people being able to adapt to change; managers need to do this to model it for others; and it enables people to do things in changing situations, and improve over time. Additionally, several recognized that some managers don't have the skills and abilities to be doing what they are trying to do. Managers rating this as 'nice to have' thought that certain aspects of this might be important, or that in an operational change context this might be an outcome.

'Monitoring and responding to actual against planned objectives' was rated by a majority to be 'important'. Many of these saw it in the context of project management, and for some individuals or organizations it was common practice. Several managers, however, acknowledged that they didn't use their action plan, or measures of progress of change, or were not experienced in this.

'Identifies and applies concepts' was acknowledged to be 'important' in many cases because: there is a need to be cognitively flexible; it's part of managing *per se*; and it results from professional training and education. Reasons for this competency merely being seen as 'desirable' or 'nice to have' include ideas that: conceptualization is a luxury; management is not necessarily an intellectual process; and the conceptual can inhibit taking action.

Reasons given by managers for the importance of 'collecting and organizing information' include the concerns that: decisions might be taken on the back of information that isn't sound; and during change there is a need to have 'soft' information to find out what people are thinking and feeling and then to determine what this implies, and what actions might need to be taken. Others were less convinced of the importance of this because it was seen as part of the 'intellectualization process', and people don't necessarily have the opportunity during change to get the 'best' information: they have to optimize on what's available.

Managers, when asked to think of any missing competencies, either spoke about elaborations of competencies already covered or identified a critical one they saw as missing:

- *A sense of humour*, because 'This helps to break the ice and reduces the temperature every so often. I'm happy when I hear my staff laughing because I know they are working hard and enjoying themselves. I feel anxious when I see quiet and furtive whispering'.
- *Being detached and not taking things too personally*: 'Although I have been instrumental in devising many of the changes here, I'm obviously only introducing change which has been sanctioned higher up, and I think if I get a negative reaction from certain people or certain quarters I would try not to take that too personally, because I am an instrument of change, even though a lot of the change has come from me'.
- *Supporting and sustaining people* at the personal level, as well as at a programme of change level.
- *Adaptability and knowhow*: 'In implementing change, the knowhow, the practical experience of change, plus the adaptability, including adapting to the type of organization you are in, understanding the business, and the way you are relating to other people'.
- *Historical understanding* of sector, organization and people: 'If you are going to manage change it is important you know the history of

where the sector/organization has come from and where it is in the present day. Otherwise other people's anxieties and concerns will seem abstract to you'.

- Being able to *react quickly* to changes in business needs, and *seeing* the most logical path to take.
- Building and maintaining *a good team* who seek success: 'The hardest thing is getting a good, effective team together. If you have such a team you can conquer the world. This, plus a desire for success. There are some people where the need to achieve and succeed burns brighter than others and if you weld them into a team then they are a great motor, a great engine'.

The concept of competencies

There is much confusion in the literature over the use of the terms 'competences' and 'competencies'. When people are described as being competent at their jobs, we imply that they perform in a satisfactory manner. But what is a satisfactory manner or standard in relation to the complex job of a manager? This was the sort of question posed by senior industrialist and government officials in the wake of several influential reports which indicated a low level of management training and development in the UK (Handy *et al.*, 1987; Constable and McCormick, 1987). These reports energized interested parties to help improve labour market efficiency through better management training and development, and thereby improving the performance of the national economy.

The UK's Management Charter Initiative (MCI) was established in 1988 to improve the quality and increase the professionalism of managers at all levels. As a recognized lead body for management, it was underpinned by the National Forum for Management Education and Development (NFMED), comprising the Confederation of British Industry (CBI), The Institute of Management (IMgt) and the Foundation for Management Education (FME). The MCI's work became part of the national approach for accreditation through an occupational standards framework. It is concerned with assessing 'the ability to perform activities in the jobs within an occupation, to the standards expected in employment' (this definition was first devised by the Manpower Services Commission in 1986 and adopted by Investors in People (1995). During the early 1990s, competence standards for three levels of management – middle, first line and supervisory management – were produced (and mapped onto the National Vocational Qualification's framework: M1S Supervisory = NVQ level 3; M1 First line management

= NVQ level 4; and M2 Middle management = NVQ level 5). The M3 standards for senior management were drafted in 1995. Such competencies are deemed generic, in that they are seen to be applicable to all effective managers, regardless of specific job or organization. The Management Standards were reviewed in 1996 and revised standards were published in 1997. The major revision was a move from four key roles to seven.

The structures for different levels of management are similar. Each comprises a number of 'units of competence' designed to describe what managers should be able to do. The units of competence are grouped into key roles: manage activities; manage resources; manage people; manage information; manage energy; manage quality; and manage projects. Each unit has a number of 'elements of competence', which reflect skills, knowledge and abilities which experienced competent managers should possess; 'performance criteria' which specify the level or standard of performance which the manager is expected to demonstrate; and 'range indicators' which describe a range of instances in which each element of competence applies. Elements of competence are identified through functional analyses of job roles and responsibilities. The focus is on the nature of managerial tasks and expectations of workplace performance; the performance criterion is an entry or threshold standard, and competence is 'owned' by national institutions and organizations, and accreditation provides a transferable qualification (Sparrow, 1995).

The term 'competencies' was applied within this context of defining what a manager should be able to do in order to achieve an acceptable standard of performance. However, others (particularly organizational psychologists) were adopting a different approach to the improvement of management performance. They were more concerned with the identification of individual qualities or abilities that differentiated the more successful from the less successful manager. The term 'competencies' was used to refer to these individual qualities. It is the meaning associated with 'competencies' with which our research study was primarily concerned.

Influential frameworks

The Boyatzis behavioural competencies model

One of the most influential frameworks or models of management competencies arose in the USA from research conducted by the McBer

Corporation and Harvard Business School (Boyatzis, 1982; Spencer and Spencer, 1993). An initiative in the late 1970s by the American Management Association sought to identify the characteristics that distinguish superior from average managerial performance. Boyatzis reported the findings of this study in which more than 2000 managers, from 12 organizations, across a variety of sectors, in 41 management roles, were assessed on a number of competencies. A job competence was defined as (Boyatzis, 1982, p. 21):

> an underlying characteristic of a person... (which)... may be a motive, trait, skill, aspect of one's self-image or social role, or a body of knowledge which he or she uses.

Richard Boyatzis, in his book *The Competent Manager* makes a distinction between a 'competence' which differentiates superior performance from average or poor performance, and a 'threshold competence' which is 'a person's generic knowledge, motive, self-image, social role or skills which is essential to performing a job, but is not causally related to superior job performance' (Boyatzis, 1982, p. 23). Boyatzis acknowledges that effective job performance depended on the specific demands of the job, and on the organizational environment. He argued that effective performance will occur when individual competencies, job demands and the organization's environment are consistent with each other. Boyatzis *et al.* (1995) have developed, applied and evaluated their model of managerial abilities at the Weatherhead School of Management. Table 11.3 summarizes the competencies that form the framework for their management development centre.

Competencies are 'soft skills' evidenced through behavioural repertoires which people 'input' to an organizational context (job, role, career stream, organization). Competencies are identified through behavioural investigation techniques, such as event interviews via job competence assessment (JCA), and focus on person-centred analyses of effectiveness. The competency is held by the individual and brought to the organization, and assessment is through the identification of potential (Sparrow, 1995).

These views on competencies relate to managing *per se*, and are not focused solely on 'managing change'. Is there a difference? There is a view that people are perceiving the environments within which organizations operate as becoming more complex and difficult to manage because the pace and magnitude of change is being driven by developments such as economic globalization, and technological innovations such as the Internet. People within organizations are experiencing dramatic internal changes, such as delayering, downsizing and

TABLE 11.3: A model of managerial abilities used in management education (Boyatzis *et al.*, 1995, pp. 84–91)

Goal and action management abilities

1 Efficiency

2 Planning

3 Initiative

4 Attention to detail

5 Self-control

6 Flexibility

People management abilities

7 Empathy

8 Persuasiveness

9 Networking

10 Negotiating

11 Self-confidence

12 Group management

13 Developing others

14 Oral communications

Analytical reasoning abilities

15 Use of concepts

16 Pattern recognition

17 Theory building

18 Using technology

19 Quantitative analysis

20 Social objectivity

21 Written communications

empowerment. One conclusion is that managing successfully nowadays is synonymous with having expertise in managing change (Clarke, 1994; Institute of Management, 1994) as one change initiative follows another in rapid succession. Hence we argue that the vital competencies for managers in today's and tomorrow's organizations are threefold: managing in a turbulent environment; to cope, adapt and change one's own roles; and to actively lead and manage change in one's area of responsibility.

TABLE 11.4: Schroder's high-performance competencies model (Schroder, 1989)

1   Cognitive: information search, concept formation, conceptual flexibility

2   Directional: impact, self-confidence, presentation

3   Motivational: interpersonal search, managing interaction, developmental orientation

4   Achievement: proactive orientation, achievement orientation

The Schroder high performance competencies model

A key model is that provided by Harry Schroder (1989). He looked at competencies needed for high performance in dynamic, turbulent environments. He divided competencies into Basic (specialist/technical/functional) or B-competencies, and more transferable skills, the high-performance or H-competencies. He proposed that H-competencies develop from our experiences in coping with interpersonal and intergroup situations in social, community and recreational activities, as well as within work organizations. For Schroder these highly complex sets of behavioural skills cannot be taught by traditional methods. The model has four clusters and 11 competencies – see Table 11.4.

Schroder believed that the changing nature of organizations (requiring organic structures and flexibility) means that H-competencies need to be developed within the workforce to build an integrated, dynamic, committed organization that can readily respond to change (i.e. organizational competencies). Research into the relationship between unit performance and high-performance managerial competencies (HPMC) has shown a strong relationship in two cases: first, where managers are attempting to change the structure of their units in response to increased change and competition in the external environment; second, when managers are responsible for enhancing the performance of units that are structured appropriately for a dynamic and competitive environment. This model has been applied and validated in the UK within National Westminster Bank (Cockerill, 1989; 1995).

The MCI personal competence model

A further model which builds on both management and managing change models is that proposed by the Management Charter Initiative. In addition to the output-based management standards, MCI developed a further model, which shares the conceptual underpinnings of other models such as those described above. These competencies are the 'personal qualities, skills and attributes that are associated with effective management behaviour'. MCI argue that the rationale for developing this model is that (Management Charter Initiative, 1994, p. 65):

> Management is a complex business, it's about developing a range of practical and technical skills associated with day-to-day work itself. But this is just the base line. Being personally effective means calling on a range of other skills that allow you to adapt to situations and get the best out of people. This part of the management jigsaw is as much about **how** we manage as **what** we actually do.... Although personal competence is implicit in the Management Standards, we decided it was too important to be left at that. Therefore we have developed what we have called the MCI Personal Competence Model.

This model is presented in Table 11.5, and will be recognized as the one that was used for the purpose of the exercise earlier on in this chapter. The MCI first published the model in 1990 alongside the

TABLE 11.5: The MCI Personal Competence Model, consisting of four clusters and 13 dimensions

1	Planning to optimize the achievement of results	1.1	Showing concern for excellence
		1.2	Setting and prioritizing objectives
		1.3	Monitoring and responding to actual against planned activities
2	Managing others to optimize results	2.1	Showing sensitivity to the needs of others
		2.2	Relating to others
		2.3	Obtaining the commitment of others
		2.4	Presenting oneself positively to others
3	Managing oneself to optimize results	3.1	Showing self confidence and personal drive
		3.2	Managing personal emotions and stress
		3.3	Managing personal learning and development
4	Using intellect to optimize results	4.1	Collecting and organizing information
		4.2	Identifying and applying concepts
		4.3	Taking decisions

Management Standards. The view is that personal competence is the 'driver' or 'engine' of improved performance, and personal competence enables managers to continuously improve themselves.

Competencies for implementing change

Discussion of results

Arriving at a model for implementing change was designed to help us to make explicit those assumptions likely to influence our thinking and behaviour. In carrying out this task we will have implicitly or explicitly identified competencies for implementing change successfully. The purpose of focusing on competencies in this chapter is to help learners explore in more depth the implications of their model for developmental purposes – their own and those for whom they are responsible. The three competency frameworks we have selected to put forward are based on significant empirical and theoretical work; but other frameworks could equally have been chosen (e.g. Pedler *et al.*, 1986; Williams and Dobson, 1993).

There are a number of ways in which we can improve the performance of individuals in implementing change once we know what the competencies are that are associated with successful performance. The three frameworks we have included in this chapter are the result of literature and empirical research to identify the competencies associated with successful performance in the role of manager. We are not too concerned that the frameworks were focusing on those competencies underlying the overall job of a manager, rather than those aspects of their job that are concerned with implementing change. Our defence for taking this stance is that, under present turbulent conditions, implementing change permeates everything they do. With a knowledge of these competencies we are in a better position (a) to select those individuals who will be successful implementers of change, and (b) to develop further an individual's competencies through appropriate learning experiences.

The raw results presented in Table 11.2 have been reduced in Table 11.6 to a single score for each of the four clusters of dimensions in the MCI model. These were calculated by (a) multiplying the numbers in the 'critical' cells by 3, those in the 'important' cells by 2 and those in the 'desirable' cell by 1; (b) adding up the total score for each dimension; and (c) adding up the total score for the dimensions in each cluster, and dividing by the number of dimensions in each cluster to

TABLE 11.6: The MCI Personal Competence Model: average rating obtained for each cluster

Score		
36.75	Managing others to optimize results	Showing sensitivity to the needs of others
		Relating to others
		Obtaining the commitment of others
		Presenting oneself positively to others
35.33	Managing oneself to optimize results	Showing self confidence and personal drive
		Managing personal emotions and stress
		Managing personal learning and development
34.66	Planning to optimize the achievement of results	Showing concern for excellence
		Setting and prioritizing objectives
		Monitoring and responding to actual against planned activities
30.66	Using intellect to optimize results	Collecting and organizing information
		Identifying and applying concepts
		Taking decisions

obtain an average rating. This average rating gives us a feel for the relative importance our sample of interviewees attached to the different clusters of competencies in relation to the management of change.

While we must be careful not to read too much into this table, three observations are worth making. First, it is the more interpersonal cluster (where one is trying to influence the behaviour of others) that is given the highest rating. Second, personal success in coping with change is perceived as being important. Third, the last two clusters are more task-oriented and intellectually loaded than the others. Given our knowledge (from the case histories and the literature) of the most difficult problems faced by managers in implementing change there are no surprises in these findings. Moreover, we would expect to obtain a different ranking if we had been asking our interviewees to rate the relative importance of the 13 dimensions in relation to another context, such as in the development of company strategy. We may confidently predict that in the latter case 'Planning to optimize the achievement of results' and 'Using intellect to optimize results' would have been rated above the other two sets of dimensions.

REFLECTION

Assuming you completed the exercise in Table 11.1, how does the pattern of your scores compare with the patterns presented in Tables 11.2 and 11.6? How do you account for any similarities or differences obtained?

A competencies framework for effective change agents

Having explored the concept of competencies within the context of three frameworks dealing with the overall role of the manager, and attempted to elicit (alongside those of our interviewees) your views as to the relative importance of different competencies for managing change, we can now focus our attention on a study that was designed specifically to identify competencies required by managers responsible for managing a change project. This is the study carried out by Buchanan and Boddy (1992). Their definition of competence was (Buchanan and Boddy, 1992, p. 92):

> actions and behaviours identified by change agents as contributing, in their experience, to the perceived effectiveness of change implementation.

In the process of identifying the behaviours, techniques or competencies that contribute to effectiveness in the management of change, Buchanan and Boddy content-analyzed the diary transcripts of eight project managers (including Chief Officer, Probation Service; Business Manager in Computer Manufacturer; Management Services manager in a Local Authority) and carried out a questionnaire survey. Analysis revealed five competence clusters (units) and 15 specific attributes (elements) relating to the handling of the project manager's process agenda. The five clusters and 15 attributes are summarized in Table 11.7. The authors view these as 'process agenda competencies', which are needed to establish a balance between public performance and backstage activity in managing and constructing an appropriate and contextually acceptable change implementation process.

They identified several problems with this competence-based analysis of the role of the change agent:

1   Survey results provided equivocal support for generalizablity.
2   The 15 competencies are not comparable – they are a mix of skills, cognitive styles and personality traits.
3   The ability to use the competencies *appropriately* is what counts; in other words, it is not sufficient to possess the competencies if they are not applied to managing the process of change in appropriate situations.

TABLE 11.7: Competencies required of change agents (Buchanan and Boddy, 1992)

1 *Goals*

  – Sensitivity to changes in key personnel, top management perceptions and market conditions, and to the way in which these impact the goals of the project in hand

  – Clarity in specifying goals, in defining the achievable

  – Flexibility in responding to changes outwith the control of the project manager, perhaps requiring major shifts in project goals and management style, and risk taking

2 *Roles*

  – Team building abilities, to bring together key stakeholders and establish effective working groups, and clearly to define and delegate respective responsibilities

  – Networking skills in establishing and maintaining appropriate contacts within and outside the organization

  – Tolerance of ambiguity, to be able to function comfortably, patiently and effectively in an uncertain environment

3 *Communication*

  – Communication skills to transmit effectively to colleagues and subordinates the need for changes in project goals and in individual tasks and responsibilities

  – Interpersonal skills across the range, including selection, listening, collecting appropriate information, identifying the concerns of others, and managing meetings

  – Personal enthusiasm, in expressing plans and ideas

  – Stimulating motivation and commitment in others involved

4 *Negotiation*

  – Selling plans and ideas to others, by creating a desirable and challenging vision of the future

  – Negotiating with key players for resources, or for changes in procedures, and to resolve conflict

5 *Managing*

  – Political awareness, in identifying potential coalitions, and in balancing conflicting goals and perceptions

  – Influencing skills, to gain commitment to project plans and ideas from potential sceptics and resisters

  – Helicopter perspective, to stand back from the immediate project and take a broader view of priorities

They argue that competencies cannot be understood independently of the process in which the change agent engages, and since this process varies from context to context, so demands made on the change agent vary. They conclude that the list of competencies is nothing more than a toolkit. It says nothing about how these competencies are to be most effectively applied; how they might relate to issues of public performance and backstage activity; or how they relate either to the process of change or to the context of change. They resolve these difficulties by drawing on the concept of 'expertise' that they see as 'the appropriate application of a tool kit to the management of change process within a given context'.

They are critical of many of the prescriptions to be found in the management of change area, pointing out: that processual and contextual analyses reveal the multi-layered and multi-variate nature of change; the central role of legitimacy; the importance of ritual and symbolic action; and the significance of cultural and historical factors. Too often, (a) project management writings advocate an unrealistic linear model of the change process; (b) participative management writings assume involvement necessarily leads to agreement and commitment; and (c) sociological accounts are too complex and lack clear prescription.

So, they ask, how do we understand the expertise of the contemporary change agent, particularly the manager operating within an organic management system and with a change programme in a complex situation? The action of the change agent must be both effective and acceptable. Effectiveness and acceptability are context-dependent, so our understanding of change agent expertise must also be context dependent. Buchanan and Boddy (1992) therefore propose a two-layer model of expertise for change agents:

Level 1: *Managerial/professional judgement*: concerns diagnostic skills, judgemental capability and behavioural flexibility. These concern developing an understanding of the changing context, identifying agenda priorities and acting accordingly (public and backstage) to construct an effective and acceptable change process.

Level 2: *Managerial/professional toolkit of competencies*: includes 15 competencies in five clusters identified and illustrated above. These concern relatively well-defined and well-understood management behaviours for which effective management development approaches have been long established.

Thus, in their view, core competencies are necessary but not sufficient in the creation of change agent expertise. The effective change agent is able to deploy these core competencies appropriately in context. These conclusions are consistent with those of others (e.g. Pedler *et al.*, 1986; Schon, 1987; Brown, 1993; McFarlane and Lomas, 1995).

Conclusions

Armed with these conclusions, and what we have learnt through the exercise involving the MCI personal competence framework, does the competencies topic give us any additional insights relating to models for implementing change? One of the main conclusions from Chapter 10 was that favourable attitudinal and behavioural consequences would follow according to the perceived level of acceptability and predictability associated with change events. In the model presented in that chapter we can identify three main sets of variables as significant determinants of acceptability and predictability, namely: learning opportunities, rewards and costs, and leadership. In the process of managing these latter variables most of the dimensions in the MCI framework are relevant, as indeed are those of the other frameworks. The value of being aware of these findings in the competencies literature is that they spell out in a more analytical and comprehensive picture what is entailed in the process of rewarding, leading and facilitating the learning of those who will be affected by change.

However, this additional information and insight may still not be sufficient for those at the front line of implementing change. Thus, knowing that 'obtaining the commitment of others' is an important competency is little help in itself. We need to know more about the knowledge and skills for obtaining the commitment, or at least the cooperation, of others. In the following chapters we shall show how selected theoretical contributions can be of practical value to managers. The two areas we have selected to focus upon are gaining cooperation and managing stress. Given our case histories, these would appear to be the most rewarding topics to explore at the present time.

REFLECTION

Consider the model you arrived at as a result of tackling the exercise in Chapter 10 (alternatively consider someone else's model which was sufficiently compatible with your mental model of implementing change). Do you feel that this model now needs to be adjusted to take into account any new insight gained from exploring management competencies? If so, what changes are needed and why?

CHAPTER TWELVE

Insights through theory: generic change models

The next three chapters focus on a sample of behavioural science theories that will increase understanding into the problems encountered in implementing change. The present chapter draws attention to some generic change, such as Lewin's three-stage model and Beer *et al.*'s critical path model. These models have a useful contribution to make to the process of developing adequate mental models of change management.

It is worth remembering a point made in Chapter 2 – learning involves conceptualization that informs future action. Mental models influence how we perceive our worlds and how we then act towards them. As Derek Pugh has stated 'every action of a manager rests upon assumptions about what has happened and upon conjectures about what will happen: that is to say it rests upon theory' (Pugh, 1971, pp. 9–10). Consequently, the adequacy of our theories will influence our recipes for implementing change. The most effective leaders will continue to strive to improve the adequacy and validity of their mental models and to share them with others.

The purpose of this chapter is to highlight a sample of behavioural science theories that will help learners develop more adequate mental models of change management. In order to do this we will first present some of the key generic theoretical ideas, and add some of our own mental models that we have found to be useful when teaching, consulting or implementing change. We shall then focus more specifically on two key issues facing managers that emerged from the analysis of our cases, namely, gaining the cooperation of others (Chapter 13) and managing stress (Chapter 14). The following illustrative discussion is by no means comprehensive; it is intended to be used as a stimulus for questioning and refining your own model(s), and for further exploring the riches of the theoretical literature.

Some models for thinking about change

Let's begin then by looking at some of the generic theoretical models in the literature. These consider why change occurs, outline the steps the manager can take to promote change, highlight the contingencies and consequences associated with the manner by which the manager makes decisions and exerts influence during change, and stress the importance of an adequate model of what the manager is attempting to change.

Lewin's Three-Stage Model

Kurt Lewin's model of change (Lewin, 1951) can be found in some guise in most management of change models. Change results from change in the forces that impinge upon the organization, group or individual. Lewin used this force-field approach to explain why individuals, groups or organizations change and consequently how change can be brought about. Change is brought about by actions that strengthen the driving forces or weaken resistances to change. Lewin makes the important point that to strengthen the driving forces without weakening the resistances results in strain. As Figure 12.1 shows, the model has three phases. First, there is an unfreezing phase in which there is a recognition that there is a need for change, followed by a period of change during which action is taken to strengthen driving forces and weaken resistances, followed by refreezing where the organization settles into a new dynamic equilibrium. One more point worthy of mention is that Lewin's model is fundamentally a power-based model:

FIGURE 12.1: Lewin's Three-Stage Model of change

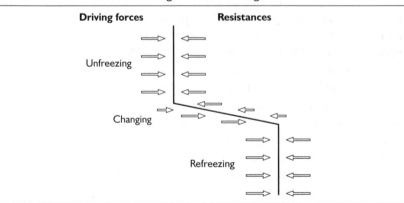

change depends upon the relative strength of the vectors (power is a topic to which we return).

Of course, it is clear that Lewin's model lacks detail. What causes individuals or groups to cooperate, what causes then to resist? For the answer we need to delve further into the determinants of the behaviour of individuals and groups, which we will do. For the present, Lewin gives us a useful general model for conceptualizing how to bring change about.

Beckhard and Harris's Model

The authors (Beckhard and Harris, 1987) present a model which is concerned with motivating change: Change = ABC > D, where:

A = Dissatisfaction with the status quo
B = A desirable future
C = A practical pathway
D = The costs of changing

Beckhard and Harris suggest that change will occur when there is dissatisfaction with the status quo, people perceive a desirable future and a practical pathway for achieving that future, and these are greater than the costs of changing. This is a motivational approach to change management. Quite rightly it has been influential and makes a valuable contribution to our understanding of how to manage planned change – we need to reduce the 'costs' of changing; we need to convince people that the present is problematic; we need to persuade people of a desirable vision of the future and that there exists a means for achieving it.

Beckhard and Harris suggest that focusing upon the future rather than the present is beneficial because it:

- means optimism replaces pessimism
- enables people to visualize their role, improving compliance
- reduces uncertainty and feelings of insecurity
- focuses attention away from problems and symptoms to a consideration of what will make the organization effective

It can be argued that Beckhard's approach has its origins in what Warren Bennis (1969) has described as the doctrine of 'truth and love' and consequently places insufficient emphasis upon the significance of power. Not everyone needs to be convinced of a desirable future, a practical pathway, and so on. Change can be imposed, and as our case studies reveal, it frequently is.

Beer et al.'s Critical Path Model (1990)

Beer *et al.* focus on change at the unit or organizational level and put forward an approach to change management that they call the critical path to corporate renewal. 'The critical path is a general manager-led process that implements task alignment at the unit level by doing the following:

1   Mobilizing energy for change among all stakeholders in the organization by involving them in a diagnosis of the problems blocking competitiveness
2   Developing a task-aligned vision of how to organize and manage for competitiveness
3   Fostering consensus that the new vision is "right", competence to enact it, and cohesion to move change along
4   Spreading revitalization to all departments of the unit in a way that avoids perception that a program is being pushed from the top, but at the same time ensures consistency with the organizational changes already under way
5   Consolidating changes through formal policies, systems, and structures that institutionalize revitalization
6   Continually monitoring and strategizing in response to predictable problems in the revitalization process' (Beer *et al.*, 1990, p. 78)

Beer *et al.* argue for involving as many employees as possible in order to develop consensus and spread revitalization. Many other authors make similar prescriptions in order to 'get everybody in the room', 'bring people on board', and develop 'ownership' or 'buy in'. Others have mentioned related advantages, including: the release of latent knowledge and skills; better solutions to problems; enhanced acceptance of decisions and greater organizational commitment; reduced stress levels; and higher job satisfaction. Certainly, involving people in change as has much to commend it.

Despite these advantages our cases mainly illustrated an autocratic approach rather than a participative approach. Indeed, there were a number of instances of covert manoeuvring to implement change, and in some cases employees were deliberately kept in the dark. Perhaps there are other factors that need to be taken into account in determining whether or not it makes sense to involve employees in change?

A generic problem-solving model

A model that we have found to be useful in teaching, consulting and implementing change is given in Figure 12.2.

Figure 12.2 is a basic problem-solving model, elements of which can be found in the action research approach of the OD school, and in the more technical approach of project management. It suggests that the steps that a manager needs to take in order to facilitate change are:

- gather data – monitor performance, undertake research, provide feedback
- analyze the data – distinguish symptoms from causes, agree importance, identify SMART change goals
- identify a solution – identify developmental actions, re-design jobs, modify company policies, recruit new skills
- plan a pathway – agree responsibilities, allocate budgets, specify timings and milestones, determine the sequencing of activities
- act and monitor success

These activities are more-or-less the same whether the manager is coaching an individual to develop their skills, managing conflict in a team, or re-engineering the work processes in a business unit. Of

FIGURE 12.2: A problem-solving model of change management

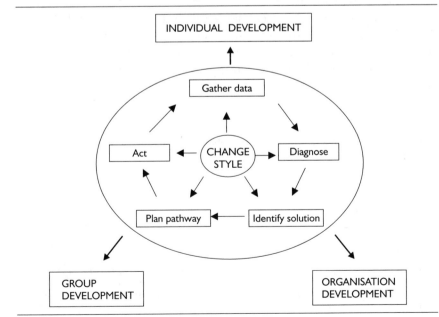

course, in reality change is a much messier problem than this. It is not a nice neat sequence of activities, but is decidedly non-linear, chaotic and political. Nonetheless, many practitioners argue that whilst our neat problem solving model is not descriptive of the reality of change, it helps to act as if it was.

A contingency approach to change management

At the centre of Figure 12.2 is an important consideration, namely change style or the manner in which the manager attempts to bring change about: this includes both the style of making decisions and of implementing solutions. Does the manager involve others in data gathering, undertake joint diagnosis, solicit ideas for a solution, empower others to implement solutions as they see fit? Or does the manager play the 'doctor' and identify the problem and impose the solution him- or herself? In our case histories all the changes taking place were initiated from the top, and one may argue that this is to be expected given the hierarchical structure of most organizations. However, some implementers of change made much greater attempts to involve and consult others. This happened in 'Implementing strategic change in a charity', but was not a feature of 'Restructuring in a processing plant'. Why these different approaches, and what situational factors make one more appropriate than another?

An adaptation of the Tannenbaum and Schmidt model (1973) is given in Figure 12.3. It suggests that there are degrees of involvement – or non-involvement – ranging from keeping employees in the dark, through informing them, explaining decisions and consulting with them, to delegation.

FIGURE 12.3: An adaptation of Tannenbaum and Schmidt's model of decision making

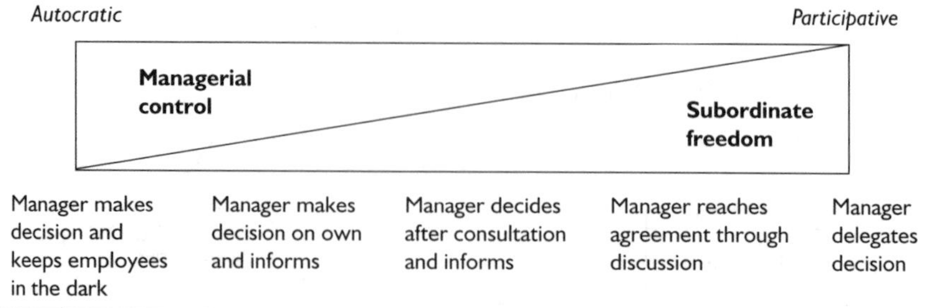

Autocratic				Participative
Managerial control			**Subordinate freedom**	
Manager makes decision and keeps employees in the dark	Manager makes decision on own and informs	Manager decides after consultation and informs	Manager reaches agreement through discussion	Manager delegates decision

Vroom and Jago (1988) suggest that the likely effectiveness of these alternative decision making styles varies with a number of contingencies, some of which are:

(a) How important is employee commitment to the decision?

(b) Do employees share the goals of change?

(c) Does the manager have sufficient information to make a high-quality decision?

(d) Are employees competent to make a high-quality decision?

(e) If the manager makes the decision, is it likely that employees would accept the decision?

(f) How much time is available to make the decision?

Let us discuss the first two of these contingency factors in a little more detail.

Importance of employee commitment

There is little doubt that organizations operating in complex, uncertain environments where innovation is at a premium must realize the potential of their human resources. In order to do so, they need to satisfy employee needs for self-determination and self-esteem. Such organizations require managers who provide these psychological strokes. In such organizations there is in Vroom and Jago's terms 'a commitment requirement'; that is, employee commitment to the decision and ensuing change is important. However, compare two organizations in our set of cases – 'Restructuring in a processing plant' and 'Merging two management consultancy units'. In the former, the jobs were prescribed and controlled. The design of the plant processes is the critical factor affecting functioning and all that is required from a large part of the human system is adequate skills and reliable role behaviour. In contrast, the jobs in a consultancy are complex, novel, unpredictable, difficult to supervise, and involve direct contact with the client. Job occupants possess specialist and possibly unique business skills, knowledge and client networks that have been learnt and developed over time, and the internal commitment, spontaneity and loyalty of staff are essential. In the consultancy firm the human system is more critical for success: employees, as opposed to production processes, create value.

One of the key questions to be considered during change is therefore how important is the human system for the achievement of the objectives of the change. If high levels of job motivation or the retention of staff is essential to achieve these objectives then a 'people focus' is appropriate during the change process. If, on the other hand, the technical system is more critical, then the commitment requirement is less important and a participative approach is less necessary. Of course, this analysis is simplistic. There are groups of employees in all organizations, for example, senior managers and boundary role workers where motivation, loyalty and retention are critical, and groups where this is less so. Nonetheless the analysis would still suggest that in order to be successful, change in a consultancy may require a different approach to that applied in a processing or manufacturing plant.

Beckhard and Harris (1987) make the point that key agents of change, for example, a unit head or integration manager, need to be committed to the change if they are expected to make it or help it to happen (to which we would add that they also need to be competent and to possess sufficient power to make change happen). They suggest a simple process of commitment mapping where the key people are identified and then their current and needed level of commitment mapped (see Figure 12.4). Involving key players in data gathering, diagnosis, designing the future and so on may well strengthen their commitment. However, as we have already pointed out, to involve them will not always make sense. It is important to be patient, but if the commitment of key players cannot be gained they will need to be replaced.

FIGURE 12.4: Commitment mapping (after Beckhard and Harris, 1987)

Key players	No commitment	Let it happen	Help it happen	Make it happen
1		X ⇐═══════⇒ O		
2			XO	
3	X ⇐══⇒ O			
4	X ⇐═══════════⇒ O			
5				
6				
7				
8				

Shared values and goals

Goal congruency would appear to be a particularly problematic contingency. People in different parts of the organization have different goals – top management have a strategic focus and, if the company is publicly quoted, are concerned with the reactions of the stock market and investors. Middle management have an operational focus and are primarily concerned with the performance of their areas of responsibility. Lower management have a job focus: they are concerned with getting the job done, normally well and with satisfaction. In many organizations there would appear to be fundamental goal differences that serve to undermine the ability of the organization to adopt a participative, let alone an empowering, style of management.

The conflict and confusion which can be caused by different goals and values at different levels of an organization can readily be seen in the case 'Unplanned change in a market research agency'. The parent company in the USA was interested in taking advantage of an expanding market in order to increase profits. Middle managers in the UK, who were having to deal face-to-face with clients and suppliers, were more concerned in satisfying clients by meeting agreed deadlines. Unfortunately, the suppliers were unable to meet the demands made upon them at short notice. Also, there was a difference of opinion between the directors of the UK firm. Some were 'externally oriented' and wanted all the time of the executives to be spent on things directly relating to immediate client needs; others were 'internally oriented' in the sense that they encouraged developmental activities which resulted in employees acquiring knowledge and skills enabling the firm to provide a better service to clients. This medley of values and goals produced certain changes that resulted in frustration and low morale among many staff. Where consensus concerning mission and strategy of the organization is not attainable, an autocratic style of management where cooperation is primarily through the compliance route may be appropriate. Indeed, when employees are opposed to change, especially if they are in a position to resist or undermine it, there is an argument for non-involvement, for keeping them in the dark until a near *fait accompli* is achieved. This is apparent in a number of our cases. Change involving downsizing, outsourcing and divestment appears to be qualitatively different to managing change where employees can envision a desirable future – turkeys don't vote for Christmas!

The issue is not, therefore, a case of involving or not involving employees, but the extent to which it makes sense to do so. Should we delegate decisions, or merely consult? Do we keep employees informed

TABLE 12.1: Motivational implications of different kinds of involvement and styles of management (after Etzioni, 1961)

Tactic	Nature of involvement	Motivational implications
Empower Persuade	Internal commitment	Spontaneous, innovative, persistent behaviour in pursuit of chosen goals
Reward	Calculative involvement	
Obligate Instruct	Compliance	Normal levels of effort, reliable role behaviour
Manoeuvre Threaten	Alienation	Minimal effort, unreliable behaviour requiring close supervision, hostility

or in the dark? The answers to these questions are dependent upon the nature of the contingency involved. For example, if we wished to develop the competence of subordinates it makes sense to involve them, at least to the extent of explaining and discussing the issues involved even though this is time-consuming and may not improve the quality of the decision. However, we would be far more wary of involving the uncommitted to this extent especially if they had power and might be inclined to use this to resist change. Our perceptions of people's motivation, and their goal commitment, are likely to be particularly influential in determining the extent to which we involve them.

Keeping people in the dark, redesigning their jobs for them, and giving them no choice over how the changes are implemented, has costs for the manager and organization. Etzioni details the likely motivational and emotional outcomes of alternative change management styles (see Table 12.1). Thus change can be imposed but there will be costs, which when individuals are a key source of value may be very significant.

A systems model

The manager of change not only needs an adequate model of why change occurs and how to bring about change, but also an adequate model of what is being changed. Figure 12.5 is a systems model of the organization that emphasizes the interdependence of the organizational components. Re-engineering the work processes, developing customer service, introducing TQM or new IT will have knock-on

FIGURE 12.5: A systems model of the organization

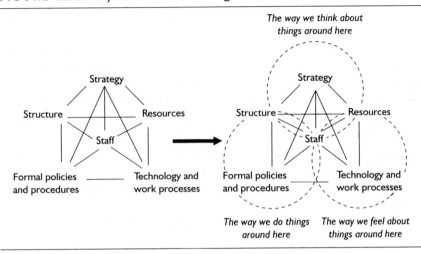

effects and require a change in other aspects of the organization, such as, staff skills, budgets, performance measurement procedures, corporate remuneration policies and so on. A change in one component is likely to require the realignment of others if it is to be effective. Whilst this model is focused at the organizational level, it is equally relevant to individual business unit or work groups.

Our model also emphasizes that there is an informal as well as a formal side to an organization, which emerges over time. The informal organization is the human side of the enterprise. Doubtless the reader has been a member of a new group at some stage and noticed how characteristic ways of thinking about and doing things emerge. Norms develop about how one is expected to dress, about timekeeping, about workloads and about standards of work. People take on informal roles as well as their formal ones. Friendships develop. An influence and power structure evolves. Shared values arise, which may or may not coincide with those of the organization. The group experiences more transient feelings, shared joy after success, despair after failure, anger and mistrust when agreements are broken, and insecurity when the future is uncertain. Change involves not just alteration to the formal aspects of the organization but also to these informal human aspects. Both the formal and informal aspects of an organization or group can serve to lever or resist change. The failure rate of business process re-engineering is often put down to not understanding and/or not sufficiently taking into account the human factor.

Similar statements could be made for a whole range of major change programmes: total quality management, downsizing, mergers and so on.

The systems model also suggests that in order to promote successful change a broad focus is necessary when data gathering, undertaking diagnosis, identifying solutions, planning implementation and monitoring success: a focus which includes both the formal and informal aspects of the group or organization. Too frequently, managers see only technical problems and identify technical solutions without any consideration for the people who will implement or be affected by them, and monitor success in terms of milestones and budgets without considering the impact of change upon motivation, commitment or morale.

Having considered some generic change models and ideas, let us next look more closely at one of the issues that emerged from our cases, namely gaining cooperation.

EXERCISE (continuation; see pp. 40–41)

To what extent does your model of implementing change incorporate any of the ideas embedded in the generic theories touched on in this chapter? If your thinking has changed then modify your model accordingly.

CHAPTER THIRTEEN

Insights through theory: gaining cooperation

One of the main challenges a manager faces when implementing change is gaining the cooperation of others. Very useful theories exist to guide them in this task, including well-known theories of motivation. This chapter outlines the essentials of several of these theories, particularly those that give us greater insight into why employees cooperate in the implementation of change.

In order to implement change plans the manager needs others to agree to do things differently or take responsibility for bringing change about – to act as an agent of change. Day to day it is the individual managers in the organization, from the CEO to the shift supervisor, who actually implement change by getting others to take action or change their behaviour. The individual manager is faced with questions such as: How do I get others to think differently about their job: it's purpose, focus and their responsibilities? How do I get others to change the way they do their job: adopt new work processes, administrative systems, and information technology? How do I get others to change the way they work together: to work in teams, share information, solve problems, provide support for each other? In order to implement change the manager needs the cooperation of others.

We observe cooperative behaviour when one or more individuals appear to be helping others to achieve their goals. In all our cases the implementers of change were striving to obtain the cooperation of others. Thus in 'Implementing strategic change in a charity', the CEO had to obtain the cooperation of a wide group of stakeholders, including Council members, full-time paid staff and voluntary unpaid staff. In 'Market testing in central government', the head of department had to gain the cooperation explicitly of his subordinate staff and implicitly of his superior. In 'Restructuring support services in a partnership', the personnel manager had to win over the cooperation of the partners. In 'Integration following a takeover in the retail industry', the finance manager and his team had to gain the cooperation of those being taken over in the merger.

The dynamics in each of these situations were quite different. In 'Implementing strategic change in a charity' the CEO had relatively little authority to order voluntary unpaid staff to do as they were told. Accordingly he had to try to retain their cooperation by winning their commitment to new strategic goals. The personnel manager in the law firm had even less authority over the partners in the firm. It was through his credibility and professionalism that he managed to win over their reluctant cooperation for change. The finance manager had, if he wished to use it, a fair amount of authority at the end of the day to impose a common financial and accounting system on the 'defeated' competitor. However, he realized the value of dialogue and consultation in introducing a common system.

Why do employees cooperate?

Let us begin our exploration of cooperative behaviour with the question why do employees cooperate? Figure 13.1 provides a framework for discussing key variables and associated theories. Cooperative behaviour results from an agreement to act cooperatively. Getting employees to agree to do something commits them, and results in an intention to act accordingly. As the left-hand side of Figure 13.1 reveals, there are a range of reasons for employees agreeing to act cooperatively. They may do so because they expect monetary rewards or a more enjoyable and satisfying job. They may do so out of friendship or loyalty to the manager. They may do so because they believe it is their job to do so – it goes with the territory so to speak. They may agree to change their behaviour because they believe they may lose their job or be overlooked for promotion if they do not. They may of course cooperate for a variety of these reasons. These factors represent what a manager can use to lever cooperation – threaten employees with redundancy, rely on friendship, offer bonuses, design a future which is enjoyable and challenging, and so on.

The right-hand side of the diagram reveals that there are degrees of commitment and motivation associated with cooperative behaviour. At one extreme, cooperation can be spontaneous, involve high levels of effort and persistence, and be undertaken enthusiastically. At the other extreme, cooperative behaviour can be entirely reactive, involve

FIGURE 13.1: The basis of cooperative behaviour

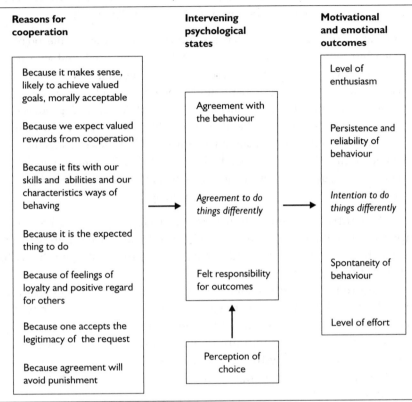

minimal effort, be unreliable and undertaken in an atmosphere of resentment and hostility, so much so that constant close supervision is required. In order to understand why this should be so, we need to consider the three intervening factors in the centre of Figure 13.1. We need to distinguish between what an individual agrees to do, and what he or she agrees with or values. Thus through obligation, obedience or threat individuals may agree to do something which they do not agree with – they may believe it does not make sense, is unlikely to be successful or is likely to be costly for them – but they nonetheless agree to cooperate. Under such conditions the individual is likely to feel coerced, and a minimal level of effort will result. In comprehending the likely strength of commitment we also need to take into account the individual's beliefs about the locus of responsibility for agreement. Do individuals feel that they have made a free choice in deciding to cooperate? If they believe so they are likely to feel personally responsible for the outcomes and engage in highly motivated and spontaneous behaviour. Chris Argyris uses the term 'internal commitment' to refer to this type of cooperative behaviour (Argyris, 1970, p. 20):

> Internal commitment means that the individual has reached the point where he is acting on the choice because it fulfils his own needs and sense of responsibility, as well as those of the system. The individual who is internally committed is acting primarily under the influence of his own forces not induced forces. The individual feels a minimal degree of dependence upon others for action. It implies that he has obtained and processed valid information and that he has made an informed and free choice. Under these conditions there is a high probability that the individual's commitment will remain strong over time (even with the reduction of external rewards), or under stress, or when the action is challenged by others.

In contrast, when individuals feel that cooperation has been imposed, they will feel less responsible for outcomes, their behaviour is likely to be less spontaneous and persistent, and the manager is likely to be blamed for any future problems.

Figure 13.1 identifies what a manager can do to gain cooperation, but it also highlights the importance for motivation of the way in which cooperation is obtained. It can be imposed, but low levels of motivation, and hostility and resentment are likely to result. On the other hand, when employees agree with the behavioural change and feel that they have freely chosen to engage in the behaviour then high levels of commitment result.

We will now look in more detail at what the manager can do to get employees to agree to do things differently or take steps to bring about change.

Gaining cooperation through rewards and punishment

Employee needs represent what individuals want from their environment. A need can be defined as an internal state of disequilibrium or deficiency that has the capacity to energize behaviour. It is assumed that when need deficiencies exist people want or are motivated to satisfy them. Change in the workplace can therefore result in an increase in employees' ability to satisfy their needs, for example through job enrichment, or result in the denial of needs and dissatisfaction. A typology of human needs is given in Table 13.1, along with a range of rewards that are frequently found in organizations and some mechanisms for their delivery. The typology is derived from Maslow's (1943) influential hierarchical theory of motivation and Alderfer's (1969) subsequent refinements of the theory.

TABLE 13.1: A typology of individual needs and examples of corresponding rewards and means of their delivery

Needs	Rewards	Mechanisms
Growth	Autonomy	Job design
Self-determination	Challenge	Performance
Need for competence	Responsibility	measurement
Self-esteem	Meaningfulness of work	Management style
	Recognition	Performance appraisal
Relatedness	Status	Career development
Approval	Advancement	Remuneration system
Affiliation	Pay	Teamworking
Affection	Friendly supervision	Fringe benefits
	Cohesive work group	Contract of employment
Existence	Pension	
Security	Job security	
Food	Safe working conditions	

Most of these needs are self-explanatory and require no further comment. The human need for competence or mastery, refers to people's wish to stretch their capabilities, to seek and conquer challenges. The need for self-determination (Deci and Ryan, 1985) refers to the desire to act out of choice – it underpins Argyris's concept of internal commitment that we discussed a little earlier in this chapter.

As need theorists such as Abraham Maslow and Clayton Alderfer state, different individuals are motivated by different needs and the same individual is motivated by different needs at different times of his or her life. Not every employee is therefore motivated by such higher order needs. People's psychological contract with, and what they want from, the workplace varies. Some are content to leave the challenge and responsibility to others. Many satisfy these higher order needs outside of the workplace. However, where these needs are potent the consequences of denying their fulfilment or removing their presence in existing jobs may include dissatisfaction, lack of commitment, absenteeism, labour turnover, hostility, stress and reduced effort – in other words, a general lack of cooperation.

The satisfaction of potent human needs is rewarding, their denial punishing. It has been repeatedly shown that people act to gain rewards and to avoid punishment. Consequently behaviour can be shaped by making rewards or the avoidance of punishment contingent upon desired behaviour, and by making punishment or the removal of rewards contingent upon undesired behaviour. By not realigning rewards and punishments to support new desired actions, change may be undermined.

Mager and Pipe (quoted in Komaki *et al.*, 1991), as an example of how punishment can discourage behaviour, describe how an 'attitude problem' on the part of physicians caused them to resist the use of computers to place prescriptions. In fact, an analysis of the situation revealed that there were a number of negative consequences associated with using the computers. The terminals were crowded, noisy and busy, with no room to work. Further, they were placed so as to make their use uncomfortable for those wearing bifocal spectacles. Not surprisingly, the physicians were less than enthusiastic about using the computers when the result was inconvenient, slightly embarrassing, and for some, even mildly painful. When these negative consequences were removed the 'attitude problem' disappeared and they began to use the computers regularly.

Porter and Lawler's (1968) expectancy theory of motivation (Figure 13.2) provides an insightful explanation of how rewards and punishments influence, or do not influence, what people do. On the basis of past experiences individuals learn that a certain behaviour is likely to result in a reward or punishment. That is, employees learn expectations that A will result in B. Thus, rather than being pushed into action by their needs, employees are pulled into action by expected rewards.

What this model suggests is that individuals will expend effort if they value the outcomes and if they expect that effort will result in these outcomes. Porter and Lawler also introduce the distinction between motivation and performance, i.e. that performing to required

FIGURE 13.2: The expectancy theory of motivation (Porter and Lawler, 1968)

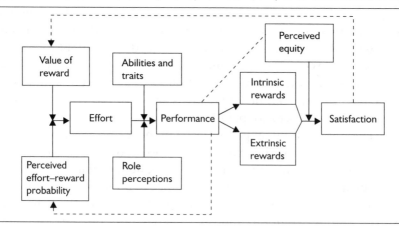

standards requires appropriate skills and abilities (to which we would add adequate resources) and clarity over what one is expected to achieve. Further, the feedback loops underline the dynamic nature of motivation – we update our initial expectation regarding the value of outcomes and the probability of effort resulting in the rewards on the basis of our experiences and perceptions of the equity of the outcomes. The model also separates the concepts of performance and satisfaction. In keeping with the empirical research findings, a happy worker may not be a productive one, nor a productive one happy.

The expectancy approach adds greatly to the understanding of the manager trying to get people to do things differently through cooperation. No longer is changing behaviour solely about encouraging the desired behaviour through the anticipation of rewards, for example through the promise of promotion or increased pay. In addition, these rewards need to be perceived as equitable – relative to the effort needed to achieve them and to the rewards gained by others – if satisfaction is to result. Further, individuals need to believe that they are capable of performing at the required level. As mentioned in Chapter 2, self-efficacy is a concept derived from *social learning theory* (Bandura, 1997) and relates to those beliefs that an individual holds in relation to their own competencies to engage in particular activities or to achieve given outcomes. Individuals with low self-efficacy beliefs may find any proposed changes to their jobs and working conditions more threatening, because they lack the self-confidence to perform well in new situations. Managers of change therefore need to take action through coaching and providing support to ensure that employees believe that they have the competence to perform at the required levels, and that they have the resources to do so. Also, they need to ensure that what is required in terms of performance is clear and that it is seen by the individual and others as a legitimate part of the job. Finally, in order to sustain motivation and promote learning, the manager needs to provide feedback on performance.

Gaining cooperation through person–job fit

Behaviour can be seen as a function of the nature of the person and the nature of the job, i.e. $B = f(P \times J)$. Note that behaviour refers not just to actions, but includes motivational and emotional aspects, for example job satisfaction and experienced stress, and that the interaction has a phenomenological basis, i.e. through the eyes of the beholder. Change invariably involves some form of job or process redesign. This is likely to change the role requirements for job incumbents in terms of the intrinsic rewards associated with doing the job, and the abilities and personality characteristics necessary for successful performance in the changed role. The redesign of jobs can therefore result in a lack of fit between the skills, needs and values of current incumbents and the changed role requirements. In the short term, this is likely to result in reduced performance, dissatisfaction and stress, and in the longer term in absenteeism, sickness and labour turnover. Note that a lack of fit can also result from change in the other side of the equation; that is, in a change in the skills and abilities available to an organization in the labour market.

Fit can be promoted by Fitting the Person to the Job (FPJ) and Fitting the Job to the Person (FJP). FPJ strategies include recruitment and selection, placement and the allocation of specific roles and responsibilities, replacement, training and development. FJP strategies include job and organizational redesign.

Individuals differ in terms of their needs and interests, abilities and skills, attitudes, values and personality. Personality and underlying abilities are considered to be the product of experience and an inherited potential. Consequently, they are relatively stable characteristics and there are limits to the extent and rate of change. The fact that people differ in their abilities has obvious implications for person–job fit: someone with below average psychomotor ability is not going to make a particular good lathe operator; someone who has below average numerical reasoning ability is unlikely to be successful in the role of a financial manager. Similarly, personality has implication for fit. Introverts do not become extroverts. Those who are typically anxious and insecure do not become confident. Those who are emotional do not become unemotional. As abilities and personality are resistant to change, selection and placement or job redesign are more likely to be effective in promoting fit than training or development. The work of Holland (1966) illustrates the fitting of individual personality and job demands through vocational choice, and the work of Hackman and Oldham (1980) provides an example of fitting individual needs and job demands through job re-design.

Holland's *Hexagonal theory of personality types* was primarily developed to help individuals in making successful vocational choices. It has been used as a tool to improve the fit between the personality of individuals and job demands, and it is one of the most researched theories of its type (Furnham, 2001). Figure 13.3 shows Holland's typology of six different personal orientations to life, and the definition of each type is provided in terms of the characteristic activities, interests, competencies and personality traits of the members. The arrangement

FIGURE 13.3: The hexagonal model of vocational interests (Holland, 1966)

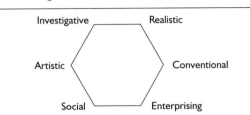

Realistic jobs, such as mechanic, surveyor and farmer, are suitable for individuals who would be described as conforming, frank, practical, genuine and uninsightful.

Investigative jobs, such as biologist, physicist and medical technologist, are suitable for individuals who would be described as analytical, critical, complex, introspective and rational.

Artistic jobs, such as composer, musician, interior decorator and actor, are suitable for individuals who would be described as emotional, expressive, impulsive, original and sensitive.

Social jobs, such as teacher, counsellor and speech therapist, are suitable for individuals who would be described as empathic, kind, understanding and warm.

Conventional jobs, such as bookkeeper, banker and tax expert, are suitable for people who would be described as conscientious, orderly, efficient and methodical.

Enterprising jobs, such as salesperson, manager and television producer, are suitable for individuals who would be described as ambitious, energetic, self-confident and sociable.

of the types around the hexagon are meaningful in that those adjacent to each other (e.g. Realistic and Investigative) have more in common than those diagonally opposite each other (e.g. Realistic and Social). An important clarification of the theory is worth mentioning – Holland is not saying that there are six types of personality, but that an individual's personality pattern will resemble more closely one of the six orientations (e.g. may be a great deal in common with the Enterprising type, less so with the Social and Conventional types, and even less with the Realistic, Investigative and Artistic types).

Hackman and Oldham's (1980) Job Characteristics Model in Figure 13.4 identifies some of the factors that result in high levels of job motivation and how the design of work processes can impact upon levels of motivation and satisfaction by providing for or denying human needs. For many, work is a central aspect of their life, but not all employees respond positively when their job is enriched with added challenge, responsibility and autonomy: hence the variable 'Employee

FIGURE 13.4: Job Characteristics Model of work motivation (Hackman and Oldham, 1980)

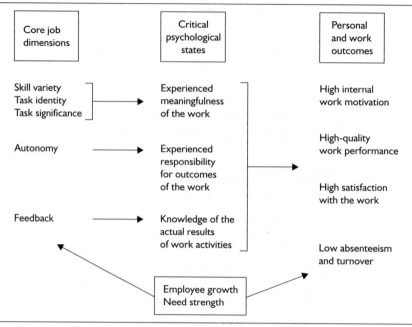

growth need strength' moderating the relationship between core job dimensions and personal work outcomes. However, there is evidence to suggest that some individuals who reluctantly cooperated by operating in 'enriched jobs' refused the option of returning to their old jobs after a period of adaptation. This can probably be explained in terms of their initial fear of being at a disadvantage when tackling unfamiliar job features, but once they had mastered new skills, and positive reinforcements had begun to flow, their whole attitude toward these changes became very positive.

Change can involve the de-skilling of people's jobs. When this occurs – that is, jobs are made more simple and routine, less varied and challenging, and with decreased responsibility and with increased supervision – many employees are likely to become demotivated and less cooperative.

Knowledge can be gained from learning (moderate), attitudes changed through persuasion, interests developed from experience and, assuming that the individual possesses the underlying ability, new skills developed through training. However, there are limits to the amount and rate of change in many human characteristics. An individual who desires and is used to autonomy is going to have difficulty adapting if the job becomes more formalized and prescribed. The graphic artist who takes pride in his hand drawing ability is unlikely to welcome the introduction of computer-based graphics. The sociable individual who enjoys chatting with colleagues is unlikely to find homeworking satisfying. Shy, introverted accountants are unlikely to be successful when their redesigned role requires them to go out and meet clients. People may well try to adapt in these circumstances and their behaviour may well change. But they might not be very successful in their changed roles; their self-esteem and self-identity may be jaded; they may feel dissatisfied and resentful; they may suffer from increased stress; and their continued cooperation may become doubtful.

The main conclusion to be drawn from this 'person–job match' section is that in the process of implementing change managers have to remember that they are trying to gain the effective cooperation of others. These 'others' are individuals, each with a unique set of characteristics as represented by their personalities, abilities and experiences. Cooperation and indeed effective performance are likely where there is a good fit between the characteristics of the individual and role demands, but where change results in an inferior fit cooperation and performance are likely to suffer.

Gaining cooperation through goal commitment

Latham and Baldes (1975) undertook some research on unionized truck driver performance in the USA. The truck drivers concerned were responsible for transporting timber to saw mills. The mill owners were concerned that the trucks were on average loaded to only 60 per cent of their legal capacity. Based upon the goal-setting theory of Edwin Locke the researchers implemented a motivational programme. A challenging goal of 94 per cent of legal capacity was agreed by the truckers, with the understanding that no one would be rewarded with monetary bonuses for achieving the goal and no one would be penalized if they disregarded it. The results of the study showed a dip in performance in the second month of the study. When the drivers were interviewed about the dip, they stated that they were testing management's statement that no punitive steps would be taken for not achieving the goal. None were taken, and an average 90 per cent-plus loading was achieved for the remaining 48 weeks of the research, and this performance level endured for the next eight years.

Locke and his colleagues have undertaken such research with many other groups with similar findings that enable us to conclude that specific, challenging and agreed goals are a major motivating force. Setting specific, challenging and agreed goals with regular feedback is a technique that can promote change; and the absence of them will act as a resistance to change. Locke and Latham (1984) identify a procedure for setting goals:

1   Specify the general objective or tasks to be done
2   Specify how the performance in question will be measured
3   Specify the standard of target to be reached
4   Specify the time span involved
5   Prioritize goals
6   Determine coordination requirements

They describe goal commitment as the *sine qua non* of goal setting. The probability that employees will agree to difficult but attainable goals is likely to be influenced by many of the factors we have already discussed; for example, employee perceptions of whether goal attainment will result in rewards, perceptions of their self-efficacy and resources available, their psychological contract with the organization, and their attitudes towards the behaviours involved. Locke and Latham identify six steps that are likely to promote goal commitment: instruction and explanation, employee participation in the goal-setting process, supervisor support, training and selection to ensure capability, and the use of incentives and rewards. They have found that factors such as trust in management, perceptions of the legitimacy of the authority of the manager, absence of threats or intimidation, and perceptions that the goals are fair and reasonable all go to promote goal commitment.

Gaining cooperation through changing attitudes

In order to gain cooperation the manager will frequently need to persuade others; that is, change people's attitudes. A person's attitudes can be defined as relatively lasting feelings, beliefs and behavioural tendencies directed towards objects, events, ideas or people. They comprise a set of beliefs about an object, person or event, and an evaluation of these beliefs in positive or negative terms, (e.g. like–dislike, good–bad) and a consequent behavioural intention towards that object or person. Obviously employees hold attitudes towards many things (e.g. their job, organization, boss, senior management), which predispose them to act in certain ways. The important thing about attitudes and values in our context is that they are relatively stable and therefore resistant to change, and they predispose some individuals to fit better with the world of work than others.

Hovland and Sherif (1957) explore the conditions when an individual's attitude towards some behaviour or goal is likely to change. Their Assimilation–Contrast Model views our attitude towards a person, object, event or behaviour as being capable of being placed on a bipolar scale which varies from extreme agreement to extreme disagreement. Thus the strong attitudes of our physicians (which we discussed in the section on rewards and punishments) are unlikely to change towards the use of the computers on the basis of information alone – as we discussed earlier, action will need to be taken to change the aversive consequences of using the terminals.

Hovland and Sherif suggest that there is a zone of acceptance around our existing attitudes and if we receive a communication from a credible source within this zone our attitude will move towards that communicated. Thus our physicians are likely to readily assimilate information which supports their view and reject information which disagrees with their view. If the communication expresses a view very different from that held, the negative attitude of our physicians is likely to harden and the credibility of the source will be undermined – the so called 'boomerang effect'. What is important in the model is the assertion that more extreme views are more strongly held and have a smaller zone of acceptance (and therefore a larger zone of rejection). Hence more extreme attitudes are much more difficult to change.

Whilst it is true that more extreme and hence more strongly held attitudes are difficult to change, it may be possible to change them incrementally over time. The foot-in-the-door research of Freedman and Fraser (1966) illustrates the point. They visited women in Californian suburbs with the intention of trying to persuade them to agree to the installation of a large safe-driving sign on their lawns for a week or so. They showed the women a picture of a rather poorly lettered sign installed in the front of an attractive house that obscured much of the house and the front entrance. Only 17 per cent agreed to the request. Another group of women had previously been visited by another interviewer and asked to put a small safe driving sign (3 inches square) in their window. 76 per cent of those who had previously agreed to the small sign later agreed to install the large sign. This work and the Assimilation–Contrast model suggest that extreme attitudes can be changed incrementally over a (long) period of time.

Of course, managers of change are normally having to implement change in the shortest possible time. What they can do is to clarify the beliefs that underpin the attitudes. Some of these are likely to be based upon misconception and misunderstanding. Some may be based upon negative consequences for the individual, and these will need to be resolved if a positive attitude is to result. And some will be based upon the individual's own perception of what makes sense and be perfectly valid from the individual's point of view. Resistance to change through disagreement is often viewed as bloodymindedness, but frequently it is a perfectly rational response from the individual's perspective.

In such cases, attitudes are unlikely to change and the manager will have to use other tactics to change behaviour. The manager can appeal to a higher value, such as 'in the interests of the unit or organiza-tion' or out of 'loyalty' but the success of such an approach will depend upon the strength of attachment to the organization or manager. If this fails then the manager has to resort to other sources of influence and use, for example, legitimate authority to coerce behavioural change or to replace the individual.

Some authors argue that attitudes are of secondary importance to behaviour. Certainly, behaviour can be changed almost regardless of attitudes; however, this is unlikely to promote positive attitudes towards work or the organization. Authority can be used to enforce compliance in the hope that experience will result in a more favourable attitude. However, research on the impact of forced compli-ance on attitude change would suggest that individuals who are coerced into doing something (normally by being paid money) contrary to their attitudes, modify their attitudes far less than those who are not so coerced.

This can be explained by Festinger's (1957) cognitive dissonance theory, according to which individuals have a need to hold compatible beliefs. Thus when new information or experiences result in cognitive dissonance, i.e. are incongruent with our existing view of the world, the individual will reject or modify the new or old beliefs in order that compatibility is achieved. The practical application of this theory can be seen operating in an early stage of many change programmes. Thus managers who are faced with staff who feel that no changes are needed may generate cognitive dissonance in their departments by enabling staff to discover for themselves the discrepancies between their beliefs concerning their efficiency and the independent evidence of a benchmarking exercise. Change in beliefs does not occur overnight. It takes time, new information, leadership and considerable social inter-action for commonly held beliefs to emerge in a department. Unfortu-nately for the manager of change, there is a tendency for individuals to deny, repress or rationalize the new dissonant information rather than change their existing beliefs.

Gaining cooperation through power

Managers of change need to be competent and committed and possess the power needed to drive change. The most frequently quoted classification of the sources of power is that of French and Raven (1958):

- *Reward-based power* – refers to the manager's control over valued rewards, such as promotion, pay increases, praise and recognition, or the removal or withholding of these.
- *Coercive power* – refers to the manager's control over punishments, such as termination of contract, criticism and admonishment, increased workload.
- *Legitimate authority* – refers to the power associated with a role.
- *Expertise* – refers to the manager's control over valued information or expertise.
- *Positional power* – refers to the power resulting from the manager's position in the organization. Centrality refers to power gained by being close to the centre of the organization and having access to decision makers. Criticality refers to the importance of ones role to the organization.
- *Personal bases of power* – refer to sources of power that reside within the individual. An individual's attractiveness, likeability, charisma, credibility and reputation are all sources of such power.

Legitimate authority

One of the most pervasive influences upon the behaviour of people at work is the authority structure. It is almost inconceivable that a change can occur in an organization without the involvement of legitimate authority. Curiously, it took many behavioural scientists 30 or so years to recognize this, for until the 1980s the terms *power* and *authority* could rarely be found in the subject index of major texts on change, and few change practitioners questioned the adequacy of the doctrine of 'truth and love'.

The theoretical concept of *legitimate authority* as a source of influence is based upon employees' acceptance that the role occupant has the legitimate right to exercise influence in certain areas. Authority is vested in a role and normally relates to the responsibilities of that role; though as many managers can testify, responsibility and authority can become divorced, and a source of frustration and conflict. Change frequently involves a change in role responsibilities and will require support from senior authority figures to legitimize authority in the changed role. The nature of authority in an organization is normative and is influenced by the nature of the psychological contract on entry to the organization and socialization experiences thereafter – acceptance of the legitimacy of authority figures is an implicit condition of entry into the organization and likely to be an explicit condition of continued membership. The authority structure of an organization is bolstered by a system of punishments and rewards. As the nature of authority is normative there are significant differences between, as well as within, organizations in what managers have authority over and what they do not. Thus, for example, authority over dress code and hair length is accepted as legitimate in the armed forces, but would not be in most university departments. A case study into culture change in the Sainsbury's supermarket chain revealed differences in opinion between line managers and the HR department in the same organization in what are mandatory and discretionary aspects of the job. Thus the HR department considered that customer service was a discretionary part of the job of checkout operators and proceeded to encourage better customer service by developing more positive attitudes towards being helpful to customers. Line management, on the other hand, considered this to be a mandatory part of the job and consequently imposed change by instructing the checkout operators that they must be helpful and smile at customers (Williams and Dobson, 1996). Being normative the nature of authority in an organization changes over time to reflect broader changes in society and legislation. Thus organizations have legitimately imposed behavioural compliance with policies on equal opportunities, race discrimination, sexual harassment, company uniforms, smoking and drinking. Thus the influence of authority is not limited to work behaviour, but can also be used to impose compliance with corporate and social values.

Stanley Milgram's classic research provides a graphic illustration of the power of authority (Milgram, 1974). Milgram concluded that obedience to authority, rather than an aggressive or psychopathological state, was capable of explaining many of mankind's atrocities. Through experimental manipulation Milgram gained the cooperation of his subjects, so much so that they were prepared to deliver severe electric shocks to others, despite the fact that it caused others and themselves considerable distress.

Milgram considered that there were a number of factors that accounted for his startling results. First, there was an antecedent condition, this being that we are socialized to accept the norm of authority and throughout our lives are rewarded when we do and punished when we do not. Second, there was the perception of an authority figure (Professor Milgram in a white coat) and an overarching rationale 'an important experiment'. And finally, there were two binding factors that locked people into the situation: their agreement to take part, and the sequential and incremental nature of the experiment.

The research placed people under considerable stress. People used various strategies to cope with the stress. They attended to the authority figure rather than the individual they were shocking. They denied responsibility: 'If it were up to me I would not administer the shocks'. They denigrated the other person 'He deserves it'. They considered it was 'For his own good'. Or they just dissented but continued.

Milgram's research reveals the power of authority and how it can influence people to do things against their will, even when it causes others and themselves considerable distress. One wonders how many managers faced with implementing painful change in their organization have denied responsibility and thought: 'If it was up to me I wouldn't do this?'.

Henry Mintzberg (1983) raises the issue of the difference between organizations in their authority structure that have implications for the management of change. He views the organization as having an external coalition of stakeholders (owners, government, trade unions, professional bodies, etc.) that may involve just one or many stakeholders. He makes the point that when there is one powerful stakeholder the authority structure within the organization can be very strong or weak, depending on whether the owner supports the CEO not. When there are many stakeholders, power passes to the internal coalition and the internal authority structure is likely to be strong. When the external coalition comprises a few divided stake-holders, the authority structure is likely to be weak and change difficult to implement.

When we look at our cases we can see differences in the authority structure and how the difference between, say, a partnership, a charity and a publicly quoted company affected the nature of change within them.

Gaining power

French and Raven's sources of power give an indication of what a manager can do to gain power in an organization. Influenced by the work of Pfeffer (1992) and Stephen Robbins (1989) a list of such strategies is shown in Table 13.2.

TABLE 13.2: Strategies to gain power

Get a powerful sponsor

Get a powerful boss

Form alliances with influential others

Establish a coalition

Gain support of peers

Develop rapport with groups capable of bring about change

Surround oneself with competent and loyal others

Publicize one's successes

Gain control over valued resources

Get promoted

Get one's role and responsibilities publicly clarified and legitimized

Develop expertise in valued areas

Move to an important unit

Move close to the centre

Develop the right image

Avoid tainted members

Appear indispensable

Be visible

Be friendly

Increase attractiveness

Do favours

Be loyal

> **REFLECTION**
>
> Think of a recent situation where you were dependent on others to achieve some goal. What was the basis of your power, if any, which you had over them? What did you do or could have done, to increase your power base?

Exercising influence

In order to gain cooperation the manager either empowers others or exercises influence. Greiner and Schein (1988) interviewed 74 managers about the strategies they had used to influence others who were not their subordinates. Their findings are presented in Table 13.3, to which

TABLE 13.3: Influence strategies

Present a persuasive viewpoint

- emphasize the innovative aspects of ideas
- quote experts, benchmarked organizations or powerful others
- frame argument in terms of important strategic issues and use favoured terminology
- tease out objections before presenting case
- collect data supporting idea
- rely on empirical observations
- demonstrate estimated savings

Involve others and share the problem

Ask others to agree

Make a moral appeal to a higher value or greater good

Work around roadblocks

- identify influential individuals and direct proposals towards them
- pre-sell idea to key decision maker
- work around the boss
- negotiate a settlement
- move/replace opponents

Exaggerate information

State that authority figures are in support

Prepare case and set deadlines/overload the agenda

Use personal attributes

Be persistent

Offer favours/monetary rewards

Use threats

Use organizational rules

Give guarantees

Discredit the opposition

---

we have added a few gleaned from Jeffrey Pfeffer's excellent book entitled *Managing with Power* (Pfeffer, 1992) and a few of our own.

Greiner and Schein focused upon influence over non-subordinates. Consequently, influence strategies based upon legitimate authority, such as instructing other to change, rewriting the rules and reallocating resources, are largely excluded from the list. Notice, however, how their respondents were clearly aware of the need to tap into the authority structure of the organization.

How power is exercised has significant implications for the potential success of change (see Etzioni, 1961). If the manager has sufficient power, he or she can impose new reward systems, new work targets and performance measures, and redesign jobs; however, such imposition will inevitably mean that employees do not feel responsible for their success. Where there is no choice, there is no ownership. Where there is no ownership, there is no care – have you ever washed a rented car?

Gaining cooperation through loyalty

Social relationships are based upon exchanges that involve a societal norm of reciprocity. Social exchange is more likely to awaken feelings of personal obligation and trust than purely economic exchange.

Compliance with another's requests, granting of favours, reliable role behaviour, and acting fairly with respect and loyalty utilize this norm and create an obligation to reciprocate. Thus managers can gain influence over their employees behaviour by treating them fairly and with respect (or lose influence by not doing so), and employees can gain influence over their boss's behaviour by acting reliably, being cooperative, loyal and so on. In times of change this can put managers in a situation of considerable conflict, and may lead them to take steps to protect their own people against consequences of change. When the Abbey National building society was gearing itself up to become more business focused prior to flotation, one of the change tactics it employed to change its culture was to move its branch managers around. Thus nearby branches would exchange managers. Abbey National reported that this had a positive effect in nearly all cases (Williams et al., 1993). One explanation that could be used to account for this was that the managers were less obligated to their new staff and felt more able to introduce needed changes.

Having illuminated some of the reasons why employees are likely, or not, to cooperate in change we can now see what the manager can do to gain cooperation – reward cooperation, punish non-cooperation, design jobs which meet employee needs and match their values, clarify and legitimize what is expected, change attitudes towards the behaviour, coach and develop appropriate competencies, allocate roles appropriate to skill and personality, and so on. These are some of the levers for cooperation.

EXERCISE (continuation; see pp. 40–41)

In the light of the theories you have encountered in this chapter, and in any other sources you have sampled, revisit your model (and/or the model presented in Chapter 10) and modify it to reflect your current understanding of the factors involved in implementing successful change.

CHAPTER FOURTEEN

Insights through theory:
managing stress

A major problem when implementing organizational change is the issue of
stress and the prevalence of stress-induced illnesses. In this chapter, we
explore some of the literature that throws light on the question: 'How can
we manage stress, and help others cope with the stress that accompanies
the implementation of change?'. We start by looking at three models of
stress, and then give three examples of interactional stress models that
are relevant in the context of managing change: person–environment fit,
job demand/decision latitude, and stress–strain models. We then move
on to explore notions of coping, and the coping process. Lastly, we assess
various ways in which managers can control stress levels accompanying
the implementation of change. In this part, we highlight organizational
properties that create workplace stressors (stimuli which have negative
consequences for a significant proportion of people exposed to them) and
suggest ways of eliminating or mitigating their effects.

Introduction

Stress affects a large proportion of organizational members. Some
writers have reported it to be 'the biggest health hazard' that
employees face at work, and in annual surveys of managers undertaken
by the Institute of Management, many report their health as being
affected in various ways by the increasing and changing demands of
work. Victor Callan (1993), in writing about strategies for coping with
organizational change, observes that traditional organizational development models emphasize the value of incremental change. Management introduces change in small measured steps that give employees
time to adapt, and the planned approach helps to reduce any likely
resistance to change. However, a large number of organizations have

determined that there is a strategic need to be transformed and revital-
l, and therefore consider incremental change as unsuitable. As a
sequence, people have been subjected to a range of different, and
n cumulative, pressures and demands. When change is not well
managed and supported, these pressures can be transformed into
sources of stress. What is the evidence for proposing that, in many
cases, the effects of organizational changes have resulted in increased
levels of stress among organizational members?

It is estimated by the Department of Health that upward of 10 per
cent of GDP is lost each year in the UK because of work related stress.
The direct cost to employers of workplace absence – as estimated by the
Confederation of British Industry's annual survey – is thought to be
around £11 billion, due to 192 million working days lost in 2000, (up
from an estimated 187 million working days lost in 1997, and a cost to
employers of £3 billion in 1992). Absence rates for manual workers have
been generally unchanged, while those for white-collar workers have
increased. Long-term absence due to physical illness is more significant
for manual workers, while stress and recurring illness are more
common among white-collar workers. Yet these figures may not reveal
the true level of the problem. While public sector workers averaged 10.2
days absence in comparison with 7.6 days for employees in the private
sector in 2000, in the central government market testing case described
in Chapter 4, the head of department acknowledged:

> Both team leaders suffered both physical and mental strain. Both took
> time off which was recorded as time out of the office (i.e. work time rather
> than sick leave).

This is hardly surprising, since there is, in many cases, a stigma associated with taking time off for stress-related illness. Organizations
seeking to compete do not want to have to 'carry' people who are
unable to cope, as the local authority competitive tendering case in
Chapter 5 shows:

> Getting the message across to the staff was important. We said 'Gone are
> the days when we can afford to carry people. It's about maximizing the
> output from the resources that we have got'. Some staff commented
> about the culture now being about 'the survival of the fittest', and I think
> that is an appropriate observation. When you have a high-unemploy-
> ment market outside you need to get across to staff that they are in this
> environment where increasing demands will be placed upon them. If
> they are unable to perform, management would have to look to the
> market to provide someone who can. That is the name of the game today.

The housing department manager also drew attention to the fact that devolved budgeting increased pressures on individual managers to keep sickness down because 'if you have someone who is long-term sick, the job still has to be done. So either the existing staff do it on over-time or we get someone in... (with cost implications), so this puts pres-sures on managers and it becomes a vicious circle with existing staff adopting increased workloads with no reward.'

Kim James and Tanya Arroba (1999) in their book *Energizing the Workplace* describe this phenomenon as the 'John Wayne syndrome', whereby people accept the extra demands placed upon them and say 'I can cope' up to cracking point. This is because, although they feel dangerously pressured, acknowledging this publicly is seen as a sign of weakness. The covert message they are hearing is that organizations do not want to employ people that cannot cope with changing circumstances.

Which models of stress are useful to consider when managing change?

There are a large number of stress models, which can be categorized into three types: response-based, stimulus-based and interactive. Stim-ulus models see stress as an environmental variable, while response-based models propose that stress is a dependent variable; that is, a response or reaction to a stressor. An interactive model includes both stimulus and response elements and possible intervening factors. The first two models are shown in Figure 14.1. In model 2, a particular pattern of responses can be taken as evidence that the person is, or has been, under pressure from a 'disturbing environment'. Factors causing stress are termed 'stressors', and in Table 14.1 we highlight the main sources of stressors.

REFLECTION

Consider both your wider organization and your immediate work situa-tion. What factors in these situations would you label as stressors? Are they temporary or permanent? Do others see them in a similar way?

Model 1 is an engineering model: it proposes that external stresses give rise to stress reactions or strains within the individual. However, this model cannot account for the fact that people don't agree in many cases on which situations can be described as stressful, and what the common characteristics of stressful situations are. There are

FIGURE 14.1: Stimulus- and response-based models of stress (source: Cox, 1978; reproduced with permission of Palgrave)

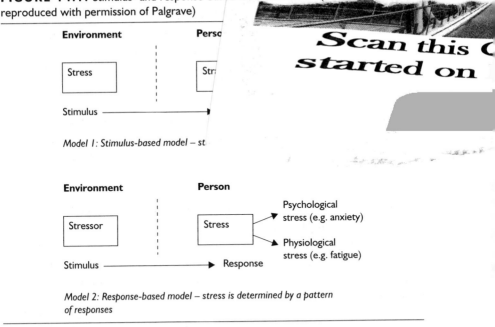

Model 1: Stimulus-based model – st

Model 2: Response-based model – stress is determined by a pattern of responses

also several weaknesses with the second response-based model. For example, there are problems in discriminating between stressors or stress responses, e.g. emotion and fatigue. Also, the same response may

TABLE 14.1: Common sources of stressors (after Furnham, 1997)

Intrinsic to the job/work: extent to which job requires making decisions; constant monitoring of machines or materials; performing unstructured tasks; repeated exchange of information with others; work overload or underload; inadequate working conditions; rigid procedures; inadequate staffing; no responsibility

Role conflict and ambiguity: role juggling – wearing many hats and switching from one type of activity to the other; required to perform tasks disliked or outside of job specification; lack of clarity about scope and responsibility of job; lack of clarity about objectives for role; inadequate information about work role

Relationships at work: lack of consideration and unrealistic job pressures by superiors; lack of support in changing situations by peers; isolation; political machinations; difficulties in managing subordinates; poor management style; responsibility for others; demanding customers; boundary roles

Social support/appraisal: friends and colleagues failing to provide emotional, financial and informational support; negative attributions made by powerful others; non-inclusion in decision making; poor or non-existent performance appraisal system

TABLE 14.1 (*continued*)

Home/work interface: conflicts over time and loyalties between work and home and family demands

Organizational structure, climate and change: mergers and acquisitions; reorganization, delayering, downsizing; cost reduction and efficiency drives; shifts in company policy; changes in organizational climate; human resource systems resulting in job insecurity, fear of redundancy or redeployment, reduction in promotion opportunities; poor communications

Environmental factors: travel to work; economic uncertainty, political uncertainty, technological innovations; competitive business environment, what competitors are doing

---

be evoked by several situations, of which only one may be seen as stressful. Accordingly, we move now to look at the interactive models.

Today, the most popular type of stress model is the interactive model. In the stimulus and response models of stress, environmental demands and individual susceptibility factors are seen as unrelated. However, in interactive models, stress occurs when a subset of environmental demands coincides with a subset of individual susceptibility factors. Interactive models focus on mechanisms through which a situation is appraised as stressful. In other words, stress is in the 'eye of the beholder'. The focus on cognitive appraisal is essentially a psychological perspective, which suggests that certain characteristics of the individual lead them to appraise an event or situation as threatening. Whether a situation is appraised as stressful or not depends, therefore, not only on the environment but also on the individual's prior experiences, learning and personality. There is evidence that certain individual difference factors predispose some people to stress while others help prevent stress. Examples of these are shown in Table 14.2.

> **REFLECTION**
>
> In what ways might your personality, past experiences and learning influence how you respond to work events and situations?

Before going on to discuss the third type of model of stress and looking at aspects of coping, we will just flag up some of the likely consequences of stress. Consequences are felt not only by individuals, but also by their families, the organizations they work for and by society. They include:

- *Individual*: decline in physical appearance, chronic fatigue, heart disease, respiratory disorders, gastro-intestinal problems, head-

TABLE 14.2: Examples of individual differences: people are more likely to be prone or resistant to stress

---

Neuroticism: people with 'negative effect', a mix of anxiety, irritability, neuroticism, and self-depreciation; people who dwell on their mistakes, disappointments and shortcomings are prone to stress.

Locus of control: people with an expectancy of internal control (a belief that life events result from their own behaviours, abilities, personalities and efforts) are likely to see threatening events at work as less stressful, and more open to their control. People with an expectancy of external control (a belief that life events are a function of luck, chance, fate, powerful others and powers beyond their control) are likely to see threatening events at work as outside of their control.

Type A behaviour: people who are driven by time urgency, excessive competitiveness, continuous involvement in deadline activities, persistent drive for recognition, intense sustained desire to achieve, aggression, impatience and consistent alertness are more likely to suffer with heart conditions.

Optimism: people who hold an optimistic and hopeful view of life, interpret situations in a positive, favourable light and expect favourable outcomes and results are more stress-resistant than pessimists. Pessimists tend to interpret situations negatively and expect unfavourable outcomes. Optimists and pessimists tend to adopt different coping strategies.

Hardiness: Hardy people tend to be stress-resistant. They are characterized by showing higher levels of commitment (such as deeper involvement in their jobs); control (the belief that they can control life events and outcomes); and challenge – change is seen as an opportunity to grow rather than as a threat.

---

aches, backaches, depression, cynicism, panic attacks, hostile behaviour, reduced concentration levels

■ *Organizational*: absenteeism, tardiness, accidents, sabotage, labour turnover, reduced productivity, reduced motivation, reduced satisfaction, poor performance, higher costs, lower profits, poor relationships

■ *Society*: high levels of drug and alcohol abuse, increased smoking and associated diseases, dropouts, broken families, higher levels of health care costs, reduction in economic output

Example of interactive models of stress

We have chosen to describe three interactive models that we feel will be of help to managers when they are in organizational change situations: person–environment fit; job demand/decision latitude; and stress–strain models.

Person–environment fit models

These models assume that stress results from the relationship between the person and the situation, and that cognitive appraisals are made of the extent to which there is congruence between the two. They propose that two kinds of 'fit' exist between the individual and the work environment:

1   the extent to which the person's skills and abilities match the demands and requirements of the job, and
2   the extent to which the environment provides opportunities for the person to meet their needs, values and goals.

In cases of mismatch, well-being is threatened and various health strains result. Readers will notice that in discussing the causes of stress the theoretical assumptions made are similar to those being made above in exploring cooperative behaviour – it would be surprising if it were otherwise.

Jeffrey Edwards (1996) looked at both versions of 'fit' and found it was likely that they are related to different forms of affect. In situations that dramatically change their values (such as with culture change), and those values are held to be important by people in the situation, this leads to displeasure and increased job dissatisfaction. Examples of this can be seen in the cases. Thus in Chapter 6, where back room work was being reorganized in an insurance company, the supervisor was adamant that her team would not adopt the proposed changes. It was only because of her retirement due to ill health that the changes could be introduced. In other cases, where people valued stability, change had introduced high levels of uncertainty and concerns about job security. This engendered a lot of dissatisfaction.

In situations where demands exceed abilities, Edwards found that this led to increased goal striving and effort expenditure, which in turn led to increased physiological arousal and subjective manifestations of tension. A good example of this happening is to be found in Chapter 9, when the market research company experienced a period of rapid growth. Expanding business and a shortage of staff led to existing staff working long hours to cope with the volume of work, and in addition to carrying out market research, also having to write proposals and deal with enquiries. The manager observed:

> trying to implement changes and cope with the running of the business at the same time... there were an awful lot of frayed tempers that year!

These approaches highlight for managers the fact that organizational changes can:

1 Bring about changes in situational attributes, whereby the organization might no longer fulfil the person's existing values, interests, motives and goals. If the nature of the job, or aspects of the working environment are changed, the person's comparison between perceived and desired 'fit' may reveal that there is no longer a 'good match'. Hence managers need to discover, when talking with their staff, where discrepancies arise and see if these can be addressed. Sometimes these cannot be addressed, as several of our cases show (see for example, Chapter 7), and it is best for the person and organization to part company. In other cases, staff dissatisfaction is ignored, because nothing can be done (e.g. loss of familiarity and increased impersonalization created by growth in employee numbers), or dissatisfaction is overcome when staff begin to value newly introduced aspects of the person–situation relationship (e.g. values of working more efficiently, or meeting targets).

2 Make additional demands on people's abilities. If the 'misfit' between demands and abilities is linked to important consequences, i.e. particular rewards or costs to the person, the manager needs to consider what these might be. What performance is required of staff? Have staff received adequate training in skills needed to perform well? Are there any situational constraints that might be removed? Are people supported in times of excess demands? For example, if workplace circumstances change, and workloads are perceived to increase dramatically, this may induce the person to improve fit by revising working methods and procedures (changing the work environment) or improving time management skills (improving self-management skills). The case in Chapter 7, the merging of two retail firms, illustrates these difficulties:

> there are ripple effects in all directions, everyone's needs are different... people are asking me for extra information at a time when I am under pressure from all sorts of other people to worry about changes that we are responsible for... everyone is in that boat, they have got a pile of their own priorities but they are also crucial to other people, so prioritizing assumes a huge importance.

Job demand/decision latitude models

The second model we consider helpful to managers in situations of change focuses more specifically on certain features of a job. During the

1970s and 1980s, research was undertaken to explore stressful aspects of work with the aim of redesigning jobs. Typical assembly line work had been found to produce dysfunctional consequences for both individuals and organizations. Hence, researchers explored different ways of improving the situation and this led to job rotation, job enlargement, job enrichment and semi-autonomous group working initiatives. The theories of psychologists such as that of Hackman and Oldham (1980) became influential in job redesign change programmes, as described in Chapter 13.

A well-respected job demand/decision latitude model is that of Karasek (1979) (Figure 14.2), and this considers how the effects of job demand on strain are moderated by the amount of job discretion and job support/constraint (with a later addition of a third dimension of social support). It proposes that psychological strain arises from the combined effects of work situation demands and decision latitude available to people to meet these demands. The model predicts that 'unresolved strain' increases as job demands increase without a commensurate increase in job discretion.

While evidence has accumulated that work characterized by high demands and low decision latitude is detrimental to employee well-being, there is doubt about the interactional effects which suggest that demands can increase with little or no strain if decision latitude is also increased. There are several reasons for this. One relates to the measurement of job demands, and a second relates to both the conceptualization and measurement of decision latitude. A development of

FIGURE 14.2: Karasek's job strain model (after Karasek, 1979)

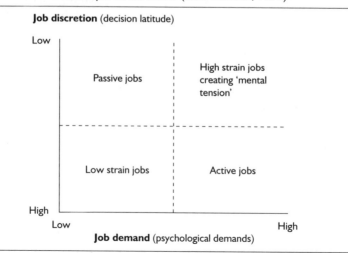

the model has led to the demand-control (residual strain) model. Control (replacing decision latitude) is thought to provide people with the opportunity to adjust to demands according to their needs and circumstances. This model proposes that when the psychological demands of a job are high and control over the task and decision latitude are both low, adverse psychological strain results. Decision latitude has two components: employees are given authority to make decisions on the job (decision authority), and to choose from a breadth of skills (skill discretion). Hence, in situations where people have high levels of decision latitude, they have sufficient discretion to change problem situations and therefore can reduce or eliminate work stressors as they arise. Jobs with both high demand and high discretion are termed 'active jobs'. In contrast, 'passive jobs' are characterized by low demands and low discretion. Such jobs result in reduced activity and no resource development, and can lead to low self-efficacy (Bandura, 1997).

This model can be seen as particularly relevant for managers in organizations that are downsizing, delayering and/or introducing 'empowerment'. In organizations that are downsizing or delayering, 'lean structures' mean that people who remain often have to pick up the work of those who have left the organization. Work may or may not have been redesigned, people may or may not have received skills training for increased skill variety, and increased responsibilities may 'just happen' by imposition on people. Initiatives to introduce empowerment do attempt to address some of these problems. Thus, from this we see that jobs can be a source of satisfaction and motivation and contribute positively to one's self-identity. However, jobs can also become a source of stress. The balance is a fine one, which needs to be considered in times of organizational change. Our cases provide examples of this, for example:

- In the market research agency (Chapter 9) members needed to rely on suppliers to provide them with services which they need when interacting with clients (such as presentational materials and data analysis). Their existing suppliers failed to give the standard of service that was expected. This caused frustrations and, because it was the market researcher's ultimate responsibility, researchers had to accept the clients' displeasure at not meeting deadlines, and were made to look unprofessional and incompetent in front of the client.
- In the oil refinery, with the introduction of teamworking (Chapter 5) '...many were happy to work out what needed to be done and then went ahead and did it. Some had to be told what to do rather than

take the initiative. They felt very uncomfortable and asked "How do I know that I have got the authority? What happens to me if something goes wrong?" They still needed written or spoken instructions to feel sure of their actions'.

Stress–strain models

The third useful model for managers of change is the stress–strain model of Richard Lazarus and Susan Folkman. This is an influential transactional model emphasizing relational aspects of both person and environmental events, such as the various daily hassles and threats that result from organizational change. Threat is seen as an imagined or anticipated future deprivation of something that is valued (and, therefore, relates to the 'self'). These writers define psychological stress as (Lazarus and Folkman, 1984, p. 21):

> ...a relationship between the person and the environment that is appraised by the person as taxing or exceeding his or her resources and endangering his or her well-being.

Hence, it shares similarities with the fit models, but the value of this model lies in its attempts to address perceptual and cognitive aspects. In this model, cognitive appraisal (i.e. attentive, perceptive and evaluative processes intervene between the encounter and the reaction) is considered in greater depth. The authors see appraisal as 'the process of categorizing an encounter, and its various facets, with respect to its significance for well-being' (Lazarus and Folkman, 1984: 31). This leads us to focus in more depth on the dynamics of stress, and gives significance to the processes of 'coping' with change.

In stressful situations, successful coping is proposed as the key to people maintaining well-being and achieving high performance. Indeed, it has been argued (O'Driscoll and Cooper, 1994, p. 343) that lack of effective coping and 'stress management':

> ...may lead to significant decrements in well-being, dissatisfaction, feelings of disengagement from the job, and reduced job performance. Prolonged maladaptive coping may ultimately induce a chronic, highly debilitating form of stress known as burnout.

As we saw from the first two types, the stimulus- and response-based models of stress, early work into stress and coping assumed a passive subject, i.e. individuals adapt to stressful situations. More recent work proposes that coping entails a broad range of responses, which include adapting some aspects of the self to stressors, but also dealing with the problem giving rise to the strain. A broad definition of coping in this vein, one that is accepted by many current writers, is (Folkman, 1984, p. 141):

> Coping is 'constantly changing cognitive and behavioural efforts to manage specific external and/or internal demands (of transactions) that are appraised as taxing or exceeding the resources of the person'.

What triggers coping?

As we discussed earlier, past research identified workplace stressors as including dimensions of the workplace, and job or occupation, with properties that acted on the individual to produce strain. But in the transactional views of stress and coping, the perceived presence of stressors does not necessarily induce stress. Only when a situation or event is *appraised* as 'stressful' is it then construed either positively or negatively, e.g. as harmful, threatening or challenging.

Some writers argue that for potential stress to be translated into actual stress, there first needs to be some uncertainty about the outcome, and second the outcomes need to be interpreted as important to the perceiver. Hence perceptions of high levels of uncertainty create high levels of stress but only when the outcome is deemed to be important.

In contrast to dimensions of stressful situations, coping targets might be internal or external. Internal targets involve adapting some aspect of the self (e.g. reducing uncomfortable feelings through resigned acceptance or cognitive redefinition), while external targets involve dealing with the problem (e.g. by changing environmental pressures, such as negotiating a new deadline rather than attempting to meet an unrealistic deadline). 'Coping' in our context, therefore, refers to cognitive and behavioural efforts to manage the taxing demands and conflicts posed by organizational changes, and encompasses both situations and targets.

This approach to the definition of coping allows three key distinctions to be made (Latack and Hovolic, 1992):

1   Defining coping in terms of behaviours and processes rather than in terms of coping styles (suggesting stable personality traits) means that coping is open to behavioural or structural intervention and training. Better stress management or coping strategies can be learnt.

2   Coping, defined in terms of what people do or think in specific situations, is separated from coping effectiveness. Effectiveness is the

assessment of appropriateness, and whether coping 'works' in terms of avoidance or control of individual distress, or improvement of organizational performance, and reduced intention to quit.

3   Coping therefore applies to both challenging and harmful/threatening situations.

In the stress–strain model, three forms of appraisal can be identified: primary, secondary and reappraisal. Primary appraisal involves the person assessing the encounter to determine its relevance to themselves (it might be irrelevant, benign and positive, or stressful). If it is perceived as 'stressful' this might be because of harm/loss sustained by the event, e.g. sudden notification of redundancy (see for example, Chapter 8); a threat which is anticipated harm or loss, e.g. possible job loss (see Chapter 5); or a challenge, e.g. possibilities for mastery or gain, as with the offer of promotion (see Chapter 8).

Secondary appraisal concerns judgements about what might or can be done given the stressful situation, i.e. what coping strategies to adopt, the likely consequences of adopting these coping strategies, and whether they will accomplish what is required.

Reappraisals result in changed appraisals based on new information about the environment or the person. Vulnerability, and its inverse, resilience, can be conceptualized in terms of deficiency or excess of coping resources; and by the significance of commitments engendered or engaged by the situation. As with their notion of stress, these concepts are relational. The most important person factors affecting cognitive appraisals are postulated to be commitments and beliefs, particularly beliefs about personal control.

Hence the key elements of the dynamic coping process include the occurrence of an event or something in the situation which impinges on the person, and appraisal of the event or situation as 'stressful'. This is followed by the identification of possible cognitive or behavioural responses, and an assessment of their likely effectiveness then occurs – a manifestation of particular responses in the situation. Finally, reappraisal of the relationship between the person and the situation occurs and acts as steering mechanism over time. The process we have been describing is shown diagrammatically in Figure 14.3.

Appraisals occur over time, which is not shown in this figure, but there are iterations between primary, secondary and reappraisals, with resulting problem-focused and emotion-focused coping behaviours, in order to seek resources and adopt different strategies to resolve each stressful encounter. The cyclical activity is demonstrated in the next section.

FIGURE 14.3: Lazarus and Folkman model of stress and coping (after Edwards, 1992)

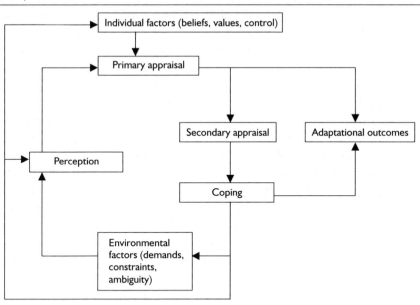

How can managers help their staff (and themselves) cope with change?

We have looked at theories and models about coping *per se*; now let us move on to look at coping in the context of organizational change. People who are directly affected by changes can experience the impact in a number of areas: demands to learn new skills, new tasks, new ways of working, new ways of viewing their role, and new ways of viewing their relationship with their employer. As changes start to happen, individuals need to be able to cope with different pressures resulting from change.

Many of those writing in the field of organizational change make the point that change has to start with ourselves, particularly when we are managing other people, for example (Clarke, 1994, p. 46):

> you [the manager] personally are one of the most powerful levers for change: your attitudes, your enthusiasm, your willingness to allow people's reactions to change the change as it goes along, the way you 'role model' the kinds of new behaviours you are seeking, your vulnerability and willingness to change yourself. How indeed can you change other people's mind-sets unless you are prepared to challenge your own?

Yet talking about changing is much easier to do than actually undergoing change ourselves. It is very hard, because learning to change not only involves gaining new skills and increasing our expertise, but also involves changing emotions. If there is no consistency between a manager's espoused values and their actual behaviours, staff make the judgement that it's all rhetoric rather than 'reality', and management is not committed to change, so why should they be? In organizational change situations 'actions always speak louder than words'.

A well-known model for managing transitions views the process of changing as involving a three-fold process: an ending, a transition and beginning anew (Bridges, 1992). These phases overlap with each other, and the degree of overlap will differ between individuals. During the transition, the manager can put support mechanisms in place that will help staff move through this difficult period. When we end a customary way of behaving or thinking, we need to let go of something we may be emotionally attached to, e.g. power, status, habits, the way we see ourselves and the role we enjoy. The greater the importance of these factors to us, the greater will be the perceived loss. Coping with loss is painful. The process of coping with change is thought to involve a number of emotional and cognitive changes that take place. For example, emotion and cognitive strategies include:

1 *Denial* of the need for change, e.g. 'We have always done it this way'; 'Look how successful we have been over the last *x* years'; 'We have tried it before and it doesn't work'.

2 *Defence*: when facing the realities of change, e.g. new type of work, new manager, different work group, changed location, or restructured department people may feel overwhelmed and try to retain the status quo. Yet this stage may not occur for everyone. Changes are happening continuously: some we recognize, and consciously adapt to meet the demands; others we skip over because they have no importance for us. If we do spend time and energy trying to maintain the status quo and resist change, we are operating inefficiently. 'The world moves on and we must move with it' is the start of the next stage.

3 *Discarding*: realizing that change is necessary or inevitable is part of coming to terms with change; seeing some positive aspects, finding out some things are not as bad as expected. This process involves changing perceptions and changing attitudes and behaviours, because of an appreciation that these are appropriate for changing circumstances and 'the way it is now'. Increased awareness is the beginning of adapting to change: people see that it is inevitable.

4   *Adaptation*: this stage involves a process of mutual adaptation through experimenting, testing out ideas, trial and error learning and slowly improving performance.
5   *Internalization*: this results when people have created a new system, process, etc. and worked out new relationships and a shared understanding of the new work situation. This 'sensemaking' process is part of enacting a 'new reality'.

Changes can affect performance in different ways: first, new systems, processes and structures will need to be learned over a period of time. This is captured in the 'learning curve' effect as performance increases with learning. Second, problems created by new systems, processes and structures are addressed and modifications enable performance to be improved. Lastly, significant changes create initial decline in self-esteem, which impacts on performance. As people cope and become more adept and confident, their performance improves.

Interestingly, the more we have experienced successful change in the past, the more likely we are to have confidence to move forward. The conviction that one can successfully execute the required behaviour has been shown to have a positive effect on performance (Wood and Bandura, 1989), and this relationship is iterative. While increased self-efficacy leads to higher performance, the converse is also true. This operates at group and organization levels, as well as at individual levels, and is manifest in virtuous or vicious cycles. The dynamic processes involved in coping with organizational change can be seen in Figures 14.4 and 14.5, where two managers are in a situation of needing to downsize their group of subordinates. The first manager is unable to cope with this situation, and a downward spiral results. The second manager can cope with this demand, and this is illustrated in an upward spiral.

One of the key managing change competencies described in Chapter 11 was the ability of the managers to manage their own emotions and feelings. If the manager is having problems in coping and adapting to change, and if insufficient support is provided, then other organizational members are likely to suffer because others' change competencies are likely to be affected. Indeed, some of the managers interviewed saw this competence as being part of 'leading change' – in the importance of acting as a role model.

FIGURE 14.4: The dynamic process of coping: the downward spiral (Mack, 1998; © International Association of Applied Psychology)

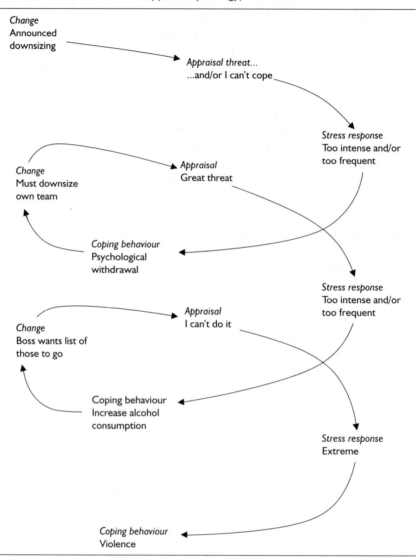

How do managers and organizations introduce and maintain low levels of stress in changing organizations?

As shown earlier, actual experienced stress sustained over a long period of time can result in many negative and unpleasant consequences.

FIGURE 14.5: The dynamic process of coping: the upward spiral (Mack, 1998; © International Association of Applied Psychology)

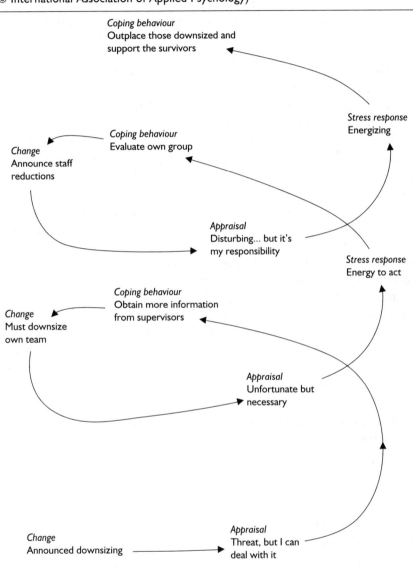

Coping behaviour
Outplace those downsized and
support the survivors

Stress response
Energizing

Coping behaviour
Evaluate own group

Change
Announce staff
reductions

Appraisal
Disturbing... but it's
my responsibility

Stress response
Energy to act

Coping behaviour
Obtain more information
from supervisors

Change
Must downsize
own team

Appraisal
Unfortunate but
necessary

Change
Announced downsizing

Appraisal
Threat, but I can
deal with it

However, there are several reasons why this need not be the case: first, people, through experience, can develop stress tolerance and resilience. Second, organizations, by introducing changes carefully and in a planned manner, can reduce the number of potential stressors in the environment. Third, stress audits can highlight unintended sources of stress. Hence there are different approaches for addressing stress: those that focus on individuals, those that focus on the individual/organizational interface and those that focus on organizational factors.

As we saw above, organizational change can bring in its wake changes in working methods and procedures, in working relationships, in required behaviours and in perceptions of what is important and appropriate in the organization. Because of the lack of slack nowadays in organizations, and because increasing demands and expectations are being placed on employees, individuals need to take responsibility for managing their stress levels. A large number of stress management techniques geared to helping individuals exist. Additionally, organizations can introduce strategies that will empower individuals to target the stressful environment themselves. Examples are shown in Table 14.3.

Some organizational factors are under management's control, such as structural elements, role and task demands, and communications. These can be changed or modified to reduce stress. Two types of strategy are possible: human-process interventions which focus on the role of interpersonal, group and intergroup processes, and techno-structural interventions that focus on job redesign, organizational structure, control, information and reward systems. In the latter part of the 1980s a number of workplace interventions had been designed and introduced to help reduce or prevent stress in employees. Three types of stress intervention were identified in a review (Murphy, 1988): primary, secondary or tertiary:

TABLE 14.3: Examples of stress management and health promotion activities for individuals

---

Access to free phone enquiry line

Access to keep-fit facilities

Workshops

Measuring stress levels

Relaxation classes

Clinical hypnosis

Counselling

Aromatherapy, reflexology, yoga and meditation classes

Biofeedback

Technical awareness training

Time management

Training in innovative coping

---

1   *Primary prevention* focuses on eliminating or reducing sources of stress that are organizational and job/task-related, such as through revising supervisory practices, installing flexible work schedules and expanding employee skills through training and development.
2   *Secondary prevention* aims to reduce the symptoms of stress (i.e. the acute reactions). It is a preventative measure open to employees before any clinical symptoms of ill health are demonstrated (i.e. chronic effects). 'Stress management' is the umbrella term referring to the group of techniques that seek to help employees. Time management skills and coping skills are examples of secondary prevention measures.
3   *Tertiary prevention* provides treatment or therapy for employees who exhibit health problems, e.g. alcoholism, heart conditions or mental breakdown. Employee assistance programmes (EAPs) offer employees an advisory and counselling service to deal with these sorts of personal and professional problems.

In the 1980s, the availability of costs and indices of workplace stress, and the litigious culture of the USA, increasingly contributed to the introduction of initiatives to reduce stress and improve health in the workplace. Interventions at secondary and tertiary levels involve health screening and health promotion activities. The former seeks to diagnose and detect existing conditions, whilst the latter aim to modify behavioural risk factors that lead to poor health. More recently, in the UK there have been high-profile court cases in which employees have been awarded large sums in compensation for employers not addressing problems arising from stress. Also, the insurance industry has a vested interest in ensuring that employers are not held liable in law for damages their employees have suffered. And, with the acceptance of the Turnbull Report in 1999, stress management can be construed as an important area for risk management attention. Thus a number of factors are causing employers to take the issue of stress more seriously.

Stress management *interventions at the individual level* can be defined as (Ivancevich *et al.*, 1990, p. 252):

> any activity, program, or opportunity initiated by an organization which focuses on reducing the presence of work related stressors or on assisting individuals to minimize the negative outcomes of exposure to these stressors. Stress management interventions represent a form of health promotion or wellness programme.

Employee Assistance Programmes are defined as (Berridge and Cooper, 1994):

programmatic interventions at the workplace... using behavioural knowledge and methods for the recognition and control of certain work- and non-work related problems... which adversely affect job performance, with the objective of enabling the individual to return to making her or his full work contribution and to attaining full functioning in personal life.

Employee Assistance Programmes are not new. The roots of EAPs can be traced back to the classic Hawthore studies conducted by Elton Mayo and colleagues in Chicago during the mid-1920s and early 1930s. Then, the purpose of the programme was to use the interview process between supervisors and other plant employees as a means of counselling people, and thereby helping them to work through, in a non-directive way, their complaints and problems. In the UK, Whitbread introduced its version, called 'Person-to-Person', in response to large-scale rationalization taking place in the late 1970s. People who were being made redundant were offered specialist redundancy counselling, while those who were staying (the 'survivors') were helped through the traumatic change process. Whitbread is believed to have benefited from this programme by reducing the number of grievances, reducing accidents, enabling management to monitor and improve employee well-being, and creating a positive approach to drug and alcohol problems.

Secondary and tertiary activities involved in managing individual stress and promoting a healthy lifestyle focus on changing the behaviour of the individual, improving their lifestyle and acquiring stress management skills, rather than changing the work situation. The emphasis is on improving the 'adaptability' of the individual to the environment.

There are a number of *organization-directed interventions* to reduce stress, many of which are directed at increasing employees' autonomy and participation. These include: redesigning tasks and work environments; introducing flexible work schedules; encouraging participative management; building cohesive teams; establishing fair employment policies; and sharing rewards. Strategies such as these mean that people feel a better fit with their job, are given greater control over work activities, and know and understand what is happening and why.

There is a movement away from viewing stress control as remedial, individually focused interventions and toward proactive organizational level responses with an emphasis on preventative measures and elimination of causes of stress. In a conscious effort employers are moving towards developing a 'healthy work organization'. This can be defined as (Cooper and Cartwright, 1994, p. 462):

an organization characterized by both financial success (i.e. profitability) and a physically and psychologically healthy workforce which is able to maintain over time a healthy and satisfying work environment, particularly through periods of turbulence and change.

A healthy work environment is characterized by low levels of stress, high levels of organizational commitment and job satisfaction; rates of sickness, absenteeism and labour turnover that are lower than the national average; good employee relations; good safety and accident record; and an absence of fear of litigation. Such an environment, argue Cooper and Cartwright, makes secondary and tertiary interventions unnecessary. Other characteristics of a healthy organization are where managers and staff work together to: pursue high performance through personal development and learning; remove operational inefficiencies; eliminate unhealthy working practices; design work and jobs to foster self-driven high performance; and develop and maintain an alert, adaptive and proactive high-performing culture that can absorb change.

Hence management should now view work stress as an issue of strategic importance, and that managing the problem of stress as an organizational responsibility. In attempts to enhance levels of organizational efficiency and effectiveness, work stress can actively impede strategy implementation. McHugh (1995) believes management writings indicate that senior management often view stress as a problem for individual employees and that senior managers often fail to recognize:

- the costly consequences to organizations of stress at work
- the interdependence of individual and organizational health
- people as a valuable resource to be supported in change
- the variety of courses of action available to address stress problems

However, with the changes in legislation and climate, this will no longer be the case.

McHugh's model (see Figure 14.6) for total stress management (TSM) can help in this process.

As the board and top management of a company have developed an increased awareness of the costs of stress, the first task 'audit' concentrates on problem identification and generates the beginnings of an organization-wide acceptance that stress is a costly problem which needs to be addressed. This task is effected not only through the collection of a wide range of data but also through investigations to determine underlying causes. Analysis of personnel data, attitude surveys, consultancy assignments by internal and external consultants, and use

FIGURE 14.6: Total Stress Management model (TSM) (McHugh, 1995; © John Wiley & Sons Ltd. Reprinted with permission)

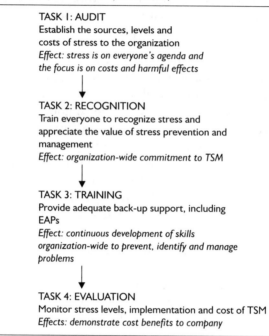

TASK 1: AUDIT
Establish the sources, levels and
costs of stress to the organization
*Effect: stress is on everyone's agenda and
the focus is on costs and harmful effects*

TASK 2: RECOGNITION
Train everyone to recognize stress and
appreciate the value of stress prevention and
management
Effect: organization-wide commitment to TSM

TASK 3: TRAINING
Provide adequate back-up support, including
EAPs
*Effect: continuous development of skills
organization-wide to prevent, identify and manage
problems*

TASK 4: EVALUATION
Monitor stress levels, implementation and cost of TSM
Effects: demonstrate cost benefits to company

of psychometric instruments, such as Cary Cooper and colleagues' 'Occupational Stress Indicator' (OSI) are examples of mechanisms that can reveal core stressors and their effects. In-depth investigations, during this phase, will provide the necessary foundational base against which future audits can be compared, to highlight trends and to determine benchmarks within or across companies. While boards and top management can act as drivers for the audit, this activity can be hindered if the focus is purely on the task itself rather than also considering what additional skills development and communications are needed as well.

The second task, 'Recognition', has an educational perspective. A culture where everyone recognizes and values stress prevention and management needs to be developed. Resources such as regular meetings throughout the organization, workshops, training, communications from top management, and actions taken to reduce stressors will help such a culture to develop. The major hindrance in this stage is the commonly held belief that stress is a problem for individuals and not for an organization and its management.

The third task involves the development of organization-wide skills so that stress can be prevented, identified or managed. A key task is to give employees the opportunity to develop generative learning techniques so they can be proactive in their work situation and address problems before they arise. Both individuals and groups can develop these new skills.

The final task is that of evaluation. Collection of a range of data, such as levels of current absenteeism, labour turnover, productivity rates, organization stress levels, qualitative data obtained from focus groups and data on the costs of implementing TSM will allow for a cost–benefit analysis. While a complete evaluation is not possible, comparisons of the analyzed data collected in this task with findings from the audit will allow some conclusions to be drawn. A summary of the main findings of the evaluation can be fed back to the organization, together with an outline of future goals, in a cyclical process, which can emphasize the organization's commitment and enable continuous improvements.

The value of this model is the acknowledgement that stress is an important outcome of organizational change, and that stress must be managed from an organizational as well as individual perspective. It also places particular emphasis on the notion that individual and organizational health are interdependent entities. By its nature, a 'healthy organization' will be better able to implement strategic change.

REFLECTION

If your current organization (or one that you are reasonably familiar with) were about to implement some major changes, what actions would you take in order to minimize dysfunctional stress experiences from arising among key staff?

CHAPTER FIFTEEN

Concluding comments: developing effective leadership in the implementation of change

Leadership has so many conceptualizations that there is a need to clarify how and why we are using the term. When individuals are instrumental in the process of helping others to identify the goals to be achieved, clarifying the pathways to these goals and learning more effective ways of achieving them, they are fulfilling a critical leadership function or role. Accordingly, all individuals in managerial roles are leaders. It is our firm belief that all those taking on managerial roles can learn to become more effective leaders. The material in this book is designed to help in this learning process. While we are advocating the merits of a particular learning approach, we also want to encourage learners to explore a rich vein of knowledge relevant to implementing change. Part 3 attempts to draw attention to a sample of knowledge that illustrates the usefulness of the theoretical literature in helping us to develop a more sophisticated mental model of how to bring about 'successful' change (the importance of what we mean by successful was discussed in Chapter 1). The sample has been mainly drawn from the work of those theorists whose outputs have withstood the criticisms of peers and practitioners. As a result their value will have been elaborated and discussed in many texts. It has not been the purpose of these chapters to carry out a comprehensive summary of relevant knowledge, nor to draw attention to speculative advances in knowledge, but to emphasize and illustrate the value of many theories to those whose job it is to provide leadership in the implementation of change.

Effective leadership emerges when those in positions of responsibility have valid mental models relating to the management of change, particularly the behavioural aspects. The approach and content of the developmental experience embodied in this book are

FIGURE 15.1: The process of learning to implement change

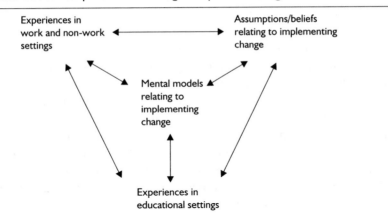

designed to enhance the understanding of those who are or will be playing a leading role in the implementation of change. A representation of the learning process that underlies our approach is shown in Figure 15.1. While a degree of understanding can be attained in an educational setting, the extent to which this understanding becomes integrated within an individual's mental models will depend upon experiences in the work setting, particularly positive reinforcements.

In Part 3 we have intentionally avoided an explicit discussion of the extensive theories of leadership. Our mental models (and the research evidence!) suggest that both transactional leadership (typically concerned with doing things right and reinforcing compatible behaviours of others) and transformational leadership (typically concerned with doing the right things and inspiring others to share common goals) are equally important in the modern organization, although there may be times when one paradigm needs to be given more emphasis than the other. Our analytical rather than prescriptive approach should provide you with the knowledge that will enable you to arrive at your own theory of leadership in the context of implementing change successfully. However, you can rest assured that our discussion of managerial competencies, and the theories we discussed when exploring the dynamics of cooperative behaviour and stress, are compatible with modern theories of leadership (Yukl, 1999). The most successful leaders in implementing change will not only inspire others to higher standards and to more stretching goals, but also gain their cooperation in bringing about change in selected organizational characteristics (e.g. structures, technologies and cultures). Hence our belief that individuals who manage others are all leaders, even though some are more effective leaders than others. The aim of this book is to contribute to the developmental process involved in bringing about more effective leaders in implementing change.

Figure 15.1 reminds us of the learning assumptions we are making in pursuing this aim. Learners are being encouraged to review, reflect and, where necessary, change their beliefs relating to the implementation of change. This process may or may not be very effective in everyday work and non-work settings because of our defensive tendency to reinforce our existing beliefs (Argyris and Schon, 1996). However, appropriate experiences can be created in an educational setting by mixing reflection with social interaction in face-to-face situations (e.g. with fellow learners) and in virtual situations (e.g. case histories of managers operating 'at the coal face'). Relevant assumptions and beliefs are shared with others, and tested out with others and against influential theories, in order to enhance understanding. Ultimately, however, any stable change to an individual's mental models is only likely to happen when there is mutual reinforcement of experiences from work and educational settings.

The interdependent and iterative learning process shown in Figure 15.1 is designed to convey the idea that understanding continues to be refined through planned and unplanned developmental experiences. One of the refinements that more effective leaders learn is to be sensitive to situational cues that will determine when a particular approach to change is better than another. The diversity of the 15 cases in this volume should help in achieving this learning outcome.

EXERCISE (continuation; see pp. 40–41)

Review and refine your visual model of key factors and relationships in the implementation of change. Has your model changed in any significant way from its initial formulation? What have been the main influences in this process? Can you draw any lessons about the process of learning that you feel will be valuable for the future?

References

Alderfer, C. P. (1969) 'An empirical test of a new theory of human needs', *Organizational Behaviour and Human Performance*, 4:142–75.

Argyris, C. (1970) *Intervention Theory and Method: A Behavioural Science View*, New York: Addison-Wesley.

Argyris, C. (1992) *On Organizational Learning*, Oxford: Blackwell.

Argyris, C. and Schon, D. (1978) *Organizational Learning*, Reading, MA: Addison-Wesley.

Argyris, C. and Schon, D. (1989) 'Participatory action research and action science compared: a commentary', *American Behavioural Scientist*, 32(5):612–23.

Argyris, C. and Schon, D. (1996) *Organization Learning II: Theory, Method, and Practice*. Reading, MA: Addison-Wesley.

Bandura, A. (1997) *Self-Efficacy*, New York: Freeman & Co.

Bartlett, F. (1933) *Remembering*, Cambridge: Cambridge University Press.

Beckhard, R. and Harris, R. T. (1987) *Organizational Transitions: Managing Complex Change*, 2nd edn, New York: Addison-Wesley.

Beckhard, R. and Prichard, W. (1992) *Changing the Essence: the Art of Changing and Leading Fundamental Change in Organizations*, San Francisco, CA: Jossey-Bass.

Beer, M., Eisenstat, R. A. and Spector, B. (1990) *The Critical Path to Corporate Renewal*. Boston, MA: Harvard Business School Press.

Bennis, W. (1969) *Organization Development: its Nature, Origins and Prospects*. New York: Addison-Wesley.

Berger, P. and Luckmann, T. (1966) *The Social Construction of Reality: A Treatise on the Sociology of Knowledge*. Harmondsworth: Penguin.

Berridge, J. R. and Cooper, C. (1994) 'The Employee Assistance Programme – its role in organizational coping and excellence', *Personnel Review*, 23(7):3–23.

Blake, R., and Mouton, J. (1964) *The Managerial Grid*. Houston: Gulf Publishing.

Boyatzis, D. A., Cowen, S. S. and Kolb, D. A. (1995) *Innovation in Professional Education*. San Francisco, CA: Jossey Bass.

Boyatzis, R. (1982) *The Competent Manager: a Model for Effective Performance*, 1st edn, New York: Wiley.

Brewer, W. F. and Nakamura, G. V. (1984) 'The nature and functions of schemas', in R. S. Wyer, and T. K. Srull (eds.) *Handbook of Social Cognition*. Hillsdale, NJ: Erlbaum.

Bridges, W. (1992) *Managing Transitions: Making the Most of Change*, Reading, MA: Addison-Wesley.

Brown, R. B. (1993) 'Metacompetence', *Personnel Review*, 22:6–13.

Buchanan, D. A. and Boddy, D. (1992) *The Expertise of the Change Agent: Public Performance and Backstage Activity*, New York: Prentice Hall International.

Buzan, T. (2000) *Use Your Head*. London: BBC Publications.

Callan, V. (1993) 'Individual and organizational strategies for dealing with organizational change', *Work and Stress*, 7(1):63–75.

Christensen, C. R. (1987) *Teaching and the Case Method*, 2nd edn, Boston, MA: Harvard Business School Press.

Clarke, L. (1994) *Essence of Change*. London: Prentice Hall.

Cockerill, T. (1989) 'The kind of competence for rapid change', *Personnel Management*, 52–6.

Cockerill, T. (1995) 'Managerial competences: fact or fiction?', *Business Strategy Review*, 6(3):1–12.

Constable, J. and McCormick, R. (1987) *The Making of British Managers*, London: BIM/CBI.

Cooper, C. L. and Cartwright, S. (1994) 'Healthy mind – healthy organization: a proactive approach to occupational stress', *Human Relations*, 47(4):455–71.

Deci, E. L. and Ryan, R. M. (1985) *Intrinsic Motivation and Self-Determination in Human Behaviour*, New York: Plenum.

Downs, S. (1995) *Learning at Work: Effective Strategies for Making Things Happen*. London: Kogan Page.

Easterby-Smith, M. M. and Burgoyne, J. (1983) 'Action learning: an evaluation', in M. Pedler (ed.) *Action Learning in Practice*, London: Gower.

Eden, C. (1989) 'Managing the environment as a means to managing complexity', in J. Rosehead (ed.) *Rational Analysis in a Problematic World*, Chichester: Wiley.

Eden, C. and Huxham, C. (1996) 'Action research for management research', *British Journal of Management*, 7(1):75–86.

Edwards, J. R. (1992) 'A cybernetic theory of stress, coping and well-being in organizations', *Academy of Management Review*, 17(2):238–275.

Edwards, J. R. (1996) 'An examination of competing versions of the person–environment fit approach to stress', *Academy of Management Journal*, 38(2):292–339.

Etzioni, A. (1961) *A Comparative Analysis of Complex Organizations*, New York: Free Press.

Festinger, L. (1957) *A Theory of Cognitive Dissonance*, Evanston, IL: Row, Peterson.

Folkman, S. (1984) 'Personal control and stress and coping processes: a theoretical analysis', *Journal of Personality and Social Psychology*, 46:839–52.

Fransella, F. and Bannister, D. (1977) *A Manual for Repertory Grid Technique*. London: Academic Press.

Freedman, J. L. and Fraser, S. C. (1966) Compliance without pressure: the foot-in-the-door technique. *Journal of Personality and Social Psychology*, 4:195–202.

French, J. and Raven, B. (1958) 'The bases of social power', in D. Cartwright (ed.) *Studies in Social Power*, Ann Arbor, MI: University of Michigan Press.

French, W. and Bell, C. (1995) *Organizational Development: Behavioural Science Interventions for Organizational Improvement*, 5th edn, Englewood Cliffs, NJ: Prentice Hall.

Furnham, A. (2001) 'Vocational preference and P–O fit: reflections on Holland's Theory of Vocational Choice', *Applied Psychology: An International Review*, 50(1).

Glaser, B. G. and Strauss, A. L. (1967) *The Discovery of Grounded Theory: Strategies for Qualitative Research*, Chicago, IL: Aldine.

Greiner, L. E. and Schein, V. E. (1988) *Power and Organization Development: Mobilizing Power to Implement Change*, New York: Addison-Wesley.

Hackman, J. and Oldham, G. (1980) *Work Redesign*, Reading, MA: Addison-Wesley.

Handy, C., Gordon, C., Gow, I., Moloney, M. and Randlesome, C. (1987) *The Making of Managers*, London: NDEC/MSC/BIM.

Herriot, P. and Pemberton, C. (1994) *Competitive Advantage Through Diversity*, London: Sage.

Holland, J. (1966) *A Psychology of Vocational Choice: a Theory of Personality Types and Environments*. Waltham, MA: Blarsdell.

Hovland, C. I., Harvey, O. J. and Sherif, M. (1957) 'Assimilation and contrast effects in reactions to communication and attitude change', *Journal of Abnormal and Social Psychology*, 55:244–52.

Institute of Management (1994) *Management Development to the Millennium: the Cannon and Taylor Reports*, London: Institute of Management.

Investors in People (1995) *The Investors in People Standard*. London: Investors in People.

Ivancevich, J. M., Matteson, M. T., Freedman, S. M., and Phillips, J. S. (1990) *American Psychologist*, 45(2):252–61.

James, K. and Arroba, T. (1999) *Energising the Workplace: A Strategic Response to Stress*, Aldershot: Gower.

Karasek, R. A. (1979) 'Job demands, job decision latitude and mental strain: implications for job redesign', *Administrative Quarterly*, 24:285–307.

Katz, D. and Kahn, R. L. (1978) *The Social Psychology of Organizations*, 2nd edn, New York: Wiley.

Kelly, G. (1955) *The Psychology of Personal Constructs*, New York: Norton.

Kolb, D. (1984) *Experiential Learning: Experience As the Source of Learning and Development*, Englewood Cliffs, NJ: Prentice Hall.

Kolb, D. A., Rubin, I. M. and Osland, J. S. (1995) *Organizational Behaviour: an Experiential Approach*, 6th edn, London: Prentice Hall.

Komaki, J. L., Coombs, T. and Schepman, S. (1991) 'Motivational implications of reinforcement theory', in R. M. Steers and L. W. Porter (eds.) *Motivation and Work Behaviour*, 5th edn, London: McGraw-Hill.

Latack, J. C. and Hovolic, S. J. (1992) 'Coping with stress: a conceptual evaluation framework for coping measures', *Journal of Organizational Behaviour*, 13(5):479–508.

Latham, G. and Baldes, J. (1975) The practical significance of Locke's theory of goal setting. *Journal of Applied Psychology*, 60:122–4.

Lawrence, P. R. (1954) 'How to deal with resistance to change', *Harvard Business Review*, 32(3):49–57.

Lazarus, R. S. and Folkman, S. (1984) *Stress, Appraisal and Coping*, New York: Springer-Verlag.

Leavitt, H. (1965) 'Applied organizational change in industry: structural, technological, and humanistic approaches', in J. March (ed.) *Handbook of Organizations*, Chicago, IL: Rand McNally.

Lewin, K. (1946) 'Action research and minority problems', *Journal of Social Issues*, 2:34–46.

Lewin, K. (1951) *Field Theory in Social Science*, New York: Harper & Row.

Likert, R. (1967) *The Human Organization*, New York: McGraw-Hill.

Locke, E. A. and Latham, G. P. (1984) *Goal Setting: A Motivational Technique That Works!*, New York: Prentice Hall.

McFarlane, B. and Lomas, L. (1995) 'Competence-based management education and the needs of the learning organization', *Education and Training*, 36(1):29–33.

McGill, I. and Beaty, L. (1992) *Action Learning: a Practitioner's Guide*, London: Kogan Page.

McHugh, M. (1995) 'Stress and strategic change', in D. E. Hussey (ed.) *Rethinking Strategic Management: Ways to Improve Competitive Performance*, Chichester: John Wiley & Sons.

Mack, D. A., Nelson, D. L. and Quick, J. C. (1998) 'The stress of organizational change: a dynamic process model', *Applied Psychology: an International Review*, 47(2):219–232.

Management Charter Initiative (1994) London: Management Charter Initiative.

Maslow, A. H. (1943) 'A theory of human motivation', *Psychological Review*, 1:370–96.

Milgram, S. (1974) *Obedience to Authority*, New York: Harper & Row.

Mintzberg, H. (1983) *Power in and Around Organizations*, New York: Prentice Hall.

Mitchell, R., Agle, B. R. and Wood, D. J. (1997) 'Toward a theory of stakeholder identification and salience: defining the principle of who and what really counts', *The Academy of Management Review*, 22(4):853–86.

Murphy, L. R. (1988) 'Employee behaviours before and after stress management', *Journal of Organizational Behaviour*, 9(2):173–82.

O'Driscoll, M. P. and Cooper, C. (1994) 'Coping with work-related stress: a critique of existing measures and proposal for an alternative methodology', *Journal of Occupational and Organizational Psychology*, 67(4):343–54.

Payne, R. (1982) 'The nature of knowledge and organizational psychology', in N. Nicholson, and T. Wall (eds.) *The Theory and Practice of Organizational Psychology: A Collection of Original Essays*, London: Academic Press.

Pedler, M., Burgoyne, J. and Boydell, T. (1986) *A Manager's Guide to Self-Development*, 2nd edn, London: McGraw-Hill.

Pepper, S. C. (1942) *World Hypotheses: A Study in Evidence*, San Francisco, CA: University of California Press.

Peters, T. J. and Waterman, R. H. (1982) *In Search of Excellence: Lessons from America's Best-Run Companies*, New York: Harper & Row.

Petty, R. E., Wegener, D. T. and Fabrigar, L. R. (1997) 'Attitudes and attitude change', *Annual Review of Psychology*, 48:609–47, Palo Alto, CA: Annual Reviews Inc.

Pfeffer, J. (1992) *Managing with Power: Politics and Influences in Organizations*, Boston, MA: Harvard Business School Press.

Porter, L. and Lawler, E. (1968) *Managerial Attitudes and Performance*, Homewood, IL: Dorsey-Irwin.

Pugh, D. S. (ed.) (1971) *Organization Theory: Selected Readings*, London: Penguin.

Rapoport, R. N. (1970) 'Three dilemmas in action research', *Human Relations*, 23:488–513.

Revans, R. (1983) *The ABC of Action Learning*, 2nd edn, Bickley, Kent: Chartwell-Bratt.

Robbins, S. P. (1989) *Training in Interpersonal Skills: Tips for Managing People at Work*, London: Prentice Hall.

Royal Society of Arts (1995) *Tomorrow's Company*, London: RSA.

Schon, D. (1983) *The Reflective Practitioner*, New York: Basic Books.

Schon, D. (1987) *Educating the Reflective Practitioner: Toward a New Design Toward Teaching and Learning in the Professions*, San Francisco, CA: Jossey-Bass.

Schroder, H. (1989) *Managerial Competence: the Key to Excellence*, 1st edn, Dubuque, IA: Kendall/Hunt.

Senge, P. (1990) *The Fifth Discipline: The Art and Practice of the Learning Organization*, London: Century Business/Doubleday.

Sparrow, J. (1998) *Knowledge in Organizations: Access to Thinking at Work*, London: Sage.

Sparrow, P. (1995) 'Organizational competences – A valid approach for the future', *International Journal of Selection and Development*, 3(3):168–77.

Spencer, L. M. and Spencer, S. M. (1993) *Competence at Work: Models for Superior Performance*, Chichester: John Wiley & Sons.

Tannenbaum, R. and Schmidt, W. H. (1973) 'How to choose a leadership pattern', *Harvard Business Review*, 51(May/June): 162–4.

Thomas, A. B. (1993) *Controversies in Management*, London: Routledge.

Vaill, P. (1989) *Managing as a Performing Art*, San Francisco, CA: Jossey-Bass.

Vosniadou, S. (1992) 'Knowledge acquisition and conceptual change', *Applied Psychology: an International Review*, 41(4):347–57.

Vroom, V. H. and Jago, A. G. (1988) *The New Leadership*, New York: Prentice Hall.

Weick, K. (1995) *Sensemaking in Organizations*, London: Sage.

White, W. F., Greenwood, D. J. and Lazes, P. (1991) 'Participatory action research: through practice to science in social research', *American Behavioural Scientist*, 32(5):513–51.

Williams, A. P. O. (2001) 'A belief-focused process model of organizational learning', *Journal of Management Studies*, 38(1):67–85.

Williams, A. P. O. and Dobson, P. (1993) 'Developmental assessment centres on MBA programmes', *International Journal of Assessment and Development*, 1(4):233–40.

Williams, A. P. O. and Dobson, P. (1996) 'Culture change through training: the case of Sainsbury', in B. Towers (ed.) *The Handbook of Human Resource Management*, 2nd edn, pp. 416–31, Oxford: Blackwell.

Williams, A. P. O., Dobson, P. and Walters, M. (1993) *Changing Culture: New Organizational Approaches*, 2nd edn, London: Institute of Personnel and Development.

Wood, R. and Bandura, A. (1989) 'Social cognitive theory of organizational management', *Academy of Management Review*, 14(3):361–84.

Worren, N., Moore, K. and Collett, P. (2000) 'When theories become tools: the pragmatic validity of conceptual models', *Templeton Working Papers*, July:1–26.

Yukl, G. (1999) 'An evaluative essay on current conceptions of effective leadership', *European Journal of Work and Organizational Psychology*, 8(1):33–48.

Index